Science in the Ancient World

Other Titles in ABC-CLIO's
History of Science
Series

Science in the Ancient World

An Encyclopedia

Russell M. Lawson

A B C · C L I O

Santa Barbara, California   Denver, Colorado   Oxford, England

© 2004 by Russell M. Lawson

Library of Congress Cataloging-in-Publication Data

Lawson, Russell M., 1957–
Science in the ancient world : an encyclopedia / Russell M. Lawson.
    p. cm.   (History of science series)
Includes bibliographical references and index.
ISBN 1-85109-534-9 (acid-free paper)–ISBN 1-85109-539-X
(eBook)
1. Science, Ancient—History—Encyclopedias.   I. Title. II. Series:
ABC-CLIO's history of science series.
Q124.95.L39 2004
509.3'03—dc22   2004017715

07 06 05 04 10 9 8 7 6 5 4 3 2 1

This book is available on the World Wide Web as an e-book. Visit abc-clio.com for details.

ABC-CLIO, Inc.
130 Cremona Drive, P.O. Box 1911
Santa Barbara, California 93116-1911

This book is printed on acid-free paper ∞.
Manufactured in the United States of America

For my sons,
Benjamin Alexander, David Brian, and Riley Russell

Contents

Introduction, xi

Science in the Ancient World: An Encyclopedia

Introduction

Ancient science strove to understand the origins and workings of nature and humanity. Science has encompassed many methods and varied disciplines over time, occupying human thought for millennia. The questions that scientists ask tend to remain constant even as the answers differ according to time and culture. The strange and sometimes simple explanations that the ancient Greeks and Romans gave for natural phenomena appear less absurd to us when we consider that the answers of today may appear ridiculous to observers a thousand years from now. Among ancient scientists—from Mesopotamia, Persia, India, China, Egypt, Greece, and Rome—the Greeks were by far the leaders in scientific inquiry because they asked the most penetrating questions, many of which still elude complete answers. (See GREEK ARCHAIC AGE; GREEK CLASSICAL AGE; GREEK HELLENISTIC AGE; PHILOSOPHY.)

There is a temptation to view the past according to the standards and precepts of the present. The historian encounters countless similarities when comparing modern and ancient science. Clearly the building blocks of today's science were formed two to three thousand years ago in the ancient Mediterranean region—in a preindustrial age before the dawn of Islam or Christianity, during a polytheistic, superstitious time. Magic and astrology were considered as legitimate as medicine and astronomy. (See MAGIC.) The earth was the center of a finite universe; the planets twinkled like gods watching from above; the moon governed the fertility of nature and woman. (See ASTRONOMY.) Fertility symbols and statuettes of priestesses and mother goddesses dot the archeological finds from the dozens of millennia BCE, reminding us of the power women once had in ancient societies before the coming of male gods reflecting male dominance. Rhea, Cybele, Artemis, Hera, Isis, and Ishtar were early fertility goddesses representing the universal mother image who brought life, love, and death to her children, the humans. (See MYTH.)

Ancient humans were animists who believed in a spiritual component to natural phenomena and pantheists who saw in nature something warm, maternal, and universal. They lived in an environment wholly alive—with the surrounding woods, mountains, and streams filled with life and spirit. Nature was an unpredictable extension of self. Humans sought to charm the spirits of nature that were mysterious, yet very familiar. Nature embraced early humans; it was all they knew. Humans joined into communities to seek the best means to yield life and happiness from the environment, which they were dependent upon yet in competition with for food and shelter. (See PAGANISM.)

The most rudimentary form of scientific thought occurred at some vague point in the distant past when the ancient human began to sense his self in his surroundings, to see other humans as like himself, and to be aware of life—and of death. This awareness of self, of mortality, of birth, of the future, of the past, allowed ancient man to detach himself not only from nature but from the moment as well, to forge a weak notion of the past-present-future continuum of time, to gain a nascent historical perspective. Perhaps he did not know *time,* but he knew the passing of days and change of the seasons and the growth of the youth and decline of the aged. Indeed, existence was sufficiently precarious to accept only the here and now and avoid being overwhelmed by contemplation of the future.

The transition from awareness to conceptualization of life, self, and nature depended in part on advancements in the human community. A secure existence with plentiful food guaranteed a growing anticipation of the future and reflection upon the past, a sense of belonging, of love and being loved. Food—that is, economic security—brought freedom to speculate on self and others, on the community and those outside of it, on nature and survival, on controlling and being controlled. To explain existence, questions were asked and answers attempted and contemplated. The once vague sense of self became a clear sense of being. The intuitive recognition of the maternal spirit-world matured into a desire to understand it. Rudolph Otto (1968) called this object of awareness the *numinous*—the awesome, majestic, sublime Other, of which humans feel a part and are called upon to respond to and to know. (See MESOPOTAMIA.)

Human science began in pursuit of understanding the *numinous* and its manifestations. Science was initially not very different from religion. Ancient scientists were religious leaders, priests who doubled as scientists in searching for signs of the divine in nature. If the motions of the planets determine the future—the secrets of life and death—then the ancient thinker must turn to the study of the heavens for religious purposes. (See PAGANISM.) The first ornithologists were prognosticators who sought in the patterns of the flight of birds messages from the gods. Soothsayers gained familiarity with animal organs in the search for abnormal lobes and other intestinal aberrations. Early humans also turned to the study of flora for the best building materials and palatable food, such as grains for bread and edible roots and flowers. Flower petals, stalks, and roots, as well as tree bark, leaves, twigs, and roots, largely composed the ancient materia medica, the potions and teas used to relieve pain, stop bleeding, reduce symptoms, and calm the hysterical. (See LIFE SCIENCES.)

In some ways ancient scientists would be scarcely recognizable to twenty-first-century scientists. The scientists described and portrayed in this book were priests, government officials, kings, emperors, slaves, merchants, farmers, and aristocrats. They wrote history, biography, and essays. (See PLINY THE ELDER; PLUTARCH.) They were artists, explorers, poets, musicians, abstract thinkers, and sensualists. The demands upon scientific study then were different from those of today. The study of astrology was necessary to know one's fate—the future. Astronomy and mathematics were essential to forming calendars to fit the cycles of nature and seasons of the year. (See ASTRONOMY.) The ancient scientist was often seeking a practical result rather than pursuing scientific thought for its own sake. At the same time, the ancient scientist was something of a wise man, a community savant who was expected to know—or at least to have thought about or investigated—all things natural, spiritual, and human. The Greeks called such a thinker *polymathes,* a word that is the origin for our word "polymath," someone who is learned in many fields of knowledge.

But ancient scientists also pursued some of the same goals as their modern counterparts. Modern physicists and chemists seek to know the basic particles that compose matter in the universe; ancient Stoics and Epicureans hypothesized the same particles and sought the same knowledge of the movement and patterns of atoms. (See AURELIUS, MARCUS; LUCRETIUS.) Albert Einstein, the theoretical physicist, wanted to know the mind of God, the ultimate secrets of the universe, a search inaugurated two and three thousand years ago in the ancient Mediterranean region. Einstein would have liked Plato; Niels Bohr, the twentieth-century Danish physicist, would have found a friend in Aristotle. (See ARISTOTLE; PLATO.) What are the abstract patterns present in the universe? Mathematicians today and millennia ago have been united in the quest to find out, to set the rational mind of man upon the most complex and least concrete inquiry. (See ARCHIMEDES; EUCLID; PTOLEMAEUS, CLAUDIUS.) Psychologists today still work in the shadow of the great psychologists of the past, although the present concern to know the human mind and the nature of personality is a more secular pursuit than it once was. (See ARISTOTLE; THUCYDIDES.) Political scientists today still rely on the initial systematic inquiries into human government that Plato and Aristotle made in the fourth century BCE. Students at modern medical schools take the Hippocratic Oath, recognizing that although the techniques of medicine have changed from the days of Hippocrates and Galen the ultimate goals and humanitarian concerns have not. (See GALEN; HIPPOCRATES.) In short, the college arts and sciences curricula and professional scientific careers of today are not a recent development. Rather, the moderns in pursuit of knowledge of man and the universe continually ascend the intellectual and methodological building blocks constructed during antiquity.

The ancient Greeks did not have a word with the precise meaning of "science," which today means a methodical, concrete, objective, workmanlike, puzzle-solving approach to understanding natural phenomena. The Greek word with the closest meaning is *episteme,* to know. The Greek scientist was someone who *knows.* To the ancient mind, science involved much that we would identify as artistic, abstract, subjective, mythical, and emotional. Especially in the last two centuries, modern science has elevated science to the unique plateau of objective knowledge. The scientist detaches himself from the environment, seeking in the here and now the means, intellectually and pragmatically, to reduce, dismantle, control, reconstruct life. The ancient scientist associated with, and attempted to recapture, nature, which was an extension of self, something from the collective past experienced in the present moment. Science at present is secular and materialistic, seeking the transcendent—the origins and meaning of life—through the reconstruction of natural history. Ancient science reveled in the spiritual, the oneness of life and being. Science and religion, reason and faith, were rarely discordant in the history of science until recent times. Today's phrase "natural theology" implies that there is something religious in nature—and something natural in religion—both of which describe the ancient scientific mind-set precisely.

The modern scientific mind-set is utilitarian, coercive, technical, and progressive; it embraces change, focusing on things rather than ideas. The ancient scientific mind-set was rather primitive, focusing on values, sentiments, morality, unity, the static and changeless, the organic and alive. Science today is progressive and historicist, focusing on what is *becoming* through the movement of time. Science in antiquity focused on *being,* what *is* regardless of the passage of time. Finally, modern science is generally a professional discipline practiced by scientists with terminal college degrees. It is well organized under prescribed methods, esoteric forms of communication, and agreed-upon theories. Modern scientists join together under the umbrella of a precise system of thought and methodology that explains clearly what the role of the scientist is in the accumulation and utilization of scientific knowledge over time. Ancient scientists were amateurs, polymaths, and generalists who were rarely well organized and who adhered to general philosophical schools of thought that were inclusive to any well-educated, thoughtful individual. (See HERODOTUS OF HALICARNASSUS; PLUTARCH.)

Science in the Ancient World pays respect to the modern definition and practice of science while meeting the ancients on their own terms. Ancient philosophy and science were usually indistinguishable because of the worldview of the ancient thinker. Aristotle was a leading scientist of antiquity, yet he was a leading philosopher as well. Hippocrates was the great student of medicine, yet much of his work was theoretical and speculative, not empirical, and focused on understanding rather than cures. Many ancient scientists were first and foremost soldiers and explorers who engaged in science on the side or out of utter necessity. (See ALEXANDER OF MACEDON; ARRIAN; CAESAR, JULIUS; NEARCHUS OF CRETE.) Lucretius, the Roman Epicurean, was a scientist who recorded his ideas in verse. Other ancient scientists were devoted to the study of magic and astrology. (See IAMBLICHUS; MAXIMUS OF EPHESUS.) Science and superstition often complemented each other in the ancient world. Moreover, ancient science was inclusive of all intellectual pursuits, not only the hard sciences. Historical inquiry, for example, was as valid an object of scientific inquiry as physics. (See POLYBIUS; TACITUS; THUCYDIDES.)

The scope of this book is science in antiquity, which is a broad epoch in the history of humankind as generally accepted by scholars and teachers in the Western world. The chronological beginning of the ancient world, for purposes of this book, is the fourth millennium BCE (about 3500 BCE), when civilization emerged in ancient Iraq, which the Greeks called Mesopotamia, centered on the lower Tigris and Euphrates rivers, and in ancient Egypt, centered on the lower Nile River in North Africa. The ancient world comes to an end with the decline of the Roman Empire during the fifth and sixth centuries CE, roughly 500 CE. The first civilizations in the history of humankind emerged during this four-thousand-year period. Science was a necessary condition for the development of civilization.

The *Oxford English Dictionary* defines civilization as a "civilized condition or state; a developed or advanced state of human society." This is sufficiently vague that a variety of more precise definitions have branched out from the original. All of them have some reference to the Latin root of the word, *civis*— "citizen"—one who is part of a body politic. Hence "civilization" generally refers to a level of society wherein the citizen has certain rights and responsibilities incumbent upon his or her particular role in the community. Citizenship requires a settled existence, which itself relies on the domestication of agriculture and livestock; the accumulation of surplus wealth; domestic and international trade; a social structure based on the distribution of wealth; a political structure that administers and protects wealth; and a system of writing to record the production, consumption, and distribution of wealth. Citizens might be farmers, tradesmen, craftsmen, and scribes. This organized division of labor requires a glue to bond it together into a working whole. The glue, in ancient as well as in modern societies, has been professionals in political, social, cultural, and religious institutions who are themselves not producers, but who administer production, distribution, and storage of wealth; who are engaged in the educational, social, and cultural systems built upon such wealth; and who express the collective thoughts and feelings of the citizenry through literature, art, music, and drama.

Science supported the thoughts, structures, and institutions of society in the ancient Near East, where civilization first began. Mesopotamian and Egyptian engineers built ziggurats and pyramids from huge blocks of stone arrayed with incredible precision. Engineers in Mesopotamia designed and implemented a complicated network of canals and dikes for flood control and irrigation. (See ENGINEERING AND TECHNOLOGY.) Agriculture appeared as early as 10,000 BCE along the banks of the Tigris and Euphrates rivers. The people who eventually immigrated to and took control of Mesopotamia, the Sumerians, were agriculturalists who learned when to plant and how to develop techniques to increase yields. Likewise the early inhabitants of the Nile River valley discovered agriculture—perhaps independently, perhaps learning it from the Sumerians—but without the need for dikes and canals. The Nile rose and fell in such a fashion as to guide farmers when to plant and harvest. (See AGRICULTURE.) Surplus food required a means of record keeping. Scribes invented a form of writing—cuneiform in Sumeria, hieroglyphics in Egypt—to track daily economic, social, and political activities. Sumerian astronomers developed calendars based on the phases of the moon to help in the preparation of almanacs to provide meteorological information for farmers. Egyptian astronomers developed solar calendars. (See ASTRONOMY.) Metallurgists of the ancient Near East figured out how to heat copper and tin to extreme temperatures to form bronze, a useful metal for tools and weapons. (See BRONZE AGE.) Inventors built wheeled vehicles for transport and wooden and papyrus reed ships for river and ocean navigation and trade. (See MARINE SCIENCE.) Sumerian sailors followed the coast and the stars as they sailed the Persian Gulf and Arabian Sea to the Indus River, where they traded with, and helped to stimulate, the emerging civilization of the Indus River valley (around 2500 BCE). (See EGYPT; MESOPOTAMIA.)

The Indus River valley, or Harappan, civilization lasted for about a millennium, during which time it exhibited many of the same accomplishments as in Mesopotamia and Egypt. The Harappan people lived in fine, well-designed, well-constructed cities (such as Mohenjo Daro). They invented writing, discovered (or learned from others) how to make bronze, and had a sophisticated agricultural system that included the production of cotton. It is possible that the Indus River civilization spread east through land or ocean contacts to influence the origins of the Yellow River civilization of China. This civilization

emerged during the middle of the second millennium BCE. It featured writing, bronze tools and weapons, dynastic leaders, and sophisticated agriculture. Meanwhile, halfway around the world, the Olmec civilization developed in Central America toward the end of the second millennium. The Olmecs were a warlike people who lived on the Yucatan Peninsula. One of their many achievements was the (apparently) independent development of a system of hieroglyphic writing. (See ASIA, EAST AND SOUTH; BRONZE AGE.)

The ancient Near East was the site of a number of other flourishing civilizations that emerged in the wake of the Sumerians and Egyptians. The Hittites of Asia Minor were a warlike people who nevertheless developed a system of writing, had an organized government, and were the first people to learn to make iron tools and weapons. (See IRON AGE.) Babylon along the Euphrates River was the center of a dynamic civilization that developed from Sumerian origins in Mesopotamia. The Babylonians made significant discoveries in astronomy, mathematics, and social organization. The law code of the Babylonian king Hammurapi showed progress toward the development of a more civil society. (See BABYLON; MESOPOTAMIA.) Toward the end of the second millennium, along the shores of the eastern Mediterranean in what is today Lebanon, several seagoing city-states emerged, their wealth and sophisticated culture based on trade. These Phoenicians developed a system of writing, later adopted by the Greeks. They had the best naval technology of the time, and, being explorers, had the most up-to-date knowledge of geography before the Greeks. The Phoenicians explored the entire extent of the Mediterranean and beyond to the European and African coasts of the Atlantic Ocean. They also came to know the Red Sea and the east African coast of the Indian Ocean. (See MARINE SCIENCE; PHOENICIANS.) Meanwhile, during the second millennium BCE, the Hebrews were developing a dynamic civilization in Palestine. Influenced by the Mesopotamian and Egyptian cultures, the Hebrews developed an astonishing culture centered upon their interpretation of the cosmos encompassed by the one god, omniscient, omnipotent, and omnipresent, Yahweh. (See OLD TESTAMENT.)

Other civilizations of the Near East that developed during the first millennium BCE included the Lydians, Assyrians, Chaldeans, and Persians stretching from the Aegean Sea east to the Indus River. The Lydians dominated Asia Minor for a brief time from their capital at Sardis. They are noteworthy for developing the first system of coinage. (See MILETUS.) The Assyrians and Chaldeans centered their respective power around Mesopotamia, particularly at the cities of Assur and Babylon. Chaldean astrologers became famous (and infamous) during subsequent centuries. (See BABYLON.) The Persian Empire existed for about two hundred years—from the sixth to the fourth centuries. The Persian gift was for organization and logistics, developing the largest and most efficient empire before the Romans. (See ASIA, EAST AND SOUTH.)

Scholars have long debated whether early civilizations, such as those in the Indus and Yellow river valleys and the Olmec civilization in Central America, that existed far from the first civilizations at Mesopotamia and Egypt, developed in isolation or through cultural contacts. Science today is an international work in progress, one of the great forces of unification crossing cultural, political, geographic, and linguistic boundaries. Has it always been this way? Clearly Renaissance European scientists had the mentality of cross-cultural scientific exchange, as did before them the scientists of Constantinople, the Arab world, and Western Europe, all of whom shared a deep interest in especially Aristotelian science. Greek was the lingua franca of the ancient world from 500 BCE to 500 CE—the Greek language was heavily dominated by philosophic and scientific terms. The scientists of the Roman Empire were typically Greek, as were teachers and physicians. (See HELLENISM; ROMAN PRINCIPATE.) The greatest period of scientific

achievement before the European Renaissance was a thousand-year period mostly in the eastern Mediterranean region at scientific capitals in Europe, Asia, and Africa. Scientists and philosophers at Magna Graecia, Athens, Miletus, Byzantium, and Alexandria conversed in Greek on a variety of scientific topics ranging from mathematics to physics to chemistry to biology. (See GREEK ARCHAIC AGE; GREEK CLASSICAL AGE.) Many scientists were great travelers, spreading information from one place to another. (See PYTHEAS OF MASSILIA.) But the Greeks were probably not the first people to engage in the sharing and communication that is the hallmark of the pursuit of knowledge. The Phoenicians, no doubt, spread widely their knowledge of world geography. Some scholars believe that before the Phoenicians other civilizations of the Near East developed naval technology that allowed the exploration of the Indian, Atlantic, and perhaps even the Pacific oceans. (See MARINE SCIENCE; PHOENICIANS.) If so, cultural exchanges included the sharing of scientific knowledge. Perhaps the similarities of culture and science throughout the ancient world in Asia, Europe, Africa, and America were due not to coincidence or isolated parallel development, but rather to intrepid explorers who brought knowledge of one people to another, thus beginning the process of world scientific achievement that we know so well today.

Science in the Ancient World is comprehensive but realistic in its focus on the Mediterranean region as the center of scientific activity during antiquity. Scientific accomplishments prior to the first millennium BCE are noted, yet the greatest period of activity was between the years 600 BCE and 200 CE. During this eight-hundred-year period the Greeks adopted the discoveries of their Egyptian, Phoenician, and Mesopotamian predecessors, while advancing their own highly original theories and observations of the natural and human world. (See GREEK ARCHAIC AGE; GREEK CLASSICAL AGE.) The Romans, who came to control North Africa, the Middle East, and most of Europe by the end of the first millennium BCE, were themselves not scientifically inclined. They recognized, however, the Greek achievement in thought and adopted Greek philosophy and learning, which became truly Greco-Roman. (See HELLENISM; ROMAN PRINCIPATE.) Ancient thinkers themselves recognized that the transition that occurred in the Mediterranean world from the third to the seventh centuries CE was the end of one epoch and the beginning of another. *Science in the Ancient World* adopts this chronological limit as well.

People rather than schools of thought or cities engage in science. Ancient science, much more than modern science, was an individual endeavor. It is anachronistic to categorize and conceptualize ancient scientists according to modern expectations of scientists, who are professional puzzle-solvers often working in teams to generate solutions to intricate and esoteric problems of interest to a very few. Hence *Science in the Ancient World* focuses heavily on the individual scientist— his or her life, discoveries, methods, tools, and writings. The primary sources for ancient science are the writings of individual scientists, the works of ancient historians, and the observations of philosophical commentators. The best way to study ancient science is to study the ancient sources.

The earliest Greek scientists left behind few writings, keeping their ideas to themselves and a few select disciples. Fortunately, there was enough interest among later scientists and philosophers to record the work of their predecessors, either by way of indicating difference or debt. Without Plato's dialogues we would scarcely know of Socrates' theories and arguments. Aristotle was such a universal thinker that he not only wrote about most scientific topics but painstakingly recorded the views of earlier thinkers as well. From Plato and Aristotle we learn about the first Ionian scientists from western Turkey and the Aegean Isles—Thales, Anaxagoras, Anaximenes, Anaximander—who initiated the scientific quest to seek rational explanations of natural phenomena. (See IONIANS; MILETUS.) Aristotle and his contemporaries also continued to rely heavily on the teachings of Greeks living in Magna Graecia in southern Italy. Some of the greatest scientists who ever lived hailed from this area: Pythagoras, Alcmaeon, Xenophanes, Leucippus, Democritus, Epicurus, and Zeno. These philosophers of what Diogenes Laertius called the Italian school tended less toward idealism and more toward materialism in their philosophic and scientific explanations. (See MAGNA GRAECIA.) These early Greek thinkers set the standard for later scientists by asking questions that required deep speculative thought and concrete analysis to answer. Doubt was an important scientific tool to the Greek intellectual. Doubt of earlier theories drove Athenian scientists. (See ATHENS.) Doubt of pat answers, of a *received tradition,* drove Epicureans, Skeptics, and Cynics. Doubt that spurred the continuing search set the standard for all subsequent scientists.

Greek science during the Archaic and Classical ages (800–323 BCE) extended beyond the physical sciences to the life sciences, social sciences, and behavioral sciences. The Ionian school of medicine at Cos, initiated by Hippocrates, investigated a wide variety of diseases and speculated on their causes. (See MEDICINE.) The Greeks were fascinated by flora and its potential for healing agents—Theophrastus, the student of Aristotle, was an early botanist. (See LIFE SCIENCES.) The origins of modern social and behavioral sciences can be found in the writings of Greek scientists of over 2,000 years ago. Historians such as Herodotus and Polybius were geographers, ethnographers, and explorers. (See GEOGRAPHY/GEODESY.) History itself was considered a science by the Greeks. (See HISTORY.) The Greek *polis* (city-state) inspired commentators and analysts to debate its origin and significance. Athenians took the lead. Aristotle's *Politics* and *Athenian Constitution* brought the study of politics and society to the realm of science. (See SOCIAL SCIENCES.) Plato's *Republic* analyzed the concept of justice, and his dialogues, particularly

Timaeus and *Phaedo,* initiated the examination of the self, the *psyche,* the study of which excited many subsequent Greek thinkers, such as the Academics, Neoplatonists, and Christians. (See PSYCHOLOGY.)

During the Roman period in the Mediterranean there were more important accomplishments in ancient science. Alexandria became the leading scientific center, from which Euclid, Eratosthenes, Ptolemy, and Hypatia introduced their ideas to the world. (See ALEXANDRIA; HELLENISM.) Science became truly an international inquiry, with research centers and scholars working in southern Europe, western Asia, and North Africa. Greeks working at Alexandria, Constantinople, and Athens dominated scientific achievements. Few Romans became involved in science; those who did were interested more in applied than in theoretical science—for example, Pliny the Elder. Others, such as the Epicurean Lucretius, expounded on Greek science and philosophy. (See ROMAN PRINCIPATE.) The Pax Romana of the Roman Empire came to an end during the third century CE. So, too, did the framework of peace and political order that maintained a fertile environment for science to grow and flower. Scientists at the end of the ancient world, during the decay of the Roman Empire, were generally unoriginal thinkers who looked back to the glory days of ancient Greece from which they continued to draw inspiration and theories. (See LATER ROMAN EMPIRE.)

The intellectual activity of ancient Mediterranean science during the first millennium BCE has rarely been equaled. Indeed, modern science, beginning with the scientific revolution during the sixteenth century CE, built upon the existing foundation of ancient science. The discoveries of Copernicus, Galileo, Kepler, and Harvey would have been something quite different without the initial work of Ptolemy of Alexandria, Aristotle of Athens, and Galen of Pergamon. Modern scientists continue to work in the shadows of the columns and stoa of ancient thought.

Ancient thought, culture, and institutions had a profound impact on the subsequent centuries of the European Middle Ages (500–1300 CE), the European Renaissance (1300–1600 CE), the Scientific Revolution (1500–1700 CE), the Enlightenment (1700–1800 CE), and the Modern World. The decline and transition of the Roman Empire during the fourth and fifth centuries CE served to bring forward ancient thought to the scattered kingdoms of Western Europe and the Byzantine Empire of the eastern Mediterranean. (See LATER ROMAN EMPIRE.) The Byzantine Empire was a Greek civilization still beholden to Greek language, ideas, and culture. Kingdoms of Western Europe, such as that of the Franks, adopted Latin language, customs, institutions, and thought. The king of the Franks, Charlemagne, for example, had himself declared Emperor of the Romans in 800 CE. Several centuries later, Otto the Great founded the Holy Roman Empire. Meanwhile Byzantines called Constantinople the "Second Rome," and emperors such as Justinian (527–565 CE) considered themselves heirs to the traditions and power of Augustus Caesar. (See CONSTANTINOPLE; SOCIAL SCIENCES.) Medieval thinkers such as Boethius and Thomas Aquinas adopted the intellectual structures of Greek philosophy. Late medieval thought, following upon developments in Islamic science, was dominated by Aristotelian science. Renaissance thinkers continued the emphasis upon Platonic and Aristotelian thought and embraced as well ancient Stoicism, skepticism, mysticism, and astrology. Catalysts of the Scientific Revolution such as Copernicus and Galileo were heavily influenced by Aristotle—and others as well, such as Claudius Ptolemy. Indeed the intellectual and scientific paradigms of the ancient world have only recently been replaced by new assumptions and theories and hitherto unimagined experiments and research technologies. (See ARISTOTLE; PLATO; PTOLE-MAEUS, CLAUDIUS.)

The Middle Ages

The problem of when and how—and even if—the Roman Empire declined and fell is complicated by the varied dimensions of cultural change in the fourth and fifth centuries CE. In both the Western Roman Empire—and subsequent European kingdoms—and the Eastern Roman Empire—and subsequent Byzantine Empire—polytheistic, superstitious, pantheistic pagans, who watched constantly for divine signs to indicate the course of the future, became monotheistic and similarly superstitious Christians who conceived of a variety of supernatural forces of both good and evil that waged war over the Christian soul. There were more similarities than differences between paganism and Christianity, so that it was common to find Christians who, like the philosopher Boethius, could not quite rid themselves of their pagan proclivities, and pagans who, like the emperor Constantine, were sufficiently attracted to Christianity to approach full conversion. (See LATER ROMAN EMPIRE; NEW TESTAMENT; PAGANISM.)

The European Dark Ages were dark from the perspective of the standards of civilization, in particular those of the cultivated and progressive cities of Renaissance Italy. Life in the Middles Ages was short and brutish; few could read the few books that survived war and conquest; great ideas vanished, as did schools; time, dates, age, years, were largely uncertain; ordered political structures were rare; the economy was agrarian and based on barter; towns were few, but not hunger and famine; death was frequent and familiar. Literacy all but vanished. Art and sculpture were primitive, anachronistic, and static. So, too, was thought—the philosophers and theologians of the Middle Ages tried to merge faith in the Scriptures with loyalty to ancient pagan sources such as Aristotle and Virgil. They developed an intricate, esoteric approach to God and the universe that relied heavily on mind-numbing logic and ontological as well as nominalist approaches to knowledge.

Augustine, Bishop of Hippo and author of *Confessions* and *City of God,* provides one of the first models for what we call "medieval philosophy." In an essay written in 395, he sought to deduce the existence of God by means of his own understanding of *knowledge.* Augustine began with three fundamental assumptions about himself: that he exists, that he is alive, and that he has understanding. Humans are separate from animals in possessing the capacity for understanding, that is, *reason.* Since humans display reason in their temporal lives, they can recognize the existence of that which transcends reason. Anticipating St. Anselm, Augustine argued that God is the being at the limit of human reason, beyond which humans cannot conceive. Reason tells us of the immutability of number. *One,* for instance, is a fundamental reality, a singularity, not dependent upon our temporal observations. Having established that, because humans possess reason, they can conceive of that which transcends reason, and because humans conceive of number and the number *one* must represent the ultimate transcendence, Augustine went on to assume that since we seek wisdom and know certain wise humans, something beyond our experience called *wisdom* necessarily exists. There are certain common assumptions that all humans share; such assumptions require wisdom to understand them; therefore, all humans share in this wisdom. Reason, number, wisdom transcend individual human existence. Likewise knowledge transcends the brief lifespan of the individual knower. In short, Augustine argued that we first know manifold truths dependent upon our own independent reason and reflection; realization of these temporal, limited truths makes us realize that something similar yet transcendent, Truth, exists—this *Truth* is God. (See AURELIUS AUGUSTINE.)

The foregoing example of a pattern of assumption and syllogism, logic and piety, reason and faith describes the religious thought not only of Augustine but of the Middle Ages in general. In the several centuries after the invasions of the northern Germanic tribes and the sack of Rome by the Goths (in 410 CE), people pursuing happiness, peace, and order arranged themselves into various communal institutions. In Italy, France, and England, for example, primitive kingdoms emerged; warlords and great landowners provided protection for farmers, peasants who soon became entangled in the unbreakable cords of feudalism. Those with a religious bent retreated from the dangers of society to form isolated communities of ascetics. Some particularly zealous believers, such as St. Anthony and St. Jerome, fled to the desert to live as hermits. Others, such as the anchorites, lived austere existences in the vain attempt to conquer the flesh so as to elevate the soul. Benedict of Nursia practiced such asceticism unsuccessfully before finding a balance between isolation and civilization in the Benedictine monastery. These varied recluses were often the few thoughtful scholars who continued to think about the past and anticipate the future.

The first scientific light to shine in the darkness of Medieval Western Europe occurred at Aix-la-Chapelle during the reign of Charles the Great, Charlemagne. The so-called Carolingian Renaissance was inspired by Charlemagne's interest in learning and interest in surrounding himself with able and intelligent counselors such as Alcuin and Einhard. Alcuin tutored Charlemagne in the basics of philosophy, mathematics, and astronomy. Carolingian scholars studied the trivium and quadrivium, the traditional liberal arts course of study. Mathematical study was primitive, focusing mostly on arithmetic. Astronomy was generally relegated to observing the stars out of wonder or, more practically, to set the calendar. Carolingian intellects focused particularly on grammar and rhetoric underpinned by logic—the dialectic. Ancient sources for such study included Cicero, Pliny, Boethius, and Aristotle, particularly within the pages of compilers and commentators such as Isidore of Seville (560–636 CE). Isidore wrote the

Etymologies, in which he tried to collect the learning and wisdom of the ancients regarding a variety of objects of inquiry, ranging from astronomy and astrology to zoology and botany to geography and law. He wrote extensively on medicine, mathematics, and rhetoric. (See ASTRONOMY; LATER ROMAN EMPIRE; LIFE SCIENCES; MATHEMATICS.)

Boethius (480–524 CE) was a transitional figure between ancient and medieval philosophy and science. He lived during the sixth century, serving under the Gothic king Theodoric, who ruled the Italian remnant of the Western Roman Empire. Boethius was gifted in both Platonic and Aristotelian thought, referring in *The Consolation of Philosophy* to Aristotle as "my philosopher." Lady Philosophy, with whom he carried on an imaginary conversation in the *Consolation,* declared that Aristotle was her "disciple" and discussed many others as well, such as the Stoics Zeno and Cicero, the Pythagoreans, Platonists, Epicureans, and Eleatics. Boethius wrote Latin commentaries on the two great philosophers Plato and Aristotle, bringing to the Latin Medieval West knowledge of classical metaphysics and logic. He was particularly interested in Aristotelian physics, ethics, and astronomy. Boethius was also a student, commentator, and translator (into Latin) of Ptolemy. (See ASTRONOMY; PHILOSOPHY.)

The legacy of ancient science on Christian Europe and the Muslim Near East is largely the story of the growing number and sophistication of commentators on Aristotle. It is difficult to underestimate the impact this one scientist and philosopher had on the subsequent two millennia of thought. After the decline of Charlemagne's empire and the Carolingian Renaissance, amid the chaos of the ninth century, students of Aristotle continued to think and to speculate using the terms and techniques of ancient science. Before the twelfth century, most of Aristotle's works were unknown to the Medieval West, and scientists often relied on compilations of ancient thought, in particular the works of the polymath Isidore. John

Scotus Eriugena, for example, in about 870 wrote *On the Division of Nature,* in which he declared that Greek philosophy is of fundamental importance in knowing the actions of the word *(logos)* in the generation of all things and the natural laws by which existence is ordered. (See LOGOS.) Eriugena incorporated Aristotelian concepts such as the First Cause, dialectic, essence *(ousia),* nature *(physis),* and knowledge *(scientia).* The latter involves the search to discover the order of all things, how life can be categorized according to genera and species, the reflection of the First Cause in nature. Eriugena set the stage for subsequent Christian Aristotelians to argue that *physics* was the best complement to theology. Eriugena had a profound impact on the twelfth-century Benedictine recluse Honorius of Autun, who wrote a compilation of undigested Greek geography, physics, and astronomy. (See PHILOSOPHY.)

Meanwhile Byzantine scholars at Constantinople, Alexandria, and Gaza continued to read, teach, and transmit to posterity the great writings in philosophy and science of the ancient past, as well as a host of more recent commentaries on, especially, Aristotle. Byzantine scholars were typically Christian (though studying and teaching pagan authors) and were usually lesser thinkers, hence rarely subsequently known, compared to the Greek masters. Typical was Procopius of Gaza, a polymath who wrote on earthquakes, mechanical devices, and theology. Timothy of Gaza wrote a zoological treatise. John Philoponus, writing at Constantinople during the reign of Justinian, wrote commentaries on Aristotelian science and philosophy. Hierocles wrote an account of the geography of the Roman Empire. Hesychius wrote commentaries on ancient writings. Anthemius and Isidore excelled as engineers and architects and created the wonderful Church of St. Sophia. Justinian sought not only to restore the Roman Empire to its ancient grandeur, but he also worked to build Constantinople into a center of beauty, learning, and Christianity. He sponsored schools and scholarship, the greatest accomplishment being the Digest of Roman Law. (See CONSTANTINOPLE; GAZA.)

That ancient Greek science, philosophy, and mathematics continued to be studied at Constantinople during the European Middle Ages is seen in the example of Michael Psellus (1018–1096), Byzantine historian, philosopher, and scientist. Psellus was extremely gifted in many ways, serving as adviser to several Byzantine emperors and holding government posts of importance. He was a Christian who believed that he could acquire knowledge through deductive and inductive thinking, mathematics, and the study of Aristotle, Plato, and Neoplatonists such as Plotinus and Porphyry. He also studied ancient texts on medicine and astronomy.

Meanwhile Muslim students of Greek philosophy and science in Western Asia, North Africa, and Spain studied and commented upon ancient literature and retained numerous writings from the ancient world unknown to the Latin West. The beginnings of Muslim interest in Greek science occurred during the Abbasid Dynasty of the eighth century. Abbasid scholars were heavily influenced by the work of Nestorian and Monophysite Christians living in Syria who had for several centuries translated and studied many Greek scientific works into Syriac. Alchemy was an especially popular topic of study, as was medicine. During the ninth century, examination and transcription of Greek scientific manuscripts was ongoing at the House of Wisdom, the intellectual center of Baghdad. A century later the leading Arabic alchemist, Jabir ibn Hayyan, was engaged in intense study of the works of the ancient alchemists of Alexandria and Aristotelian scientific principles. It was partly by means of Arab scholars that the West was generally reintroduced to the writings of Galen and Hippocrates. (See MEDICINE; PHYSICAL SCIENCES.)

The Muslims Avicenna and Averroes had a central role in bringing an Aristotelian Renaissance to Western Europe. Avicenna, Ibn Sina (980–1037), was, at the beginning of the eleventh century, the greatest living Aristotelian scholar. He had an encyclopedic mind, wrote many commentaries, and was best known for his studies of medicine. European scientists relied on his works for centuries. Averroes, Ibn Rushd (1126–1198), was known as the "commentator," a title that he earned from his numerous works of study on Aristotle and from using Aristotle to tackle metaphysical topics. A Jew born in Muslim Spain who wrote medical and scientific treatises in Arabic, Maimonides (1135–1204), was another Aristotelian commentator and student of a wide range of Peripatetic writings. (See COMMENTATORS; PERIPATETIC SCHOOL.)

The greatest Aristotelian of the European Middle Ages, the Christian philosopher Thomas Aquinas (1225–1274), attempted to reconcile Greek philosophy and science with Christian theology. The writings of Muslim commentators on Aristotle had become known through Latin translations by the early to mid- thirteenth century. Aquinas therefore had at his disposal a vast corpus of Aristotle's works. He made great use of them in his own writings, in particular the *Summa Theologica*. Aquinas relied heavily on Aristotelian methods to arrive at logical deductions about the existence and nature of God and God's works. Repeatedly Aquinas referred to Aristotle as simply "the Philosopher." Like the Philosopher, Aquinas used logical syllogisms of common everyday things, such as wood and fire, to arrive at correct answers to the questions he posed throughout the *Summa*. Aquinas's use of science was, of course, limited by his methodology—it was not empirical—and by his focus on Christian theology. His successors in the European Renaissance were quick to point out his shortcomings, as they attempted to use ancient scientific literature as the basis for a full study of all natural phenomena. (See ARISTOTLE; PHILOSOPHY.)

The Renaissance

The European Renaissance (1300–1600) was a time of political, cultural, and scientific rebirth of ancient learning. Whereas the medieval focus on ancient science was generally limited to an ongoing commentary on Aristotle's thought and writings, Renaissance thinkers developed a broader understanding of ancient thought because of the rediscovery of ancient texts, many of which had nothing to do with Aristotle. Renaissance philologists engaged in the painstaking work of studying the varied surviving handwritten copies of ancient works, attempting and succeeding in providing accurate texts close to the original. Few scholars could read classical Greek, but there was enough demand that some Italian printers issued editions of Aristotle, his Peripatetic followers, the geographer Strabo, and similar works in the original Greek. Latin was the language of scholarship and learning during the Renaissance; printers issued Latin translations of Greek writers such as Euclid, Ptolemy, Galen, and Plato. All of these added to the growing corpus of knowledge about ancient Greek science.

The trivium and quadrivium continued to orient Renaissance academic studies. As in the ancient world, specialization and professionalization of science was still long in the future. From this comes the idea of the "Renaissance man" who engaged in the study of all phenomena, human as well as natural. The study of Aristotle and Plato continued to orient Renaissance pursuits of knowledge. Aristotelian logic was considered by some Renaissance scholars to be "scholastic," a derogatory term for a medieval thinker who relied on frozen formulas of thought. Indeed there was more fluidity to Renaissance thinking, more openness and a broadening range of interests, not all of them religious. Christianity still dominated the Renaissance worldview, though there was more freedom to inquire into secular topics, perhaps because the world itself—the expanding trade, growing cities, increasing wealth—was becoming more secular. (See PHILOSOPHY.)

Most important, the Renaissance became a great time of questioning. Intellectuals of the fourteenth century, such as Francesco Petrarca, not only studied the ancient classics, but questioned the foundations of ancient thought—indeed questioned ancient thinkers themselves. Petrarch gained a literary as well as vicarious personal familiarity with his hero Cicero, the Roman Republican and orator of the first century BCE. Petrarch discovered many of Cicero's letters, which gave him a true sense of Cicero's personality and opened the doors to a critical understanding of Cicero and his work. In time, others imitated Petrarch in their willingness to question the ancients. The great challenge would be to question the universally recognized Philosopher and Scientist of ancient Greece, Aristotle. (See ARISTOTLE; CICERO.)

The Scientific Revolution

The initial realization of possible errors in ancient scientific thought occurred during the fifteenth century when Renaissance explorers began to break from the bonds of ancient geographic thinking to arrive at a new and more accurate picture of the world. Portuguese and Italian explorers from the mid to the late fifteenth century showed the willingness and courage to question the legends and myths of the world initiated during antiquity and accepted as truth during the Middle Ages. The ancient picture of the world was limited to three continents, Europe, Asia, and Africa, and two oceans, the Atlantic and the Indian. Ancient Greek philosophers had established the sphericity of the earth and its hemispheric nature. But there were many misconceptions in Greek geography. There was the notion of a fiery barrier that separated the northern and southern hemispheres, through which no person or ship could pass. Claudius Ptolemy, whose works, translated into Latin, were more available by the fifteenth century, taught that Africa and Asia were joined by a terra incognita, an unknown land to the south, which made the Indian Ocean an inland sea. Ptolemy also overestimated the size of

Asia and underestimated the circumference of the earth, making it appear that the Atlantic Ocean—that is, the distance from Europe to Asia—was much shorter than it is. The Portuguese proved in the late fifteenth century that the equatorial zone of fire was a myth, that one could sail from north to south and vice versa, and that Ptolemy was wrong in assuming that Africa could not be circumnavigated. The four voyages of Christopher Columbus, the Genoese sailor, showed that Ptolemy's geography of the earth was erroneous, that the distance from Europe to Asia was much greater than Ptolemy thought, and that there were peoples and continents— North and South America—unknown to the ancients. Michel de Montaigne, the French thinker, wondered in one of his essays what Plato, who imagined the lost city of Atlantis, would have made of the inhabitants of the Americas and the rich civilizations of the Aztecs and Incas. The Portuguese sailor Magellan showed, in circumnavigating South America and sailing across the Pacific Ocean, just how rudimentary ancient geographical knowledge was. (See GEOGRAPHY; MARINE SCIENCE; PTOLEMAEUS, CLAUDIUS.)

Renaissance discoveries in the science of geography were the initial steps in a new way of thinking about science, which historians call the Scientific Revolution. The great thinkers at the dawn of modern science— Copernicus, Galileo, Kepler, da Vinci, Bacon, Harvey, and Vesalius—worked in the shadow of Ptolemy, Hipparchus, Aristotle, Pliny, Hippocrates, and Galen.

Italian cities such as Florence, Padua, Pisa, Genoa, Bologna, and Venice were the most flourishing commercial and cultural centers of the Renaissance; naturally they were often the centers of the new focus on science. Padua, for example, was a center of Aristotelian studies, particularly as applied to medicine. At Florence at the end of the fifteenth century, Leonardo da Vinci (1452–1519) studied Greek philosophy and science, Aristotle and Galen, which encouraged his studies in physics and anatomy.

Nicholas Copernicus (1473–1543), as a student in Bologna, came in contact with scientists and philosophers rediscovering the importance of Pythagoras and Plato in the history of rational and mathematical thought. (See PYTHAGORAS.) Indeed Copernicus, in the dedication to Pope Paul III that opened his landmark *On the Revolutions of the Heavenly Spheres,* commented on his debt to Claudius Ptolemy and the inspiration that he received at the hands of Plutarch, who had recorded the Pythagorean hypothesis of a moving and orbiting earth. Sir Thomas Heath claims that Copernicus knew as well the heliocentric theory of Aristarchus of Samos. (See ARISTARCHUS OF SAMOS; ASTRONOMY; PTOLEMAEUS, CLAUDIUS.)

Johannes Kepler (1571–1630) was a student of Ptolemy in imitation of his mentor Tycho Brahe (1546–1601), the Danish astronomer, who was a lifelong defender of Ptolemy's world system. Kepler, however, converted to Copernicus's world system, partly because he was also convinced by Platonic and Pythagorean theories of harmony and mathematics. Like other Renaissance Neoplatonists, Kepler believed that geometric forms mirrored Plato's ideal forms and that the patterns of the universe reflected both. Kepler wrote *The Harmony of the Spheres,* revealing his belief that Pythagorean harmonies are reflected in the movement of the planets. Like the Neoplatonists of the ancient world, Kepler assumed that the sun, the source of light and power, must be the center of all things. (See NEOPLATONISM; PYTHAGORAS.)

Galileo Galilei (1564–1642), who perhaps more than any other Renaissance scientist inaugurated the Scientific Revolution, used the works of Archimedes, Ptolemy, and Aristotle as the foundation for his own discoveries and repudiation of ancient theories about motion and the heavens. Galileo was Italian, a native of Pisa. A gifted mathematician, he mastered Euclid's *Elements* as a student. He reputedly was the first scientist to study the solar system and Milky Way with the telescope. Although many of his discoveries contradicted Aristotle, Galileo sympathized with the ancient scientist, believing that had Aristotle had the advantages of seventeenth-century thought, he too would have discovered the errors of his theories of motion and the universe. (See ASTRONOMY; MATHEMATICS; PHYSICAL SCIENCES.)

With Galileo in the lead, other scientists took up the cause of empiricism. Francis Bacon (1561–1626) arrogantly tossed aside the ancients even as he relied on them for his initial assumptions. Andreas Vesalius was an ardent student of Galen, using the Roman's works and theories in the process of making new discoveries to undermine them. William Harvey (1578–1657) likewise developed the theory of the circulation of the blood by first wondering whether or not Galen's theories were correct. (See GALEN; MEDICINE.) Pierre Gassendi (1592–1655), a skeptic who embraced the theories of the ancient philosophers Sextus Empiricus and Pyrrho, declared emphatically that Aristotelian philosophy is not science. René Descartes, like Francis Bacon, was declaring revolution from ancient science and philosophy as well, rather as a child rebels from the parental strictures of the past.

The Enlightenment and the Modern World

In the year that Isaac Newton published his *Principia Mathematica,* 1687, the curriculum at America's foremost college, Harvard, continued to be devoted to Aristotle in logic and physics and Ptolemy in astronomy. Copernicus had made little headway in the American colonies, although a few almanacs were beginning to include descriptions of the Copernican worldview. Even into the eighteenth century, Newton was thought to be difficult reading for American scientists, and college curricula struggled to abandon the influence of classical physics and astronomy. Medicine continued its relationship with Galen. Aristotle's *Politics* was read alongside Hobbes, Locke, and Montesquieu. Stoic thinkers such as Cicero and Seneca continued to intrigue American philosophers. Plutarch was still the biographer of choice. That Thomas Jefferson, arguably the most brilliant and revolutionary eighteenth-century American thinker, was also the most learned student of the Greek and Roman classics, might seem ironic today, but not during his time, when fluency in Greek and Latin was still the mark of the educated person. (See EPICUREANISM; MEDICINE; PHILOSOPHY; STOICISM.)

The modern world has in many ways never entirely broken away from the influence of ancient scientists and philosophers. The liberal arts education still promoted in colleges and universities derives from Greek models of education developed 2,500 years ago and then resurrected during the Renaissance. Monumental architecture is still classical. Historical inquiry remains beholden to the likes of Thucydides and Tacitus. The philosophers and artists upon which we base our cultural expression and institutions—past masters such as Shakespeare, Locke, Montaigne, Jefferson—were themselves heavily dependent upon Plutarch, Aristotle, Cicero, and Pliny. I. Bernard Cohen has recently noted, in *The Birth of a New Physics,* that our conceptions of the world are still Aristotelian, even though we live in a world in which science is dominated by the Newtonian and Einsteinian paradigms. So subtle has been the influence of ancient science that, try as we might, we still cannot help but think that the sun rises and sets, the moon benevolently shines down upon us, that when we stand still we are motionless, at rest on a still earth, and that heavy objects fall faster than lighter ones. Modern science appears to contradict experience, what we daily observe and sense, which explains why it required a revolution in thought to begin to break the spell that ancient science has cast upon the unconscious and conscious minds of humans. One wonders whether the works of the ancient Greeks will ever cease to have a hypnotic effect upon the modern mind.

References

Cohen, I. Bernard. *The Birth of a New Physics.* New York: W. W. Norton and Co., 1985.

Otto, Rudolf. *The Idea of the Holy.* New York: Oxford University Press, 1968.

St. Augustine. *City of God.* Translated by Henry Bettenson. London: Penguin Books, 1984.

———. *Confessions.* Translated by R. S. Pine-Coffin. Harmondsworth, Middlesex: Penguin Books, 1961.

Sullivan, Richard E. *Aix-la-Chapelle in the Age of Charlemagne.* Norman: University of Oklahoma Press, 1963.

A

Academy

The words academy, academe, and academic derive from the fourth-century Athenian school founded by the Greek philosopher and scientist Plato. Plato founded his academy in the years after he had been a student of Socrates, had experienced his teacher's death in 399, and had traveled to places throughout the Mediterranean, ending up at Syracuse where he had failed in trying to make the tyrant of that city, Dionysus, into a philosopher-king. Plato decided that if he could not turn kings into philosophers, at least he could train the sons of Athens in the art of thinking, the understanding of what is real and true, the best way to live, and the art of citizenship.

The Academy was named for a local god and was dedicated to Zeus's daughters, the Muses. Men and women were admitted on equal terms to the Academy, the two requirements being a good understanding of mathematics, particularly geometry, and wealth—the school was free but relied on donations of wealthy alumni. Mathematics formed the core of the curriculum: arithmetic, geometry, and related subjects such as astronomy and music. Plato used Socrates' technique of the dialogue supplemented by lectures and discussions.

Upon Plato's death in 346, the directorship of the school was assumed by Speusippus and then Xenocrates. Xenocrates was the epitome of the philosopher: dedicated to wisdom, chaste, and poor by choice. Students of the Academy taught others the Socratic approach to knowledge and life, engendering a school of thought focusing on transcendent realities perceived by human reason and intuition, subsequently termed "academic." Many of the great mathematical accomplishments of the age were initiated by the Academics. Plato's most famous student, Aristotle, attended the Academy but never became head of the school. Instead, Aristotle eventually (in 334 BCE) opened a rival school at Athens, the Lyceum, the curriculum of which was based on Aristotle's inductive scientific approach rather than Plato's deductive, rational, and intuitive approach. As time passed, the Academy gained the reputation for sophistry and for splitting hairs over minute philosophical issues, as opposed to Aristotle's successors who focused on practical solutions to the many questions of life and nature. An example was Carneades, who led the Academy in the second century BCE and who could not find anything in the daily happenings of life in Athens—or anywhere else, for that matter—that resembled *reality,* which is unseen, unknown. Academics of the first century, such as Philo and Antiochus, were less concerned with finding reality and more concerned with their reputations in comparison to other schools of thought. Significantly, Philo and Antiochus were teachers of Marcus Tullius Cicero: hence the Academy began to influence Roman philosophy and culture, as had other schools of thought—the Epicurean, the Stoic—before it.

See also Aristotle; Athens; Greek Classical Age; Lyceum; Plato; Socrates

References

Durant, Will. *The Life of Greece.* New York: Simon and Schuster, 1939.

Hare, R. M. *Plato.* Oxford: Oxford University Press, 1982.

Ogilvie, R. M. *Roman Literature and Society.* Harmondsworth, Middlesex: Penguin Books, 1980.

Aelian, Claudius (floruit early third century CE)

Aelian was a Roman who wrote in Greek during the first half of the third century CE. He was a Sophist, connected, perhaps, to the court of Julia Domna, the empress and wife of Septimius Severus and the patroness of philosophers. Philostratus, who knew him, wrote a brief life of Aelian in his *Lives of the Sophists.* Aelian's *On the Characteristics of Animals* is an eclectic compilation of facts about animals purporting to illustrate their moral (and immoral) behavior. Aelian's work is not an original contribution to science—it is heavily reliant upon earlier authors. As such it furnishes us with a varied catalog of ancient writers and commentators. Aelian took as his model such writers as Herodotus, who wrote of places in Europe, Asia, and Africa and presented, uncritically, fact and fancy. Aelian never traveled the Mediterranean to learn firsthand the facts and stories about which he wrote. Aelian's work proceeds from one topic to another in an apparently random fashion, order being determined only by specific animals under discussion according to hearsay, legend, and myth.

On the Characteristics of Animals is anecdotal and filled with comparisons to current practices, beliefs, and verbal expressions. For example, Aelian described the Egyptian veneration for lions, which come to people in their dreams and give them a sense of the future. Following Democritus, he attributed to hot weather and warm south winds a more rapid birth in animals because the organs and tissues are warm and fluid. He wrote that bitches have many babies in a litter because they have many wombs. Ancient myth informed the credulous mind of Aelian that some animals are particularly loved by the gods, who use animals to send their messages and do their will. According to Aelian, many animals have human characteristics. Some nurture and raise infant humans (one thinks of the she-wolf raising Romulus and Remus). Others come to the aid of humans, as when the dolphin saved Arion. Animals such as dolphins, mares, and stingrays enjoy human music; others enjoy dancing. Indian elephants take pleasure in the scent of flowers, drink wine, and are grateful when the forerunners of veterinarians apply salves and other concoctions to heal their wounds. Aelian reported on a thieving octopus, a male hare that bore baby rabbits, on tritons (half human, half fish) seen at sea, and on the two hearts of the elephant—one good, one bad. Interested in medicine, Aelian described remedies for physical ailments derived from various animal parts. The sea urchin is good for stomach problems; the ashes of the hedgehog mixed with pitch is good for hair loss; hedgehog ashes and wine help purify the kidneys.

If Aelian was not a discriminating scientist, he was at least a writer interested in compiling all that he had learned on natural history. His *On the Characteristics of Animals* helps scholars supplement surviving fragments of earlier philosophers. Most importantly, Aelian's work reveals the amazing degree to which people of the Later Roman Empire bought into the claims and stories of pseudoscientists.

See also Later Roman Empire; Life Sciences; Philostratus

References

Aelian. *On the Characteristics of Animals.* 3 vols. Translated by A. F. Scholfield. Cambridge: Harvard University Press, 1971.

Philostratus. *Lives of the Sophists.* Translated by W. C. Wright. Cambridge: Harvard University Press, 1921.

Agathemerus (floruit first century CE)

Little is known of Agathemerus, except that he wrote the treatise *Geography* that has survived in fragments. Perhaps he lived at the beginning of the Common Era, making him a contemporary of Strabo. Agathemerus appears to have been a Roman. He was intrigued by Greek geographers who hypothesized the spherical nature of the earth and believed that Delphi, sacred to Apollo, formed the center. He lauded Democritus for his conception of an earth more wide than long. He claimed that Anaxagoras was the first to draw a world map. Agathemerus had the benefit of having the works of Hecataeus and Herodotus before him and the increased knowledge of the world brought about by Alexander's conquests and the explorations of Pytheas of Massilia and Nearchus of Crete.

See also Geography/Geodesy; Roman Principate
Reference
Barnes, Jonathan, trans. *Early Greek Philosophy.* London: Penguin Books, 1987.

Agriculture

Perhaps the greatest of all human revolutions in science was the invention and development of agriculture nearly twelve thousand years ago in western Asia. The domestication of plants—the process of planting the seed; waiting for germination; cultivating the plant; harvesting the mature grain, vegetable, or fruit; collecting the seed; and then planting again as before—ushered in the Neolithic Age. How purposeful this process was in the beginning is unclear. Perhaps accident played a large role in the initial discovery—indeed much of science has occurred serendipitously. Some gatherer of wild grain used his or her observation and reason to figure out the process, which resulted in a complete change in all aspects of life. Agriculture suggested the possibility, eventually accomplished, of sufficient food production to last more than just a day or two. Surplus food meant that the nomadic ways of the past were over—that there was little reason to keep on the move searching for food and that stability and order beckoned. Agriculture allowed for the first stable communities to be made permanent where the soil was rich, moisture plentiful, and enemies at a distance. These first villages were at places such as Catal Huyuk in eastern Turkey and Jericho near the Dead Sea. Surplus food provided a sense of well-being and wealth, an opportunity for rest and planning for the future, and a sense of time's passing in the seasons as planting and harvesting occurred. Writing was a consequence of the need to keep track of surplus goods from year to year—the first pictographs simply recorded agricultural data. This sense of time, the continuum of past, present, and future, was a prerequisite for scientific thought. Science is fundamentally an intellectual activity involving a historical perspective, wherein the data of experience (natural and human) is accumulated and examined in the present in order to speculate upon, and perhaps predict, the future. The sense of time incumbent upon agriculture was therefore fundamental to the emergence of science.

The first civilizations were built upon the banks of rivers because of the need to irrigate crops in a dry climate. Agriculture in Mesopotamia involved tremendous human labor and organization to control the waters of the Tigris and Euphrates—to build canals for irrigation and dikes for flood control. Sumerian agriculture involved simple bronze tools—spades, hoes, scythes, and sickles. Plows had plowshares and seed feeders, a device to allow the immediate dropping of seed into the furrow. The Sumerians, according to Kramer (1980), performed simple agricultural experiments such as "shade-tree gardening" to see how plants growing under broad shade trees, like the fig or sycamore, would perform.

An Egyptian man plowing and an Egyptian woman sowing seed. (Instructional Resources Corporation)

Egyptian Agriculture

The Nile River was at the center of agriculture in Egypt. Only the simplest tools were required to prepare the soil once the waters of the Nile had receded after its annual flooding leaving behind a rich layer of extremely fertile silt. When Herodotus visited Egypt about 450 BCE he was astonished at the ease with which the Egyptians farmed, the Nile literally doing all of the work. In areas that were not inundated by the Nile, the *shaduf,* a simple device to hoist water in a vessel and then rotate to a holding area or canal, was used to irrigate fields. Egyptian farmers used a simple two-handled plow drawn by oxen to prepare the soil for seed. The plowshare that cut through the soil was made of wood. Egyptian farmers devised a two-handled, two-bladed hoe for breaking up dirt clods. After the scattering of seed, sheep or hogs were driven through the field to trample the seed into the soil. At harvest, the grain of wheat, barley, or millet was cut with a sickle, bound into sheaves, and brought to a threshing floor to be threshed—donkeys were used to separate the fruit from the stalk. The threshed grain was then winnowed by tossing in the air, the heavier grain falling down and the lighter chaff being blown away by the wind.

Greek Agriculture

The mountainous peninsula of Greece did not easily support agriculture, although we find in the *Works and Days* of Hesiod, written about 700 BCE, a portrait of the pastoral existence of the farmer and herder. Hesiod gave directions for planting and harvesting based on astronomical phenomena. Homer's *Odyssey* emphasized the agricultural wealth of landowners at the beginning of the first millennium; the details of production of grain, hogs, wine, and beef could hardly have been based on mere poetic imagination. Greece was fit more for the cultivation of wine and olives, the latter requiring little effort to cultivate properly, the former perfectly adapted to the climate of the Mediterranean. The rocky soil hosted enough successful viticulture, olive production, farming of grains, and raising of cattle and goats for milk and cheese that the population of Greece grew—such that by the time of Homer and Hesiod various city-states sent colonists elsewhere in the Mediterranean region to find fertile land to raise crops and establish trade. Another reason for colonization appears to have been declining yields of grain due to the lack of the fertility of the soil and soil erosion. Archaic Age Greeks knew little about fertilization and vainly hoped prayers to fertility gods and goddesses would increase yields. It was no coincidence that during this time Bolos of Mende wrote treatises on both agriculture and signs from the heavens.

Roman Agriculture

The Roman Empire was initially built on successful cultivation of the Italian soil by hardy farmers and shepherds. Roman writers including Livy eulogized the sturdy farmers, such as Cincinnatus, who were loyal to Rome and formed the basis for middle-class armies of freeholders who could defeat any army in the Mediterranean world. The practical Roman mind-set produced quite a few agricultural writers. Examples include the Elder Cato, Varro, Celsus, Columella, the Elder Pliny, and Palladius. These writers emphasized the pastoral, the valuable peace that accompanied the farm life. Some, such as Cato, wrote to the increasing number of wealthy plantation owners who rarely got their hands dirty but rather had armies of slaves, captured in war, who performed the manual labor. Roman politics of the second century BCE revealed the conflict over land, as small freeholders were being forced to sell to the grasping owners of slave plantations, *latifundia*. Palladius, writing in the fourth century CE, indicated that Roman agricultural methods were the same throughout the thousand-year history of the Roman Empire. The sandy Mediterranean soil required simple methods and tools; the heavy plow of the Middle Ages was developed later in response to the thick and rocky soil of northern Europe. The Romans practiced an elementary form of crop rotation involving leaving land fallow in intermittent years. Palladius suggested leaving land burned by fire for five years, at which time its fertility would be astonishing. Dung had different purposes, depending on the animal and how the dung was kept. Palladius provided detailed information on when crops and fruits should be sown according to the season and phases of the moon. He provided a full listing of the types of tools the Mediterranean farmer should use. For example, he described an ox-drawn cart with a toothed jaw at the front that gathered the wheat and separated the chaff from the grain. The husbandmen, like hunters, wore leather coats and hoods to protect themselves from the countless thorn-bushes in the woods.

The staple of the ancient Mediterranean diet was bread made from grains such as barley, millet, and wheat. Mills ground the grain into flour. Roman mills, for example, relied on two massive millstones, lying flat and parallel against each other, one being driven around by human or animal power to grind the grain.

Palladius counseled hard work to achieve high yields. By the time of his writing in the mid-fourth century, however, most of those working the land were agricultural laborers rather than independent freeholders. The major change in Roman agriculture from the first millennium BCE to the first millennium CE was the increasing number of slaves and peasants involved in cultivation of land that they did not own. The inequality of Later Roman agriculture meant that there was a small class of the very rich who were looked to for leadership in war and local politics and a huge dependent class of agriculture laborers, the *coloni*.

Agriculture in the New Testament

The Greek New Testament provides an interesting portrait of agriculture during the first century CE in the eastern Mediterranean of the Roman Empire. Jesus moved among a people who were intimately tied to the land. The soil of the valleys that sometimes had sufficient rainfall and was therefore a rich loam was prepared for the seed by a simple plow used as a hoe by the farmer. Soil in dry upland areas could rarely hold the seed, the thin soil covering often exposing rock just below the surface. According to the Gospel of Luke (8:5–8), "a sower went out to sow his seed: and as he sowed, some fell by the way side; and it was trodden down, and the fowls of the air devoured it. And some fell upon a rock; and as soon as it was sprung up, it withered away, because it lacked moisture. And some fell among thorns; and the thorns sprang up with it, and choked it. And other fell on good ground, and sprang up, and bore fruit an hundred-fold." Jesus's use of agricultural terms to describe the process of judgment was not lost on the simple Palestinian farm folk: God, "whose fan is in his hand, . . . will thoroughly purge his floor, and will gather the wheat into his garner; but the chaff he will burn with fire unquenchable" (Luke 3:17).

Agriculture and the Fall of Rome

Some scholars have argued that the principal cause of the decline of the Roman Empire, particularly in the Western Roman Empire (Britain, Spain, Gaul, Italy, North Africa), was that agriculture, the dominant feature in the Roman economy, declined in the third and fourth centuries. Declining agricultural productivity and food surpluses spelled disaster for the lower classes, who frequently were victims of famine, malnutrition, and disease. The population of the Roman Empire was dramatically reduced during the third century. More and more thousands of acres went untilled. Declining food reserves encouraged declining population, leading to less acreage under cultivation. The problem did not go away for centuries—in the meantime the Western Empire fell to Germanic tribes who knew little about agriculture, which helped to bring about the Dark Ages in Europe.

See also Cato, Marcus Porcius; Celsus; Columella; Egypt; Hesiod; Irrigation Techniques; Later Roman Empire; Mesopotamia; New Testament; Palladius; Pliny the Elder

References

Erman, Adolf. *Life in Ancient Egypt.* Translated by H. M. Tirard. New York: Dover Books, 1894.

French, A. "The Economic Background to Solon's Reforms." *Classical Quarterly* 6 (1956).

Jones, A. H. M. *The Decline of the Ancient World.* London: Longman, 1966.

Kramer, Samuel Noah. *History Begins at Sumer.* Philadelphia: University of Pennsylvania Press, 1980.

Palladius. *On Husbandrie.* Translated by Barton Lodge. London: Early English Text Society, 1879.

The Holy Bible, Containing the Old and New Testaments. New York: American Bible Society, 1865.

Von Hagen, Victor W. *Roman Roads.* London: Werdenfeld and Nicholson, 1966.

Alchemy

See Physical Sciences

Alcmaeon (floruit early sixth century BCE)

Alcmaeon was a younger contemporary of Pythagoras—perhaps his student. Like Pythagoras he lived at Croton in southern Italy. Alcmaeon was a naturalist and physician in addition to being a philosopher. Diogenes Laertius, in the *Lives of the Philosophers,* claimed that Alcmaeon wrote a natural history, the first of its kind, and that like Pythagoras he believed in the transcendent soul and the spiritual make-up of the stars, planets, and moon. He was known as a teacher who was true to the basic teachings of the Pythagorean school. He believed that the spiritual is not still but rather in constant movement. The soul is eternal, unlike the body. Human bodily existence is transient rather than transcendent, subject to time and hence death. One's birth and death are always at opposite ends.

Alcmaeon as a physician was more the philosopher, believing that all life exists in pairs, or opposites, such as wet and dry, good and bad, angry and happy. Illness in humans derives from an imbalance of these opposites. The well person does not want to be more hot than cold, and vice versa. Aristotle's student Theophrastus quoted Alcmaeon as believing that sound is caused by echoes in the ear canal, that the nose brings air to the brain to detect scent, that taste is dictated by the tongue and its saliva, and that the eyes have water that helps reflect an image that is external to it. Alcmaeon hypothesized that the brain and the senses are somehow or other connected, and that should the former fail the latter will fail too.

Alcmaeon also made his mark as an astronomer. A Pythagorean, he doubtless believed in the sphericity of the earth and its place in the center of the universe surrounded by planets and the fixed stars. The Pythagoreans also believed in the geocentric universe. He advocated (and perhaps conceived of) the theory that "the planets have a motion from west to east, in a direction opposite to that of the fixed stars," which move east to west (Heath 1913). Such a conclusion about the movement of the stars demanded patient observation and a willingness to puzzle over the major problem of ancient planetary astronomy: the retrograde motion of the planets, the "wanderers."

See also Astronomy; Greek Archaic Age;
    Hippocrates; Medicine; Pythagoras
References
Barnes, Jonathan, trans. *Early Greek Philosophy.*
    London: Penguin Books, 1987.
Heath, Sir Thomas. *Aristarchus of Samos.* 1913;
    reprint ed., New York: Dover Books, 1981.

Alexander of Macedon (356–323 BCE)

The original thinking, unique personality, and irrepressible will of Alexander the Great inaugurated the Hellenistic Age (323–31 BCE). Alexander's conquest of the Persian Empire and his vision to link the Greeks and Macedonians of Europe with the Africans of Egypt and the Asians of Anatolia, Palestine, Mesopotamia, and Iran resulted in a mixture of unique cultures that stimulated a new epoch of intellectual and scientific achievement. The diversity of thinkers brought together at such centers of learning as Alexandria, Egypt, founded by Alexander in 331 BCE, resulted in significant scientific writings and theories that have influenced subsequent scientists and philosophers for centuries even to the present. Alexander himself, as the student of Aristotle, was a scientist, a philosopher-king, who appended curiosity and scientific discovery to his principal aims of conquest and military glory.

Alexander was raised in a kingdom that valued brutal strength and military prowess. Fourth-century BCE Macedonians had faith in the traditional Greek gods who were themselves divine and eternal symbols of raw human emotions and violent confrontations. Not surprisingly, Alexander identified with the great Homeric hero and warrior Achilles and the legendary strongman Heracles. His conquest of Asia was motivated in part by his desire to exceed Achilles and Heracles in glory. His mother, Olympias, reputedly believed that she had conceived Alexander with the seed of Zeus, king of the gods; Alexander grew up thinking of himself as (perhaps) the son of Zeus. Olympias, a princess from the kingdom of Epirus west of Macedonia, was a snake charmer who introduced Alexander to other deities, such as Bacchus, the god of wine, whose worship involved orgiastic rituals brought on by divine intoxication. Alexander learned as well that the gods often revealed truth and destiny by means of oracles. Alexander traveled to the Oracle of Zeus-Ammon at Siwah in the Sahara Desert after his conquest of Egypt in 331. Alexander regarded Homer's tale in the *Iliad* to have been an accurate account of valor, conduct, and relations between humans and gods. Throughout his life he tried to live up to the poetic, heroic model wrought by Homer.

Alexander the Great. Anonymous, ca. 320 BCE. (Kathleen Cohen/J. Paul Getty Museum)

Another important influence on Alexander's life was the scientist and philosopher Aristotle and his teachings. Aristotle served as Alexander's tutor for three years, from 343 to 340. Aristotle's approach to the divine (and to every other form of human inquiry) was much more sophisticated than the young Alexander had hitherto experienced. The philosopher helped Alexander to see that besides Homeric valor and beliefs are the values of civilized culture and the understanding of the divine by means of the intellect rather than blind superstition. Aristotle opened up Alexander's mind to the infinite possibilities of life and the potential diversity of human behavior and belief.

No precise record survives to indicate what Aristotle taught and Alexander learned. One can hypothesize that Aristotle brought to Alexander many of the theories and observations that would make up the philosopher's immense corpus of writings. Aristotle rejected the Homeric worldview, arguing instead that truth is metaphysical and that the gods are elementary representations of being *(ousia),* which is the transcendent creative force in the universe. Whereas strength mattered most in Macedonia, Aristotle argued that the best form of government is the state that is run according to virtue and which encourages virtue in its citizens. Aristotle taught the young prince techniques of observation, inductive reasoning, and deductive logic. He encouraged Alexander to become more than a king—to be a philosopher as well. Plutarch, in his *Life of Alexander,* wrote that Alexander, upon learning that Aristotle had published his book of *Metaphysics,* wrote the philosopher from Asia chiding him for publishing his teachings hence allowing others to be privy to the same information that Alexander himself had been taught. What is the point in being a king if one's subjects have the same knowledge? Plutarch added that Alexander was particularly interested in what Aristotle taught him about medicine. The philosopher's influence upon the student was so great that Alexander acted as a physician to his friends, making diagnoses and recommending cures and regimens to restore health.

Alexander never attended Aristotle's school, the Lyceum, at Athens, though the king admired the Athenians for their many scientific and philosophic accomplishments. Perhaps the model of Athens inspired Alexander's vision of a center of learning in his new empire that would eclipse the old—the grand but limited ideas of Athens and its philosophers. When in 331 Alexander saw Pharos Island near the mouth of the Nile River in Egypt, he knew he had found the site for his city. Indeed, within a generation of his death, Alexandria had already emerged as one of the leading centers of trade and science in the Mediterranean world.

Alexander led not only a host of warriors to conquer the Persian Empire but a host of scientists as well. Aristotle's grandnephew Callisthenes accompanied the king, serving as official historian. Other historians, such as Aristander of Telmessus and Cleitarch of Colophon, accompanied Alexander, as well as Sophists such as Anaxarchus of Abdera, Indian sages such as Calanus, and soothsayers such as Aristobulus of Cassandreia. His interest in geographic exploration inspired Alexander to send Nearchus to explore the Arabian Sea; Archias, Androsthenes, and Hieron on separate expeditions to explore the Arabian peninsula; and unnamed explorers to explore the Caspian Sea. Arrian, the Greek biographer of Alexander, wrote that Alexander had many questions regarding the Caspian: whether or not it was linked to the Black Sea or connected to an outer ocean, and if not, what rivers fed the Caspian.

Alexander has been the object of much discussion among ancient and modern historians, who debate what his motives were in planning and carrying out his ten-year conquest of the Persian Empire. Some see Alexander driven by an idealist desire to unite all humans under his sole rule. Others argue that Alexander was a megalomaniac conqueror like so many other tyrants before and since. A possible interpretation for the historian of science is that Alexander's conquests were fueled by a deep personal motivation for glory and power as well as a strong desire to confront and conquer the unknown. Arrian's *Anabasis* quoted unnamed sources, perhaps Nearchus, that Alexander used a specific word, *pothos,* to describe this longing to explore the unknown. Arrian cited several examples of Alexander's use of the word. Upon the death of King Philip, Alexander, trying to solidify his hold on power, marched north to the Danube River to put down rebellions. Upon reaching the Danube, according to Arrian, Alexander longed to cross the river. This longing was partly an insatiable curiosity to know. Likewise in his *Indica,* Arrian quoted Nearchus's sense that Alexander's desire (*pothos*) to know was the origin of his plan to send Nearchus to explore the Arabian Sea and Persian Gulf. Again, when Alexander had returned from his conquests and the disastrous journey across the Gedrosian Desert, upon reaching Persepolis he again felt the yearning for discovery, and wished to see the Persian Gulf for himself. Arrian cited various

writers who claimed that Alexander had a longing to see and conquer much more, including Arabia and Africa, both of which he proposed to circumnavigate, the latter all the way to the Pillars of Heracles at the Strait of Gibraltar. He was also interested in Sicily and Italy, having heard of the Romans' growing strength, and also longed to explore the Euxine Sea (as the Black Sea was called in antiquity) and conquer the savage Scythians to the north.

See also Aristotle; Arrian; Geography/Geodesy; Hellenism; Nearchus of Crete; Plutarch

References
Arrian. *Anabasis* and *Indica*. Translated by P. A. Brunt and E. Iliff Robson. 2 vols. Cambridge: Harvard University Press, 1933, 1976.
Ehrenberg, Victor. *Alexander and the Greeks.* Oxford: Oxford University Press, 1938.
Fox, Robin Lane. *The Search for Alexander.* Boston: Little, Brown, 1979.
Plutarch. *The Lives of the Noble Grecians and Romans.* Translated by John Dryden; revised by Arthur Hugh Clough. 1864; reprint ed., New York: Random House, 1992.

Alexandria

Alexandria, founded and named by Alexander the Great in 331 BCE, became the leading center of science and thought in the ancient world from 300 BCE to 500 CE. As the center of Hellenistic culture after Alexander's death in 323 and supported by Ptolemy I and his successors, Alexandria brought together a host of different scientists, philosophers, cultures, and peoples. This dynamic, cosmopolitan mix ensured that the city would be vibrant, diverse, sometimes chaotic, and calm neither in its political affairs nor in its intellectual debates.

Alexandria was the namesake of Alexander the Great, the enigmatic Macedonian conqueror who founded the city after having recently sacked the Phoenician city of Tyre and the Palestinian city of Gaza. Alexander had arrived in Egypt fresh also from defeating Darius III at the Battle of Issus. He came to Egypt as a liberator for Egypt from Persian control; the Egyptians responded by naming him pharaoh of Egypt. Alexander knew that his emerging empire encompassing Eastern Europe, northern Africa, and western Asia would require a center of trade, government, and learning. He had the foresight to see that a city at the mouth of the Nile River would fulfill that role.

The ancient biographers Arrian and Plutarch related that Alexander sailed down the Nile to its mouth, then along the Mediterranean coast a brief distance to a natural harbor, formed by a quiet lagoon situated between the mainland and an island called Pharos. The harbor was protected from the fresh westerly breeze, and the island hinted of its importance as a seamark for sailors. Alexander decided that such a location would be perfect for the kind of city he envisioned. He himself eagerly set out the plan of the town, using barley meal to set the boundaries. According to Plutarch, Alexander conceived of the city as a semicircular arc proceeding from one point in equal segments. Alexander wanted a city built according to the theories of Hippodamus of Miletus, who believed in an ordered city of rectangular streets and buildings where the predominant shape would be the right angle. Alexander departed, leaving others to complete his vision; he appointed a student of Hippodamus, Deinocrates of Rhodes, as lead architect and planner. Deinocrates was notable for building the Temple of Artemis at Ephesus, a wonder of the world, and for accompanying Alexander on his conquest of Persia; he built the fabulous funeral pyre in honor of Alexander's friend Hephaistion. Deinocrates designed the city to be wide, with a central boulevard connecting different quarters of peoples and places. A series of canals and other hydraulic masterpieces were built by Crates of Olynthus. A causeway connected the island of Pharos to the mainland, which itself was a vast peninsula practically surrounded by water. The causeway formed two harbors on either side; the harbor to the east was enclosed and able to host scores of ships. The southern part of the city had important harbors on Lake Mareotis. Upon Alexander's death, one of his successors, Ptolemy, marched to Egypt with Alexander's embalmed corpse, set himself up as pharaoh, and built a tomb for Alexander.

Ptolemy I inaugurated the idea of a massive lighthouse constructed on Pharos; his successor Ptolemy II Philadelphus completed it, using the talents of the architect Sostratus of Cnidus. The lighthouse, subsequently called simply Pharos, was justifiably considered one of the seven wonders of the ancient world. It was built in three levels— the first rectangular, the second hexagonal, the third a cylinder culminating in the pinnacle, where stood a massive fire fed by wood and resin. The Elder Pliny implied that the fire burned continuously. Some scholars have hypothesized the existence of mirrors that illuminated the flame. Its builders dedicated Pharos to Zeus and Poseidon. One inscription states that Sostratos called upon the gods to preserve the lives of mariners. Pliny praised Ptolemy II for allowing Sostratos the honor of an inscription with his name as builder. Pharos survived for nearly fifteen hundred years, during which it fascinated scores of travelers, sailors, writers, and scientists. It helped to make Alexandria a center of trade, culture, and learning.

Other prime attractions in Hellenistic Alexandria were the museum and the library. The museum, reputedly sponsored by Ptolemy I working with Aristotle's student Demetrius of Phaleron, housed scholars who engaged in research, writing, speaking, and symposia, which even included the pharaohs. The library adjoined the museum and held up to seven hundred thousand papyrus scrolls. Pliny the Elder claimed that papyrus parchment came into being with the creation of Alexandria. Directors of the library included the likes of Apollonius of Rhodes, the author of *Argonautica,* and Eratosthenes of Cyrene, the geographer. Great thinkers lived and worked in Alexandria—Euclid, the mathematician, author of *Elements;* Ctesibius, the pneumatic engineer, thought to have worked with water clocks; Timochares, an architect who worked with magnets; Hero, the mathematician and engineer; Potamo, founder of the Eclectic school of philosophy and author of *Elements of Philosophy;* and physicians such as Herophilus, Erasistratus, and Serapion. One of the great thinkers of the ancient world, Claudius Ptolemaeus, the astronomer, geographer, and mathematician, lived and worked in Alexandria. Such scholars made Alexandria the leading center of thought in the ancient world, eclipsing even Athens, Antioch, Rome, and Constantinople.

As the years passed, even as the Roman Empire began to have problems and decline, Alexandria continued to be a bright light of learning in the eastern Mediterranean. During the age of Constantine, for example, the mathematician Hypatia lived and taught at Alexandria, as did her father, Theon, also a mathematician as well as a physicist, astronomer, and commentator on the works, the *Almagest,* of Ptolemy. Other important mathematicians included Diophantus, Pappas, and Proclus.

See also Alexander of Macedon; Apollonius of Perga; Engineering and Technology; Erasistratus; Eratosthenes; Euclid; Hellenism; Hero; Hypatia of Alexandria; Mathematics; Ptolemaeus, Claudius; Seven Wonders of the Ancient World

References

Arrian. *Anabasis* and *Indica.* Translated by P. A. Brunt and E. Iliff Robson. 2 vols. Cambridge: Harvard University Press, 1933, 1976.

Casson, Lionel. *Libraries in the Ancient World.* New Haven: Yale University Press, 2001.

Empereur, Jean-Yves. *Alexandria Rediscovered.* New York: George Brazziler, 1998.

Grant, Michael. *From Alexander to Cleopatra: The Hellenistic World.* New York: History Book Club, 2000.

Hamilton, J. R. *Alexander the Great.* Pittsburgh: University of Pittsburgh Press, 1974.

Jones, Tom B. *In the Twilight of Antiquity.* Minneapolis: University of Minnesota Press, 1978.

Pliny the Elder. *Natural History.* Translated by John F. Healy. London: Penguin Books, 1991.

Plutarch. *Life of Alexander.* Translated by Bernadotte Perrin. Cambridge: Harvard University Press, 1986.

Ammianus Marcellinus (325–395 CE)

Ammianus Marcellinus was a soldier turned historian during the Later Roman Empire. He was a native of Antioch in Syria, a Greek from an aristocratic family who served in the Roman military under the emperors Constantius II and Julian. As a soldier he traveled throughout the Roman Empire, from Gaul (France) in the west to the eastern extreme of the empire at Mesopotamia (Tigris and Euphrates river valleys). Marcellinus was a well-educated man who in his surviving *History* was willing to discuss and speculate upon a variety of natural and human phenomena. In the role of a man of affairs and historian who occasionally dipped into the world of the scientist, he mirrored his hero Cornelius Tacitus, the great historian of the Roman Principate. Indeed, Ammianus Marcellinus conceived his massive *History* to be a continuation of the *Histories* of Tacitus. The first fourteen books of Marcellinus's *History* are lost. In the surviving books, however, we have a full narrative account of many of the events of fourth-century Rome, as well as plentiful discussions of the lands and peoples of Rome and its enemies. Marcellinus was a pagan during a time when Christianity was becoming more widespread throughout the Roman Empire and most emperors (except Marcellinus's hero Julian) were Christian. Antioch was one of the cultural centers of the eastern Mediterranean. Marcellinus had a classical education and was familiar with the best writers and thinkers of the Greco-Roman world.

Because of the many years in which Ammianus Marcellinus traveled about the Roman Empire as a soldier and the wide variety of peoples and places he saw, his *History* is particularly useful in its geographic and ethnographic descriptions. In Book 14, for example, Marcellinus described the Saracens, a nomadic people living on the fringes of the empire near Arabia. The men were great horsemen but not agriculturalists. Plowing the soil was eschewed by men who lived on horseback under the great canopy of the open sky and twinkling stars of night. Of the Gauls, whom Marcellinus had come to know in war, he wrote of their irrepressible courage, particularly exhibited by Gaulish matrons who fought with the same fury and strength as their husbands. Marcellinus was particularly good at describing the Alps, the Rhine River, the Rhone River, Mesopotamia, and other places that he had seen on his travels.

At other times, eschewing experience for the wisdom of other sources, Marcellinus relied on authors whom he considered like-minded, such as Strabo the geographer and Pliny the natural historian. For his long and fascinating discussion of the Euxine (Black) Sea, in which he mixed legend, myth, and natural history, Marcellinus used Pliny and Strabo extensively. From Strabo, Marcellinus learned of the Druids, whom he compared to Pythagorean philosophers in their attempts to uncover the essence of things, and the Euhages, also of Britain, who pried into the mysteries of nature. For his description of Egyptian hieroglyphics, he relied on Plutarch, Seneca, and Diodorus Siculus. Pliny the Elder's *Natural History* assisted Marcellinus in wading through the varied theories to account for the rising of the Nile River in Egypt. Marcellinus knew from Eratosthenes that the sun was directly overhead at the summer solstice at Syrene. He identified the source of the word "pyramid" from the Greek *pyre,* or fire, the flames of which form a point as they rise. Marcellinus was heavily dependent upon Herodotus for his discussion of Persia. However, when he took time to consider the origins of pearls, that they are formed by the rays of the moon, he relied upon his own singular imagination.

As an astronomer Marcellinus was not, of course, original, relying heavily on his forebears, particularly Claudius Ptolemy. The universe of the Later Roman Empire was geocentric, the moon closest to the earth, the sun in the third spot between Venus and Mars. The inaccuracies of such a system were daunting for an Aristotle or a Ptolemy and

simply overwhelming for a lesser thinker such as Marcellinus. His account of a solar eclipse in 360 CE is fascinating for its description of the darkness of the day such that stars could be seen. Marcellinus knew that a lunar eclipse occurred when the moon stood at the opposite extreme of the spherical path or elliptic of the sun. Marcellinus's explanation of rainbows was accurate that the light of the sun confronting mist in the atmosphere forms the rainbow. He thought, however, that the rainbow is opposite in respect to the sun, rather like what happens in his theory of the lunar eclipse, and it extends across the entire starry vault of the heavens. Marcellinus's theory of meteors fit perfectly the ancient conception of the spiritual nature of the heavenly bodies. He condemned the idea that meteors are physical bodies— rather they are sparks of heaven, or at least rays of light produced by the confrontation of sunlight and dense clouds.

Northwestern Turkey, even today subject to frequent tremors of the earth, experienced an earthquake in August of 358: Marcellinus was (perhaps) an eyewitness. The city of Nicomedia was flattened by the earthquake, which indicated its coming by the darkness of the sky and terrible thunderstorms revealing the anger of the gods. Marcellinus duly presented an extensive discussion on the cause of earthquakes, describing the views of Aristotle, that water surging through fissures in the earth is the cause; of Anaxagoras, that it is subterranean winds; and Anaximander, that it is an earth either too dry or soaked by rains that succumbs to the force of wind.

Marcellinus's history is a narrative of cause and effect, with arbitrary actions of Adrastia (Nemesis) underlying this. As the universal spiritual power pervades the earth and cosmos, some humans, exercising prescience, gain knowledge of the future with the help of Themis, who makes known what fate has determined. The gods send birds, the flight of which, the noises they make, the path they pursue, indicate the future for the clever augur. Another source of future knowledge comes from the sun, Helios, the life and breath of the universe who sends thought (divine sparks) to the human seeking mental awareness.

Ammianus Marcellinus was a supporter of Julian, the emperor and Neoplatonist. Marcellinus's conception of human and natural history was that of a Neoplatonist—believing that the source of all being exudes from the invisible One. Like Julian as well, he had the Stoic belief in the order of things and in the importance of human experience in the acquisition of knowledge.

See also Astronomy; History; Julian; Later
   Roman Empire; Neoplatonism; Pliny the
   Elder; Stoicism; Strabo; Tacitus

References

Rolfe, John C., trans. Ammianus Marcellinus. 2 vols.
   Cambridge: Harvard University Press, 1950.
Rowell, H. Ammianus Marcellinus, Soldier Historian
   of the Late Roman Empire. 1964.
Thompson, E. A. The Historical Work of Ammianus
   Marcellinus. Cambridge: Cambridge University
   Press, 1947.

Anaxagoras of Clazomenae (500–428 BCE)

Anaxagoras, a native of the Ionian town of Clazomenae, was one of the last members of the Ionian school. He was influenced by his predecessors Thales, Anaximander, and Anaximenes. Anaxagoras was a questioner who sought explanations for the ultimate origins of all phenomena. According to Diogenes Laertius, Linus of Thebes, a poet who wrote a cosmology that featured a central causative power, mind (nous), influenced Anaxagoras. Anaxagoras spent his youth during a period of Persian occupation of western Turkey. After the Persian Wars he migrated to Athens at the invitation of Pericles, the great general and leader. Plutarch claimed in his Life of Pericles that Anaxagoras, who was nicknamed nous, helped to form the philosophic mind of Pericles. Some historians believe that Pericles' concubine Aspasia, a native Milesian inclined toward philosophy, was influential in bringing Anaxagoras to Athens. Anaxagoras, the student of the Milesian Anaximenes, had a major impact on the development of scientific speculation in Athens, as his students included Archelaus, who was himself the teacher of Socrates.

Anaxagoras reputedly wrote a treatise, Physics, in which he stated his belief that all existence is encompassed by nous, an infinite and transcendent presence of which humans partake, and by which humans can know reality. Anaxagoras, according to Plutarch, initiated among philosophers the cosmology of a universe that is not the result of chance or whim but reason. One can clearly see the influence of Anaximander and Anaximenes on Anaxagoras's conception of infinity. Anaxagoras hypothesized that there are infinite particles moving in an infinite space of ether. Here he anticipated the atomists. The glue, as it were, that holds this infinite multiplicity together is mind.

Anaxagoras's concept of mind is a highly original idea similar to the Hebrew Yahweh, the Egyptian pharaoh Akhenaten's Aten, and the Stoic logos. Mind (nous) is a universal force, the first cause, the knower of all things, yet unique in its singularity, its aloofness from human concerns. Mind is self-reliant, having no need for anything besides itself. Infinite and eternal, it encompasses time and knowledge.

As an astronomer and physicist, Anaxagoras made some startling discoveries. He was the first to understand the true nature of lunar and solar eclipses because he was the first to understand that the moon produces no light of its own but merely reflects the light of the sun. The commentator Aëtius wrote that "Anaxagoras, in agreement with the mathematicians, held that the moon's obscurations month by month were due to its following the course of the sun by which it is illuminated, and that the eclipses of the moon were caused by its falling within the shadow of the earth, which then comes between the sun and the moon, while the eclipses of the sun were due to the interposition of the moon" (Heath 1913).

Ionian philosopher and scientist Anaxagoras (500–428 BCE), tutor to Pericles and Archelaus. Engraving from ca. 1493. (From Hartmann Schedel, Liber Chronicorum Mundi, *Nuremberg Chronicle.) (Hulton Archive)*

Anaxagoras also had a remarkable interpretation of the origins of the universe. In the beginning "all things were together" and nothing was separate. Mind made the whole to revolve. As it turned, "in consequence of the violence of the whirling motion, the surrounding fiery aether tore stones away from the earth and kindled them into stars" (Heath 1913). In time, the air and ether were separated and formed two realms wherein were the opposites of wet and dry, cold and hot, dark and light. Echoing Thales, Anaxagoras believed that the moist and cold produced the earth and the dry and hot the heavens. The heavenly bodies, he agreed with his teacher Anaximenes, are stones of fire. Anaxagoras broke from most ancient astronomers in his belief that the order of the heavenly bodies orbiting Earth was Moon, Sun, Mercury, Venus, Mars, Jupiter, and Saturn.

One can see a direct influence of the thought of Anaxagoras upon Socrates and Plato, and therefore all of Western philosophy and science. The Platonic vision of a reality unperceived by the senses was inspired by Ionian philosophers such as Anaxagoras. Socrates, in the *Phaedo,* claimed that Anaxagoras set him on the path of seeking the essence of what is in mind.

See also Anaximenes of Miletus; Archelaus of
    Athens; Astronomy; Athens; Greek Classical
    Age; Ionians; Physical Sciences; Socrates

References

Barnes, Jonathan, trans. *Early Greek Philosophy.* London: Penguin Books, 1987.

Heath, Sir Thomas. *Aristarchus of Samos.* 1913; reprint ed., New York: Dover Books, 1981.

Laertius, Diogenes. *Lives of the Philosophers.* Translated by R. D. Hicks. 2 vols. Cambridge: Harvard University Press, 1931, 1938.

Plutarch. *The Lives of the Noble Grecians and Romans.* Translated by John Dryden; revised by Arthur Hugh Clough. 1864; reprint ed., New York: Random House, 1992.

Anaximander of Miletus (610–540 BCE)

Anaximander was the student of Thales, a leader in the early development of the Ionian school of thought. He continued his teacher's search to discover the one source of all things, whether material or spiritual. Thales had argued for the origin of all things in water; Anaximander sought the unity of all things in the uncreated, unlimited infinite *(apeiron)*. Anaximander engaged in the contradictory pursuit of imposing limits and definitions on the limitless that by its very nature is indefinable. Yet he was the first ancient scientist to try to explain all phenomena according to a single principle.

Anaximander reputedly wrote a book, *On Nature,* but nothing survives from it except by paraphrase and a quote or two found in the commentators of later antiquity. Plutarch, Simplicius, Hippolytus, and Diogenes Laertius, among others, recorded the general outline of Anaximander's principle of the infinite and its necessary corollaries, that there has been, is, and will always exist an unending cycle of creation and destruction, for what purpose is unclear. This infinite is an anonymous, impersonal force, not a personal deity but rather an amoral, eternal absolute that is truly unrecognizable to humans. The infinite as a creative principle made the earth, which is a cylinder that rests in air surrounded by the moon, sun, planets, and stars, all made of fire. Parenthetically, Anaximander would add that an infinite universe must accommodate an infinite number of worlds. We see the heavenly bodies because the fire protrudes through gaps or holes in the air. The heavenly bodies vary in size, though they are all equally distant from the earth. The sun, the source of warmth, acting upon water produces life. The first form of life, rather like a fish, crawled up on land and eventually ended up looking remarkably like humans. Not surprisingly, Anaximander rarely had fish for dinner.

The ancients claimed other accomplishments for Anaximander. The geographer Agathemerus wrote that Anaximander was the first to draw a map of the earth, which must have been on a long and narrow parchment. Hecataeus reputedly used Anaximander's map as the basis for his own. Pliny the Elder believed that Anaximander was the first to use a globe, even if it was awkwardly shaped. Diogenes Laertius recorded that Anaximander was the first to introduce to the Greeks the sundial or gnomon, with which to gauge time by day and to approximate the summer and winter solstices and the fall and spring equinoxes. Herodotus, however, assigned these scientific accomplishments to the Mesopotamians, from whom, perhaps, Anaximander took his own ideas. Many of Anaximander's ideas were carried forward by his fellow Milesian and disciple, Anaximenes.

See also Anaximenes of Miletus; Geography/Geodesy; Greek Archaic Age; Hecataeus of Miletus; Physical Sciences; Thales

References

Barnes, Jonathan, trans. *Early Greek Philosophy.* London: Penguin Books, 1987.

Heath, Sir Thomas. *Aristarchus of Samos.* 1913; reprint ed., New York: Dover Books, 1981.

Laertius, Diogenes. *Lives of the Philosophers.* Translated by R. D. Hicks. 2 vols. Cambridge: Harvard University Press, 1931, 1938.

Leicester, Henry M. *The Historical Background of Chemistry.* New York: Dover Books, 1971.

Anaximenes of Miletus (585–525 BCE)

Anaximenes of Miletus was the student of Anaximander and the teacher of Anaxagoras. He was an important figure in the development of the Ionian school because he continued the focus of inquiry established by his predecessors Thales and Anaximander. Anaximenes, like his teacher, believed that there is a constant indivisible source of all being, all existence. Thales believed water was the primal element and Anaximander thought it was the infinite, but Anaximenes pointed to air as the source of all things. Air is always changing, always in movement; its condition of relative heat or cold generates other founding substances such as water, fire, and earth.

Like his predecessors, nothing survives from Anaximenes' own pen. Later commentators, notably Hippolytus, Plutarch, and Aristotle, summarized and assessed his beliefs. Anaximenes believed that the earth, planets, sun, and moon are literally "suspended in mid-air"—all heavenly bodies are round, flat disks that ride upon the all-encompassing air. The earth existed first, and then moisture from the earth became rarified and produced the bright, fiery heavenly bodies. The planets and sun orbit about the flat inhabited top of the earth, but they never pass underneath. The sun is sometimes hidden (night) because it is obscured by highlands to the west. Sir Thomas Heath (1913) argued that Anaximenes understood the planets ("wanderers") to behave differently from the stars—the former were moved about by the air; the latter were fixed to the vault of heaven. Anaximenes also believed that the stars were a much greater distance from the earth. The sun gives off heat because of its relatively close proximity to the earth.

Anaximenes' meteorological beliefs appear more sophisticated. He had realistic assessments of rainbows, caused by the light of the sun and the moisture of the clouds. He realized that moisture dropping from the clouds could become cold and solid: hail and snow. Anaximenes clearly believed that hot and cold had a tremendous impact upon the earth, producing, among other things, earthquakes.

The impact of heat and cold on matter plays an important role in the physical universe. Plutarch recorded Anaximenes' view that hard substances are cold, and fluid substances are hot. Anaximenes' argument that the cooling of air is the cause of much that exists laid the groundwork for later generations to seek the chemical properties of the basic substances of existence: earth, air, fire, water. Atomists especially appreciated Anaximenes' work. One can see his influence on the thinking of Lucretius the Epicurean. Anaximenes also had a direct impact on Anaxagoras and through him the philosophers and scientists of fifth-century Athens.

> *See also* Anaxagoras of Clazomenae; Anaximander of Miletus; Astronomy; Ionians; Meteorology; Miletus; Physical Sciences
> *References*
> Barnes, Jonathan, trans. *Early Greek Philosophy.* London: Penguin Books, 1987.
> Heath, Sir Thomas. *Aristarchus of Samos.* 1913; reprint ed., New York: Dover Books, 1987.
> Laertius, Diogenes. *Lives of the Philosophers.* Translated by R. D. Hicks. 2 vols. Loeb Classical Library, 1931, 1938.

Apollonius of Perga (floruit 235 BCE)

Apollonius of Perga was a Hellenistic mathematician, geometer, and astronomer. Like many of the great Hellenistic mathematicians, Apollonius studied and taught at Alexandria. An Ionian, he also taught at Ephesus in Asia Minor. Apollonius wrote one of the definitive works on geometry of the ancient world. His *Conics* was a masterpiece of examining the intersection of the cone and plane. He coined the terms for many geometrical shapes, such as the hyperbola, ellipse, and parabola. Apollonius was a prolific writer of treatises on geometric shapes. His *Universal Treatise* tried to show in Platonic fashion that geometry is the fundamental basis of thought and the means to uncover the truth. Apollonius also wrote on irrational numbers and the means to arrive at quick computations. The latter treatise revealed a deep thinker with a practical mind. Apollonius was not just a theoretician but an inventor as well, working with hydraulics and time measurement. He built a highly accurate sundial at the same time that other Hellenistic astronomers, such as Aristarchus, were experimenting with such devices. Apollonius influenced the mathematics and astronomy of Hipparchus and anticipated the theories of epicycles and eccentrics used by Ptolemy in the *Almagest*.

See also Astronomy; Euclid; Hipparchus; Mathematics; Ptolemaeus, Claudius

References

Crowe, Michael J. *Theories of the World from Antiquity to the Copernican Revolution*. New York: Dover Books, 1990.

Durant, Will. *The Life of Greece*. New York: Simon and Schuster, 1939.

Heath, Sir Thomas. *Aristarchus of Samos*. New York: Dover Books, 1913.

Technology Museum of Thessaloniki website: www.tmth.edu.

Archelaus of Athens (floruit fifth century BCE)

Archelaus was the student of Anaxagoras and the teacher of Socrates. He was a transitional figure in the movement of the Ionian school of thought to Athens where it would find its greatest exponents in Socrates, Plato, and Aristotle. Archelaus was probably born at Athens, though some accounts claim he was a native of Miletus. At any rate he had the same scientific interests as the Milesians. This debt is clearly seen in Archelaus's ideas that heat and cold are the two basic principles of matter and that life emerged from mud. Like Anaxagoras he believed that mind *(nous)* is the initial cause, the essence of being. He anticipated Aristotle by arguing that hot is movement and cold is rest. Hippolytus, the Late Roman writer, noted that Archelaus believed in the four elements of air, water, fire, and earth, arguing like Thales that water becoming rarefied generates air and earth—the latter being at rest in the center of the universe, the former being the substance upon which the earth is suspended. As an astronomer, Archelaus was hardly original, although Hippolytus recorded Archelaus's belief that the earth must be spherical because it is hollow.

Archelaus assigned thought to animals as well as humans, though by degree of complexity one excels the other in the development of the attributes of civilization.

How precisely Archelaus influenced Socrates is unclear. Diogenes Laertius claimed that philosophy took a turn with Socrates because of his development of ethics, a field of thought he learned from Archelaus. More important, Socrates believed mind was the essence of all things and reality is immaterial and transcendent, which were ideas clearly developed by the Ionian school of thought, in particular by Anaxagoras.

See also Anaxagoras of Clazomenae; Athens; Elements; Ionians; Miletus; Socrates

References

Barnes, Jonathan, trans. *Early Greek Philosophy*. London: Penguin Books, 1987.

Heath, Sir Thomas. *Aristarchus of Samos*. New York: Dover Books, 1913.

Laertius, Diogenes. *Lives of the Philosophers*. Translated by R. D. Hicks. 2 vols. Cambridge: Harvard University Press, 1931, 1938.

Archimedes (287–212 BCE)

Archimedes of Syracuse was one of the ancient world's great scientists, mathematicians, and engineers. In mathematics, his work on geometry, particularly cones, spheres, and cylinders, was unsurpassed. He anticipated calculus and studied in depth hydrostatics, mechanics, matter, and force. He perfected the screw used in irrigation and solved many engineering problems associated with the use of the pulley, wedge, and lever. In geodesy, Archimedes estimated the circumference of the earth to be 300,000 stadia. Archimedes was the first to study and make an accurate approximation of pi (π).

Archimedes, like other ancient engineers, plied his craft in making fascinating inventions, particularly in military science. During the Second Punic War and the battle for Sicily in 212 BCE, the Romans laid siege to the Greek city of Syracuse, ruled by Hiero. The king compelled Archimedes to

Renaissance engraving of Archimedes (ca. 287–212 BCE), Greek mathematician and inventor. (Bettmann/Corbis)

apply his inventions based on research into the principles of mechanics to help defend the city. Plutarch, in his *Life of Marcellus,* described the fascinating array of military devices that Archimedes had invented. Although the Romans took the city and though the Romans took the city and Archimedes was killed, they were astonished by the incredible power of Archimedes' machines. Huge cranes were able to latch onto Roman triremes and pick them up and dash them against the walls of the city and rocks below.

As Mathematician and Astronomer

Archimedes reputedly discovered thirteen solids that are known by means of the *Mathematical Collection* of Pappus of Alexandria. These solids were as follows: the truncated tetrahedron, the cuboctahedron, the truncated octahedron, the truncated cube, the rhombicuboctahedron, the truncated cuboctahedron, the icosidodecahedron, the truncated icosahedron, the truncated dodecahedron, the snub cube, the rhombicosidodecahedron, the truncated icosidodecahedron, and the snub dodecahedron. He claimed to be the first to form explanatory postulates on the surface of the sphere, the radii of circles, and the measurements of the cylinder. Aristarchus applied such principles to astronomy, declaring that the "universe" is a "sphere, the centre of which is the centre of the earth, while its radius is equal to the straight line between the centre of the sun and the centre of the earth" (Heath 1913).

As Hydraulic Engineer

Archimedes developed several basic propositions of hydraulics that became a basis for many of his inventions. His studies of fluid displacement showed that when pressure is applied to a given volume of water the part under pressure will necessarily displace another part not under the same pressure. He examined the weight of objects relative to volume of water: a solid of the same weight as a proportional amount of fluid will float at just below the surface. A solid of lesser weight than a proportional amount of fluid will extend part of its surface above the water. The amount of water displaced by the solid is of the same weight as the water. If a solid is forced into water the reciprocal force is proportional to the weight of the water and weight of the water displaced.

See also Engineering and Technology; Hellenism; Irrigation Techniques; Mathematics; Plutarch
References
Durant, Will. *The Life of Greece.* New York: Simon and Schuster, 1939.

Grant, Michael. *From Alexander to Cleopatra: The Hellenistic World.* New York: History Book Club, 2000.
Heath, Sir Thomas. *Aristarchus of Samos.* New York: Dover Books, 1913.
Plutarch. *Makers of Rome.* Translated by Ian Scott-Kilvert. Harmondsworth, Middlesex: Penguin Books, 1965.
Thatcher, Oliver J., ed. *The Library of Original Sources.* Vol. 3, *The Roman World,* pp. 286–292. Milwaukee: University Research Extension, 1907.

Architecture
See Engineering and Technology

Aristarchus of Samos (310–230 BCE)

Aristarchus of Samos was a mathematician who was the first human to argue that the sun, not the earth, was the center of the universe. Aristarchus was a theorist more than an empiricist. His treatise, *On the Sizes and Distances of the Sun and Moon,* provided the theoretical, mathematical basis for measurements of the heavenly bodies and calculations of their distances. Aristarchus was a Peripatetic philosopher, the student of Strato who was himself the student of Theophrastus.

On the Sizes and Distances of the Sun and Moon suggests the respective size of the moon and sun based on measuring their radii and, using geometric and trigonometric techniques based on angles of observation, estimates of the relative distances of the sun and moon from the earth. Aristarchus's estimate that the sun is almost twenty times the distance from the earth as the moon was an underestimate of 50 percent. His estimate that the sun's diameter is seven times that of the earth was a dramatic underestimate (109 times). Aristarchus's hypothesis that the earth moves about the sun, which is the true center of the universe, is known from Archimedes and Plutarch. Archimedes reported that Aristarchus conceived of the earth's orbit as circular and the distance of the fixed stars from the center of the universe (sun) to be much greater than hitherto thought. This awareness of the astonishing distances of the stars allowed him to realize that the real movements of the stars respective to the earth (parallax) cannot be observed (without precise scientific instruments). Following Heraclides of Pontus, Aristarchus also argued that the earth orbits on its own axis.

How Aristarchus conceived of this theory is subject to speculation. One possibility is that he assumed that the sun's greater size necessitated that the earth orbit it rather than vice versa. He could also have been influenced by Pythagorean philosophers such as Philolaus who suggested that all the heavenly bodies orbit about a central fire.

See also Archimedes; Astronomy; Hellenism; Heraclides of Pontus; Peripatetic School; Philolaus

References

Aristarchus. "On the Sizes and Distances of the Sun and Moon." In Sir Thomas Heath. *Aristarchus of Samos.* 1913; reprint ed., New York: Dover Books, 1987.

Crowe, Michael J. *Theories of the World from Antiquity to the Copernican Revolution.* New York: Dover Books, 1990.

Heath, Sir Thomas. *Aristarchus of Samos.* 1913; reprint ed., New York: Dover Books, 1987.

Aristotle (384–322 BCE)

Aristotle was the greatest scientist of the ancient world. A student of Plato, Aristotle was the teacher of Alexander the Great and the founder of the Peripatetic school of thought. Aristotle mastered all objects of inquiry, including metaphysics, physics, logic, politics, ethics, poetry, zoology, biology, astronomy, geography, natural history, psychology, and magic and astrology. His vast writings include *Metaphysics, Physics, Nichomachean Ethics, Politics,* and *Poetics.* Aristotle was one of the first empirical thinkers, although he generally relied on tried-and-true methods of science: observation, collection, and categorization of specimens, analysis of data, induction, and deduction. Aristotle's mastery of the subjects he studied gained him the

reputation in subsequent centuries as an infallible guide to natural phenomena and philosophy. After 1500 CE, in light of new discoveries by Copernicus, Galileo, Newton, and others, many of Aristotle's theories were rejected, although his influence on modern science is undeniable.

Aristotle was born in the small town of Stagira in Thrace, a primitive outpost of Greek culture east of Macedonia. His father was a wealthy court physician to the kings of Macedonia. Thus Aristotle spent his early years at Pella, the capital of King Amyntas and his successor King Philip II. Aristotle, seeking to follow in his father's footsteps as a scientist and physician, journeyed south to Athens in 366. He became a student at the Academy, Plato's school in Athens. Aristotle became the philosopher's most famous student. At the Academy, Aristotle fit in as a wealthy aristocrat, but his Thracian/Macedonian background plagued him among condescending Athenians. In the end, Aristotle's superior intellect silenced all criticism.

From Plato, Aristotle learned of the universal truth, which Socrates termed "the Good." Plato and his teacher Socrates believed that the Good and other transcendent ideals such as Justice and Beauty cannot be known or seen but rather are beyond human conception—what we call the good, justice, and beauty are mere shadows of the truth. Aristotle, however, questioned whether such truths are beyond human comprehension—perhaps they are every bit a part of human experience. Plato taught his students at the Academy that the best means to approach an understanding of truth was through reason, the study of mathematics and music, intuition, and intense and deep contemplation. Aristotle, less the mystical and more the pragmatic thinker, broke from his teacher by adopting the scientific approach to human behavior, natural philosophy, natural science, ethics, and metaphysics. Aristotle also learned from Plato of *being* (*ousia*), the divine essence, from which all things derive. Aristotle did not abandon this religious interpretation of the ultimate reality but brought science to bear to discover and to understand it. For Aristotle, then, science is a pious act to discover the nature of goodness, justice, virtue, and being. Human experience is an essential matter for study, since the better sort of human beings echo *being* itself.

Upon Plato's death, Aristotle left what was no doubt a hostile and competitive situation among Plato's students, each jockeying to take the place of the master. Aristotle journeyed to a small kingdom in Asia Minor (present-day Turkey) where he became court philosopher to King Hermias. Aristotle married the king's daughter but soon fled (with his wife) upon the tragic assassination of the king. Aristotle ended up back in Macedonia in 343, this time as tutor to the royal prince Alexander. Legend has it that Philip enticed Aristotle to return to Pella, an intellectual and cultural backwater compared to Athens, with a tempting salary and a promise: Stagira having been destroyed and its population enslaved in one of Philip's campaigns, Philip proposed that in return for Aristotle's services the king would rebuild the town and bring the inhabitants out of slavery. Aristotle agreed to the terms.

Alexander eventually became king of Macedonia in 336 upon his father's assassination and then spent the next thirteen years of his life conquering Greece, Asia Minor, Palestine, Egypt, Iran, Iraq, and Afghanistan—all of which made up the Persian Empire. Alexander was a warrior, conqueror, and megalomaniac who thought himself to be the heroic son of the king of the gods, Zeus. And yet, strangely, Aristotle, who eschewed the life of a warrior, had been his teacher for three years during the impressionable years from thirteen to sixteen. Indeed, below the surface of Alexander's actions one can see hints that Alexander had adopted the life of a philosopher, that he thought of himself as a scientist, even a physician. Alexander, for example, composed letters to Aristotle that included samples of plant and animal life that the king had gathered for his teacher's collection.

Aristotle (384–322 BCE), Greek philosopher and scientist, student of Plato, and teacher of Alexander the Great. Statue in the village of Stayira, Halkidiki, Greece. (Corel Corporation)

In the meantime Aristotle had left Macedonia for Athens, where he opened his school, the Lyceum. The philosopher eventually broke with Alexander over the death of Aristotle's grandnephew Callisthenes, a philosopher and historian who accompanied Alexander's expedition. Callisthenes was implicated in a plot to assassinate the king and was executed. Even so, the Athenians associated Aristotle with Alexander, who was very unpopular in Athens. Upon Alexander's death in 323, the Athenians felt free enough to throw off the shackles imposed on them by Alexander—and one shackle was represented by Alexander's former teacher. Aristotle was eventually forced to flee the city and abandon his school. He died soon after, in 322 BCE.

Logic

Aristotle is perhaps best known today as a logician. He created a system of thought based on fundamental assumptions that one cannot doubt—the famous *a priori* truths. Whereas Plato believed that one must accomplish knowledge of truth by means of reason and intuition, Aristotle believed that the philosopher must observe particular phenomena to arrive at an understanding of reality, a scientific technique known as *induction*. Once truth is known through induction from the particular to the universal, the philosopher can engage in the process of *deduction* from the basis of the universal to arrive at other particular truths. Aristotle's system of logic is known as *syllogism*. For example, assume the following:

Each human can know things, each
    human is a knower (A).
What humans collectively know (A) we
    call knowledge (B).
Knowledge (B) is synonymous to reality,
    the truth (C).
Therefore, each individual human can
    know what is the truth. If A=B and
    B=C, then A=C.

Metaphysics

Metaphysics is the study of reality that transcends the physical world. Once again *a priori* truths are the basis for metaphysical studies. Aristotle assumed that there is a *First Cause,* an "unmoved mover," that he defined as *actuality,* in contrast to *potency,* the potential, which represents movement. Aristotle argued that all reality can be explained according to cause and effect, act and potential. For example, time is an actual phenomenon—it has existence as a form or essence *(ousia).* Time acts upon human movement, providing a temporal context in which humans are born, live, and die, all the while measuring their lives according to the standard of time. Aristotle further argued in *Metaphysics* that one must distinguish between art and experience. Art as essence is based on abstract thought—what the Greeks termed the logos—whereas experience is based on a series of particular events occurring in time. In *Poetics,* Aristotle argued that poetry (art) explores universals, how things *ought to be,* while history *(historia)* explains the particulars of human existence, how things *are.* Wisdom represents the unification of art and experience.

Natural Science

Aristotle's treatise on natural science was *Physics.* Natural science, he wrote, is concerned with physical movement from the first principles of nature. Aristotle associated nature with the first cause. His unmoved mover was an amorphous divine force of creation, which establishes the laws through which movement—plant, animal, human existence—occurs. The four causal determinants expressed in nature are:

The material substance that forms a
    physical object.
The type or class of phenomenon *(genos)*
    to which an object belongs.
The cause of change in or movement of
    an object.
The goal or purpose *(telos)* of movement.

Aristotle's categorizations had a profound impact on the formation of a vocabulary of science. His notion of type or class is the basis for our notion that a species in nature comprises a set genus. Aristotle's idea of goal or purpose forms the philosophical concept of teleology, the study of the end of natural phenomena, the future pole or stopping point of time itself.

Psychology

Aristotle was one of the first students of the human psyche. He wrote treatises on dreams, memory, the senses, prophecy, sleep, and the soul. Aristotle believed that the soul is the actuality within the potency of the body. It is the unmoved mover within each individual human. The mind *(nous)* is an expression of the soul. Aristotle argued that each human soul is part of a universal whole, a world soul, the ultimate actuality, the first cause. The idea of a soul, of course, seems to be outside the realm of scientific study. But Aristotle believed that philosophy and science are completely united—that one cannot understand nature without understanding thought or understand movement without understanding being. For Greek philosophers, the principle of truth, the meaning of any phenomenon, is the *logos,* which literally means *word.* The human soul, the world soul, is therefore the *logos.*

Aristotle's study of dreams provided a rational explanation of what the ancients often considered a supernatural phenomenon. Aristotle argued that the only thing "divine" about a dream is that it is part of nature, which is itself the creation of God, hence divine. That events turn out according to one's dream is either coincidence or the result of the subtle impact of a dream on an individual's actions. No matter if a person is asleep or awake, he argued, the same quality of sense-perception is active in acquiring information and making sense of the world.

Along with dreams, Aristotle was interested in magic as an object of inquiry. He wrote about the Asian magi, claiming that they were even more ancient than Egyptian astrologers and magicians.

Zoology

Aristotle's contributions to zoological study included several treatises, *Description of Animals, Parts of Animals,* and *Generation of Animals.* In *Parts of Animals,* Aristotle noted that although animals are a less profound area of study than the metaphysical, nevertheless it is an inquiry accessible to anyone willing to explore natural history. Consistent with his Platonic background, Aristotle studied animals for the sake of understanding the whole of natural history. He assumed that the source of all good and beauty is the same source of animal and biological phenomena. Hence even animals mirror the divine. Aristotle's *Description of Animals* assigns to animals human characteristics of behavior such as treachery and courage, although humans are superior to animals because of their deliberative capacity of

thought, especially the ability of humans to recall and analyze past experience. Aristotle discussed the bone structure of vertebrates as being linked into a whole system, which includes cartilage and muscles; likewise the movement of blood throughout the body is part of a unified whole. The male animal's role in reproduction, according to Aristotle, is an active, creative role that is not permanently linked to the resulting product, just as God creates material things but is not Himself present in His creation. In *Generation of Animals,* as in other works, Aristotle maintained a sense of humility in respect to some of the mysteries of animal generation, characteristics, and behavior. He confessed in *Description of Animals* that notwithstanding his desire to form a clear system of classification, he found the object of inquiry too daunting to truly master.

Ethics

How, one might ask, can ethics, the ultimate basis of behavior, the set of rules that establishes the good, be understood according to science? Aristotle believed that the tools of science—observation, categorization, logic, induction—could be brought to bear on the study of human behavior. The scientist studies human behavior in its incredible variety of contexts to arrive at general laws of how humans act and how they should act. How humans act is the realm of the scientist; how humans should act is the realm of the philosopher. Once again, Aristotle combined science and philosophy into one organized study. Aristotle believed that the ultimate end of human existence is happiness, which occurs when humans conform to "the good." The good is accomplished when humans exercise reason in accordance with virtue. But what is virtue? Aristotle studied human behavior to arrive at a definition: virtue is an action performed for its own sake, that is, an action performed for the sake of the good, an action performed out of principle. Vice, the opposite of virtue, derives from actions committed for selfish reasons, for personal motives. Actions that occur not because of the search for power, wealth, fame, and security are virtuous actions.

Politics

The Greek philosophers before and during Aristotle's time were the first political scientists. Aristotle's contribution, *The Politics,* applied his philosophical methods and assumptions to the understanding of statecraft. He argued that the state is, as it were, the actual, while the citizens are the potential. The latter are the parts (the particulars) that made up the whole, the universal body politic. Aristotle conceived of a pluralistic society operating according to natural laws based in part on reason and necessity, a social compact among people to promote security and serve the needs of survival. Within this concept of the state (which represents virtue) people move, act, and struggle for power and wealth. Nature has created a hierarchical state of being—in society this is realized through unequal ranks of people according to intelligence, property, gender, and personal freedom. Aristotle argued, based on his experience at Athens, that slavery was justified because of the inferior intellect of slaves. Likewise, he assumed that women lacked the cognitive abilities of males and therefore should not participate in democracy. In *The Athenian Constitution,* Aristotle provided a detailed analysis of Athenian democracy, providing details into the life and political science of the great Athenian lawgiver Solon.

In short, the overall goal of the state is the good of the whole, the achievement of general happiness for all people. To Aristotle, the state is the agency through which the citizen exercises virtue, which is how the individual attains the good, that is, happiness.

Astronomy

Aristotle explored his ideas on astronomy in *On the Heavens* and *Meteorology.* Based on observation, Aristotle established the spherical nature of the earth. Viewing a lunar eclipse, Aristotle detected a slight curvature of the shadow of the earth on the moon's surface. He also observed that the altitude of stars changes according to changes in latitude. He also believed, following Plato, that the sphere was the most perfect surface, hence the logical shape of the earth. In *On the Heavens,* Aristotle concluded that the earth's circumference is 400,000 stadia (40,000–50,000 miles, which was an overestimate of 45 percent). He advocated the view that there is more water than land on the earth's surface. The study of meteors, or falling objects from heaven, was the focus of *Meteorology.* Aristotle covered falling objects such as rain, hail, snow, and sleet, as well as cloud formations, wind patterns, and storms.

Much of Aristotle's thought on astronomy, however, was erroneous. Observation with the naked eye was insufficient for the study of the nature of the stars and planets. His theories, though logical, were not empirically based and hence were suspect. Observation tells us that the sun rises and sets, moving across the sky of an earth that appears perfectly still. If the earth were moving, would we not feel the motion? Further support for the theory that the earth is at rest, the stable center of the solar system (the universe), was the direction of falling objects. Would a rock fall to the ground in a straight line if the earth were moving? Aristotle assumed that the earth must be the center of things toward which terrestrial objects move. Extraterrestrial, planetary objects have form yet are nevertheless perfect spheres, perhaps heavenly beings, that move in perfect spherical orbits around the stable earth. The universe is finite, the extreme edge being the starry vault, the fixed stars that move in an unchanging pattern around the planetary solar system.

The Peripatetic School

Aristotle's ideas, such as the model of the geocentric universe described above, were advocated and defended for centuries after the philosopher's death. Theophrastus took over the helm of the Lyceum, Aristotle's school at Athens. He organized Aristotle's papers and writings and pursued Aristotle's theories and investigations in the physical and metaphysical worlds. After Theophrastus's death in 287 BCE, Strato assumed leadership of the Lyceum and the Peripatetic philosophers. A peripatetic is one who moves about or walks while engaged in discussion or disputation. Aristotle enjoyed teaching in such a way at the Lyceum. For centuries Aristotle's disciples were known by the master's teaching style.

Aristotle's Legacy

Aristotle's teaching and writings, along with Plato's, dominated philosophic and scientific thought for over two thousand years. During the Hellenistic Age (323–31 BCE) and during the period of Imperial Rome (31 BCE-476 CE), ancient philosophers, orators, botanists, physicians, astronomers, astrologers, and teachers, both pagan and Christian, began their studies with one of the many surviving texts of Aristotle's works. The greatest astronomer of the centuries after the birth of Christ, Claudius Ptolemy, relied heavily on Aristotle's conceptions of the earth and heavens. Aristotle's theories of motion and his reliance upon deductive reasoning attracted disciples during the European Middle Ages, not only in the primitive feudal environment of Western Europe but in Eastern Europe as well, especially at the great capital of the Byzantine Empire, Constantinople. Indeed, Muslim scientists came into contact with Aristotle's writings, had the Greek translated into Arabic, and circulated them throughout the Muslim world, from Iran to Egypt to Morocco to southern Spain. Muslim scholars such as Averroes became Aristotelians. Eventually, after 1100 CE, Western European intellectuals translated Aristotle's works into Latin, which attracted the attention of theologians such as Thomas Aquinas. Aquinas's massive treatises on philosophy, theology, and science, in particular *Summa Theologica,* were heavily dependent on Aristotle, whom Aquinas referred to simply as The Philosopher. During subsequent centuries of the Renaissance, intellectuals divided themselves into competing camps, the Platonists and Aristotelians. Aristotle's theories on astronomy and motion became the starting point for Renaissance scientists such as Galileo, who disproved, but still owed much to, Aristotle's theories. Even up to 1700 in Europe and America, intellectuals and college curricula relied heavily on Aristotle's teachings. Today's courses in logic still go back to the fourth-century BCE teachings of Aristotle.

See also Alexander of Macedon; Astronomy; Hellenism; Life Sciences; Meteorology; Peripatetic School; Plato; Psychology; Social Sciences; Theophrastus

References

Bambrough, Renford, ed. and trans. *The Philosophy of Aristotle.* New York: New American Library, 1963.

Barnes, Jonathan. *Aristotle.* Oxford: Oxford University Press, 1982.

Schmitt, Charles B. *Aristotle and the Renaissance.* Cambridge: Harvard University Press, 1983.

Turner, William. "Aristotle." *Catholic Encyclopedia.* New York: The Encyclopedia Press, 1913.

Wheelwright, Philip, ed. and trans. *Aristotle.* New York: Odyssey Press, 1951.

Arrian (89–180 CE)

Flavius Arrianus Xenophon, Arrian, is important to the history of science as a compiler and commentator on the works of others. Arrian wrote the *Anabasis,* one of the most important sources for the study of the reign of Alexander the Great, in which Alexander's scientific interests are discussed at length. Arrian's *Indica,* a literary and scientific appendage to the *Anabasis,* is the account of Nearchus's voyage from the Indus River to the Tigris River in 325 BCE. In both of these works Arrian discussed Greek exploration, the geography and anthropology of Asia, and the scientific inclinations of these violent, warring Macedonians. Arrian's third major contribution to the literature of ancient science was his compilation of the writings of the Stoic philosopher Epictetus.

Arrian was a Greek, a native of Nicomedia in western Turkey, who rose to prominence among the Romans in the second century CE. He was a student of the philosopher Epictetus in the Epiran town of Nicopolis. Subsequently Arrian served as a soldier, became a consul of Rome, was a priest in his native Bithynia, and crowned his career as governor of Cappadocia in Turkey. Cappadocia was one of Rome's frontier provinces; Arrian was involved in many battles against outside aggressors. For a Greek to become governor of an important province was at this time exceptional. Reasons for his success include his wealth and his father's Roman citizenship; Arrian became a citizen of Rome at birth. Stoic philosophy, learned from Epictetus, gave Arrian the training and mind-set of successful Roman men of action. Also, Arrian was a student of the fourth-century BCE historian, philosopher, and adventurer Xenophon, whose interest in military affairs, horsemanship, and the hunt became passions for Arrian as well. Xenophon wrote an account, the *Anabasis,* of the Greek incursion into Persia that inspired Alexander's own expedition into the Persian Empire. Arrian modeled himself after Xenophon and named his account of Alexander's journey *Anabasis.*

One would hardly call Arrian a scientist, but in his interests and writings he was clearly one of a growing number of historians of science of the Pax Romana and Later Roman Empire. In his *Anabasis* Arrian described the scientific interests of Alexander and the activities of the numerous philosophers and scientists that the conqueror brought with him. Arrian's *Indica* is an account of the voyage of exploration and science of Alexander's lieutenant Nearchus. Arrian also wrote a fascinating treatise of geographic exploration, the *Circumnavigation of the Black Sea,* in which he described a journey taken in the early 130s CE to explore the entire coastal reaches of the Black (Euxine) Sea.

Arrian's writings are typically modeled on Attic and Ionic Greek of centuries past. An exception is his compilation of the works of the Stoic philosopher Epictetus. As a young man Arrian attended the lectures of this ex-slave and formidable teacher. Epictetus did not record his lectures or write anything at all, and the student Arrian decided to record the teachings of the master. He did so in the spoken Greek of the period, the *koine.* Arrian claimed, in an opening letter to a friend that introduces the *Discourses* of Epictetus, that he took notes of the lectures, not intending them to be published.

In the *Anabasis,* Arrian relied on the extant sources of his time, many of which were by scientists or written in a scientific style. Of the latter type is Nearchus's *Indica,* an account of the coastal wastelands from the Indus to the Euphrates rivers. Arrian also used the incomplete account of Alexander's conquests by Callisthenes, who was a grandnephew of Aristotle and a scientist and philosopher. Also of importance was the account of Alexander written by Aristobulus, a scientist who accompanied the expedition and who wrote of his experiences with Alexander.

See also Alexander of Macedon; Epictetus; Geography/Geodesy; Nearchus of Crete; Stoicism

References

Arrian. *Anabasis* and *Indica.* Translated by P. A. Brunt and E. Iliff Robson. 2 vols. Cambridge: Harvard University Press, 1933, 1976.

———. *The Campaigns of Alexander.* Translated by Aubrey de Selincourt. Harmondsworth, Middlesex: Penguin Book, 1971.

Epictetus. *The Discourses.* Edited by Christopher Gill. Everyman's Library. Rutland, Vt.: Tuttle Publishing, 2001.

Hamilton, J. R. *Alexander the Great.* Pittsburgh: University of Pittsburgh Press, 1974.

Asclepiades (floruit first century BCE)

Asclepiades was a Greek from Bithynia who embraced the doctrines of the atomists and materialists, such as Democritus and Epicurus. Asclepiades adapted Greek medicine to Roman society and thought. As an Epicurean, Asclepiades was a thoroughgoing materialist in science and medicine, believing that there was nothing spiritual or holistic in healing. Neither was he concerned with the impact of

Engraving of the Roman physician Asclepiades (floruit first century BCE). (Courtesy of the National Library of Medicine)

taken and kept by the king. Asclepiades advised medicated wine to treat various illnesses and believed that onion juice was an important remedy for digestive complaints and illness of the eyes. He also used "hydrotherapy" in various ways—baths of varying temperature and the plentiful use of cold water applied to the body and, in copious amounts, as a remedy for various ailments.

> *See also* Galen; Hellenism; Hippocrates;
> Medicine; Pliny the Elder
> **References**
> Galen. *On the Natural Faculties.* Translated by A. J.
> Brock. Cambridge: Harvard University Press,
> 1916.
> Pliny the Elder. *Natural History.* Translated by John
> F. Healy. London: Penguin Books, 1991.

the environment and the particulars of the individual case. There was no "art" in Asclepiades' healing. Breaking, then, from the Hippocratic school, Asclepiades and other such "Methodists" argued that disease was the result of constriction or dilation of tissues by which fluids flowed with ease or not. The Methodists believed that treatment must abide by opposites, that is, either a reversal of the constriction or dilation.

According to the Elder Pliny, Asclepiades corresponded with King Mithridates of Pontus, advising him on the king's materia medica, especially his obsession with antidotes. Mithridates reputedly took small amounts of poison to inure his body to it and to test various antidotes. Pliny claimed that after Gnaeus Pompey defeated Mithridates in 63 BCE he discovered a corpus of medical notes

Asclepius/Asclepiads

Asclepius was the god of healing worshipped by the Greeks as well as the Romans. Homer's *Iliad* first identifies Asclepius, not as a god but rather as a human, a contemporary of Heracles, Theseus, and Jason. Chiron the Centaur, the teacher of Achilles the warrior and Jason the sailor and adventurer, imparted his knowledge of medicine and surgery to Asclepius. Asclepius in turn taught his sons Machaon and Podalirios the art of healing and they their sons, so that as time passed the Greeks believed that the progeny of Asclepius existed among them, teaching medicine and healing the sick. Asclepius himself was eventually given the patrimony of the original god of healing, Apollo. The story goes that Apollo's mortal lover, Coronis, pregnant with his child, was killed by the angry god for loving another. Upon her death, the babe Asclepius, taken from her womb, was given to Chiron to raise. As the son of Apollo, he was deified by the Greeks to become the god of medicine. The *Homeric Hymns,* composed at some point around 1000 BCE, include a hymn to the god Asclepius. The story of the mortal Asclepius becoming the deified patron of medicine was perhaps a Greek borrowing of the Egyptian story of the early hero

Imhotep, who was deified to become the Egyptian god of healing and magic.

Temples hosting cults of Asclepius were found throughout the Greek world. Epidaurus on the east coast of the Peloponnesian peninsula and Cos in the Aegean Sea were centers of the worship of Asclepius. The cult at Cos featured priests and physicians who considered themselves descendants of Asclepius—the Asclepiads. The most famous Asclepiad of Cos was Hippocrates, the fifth-century physician and writer. The Hippocratic Oath begins with an oath to Asclepius and his daughters Hygeia (health) and Panacea (all-heal). Statues of Asclepius typically show the god holding a staff around which the "asclepian snake" is coiled. Priests, to honor the god, allowed the small, brown, nonpoisonous snake to inhabit the temples of Asclepius. Snakes symbolized regeneration, the hope of many worshippers of Asclepius. Asclepiads were known to use the mistletoe and bark of the willow tree in cures of physical ailments. The Elder Pliny recorded an inscription found at the temple of Cos that described an antidote for snake venom being comprised of thyme, vetch, various seeds, and parsley formed into something like pills that were dropped into a cup of wine and ingested.

The cult of Asclepius grew during the Hellenistic Age and after, as Romans adopted the worship of the healing god (known as Aesculapius). As early as the third century BCE, a temple of Asclepius existed at an island in the Tiber River in Rome, the Tiberine, where the sick went for medical and spiritual aid. The historian Cassius Dio (in his *History*) recorded that, after the Battle of Actium, Octavian Caesar, at Cos, had executed one of the assassins of Julius Caesar, Turullius, who had added to his crime by cutting down trees in the sacred grove of the Asclepian shrine at Cos, using the wood to help construct Mark Antony's navy. The writings of Aelius Aristides during the second century CE gives a detailed description of Aristides' personal relationship with Asclepius. In his *Sacred Teachings,* Aristides recorded his dreams in which the god advised him on medical concerns. Aristides believed that he and Asclepius experienced a healing union initiated by the god himself. Aristides had numerous health problems—real or imagined—that drove him to the worship of Asclepius. The god prescribed in dreams ritual acts of healing and atonement. Aristides was to go barefoot in winter, take mud baths, and bathe in cold water during all seasons. Aristides apparently sought to expiate guilt by such extraordinary measures. His gastrointestinal and nervous illnesses demanded the healing of his mind and soul more than anything else.

The cult of Asclepius thrived during the Principate into the Later Roman Empire. The pagan writer Celsus wrote matter-of-factly of the numerous people who relied on their personal relationship with Asclepius. Marcus Aurelius, perhaps encouraged by his physician Galen, benefited from the counsel of Asclepius. During the third century, however, the cult of Asclepius declined. Devotees to Asclepius, such as the pagan Neoplatonist Porphyry, in *Against the Christians,* claimed that Christian opposition, in particular the counter claims of the healing presence of Christ, led to a decline in the worship of Asclepius and increased sickness in the empire. Christians found in their dreams the answers to physical, mental, and emotional complaints. And the expiation of guilt and illness required nothing so harsh as a mud bath in winter.

See also Hippocrates; Homer; Later Roman
Empire; Medicine; Myth; Porphyry

References
Dodds, E. R. *Pagan and Christian in an Age of Anxiety.* New York: W. W. Norton, 1965.
Graves, Robert. *The Greek Myths.* Vol. 1. Harmondsworth, Middlesex: Penguin Books, 1960.
Hesiod. *Homeric Hymns, Epic Cycle, Homerica.* Translated by Hugh G. Evelyn-White. Cambridge: Harvard University Press, 1936.
Jones, W. H. S., trans. *Hippocrates.* Vol. 1. Cambridge: Harvard University Press, 1923.
Pliny the Elder: A Selection. Translated by John F. Healy. London: Penguin Books, 1991.
Radice, Betty. *Who's Who in the Ancient World.* Harmondsworth, Middlesex: Penguin Books, 1973.

Asia, East and South

China

Science in ancient China, from the beginnings of the Yellow River Civilization to the Han Dynasty, emerged in relative isolation from the more dynamic scientific cultures of western Asia, Europe, and northern Africa. The first Chinese civilization developed along the Yellow River in the second millennium BCE. This was the Shang culture of cities based on surplus agriculture that resulted in a sophisticated society that included the invention of writing as well as bronze. The Yellow River is prone to flooding because it is on a higher plane than the surrounding countryside; dwellers of the Yellow Valley developed the means to control the river with dikes and canals. This required, of course, techniques of irrigation, which the Shang people devised. One type involved workers trudging on rotating paddles that were attached to an axle and then to a gear that would bring water up from a stream on multiple pallets. Another irrigation technique was the use of the windlass—a manual crank tied to a basket that was drawn up and emptied into a canal leading to the fields.

The Chinese developed theories based on speculation and observation to explain human and natural history. One of the most important ideas developed in ancient China was the cosmic dialectic of yin-yang. The primal forces of the feminine (yin) were symbolized by the moon, cold, water, earth, nourishment, autumn, and winter; those of the masculine (yang) were symbolized by the sun, fire, heat, spring, and summer. Yin-yang was initially introduced in the *I Ching*, the *Book of Changes*. The *I Ching* presents a worldview that is an organic, eternal whole. The cosmic process is cyclical, with no beginning or end. Confucius (K'ung-Fu-tzu) advocated such a universe, in which the *ju* or wise man discovers through knowledge of self and nature the harmony within and without. Han Dynasty documents reveal that yin-yang was applied to medicine in the same way as Hippocratic humors. When yin-yang is out of balance in the human body, such as cold overwhelming hot, illness can result—one must reestablish the balance through proper living and thinking to regain health.

One of the great accomplishments of ancient Chinese thought was in the field of history. Traditionally, Confucius was the first Chinese historian, the author of the *Spring and Autumn Annals*. Another early historian was Liu Chih-Chi, who wrote *Generalities of History (Shih-T'ung)* in the seventh century BCE, which was didactic history written to inform the reader about political systems. Liu was noteworthy for practicing internal source criticism. The most famous ancient historian was Ssu-Ma Ch'ien (145–90 BCE), author of *Records of the Historian (Shih Chi)*, who, like his Greek and Roman counterparts, wrote didactic history based on a cyclical perception of time and the cosmos. Ssu and other early Chinese historians were semi-religious moralists, even though they wrote realistic, rational history. Tso Chuan, for example, a third-century BCE text, provides a rational view toward humans, seeing man as a free moral agent choosing between a clear division of right and wrong. The Confucian *ju* was a shaman, a keeper of records, including heavenly records, that is, astronomical data. Ssu-Ma Ch'ien, in *Shih Chi,* discussed astronomy for astrological purposes. Chinese intellectuals such as Ssu believed that time and history match the movement of the stars, which are the "heavenly governors" of the universe. This astrological view also included the idea of the "mandate of heaven" in human and natural affairs, which was the core belief that all life is a cycle of growth and decay. The world consists of five elements: earth, fire, water, metal, and wood. These interact with other sets of five and can be understood through astrology and numerology.

Important Chinese astronomers included Gan De, who in the fourth century BCE wrote *Treatise on Jupiter*. Chinese astronomers at the end of the first millennium BCE wrote astronomical treatises, using the gnomon to pinpoint the position of stars, planets, and the sun. Luoxia Hong in the first century BCE made a calendar that combined lunar and solar elements with months of twenty-nine or thirty days and a Metonic cycle of nineteen years. The Chinese mandate of heaven during the Han Dynasty required a new calendar for each new emperor. Ancient Chinese astronomers also developed precise star charts. Like the Greeks, the Chinese universe was geocentric.

India

Civilization appeared in the Indus Valley about 2500 BCE. These early Harappan peoples of the upper Indus Valley had the typical characteristics of civilization, agricultural surplus, trade, writing and numbers to record trade, and urban centers. They used a decimal system for weights and measures, engaged in astronomical observations, and developed simple geometric constructs. By about 1000 BCE, certain cultural groups in India, notably the Jains, worked with numbers and geometry and speculated on infinity. The Indians, like most ancient peoples, developed a lunar calendar. Contact with Greco-Roman and Mesopotamian civilization at the beginning of the Common Era led to sophisticated lunar and solar calendars that included the nineteen-year Metonic cycle. Hindu astronomical writings included computations describing eclipses, charts of astronomical observations, and ephemerides. By the seventh century, the use of zero as an actual number was known in India.

> **See also** Astronomy; History; Mathematics; Medicine
>
> **References**
>
> Beasley, W. G., and E. G. Pulleyblank, eds. *Historians of China and Japan.* London: Oxford University Press, 1961.
>
> Fairbank, John K., Edwin O. Reischauer, and Albert M. Craig. *East Asia: Tradition and Transformation.* Boston: Houghton Mifflin, 1978.
>
> Mote, Frederick W. *Intellectual Foundations of China.* New York: Knopf, 1971.

Neugebauer, O. *The Exact Sciences in Antiquity.* New York: Dover Books, 1969.

O'Connor, J. J., and E. F. Robertson. *History of Mathematics:* http://www-history.mcs.st-andrews.ac.uk/history/References/Heron.html (website of School of Mathematics and Statistics, University of St. Andrew's Scotland).

Watson, Burton. *Early Chinese Literature.* New York: Columbia University Press, 1962.

_____. *Ssu-Ma Ch'ien: Grand Historian of China.* New York: Columbia University Press, 1958.

Astronomy

Astronomy developed during the fourth, third, and second millennia BCE in Europe, Africa, Asia, and America, with the erection of megaliths to track astronomical phenomena, the development of lunar and solar calendars and star catalogs and charts, the recording of astronomical observations, the creation of sundials, and the creation of the pseudo-science astrology. The earliest Chinese calendar dates to 1300 BCE—an extremely accurate solar calendar with 365 1/4 days in the year. Chinese astronomers observed comets, sunspots, novas, and meteors, although accurate explanations eluded them. Chinese scholar Shih Shen in the fourth century BCE developed a catalog of eight hundred stars. Meanwhile in the Middle East, Babylonian scholars developed a lunar calendar of thirteen months, and Egyptian scientists formed a calendar based on the rising of the Dog Star, Sirius, in the eastern horizon, which conformed to the rising of the Nile River. Ancient Mayans of Central America developed calendars, while ancient Polynesians sailed the Pacific Ocean using nautical astronomy. Ancient astronomy was mostly employed for religious and magical purposes, but sometimes to create calendars for society and agriculture.

Archaeoastronomy

Stonehenge is the most famous of the hundreds of megalithic sites throughout the world. Megaliths are huge stone structures set up by Neolithic peoples for religious and scientific purposes. Stonehenge, a series of megalithic structures conceived and built over the

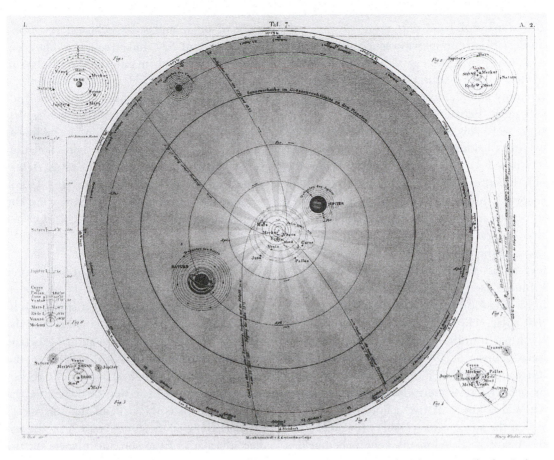

Chart comparing the planetary systems of the ancient Egyptians, the Greek astronomer and mathematician Claudius Ptolemy, and the Renaissance astronomers Tycho Brahe and Copernicus. In Iconographic Encyclopaedia of Science, Literature, and Art, *Johann G. Heck (New York: Rudolph Garrigue, 1851, vol. 1, division 1, vol. 2, pl. 7). (Library of Congress)*

space of thirteen hundred years (2800–1500 BCE), served as the means for these ancient peoples to identify and predict solar and lunar phenomena. The debate about exactly what the purpose of Stonehenge was and how precise and intentional were its astronomical observations continues to rage among scholars who call themselves archaeoastronomers. It appears that the ancient astronomers at Stonehenge aligned the massive stones with moonrise and sunrise at various times of the year. Possibly, these Neolithic astronomers also predicted or at least traced eclipses using the arrangement of the monoliths.

Ancient peoples assigned special qualities to the planets, stars, moon, and sun. The sun as the source of warmth and light early on gained more significance than the other bodies. Ancient humans were naturally sun worshippers, whether it was Ra and Amen of the Egyptians, Helios and Apollo of the Greeks, or the One of the Neoplatonists. The moon, imitating the female reproductive cycle of 29 1/2 days, appeared to be involved in fertility and feminine matters. Likewise the morning star was seen by many ancient cultures as representing a feminine, reproductive power—Ishtar, Aphrodite, and Venus personified the morning star. The other morning star, Mercury, was the herald of day—Hermes, the messenger. The red planet Mars heralded conflict and war. Planets represented metals, too: Mars was iron, Mercury, tin, and Venus, copper. The sun, of course, was gold.

Babylonian Astronomy

Sumerian astronomy was vague and inconclusive, except for the examination of stars and planets as representing deities. Babylonian astronomy was theoretical rather than empirical; many Babylonian astronomical observations were anecdotal and not based on actual events. Chaldean wisdom was proverbial but not based on actual observations. After the eighth century BCE, Babylonian astronomers recorded lunar and solar eclipses, but they were not able to predict them, and the story that Thales learned how to predict eclipses (such as the one of 585 BCE) from the Babylonians is a fable. The Greek astronomer Ptolemy used Babylonian records of eclipses in his astronomy. The Babylonians discovered that solar eclipses occur at the beginning of the lunar month, at the new moon, whereas lunar eclipses occur during the middle of the lunar month at full moon. The universe comprised separate spheres for planets and stars. They also knew of the ecliptic, the path in which the sun makes its daily progress across the heavens. Babylonians kept ephemerides for planet positions. They also had a geocentric planetary theory that was remarkably like that of Ptolemy—Ptolemy must have borrowed from it. The Babylonians conceived of the sun orbiting the earth and the planets orbiting the sun. Their observations were particularly directed toward trying to determine the position of planets relative to fixed stars, and especially the rise of the star Sirius.

Egyptian Astronomy

Egyptian astronomy relied very little on sophisticated mathematics and was rather practical, used to develop agricultural solar calendars. Egyptian astronomers kept track of the heliacal rising of Sirius, the appearance of which indicates the rising of the Nile River. Hence Egyptian priests, the astronomers in ancient Egypt, could always accurately predict the rising of the Nile by means of astronomical observations. Egyptians used a 360-day solar calendar. Diogenes Laertius reported that Egyptian astronomers kept track of lunar and solar eclipses, recording 373 solar and 832 lunar eclipses. They believed that the gods manifested themselves in the heavenly bodies. Hence the sun was, at various times in Egypt's long history, the gods Ra, Amun, Aten, and Osiris. The goddess Isis manifests herself as the moon. In addition, the Egyptians conceived of a spherical universe. The stars, flames in the heavens, determine human destiny. Herodotus the Greek traveler claimed that the Egyptians were the first astrologers.

Greek Astronomy

The greatest astronomers of antiquity were the Greeks. Early Greek scientists developed the idea of the heavens as a great sphere arching over the earth. Astronomers observed the continually changing horizon and tracked the appearance of stars in the direction of the earth's rotation. Greek astronomers recognized the eastward rotation of the earth; the ecliptic, which is the path of the sun across the horizon over the course of a year; the zodiac, the path of the sun and planets on the ecliptic; and scores of constellations, which they named according to their own myths and legends.

Greek astronomy began during the eighth century BCE. The earliest surviving sundial of antiquity dates from that century. The Greek poet Hesiod, in *Works and Days,* wrote that the wise husbandman knows when to engage in agricultural tasks according to the appearance and movements of the Pleiades, Sirius, and Orion. Homer's poems identified similar celestial phenomena as well. The Greeks, like the Babylonians and Egyptians, brought their mythology to the heavens, naming groups of stars according to great heroes, legendary figures, and animals. The fixed stars formed the background for the wandering heavenly bodies, the planets, which move on the same plane in the band of the zodiac.

Ionian Greeks such as Thales and Pythagoras formed the first sophisticated school of Greek astronomy. Pythagoras reputedly developed the idea of separate perfect spheres that define the orbits of the planets, moon, and earth. Planets rubbing against each other cause a sound, the harmony of the spheres. Pythagoras or his followers realized that the moon reflects the light of the sun, and that the varying shapes of the moon prove its sphericity, which led to the deduction of the earth's similarity in this regard. Lunar eclipses as well reveal the curved earth surface. Philolaus, a follower of Pythagoras, hypothesized the moving earth. He conceived that the earth cannot be the center of the universe, but rather there must be a central fire around which all the celestial bodies orbit. The sun, moon, and seven planets make nine spheres orbiting around the central fire. Nine is not such a significant number, however, compared to ten (the sum of 1, 2, 3, and 4). There must be a tenth sphere, which Philolaus imagined to be the antichthon, the "counter earth," which always stays hidden from humans—being precisely on the other side of the sun, it is never seen.

The Pythagorean concept of the central fire was a heliocentric theory based upon philosophy rather than observations and mathematics. Aristotle, the leading scientist of his age, rejected such a scheme for the geocentric universe. Besides the obvious experience of the sun passing daily from east to west, which according to common sense reveals that it moves while the earth is still, Aristotle argued that for the earth to be orbiting the sun the stars would pass, rise, and set like the sun and moon, which is not the case. Aristotle was too much the practical observer to realize that the distance of the stars from the earth prevents any significant movement in the night sky. In other words, there is very little parallax, stellar movement respective to the earth, a phenomenon that escaped Aristotle.

Hellenistic Astronomy

An understanding of parallax did not, however, escape Aristarchus of Samos, the first astronomer to argue for the heliocentric universe. Aristarchus assumed that the stars are at such a distance from the earth that their movements respective to the earth are scarcely noticed. He used geometry to try to discover the relative distances and sizes of the sun and moon to each other and to the earth. His estimates were erroneous yet still revolutionary in the attempt.

Hipparchus of Nicaea was a greater astronomer than Aristarchus, even though Hipparchus advocated the geocentric universe. Hipparchus worked at Alexandria and Rhodes—at the latter city creating something like an astronomical research center in which he cataloged the stars according to brightness, which indicated to him relative distance from the earth and location. He ended up with a star chart of about 850 stars. Hipparchus made more accurate measurements than Aristarchus did of the distance of the moon and sun from the earth. He discovered that the earth's axis changes over time. And to try to account for the orbit of the sun around the earth he developed the idea of the eccentric, which Ptolemy of Alexandria would expand upon.

Other Hellenistic astronomers included Callippus of Cyzicus, a student of Eudoxus and Aristotle, who studied the theory of concentric spheres of heavens, theorizing one for each planet. He charted and wrote on the rising and the setting of stars. Callippus is remembered for his *On the System of the Planets*. His contemporary, Heraclides of Pontus, developed a system combining geocentric and heliocentric systems, in which the sun and moon and outer planets orbit earth, but Mercury and Venus orbit the sun. Heraclides believed that the earth rotates on its axis every twenty-four hours. Autolycus of Pitane (ca. 300 BCE) wrote treatises on the heavenly spheres and the movement of the stars. Aratus of Soli (315–240 BCE) penned *Phaenomena*, a treatise in verse on constellations and stars. Alexandrian astronomers included Menelaus working in the late first century CE, who used trigonometry and the geometry of the sphere; Hypsicles, a second-century CE mathematician and astronomer who calculated the length of each day at Alexandria and the extent of the zodiac; and Claudius Ptolemaeus, Ptolemy, the greatest astronomer of the Roman Principate.

Ptolemy

Ptolemy's accomplishment was a reasonable explanation for the problem of the wandering planets, retrograde motion, which occurs when a planet farther from the sun than earth is "passed" by earth in their respective orbits. The position of the planet in the night sky alters—seemingly reverses and then resumes its previous course. Retrograde motion of outer planets was confusing to the ancients until Ptolemy came up with his explanation of epicycles, equants, eccentrics, and deferents. Ptolemy's scheme was, of course, based on an earth-centered universe. He imagined that as planets orbit the earth they also orbit about a point in their earth-orbit called the epicycle. The deferent is the orbital pattern around the earth. The eccentric is the center point of the orbital scheme. Earth is not directly in the center of the orbiting planet's deferent. The equant is the true point about which the planet orbits. If this sounds confusing, it was, and it did not reflect reality in the least—but Ptolemy was not concerned about reality, he was concerned about a mathematical scheme that could predict the motions of the planets. In this goal he succeeded brilliantly.

The Romans

The Elder Pliny's *Natural History* provides a good summary of how Roman scientists absorbed Greek astronomy. Pliny assumed that the universe is godlike, possibly infinite, yet unknowable. The spherical earth, revolving at a tremendous rate of speed, is at the center of the universe. For Pliny, the universe is harmonious and regular, the product of a divine mind utterly beyond human understanding. Perhaps the harmony of the planets produces a beautiful sound, although we earthlings cannot hear it. The planets are distant to the earth in the sense of their respective elevation approaching the starry vault. Each revolves around the earth in a set period; each has a certain character that gives a particular identity. Venus and Mercury, unlike Mars, Jupiter, and Saturn, rarely extend much above the horizon, in morning or in evening. Venus's light is third only to the sun and moon—and thus like those two bodies has a clear impact on human events. The moon is easily as large as the earth, though the sun dwarfs them both. Pliny discussed the phases of the moon, the solstices and equinoxes of the sun, and the varied forms of eclipse. He discussed comets and their influence on earth events. Indeed, Pliny discussed meteorology in light of astronomy, believing that storms, thunderbolts, climatic change, and the like are influenced by the sun, moon, planets, and stars. He was willing to believe in astronomical portents of changes in human affairs, yet such credulity was countered by some interesting discussions, such as his account of rainbows as being the contact of sunlight with clouds, which is a close approximation to the modern view that molecules of light are refracted by water vapor.

Other astronomers of the Roman Empire included Theodosius of Tripolis, an astrologer and astronomer of first century CE; Posidonius of Rhodes, who influenced Geminus of Rhodes, the latter of whom wrote the treatise *Introduction of Astronomy;* Heliodorus of Alexandria, late fourth century CE, who wrote a commentary on Ptolemy; and Manilius, first century CE, who wrote a poem, the *Astronomica.*

Astrology

For most periods in the history of science, astrology and astronomy were scarcely distinct studies. In the ancient world, for example, astrology provided a big impetus to the development of astronomy, as astrologers wanted to know the positions of planets, the moon, and the sun at various times. Astrologers believed that the movement and position of the planets had a determining effect on the future. Mesopotamian, Egyptian, Greek, and

Roman astronomers practiced astrology. Theophrastus the Peripatetic scientist thought the Chaldeans (Babylonians) and Herodotus thought the Egyptians could predict the future through astrology. Ptolemy wrote a treatise on astrology, the *Tetrabiblos.* Astrology became personalized during the Greek Classical and Hellenistic periods. Each individual had a particular destiny according to the position of the heavenly bodies at his or her birth. A horoscope, determining the position of the planets and stars at one's birth, indicated the future. The earliest recorded horoscope is from 410 BCE. The astrologer determines the position of the planets on the day of an individual's birth to see what zodiacal sign the individual was born under. Each of the twelve signs of the zodiac determines a person's character and destiny. The zodiac is made up of twelve thirty-degree planetary regions set within the ecliptic, the thirty-degree path of the fixed stars. Babylonian astrologers conceived of the zodiac in the fourth century BCE.

Astrology without the nonsense is based on astronomical principles and examines the impact of heavenly bodies on each other and the earth, which is exactly what modern science does. The difference, of course, is that ancient astrologers gave the heavenly bodies a significance that modern astronomers do not accept. The ancient universe was one of mysterious divine forces; the planets were conceived of as being perfect spherical bodies associated with the divine. Modern astronomers have determined that the planets are made of particles that have no spiritual basis or connection. Dead planets of gas and rock can hardly have an impact on human destiny.

See also Aristarchus of Samos; Aristotle; Constellations; Egypt; Hipparchus; Mathematics; Mesopotamia; Physical Sciences; Pliny the Elder; Ptolemaeus, Claudius; Pythagoras

References
Abell, George O. *Exploration of the Universe.* 3d ed. New York: Holt, Rinehart Winston, 1975.
Crowe, Michael J. *Theories of the World from Antiquity to the Copernican Revolution.* New York: Dover Books, 1990.
Heath, Sir Thomas. *Aristarchus of Samos.* New York: Dover Books, 1913.
Leicester, Henry M. *The Historical Background of Chemistry.* New York: Dover Books, 1971.
Neugebauer, O. *The Exact Sciences in Antiquity.* New York: Dover Books, 1969.
Pliny the Elder. *Natural History.* Translated by John F. Healy. London: Penguin Books, 1991.

Astrology
See Astronomy

Athenaeus (floruit early third century CE)

Athenaeus, who lived at Naucratis, Egypt, was a commentator and satirist on Sophists and scientists. Author of *Deipnosophists,* an account of Sophists or philosophers conversing at a dinner party, Athenaeus was connected to the court of Julia Domna in the early third century. The precise translation of his book is "Sophists at dinner" discussing science and philosophy.

The *Deipnosophists* records interesting tidbits from the early history of Greek science and philosophy. Athenaeus preserved, for example, fragments from the writings of Ionian scientists such as Anaxagoras and some of the theories of the Pythagoreans. Some of his comments reveal wit and mirth, especially when writing about the ridiculous habits of Pythagorean vegetarians in their attempt to avoid all flesh.

See also Later Roman Empire; Pythagoras
References
Athenaeus. *The Deipnosophists.* Translated by C. B. Gulick. 7 vols. Cambridge: Harvard University Press, 1963.
Barnes, Jonathan, trans. *Early Greek Philosophy.* London: Penguin Books, 1987.

Athens

The center of science in the Archaic and Classical periods of ancient Greece was the city of Athens, located in eastern Greece on the Attic peninsula. Athens harked back to the Mycenaean period of the second millennium

BCE. It withstood the Dorian invasions of the twelfth and eleventh centuries sufficiently to emerge as the center of culture on the mainland in the ninth and eighth centuries. The Athenians at the beginning of the Archaic Age, ca. 800 BCE, identified with the Greeks of the Aegean islands and western Turkey, the Ionians, and not with the Dorians to the south and west. Athens prided itself on its intellectual and cultural stature, a preeminence rarely matched for over a thousand years.

The foundations of Athenian intellectual greatness were built during the Archaic Age from 800–500 BCE. During this time Athens went through dramatic changes in government, society, economy, and thought. Increasing agricultural production and surplus allowed for the growth of population and trade, so much so that Athens, like other Greek city-states *(poleis)*, sent citizens abroad to found new colonies. Wealth and trade led to the rise of the middle class, which demanded more input into local government, which resulted in the world's first *rule of the people*, democracy, as well as a greater role in military affairs. The development of the heavily armed infantry of Athens, the hoplite soldier, signified the social and economic ferment of Archaic Age Athens.

Social, economic, and political change always accompanies intellectual change. At the same time that Athenian hoplites were leading Greeks in the defense of Hellas from Persian invasion, and as the Athenian empire grew and its political and economic dominance carried forth into the Aegean islands and Ionia, there were dramatic changes in philosophy and science. Around the time that Pericles came to power in Athens, an Ionian philosopher arrived from Asia Minor, Anaxagoras of Clazomenae. Anaxagoras brought with him the general beliefs of Ionian philosophers—a confidence in human thought, a questioning attitude, a search for the causes of natural phenomena, an attempt to explain the nature of man and the universe—as well as his own specific ideas, the chief of which was his belief that Mind *(nous)* governs all things. This notion that a transcendent, spiritual force, an idea, is the ultimate reality of which all being partakes was revolutionary for its time. Many Athenians distrusted Anaxagoras's ideas and thought he was impious, atheistic, and dangerous. But not Pericles, the great Athenian who became Anaxagoras's pupil, who took the philosopher's truths to heart, according to ancient writers such as Plutarch, and who developed into a genuinely good man who could weather the storms of human existence.

Democracy

At the beginning of the Peloponnesian War, Pericles, the Athenian general, gave a funeral oration, as recorded by the historian Thucydides. In the speech Pericles praised Athens as a democracy, where the people rule and equality among citizens exists. Athens is an open society, he said, where goods are freely exchanged in the agora, or marketplace, and ideas are freely exchanged in the open air and bright light of free speech and movement. Athens, said Pericles, is the center of thought and culture in Greece insofar as the political and intellectual freedom brought about by democracy leads to dramatic advances in culture, art, literature, philosophy, and science.

That scholars debate whether or not Athens, an imperialistic state that denied rights to women and slaves, should be called a democracy should not prevent us from recognizing the incredible intellectual accomplishments of Periclean Athens. Fifth-century Athenians made a study of the science of government. Ancient political and social scientists such as Solon, Thucydides, Pericles, Socrates, and Plato studied the nature of government and society not according to the random acts of gods and men but according to the actions and movements of people, the *demos*, over time. These thinkers and others explained the role of virtue *(arete)* and restraint *(sophrosyne)* in the functioning of the state, that the mind and the will and not brute passions govern a people. The arrogant pursuit of power in the individual is overcome by

The Athenian acropolis, from a nineteenth-century illustration, in Excursions Daguerriennes *(Paris: Rittner et Goupil, 1842, plate 21). Print based on daguerreotype by N. P. Lerebours. (Library of Congress)*

the common needs of the whole as acted out in the Council of 500, the Assembly of free citizens, the court system and trial by jury, and the institution of ostracism, meant to curtail the power of demagogues. The key to such political and social success was simply freedom. Writers such as Herodotus, Aeschylus, and Demosthenes commented on the Athenians' great fear of slavery to foreign powers and despots.

Notwithstanding its manifold limitations, Athenian freedom allowed a commoner such as Socrates to become one of the great thinkers of all time, to develop sophisticated ideas on government, society, and philosophy, and to influence scores of Athenians—so influential was he that those jealous of his intellect sought to and succeeded in getting rid of him. Socrates, according to his student Plato, elevated the workings of the state and varied

roles of the people into an abstract conceptual framework wherein the practical aspects of rights and wrongs, of justice and injustice, were understandable according to the idea of justice itself. How, Socrates asked, can we know whether or not justice is accomplished at the Athenian courts if we are ignorant of what true justice is regardless of time and place? With Socrates we find the beginnings of a rigorous examination of thought and practice that formed the basis for the social and political theories of today's social sciences.

The Socratic School

The shadow of Anaxagoras and the Ionian philosophers and scientists hung over Athens during the fifth century. This was in part because the aggressive militaristic and imperialistic actions of the Athenians contradicted their professed beliefs in democracy and equality. Perhaps more important, Anaxagoras's pupil Archelaus was the teacher of Socrates who was the teacher of Plato. Hence, the great thinkers throughout Hellas of the fifth century were centered at Athens. Socrates had a reputation as a Sophist, although his disciple Plato vehemently disagreed with the assertion, pointing out that Socrates did not take money for his teachings, unlike true Sophists such as Protagoras. In the dialogue *Protagoras,* Plato imagined or recreated a debate between Protagoras and Socrates, in which Socrates' dialectic method of interrogatives and logical deduction overwhelms Protagoras's reliance upon rhetoric. Protagoras signifies the use of the spoken word to persuade, to create as it were a momentary truth, whereas Socrates advocates the view, which Anaxagoras would have found acceptable, that truth is everlasting for all times and places and only the thinker who trains his mind to seek the truth will be able to find it.

Besides philosophers, Athens was home to many other thinkers. The architect Callicrates designed and oversaw construction of the majestic Parthenon during the 440s. Herodotus, originally from Halicarnassus in western Turkey, spent time in Athens promoting his *Histories*—for the first time Athenians heard of the geography, history, and peoples of the eastern Mediterranean. One thinker was not impressed: Thucydides composed his *History* of the Peloponnesian War using an exact, chronological style, in contrast to Herodotus's more rambling account. Thucydides used history as a route to uncover general patterns in human behavior. Playwrights such as Aeschylus, Sophocles, and Euripides likewise used the stage to develop themes of human behavior and its consequences, the relation of humans to the divine, and the conflict between good and evil. Aspasia, the consort of Pericles, was a well-known thinker and philosopher. Antisthenes and Diogenes, founders of the Cynic school of thought, preached philosophy and poverty at Athens.

The Academy and the Lyceum

The best-known figures of science and thought in fifth and fourth century Athens BCE were Plato and Aristotle. Plato was a polymath and student of Socrates, an aristocrat who despised democracy, a Pythagorean who opened a school at Athens called the Academy. Plato's students were mostly the rich and included some women. They studied mathematics, harmony, astronomy, history, ethics, dialectic, and politics. One of his students was Aristotle, a native from the Thracian town of Stagira. Aristotle founded the Lyceum at Athens, teaching the same subjects as Plato but with less of an intuitive, mystical sense, and more of a concrete, scientific focus. Before Aristotle founded his school he was tutor for three years to the teenage Alexander of Macedonia. After Alexander succeeded his father Philip and inaugurated a campaign to liberate Ionia and conquer the Persians, Aristotle at Athens received periodic communications from his student, which included specimens from distant lands. Aristotle's followers the Peripatetics included Theophrastus, who wrote a fundamental treatise on plants and their healing properties. While the Lyceum focused on scientific studies, Plato's Academy, under the leadership of Speusippus and Xenocrates during the fourth century BCE, continued the master's concern with philosophy. For the next few centuries, Athens continued to host some of the great philosophers and scientists in the Mediterranean world: Chrysippus, Carneades, Arcesilaus, Zeno, and Epicurus. The last, during the third century, used Athens as his philosophical retreat as he developed the theories that became the philosophy of Epicureanism. Only Zeno rivaled Epicurus. Zeno taught among the stoa of Athens, and thus his followers called themselves Stoics. Like the Epicureans, the Stoics rejected Platonic idealism for a materialist philosophy that explained the universe according to atoms.

The Legacy of Athens

The impact of classical Athens upon subsequent science and philosophy is profound. Plato and Aristotle, Epicurus and Zeno, the Academy and the Lyceum, have provided the chief philosophical and scientific divisions during the Later Roman Empire, Medieval Europe, the Renaissance, the Enlightenment, and today. One can see, over the course of Western thought, a dichotomy between two great philosophical systems: the Platonic with its focus on subjective thought, intuition, and pure reason, and the Aristotelian with its focus on empiricism, observation and the use of the senses, and finding truth in nature. Solon, Anaxagoras, Socrates, Plato, Aristotle, Zeno, and Epicurus sought answers to the most penetrating questions: What is the nature of being? Is there a soul, and of what is it made? What is the role of the divine in our lives? What is the good, and is there a contrasting presence of evil? What is the duty of man? Is there a universal code of ethics upon which to mold behavior? Is the state necessary, and if so what is its purpose? What is virtue, and is it possible to obtain? Is there an objective truth? What role does the self have in the acquisition of knowledge? These questions and so many more, asked by the Athenians of the ancient world, are Athen's greatest legacy.

See also Academy; Anaxagoras of Clazomenae; Aristotle; Epicureanism; Epicurus; Greek Classical Age; Hellenism; Lyceum; Peripatetic School; Plato; Social Sciences; Socrates; Solon; Stoicism; Theophrastus

References

Durant, Will. *The Life of Greece*. New York: Simon and Schuster, 1939.

Jowett, Benjamin, trans. *The Portable Plato*. Harmondsworth, Middlesex: Penguin Books, 1976.

Robinson, Charles A., Jr. *Athens in the Age of Pericles*. Norman: University of Oklahoma Press, 1959.

Thucydides. *The Peloponnesian War*. Translated by Rex Warner. Harmondsworth, Middlesex: Penguin Books, 1972.

Wheelwright, Philip, ed. and trans. *Aristotle*. New York: Odyssey Press, 1951.

Atoms

In a remarkable and stunning insight that anticipated modern science by two thousand years, Greek philosophers hypothesized the existence of atoms. The countless mysteries of life and nature could not be adequately explained by reference to the gods, or to obscure, ephemeral, metaphysical forces such as mind, logos, number, and the infinite. Speculation on the spiritual world can be unending and unsubstantiated by the senses and experience. The atomist demanded that explanations of existence be reduced to common sense and the evidence of the senses. This radical empiricism required a disbelief in anything that could not be seen, heard, smelled, touched, and tasted. Everything else must be the product of overactive imaginations. The atomist allowed himself one general supposition: There must be a force that causes the movement in things detected by humans. This force must be the basis of cause, of the nature of things, and hence the fundamental force of being and matter in the universe. But this force of being, cause, and matter must result from a thing—something material, composed of matter—not an idea.

Two ancient schools of thought, the Epicurean and the Stoic, embraced the science of the atom. The most famous atomists were Leucippus, Democritus, Epicurus, Zeno, and Lucretius. The forerunners of the atomists, such as Empedocles, had hypothesized the existence of material elements, four in number, which the atomists embraced as the basic atomic phenomena: earth, air, fire, and water. Democritus argued that only two things really exist, atoms and void, but the former combines into various other forms, initially the four elements and eventually everything else in existence. Atoms have no quality, whether color, odor, temperature, or taste, though they form into things of color and taste. Lucretius, in *On the Nature of Things,* went further, giving to atoms specific shapes that allow them to combine and recombine to form all things. Some are more dense, some of a distinctive texture, some with hook-like features that are highly resistant to change. The Epicureans believed that atoms swerve at times without warning, being totally random in their movement. The randomness of atomic movement (of electrons) forms the basis of the modern Uncertainty Principle advanced by the German physicist Werner Heisenberg. Random movement and collision is the essence of causation and, because unpredictable, free will. Lucretius anticipated Galileo in arguing that atoms constantly move at a uniform rate through a void of no resistance that does not alter the rate of movement. Like the corpuscular theorists of the Scientific Revolution, such as Boyle and Descartes, the ancient atomists believed that atoms are completely material, without mind or soul, and of infinite number, producing infinite and recurrent possibilities.

See also Aurelius, Marcus; Democritus; Elements; Epicureanism; Epicurus; Lucretius; Stoicism

References

Barnes, Jonathan, trans. *Early Greek Philosophy.* London: Penguin Books, 1987.

Lucretius. *The Nature of the Universe.* Translated by R. E. Latham. Harmondsworth, Middlesex: Penguin Books, 1951.

Russell, Bertrand. *A History of Western Philosophy.* New York: Simon and Schuster, 1945.

Aurelius, Marcus (121–180 CE)

One of the great exponents of Zeno's philosophy of Stoicism was the Roman emperor Marcus Aurelius, the author of *Meditations.* By the time of his reign in the mid- to late second century CE, Stoicism was firmly entrenched as the most popular philosophy among Romans. Marcus Aurelius had trained himself as a philosopher even before he was adopted by the emperor Antoninus Pius. The Stoics believed that fate directs all human affairs. In 161, fate thrust the Stoic Marcus into a position of great responsibility as leader of tens of millions of people in an empire suffering from military disasters and plague. The emperor usually found himself not at Rome, where one could pursue philosophical study, but encamped on the Danube in a cold wilderness facing Germanic invaders. That Stoicism taught human equality and the brotherhood of all mankind was not lost on Aurelius, who resented his military duties and ruminated about the nature and meaning of life. He based his ideas on the brevity and insignificance of life, the irrelevance of fame and glory, and the ignorance and depravity of humanity. He considered his own thoughts and experiences in light of the thoughts and experiences of other past humans, especially Stoic philosophers such as Epictetus. Aurelius's *Meditations* is a diary meant only for himself and written sporadically in consolation, expression, rumination, joy, and sorrow. And yet *Meditations* is also an account of the scientific worldview of the ancient Stoic philosopher.

The study of physics, that is, the natural world, its causes and effects, was one of the chief topics of Stoic inquiry. Aurelius studied human behavior and natural phenomena to arrive at the notion that there is a universal law of nature that governs and orders all things. Believing that this law was not the product of chance in a universe completely oriented around fate, Aurelius, like other Stoics, assumed the existence of a universal mind, the holy spirit, the *logos.* The logos was a creative yet impersonal force of reason that erects, controls, and destroys successive universes in infinite time. Aurelius believed that the logos is a thrifty creator that allows only such beings as are necessary in an economical universe. A materialist, Aurelius believed that all things, even being, the soul, the logos, are physical phenomena. He confided to himself in *Meditations* that his own soul, having derived from the material of the universe, would upon death return to its original state.

Marcus Aurelius was also an important philosopher on the nature of time. He clearly perceived existence in terms of the present as a "moment" in time. But this awareness was based not on a restricted perception of time and existence, but rather on a broad perspec-

Stoic philosopher and Roman emperor Marcus Aurelius. (Archivo Iconografico, S.A. / Corbis)

tive, to the degree that Aurelius could conceive of one's life as a solitary moment amid the many moments that make up existence as a whole. Time, like the universe, like being, is interconnected, a unity embraced in its totality by the logos.

The *Meditations* is hardly the work of a man content with himself, his life, his destiny, and the cosmos. Stoicism in theory taught the acceptance, hence the conquest, of death. Aurelius repeatedly tried to convince himself that death is nothing to fear—

and yet the fear crept in daily, weekly, yearly, recurrently. The Stoic promise, based on materialism, that one's destiny lies in the return of one's atoms to the universe, never to know or to love again, led to despair rather than happiness in the life and writings of Marcus Aurelius.

> **See also** Epictetus; Logos; Roman Principate; Stoicism; Time

> **References**
> Aurelius, Marcus. *Meditations.* Translated by Maxwell Staniforth. Harmondsworth, Middlesex: Penguin Books, 1964.
> Birley, Anthony. *Marcus Aurelius.* Boston: Little, Brown, and Co., 1966.
> Lawson, Russell. "The Lost Promise of History." *Journal of Unconventional History.* Volume 7, 1996.

Aurelius Augustine (354–430 CE)

Aurelius Augustine was a theologian and philosopher and one of the great thinkers of all time in the fields of psychology, the theory of knowledge, and the nature of time. Augustine was a prolific writer best known for his *Confessions* and *City of God.* The former is an autobiographical portrait of his struggle with sin and redemption through conversion and faith in God. The *City of God* is a massive treatise on history and the human relationship with God. Both works became fundamental sources of Christian theology, spirituality, and faith. Ironically they are also sophisticated analyses of human nature. Augustine's works also allow us to see the intellectual perceptions of the Later Roman Empire. Augustine was at various times in his life a student of Stoicism, Neoplatonism, Manicheism, and, of course, Christianity.

Augustine was born and raised in the North African city of Thagaste. By his own account, he was intellectually precocious and thus arrogant and vain; he rejected the Christian teachings of his mother, Monica, to pursue success and fame as a scholar and orator. Sin drove him to unhappiness even as he sought happiness through philosophy. Cicero and Roman Stoicism had an early influence on Augustine, who found the Stoic notions of *humanitas* appealing: a common humanity, equality, and the dignity of humankind. The Stoics emphasized human experience as the key to happiness, but all of Augustine's attempts to unlock the door failed. During these years of his late teens and twenties Augustine was a materialist who, when Stoicism could not provide sufficient answers, sought them elsewhere. The words of *Confessions* exude the pain of recollection that he had strayed so far as to embrace an eastern materialistic philosophy, Manicheism. Augustine sought from the Manicheists an explanation of the pain and sorrow he felt and the evil within him. The Manicheist solution was simple: evil has a material presence within oneself; likewise the material of good can be increased or decreased depending upon one's bodily habits. It did not take Augustine long to discover how ludicrous were the teachings of the Manicheists.

In pursuit of success and elusive happiness, Augustine migrated to Rome and then to Milan, Italy, where he taught rhetoric. At Milan he came under the influence of the Christian bishop, Ambrose. Augustine admired Ambrose, who influenced Augustine to begin a reassessment of Christian scripture, which Augustine had long considered with disdain as filled with fantastic stories that did not even make eloquent reading. Ambrose suggested and Augustine considered that the stories of the Old Testament and New Testament were allegories of more profound spiritual phenomena. Meanwhile Augustine read Neoplatonist philosophers such as Plotinus, who helped to convince Augustine that truth is spiritual, not material, and that sin is not a substance but willful error in behavior.

At this point, living in Milan, wealthy, successful, and famous, understanding the contributions to human understanding of the Stoics, Neoplatonists, and Manicheists, and deeply influenced by Ambrose and his mother, Monica, Augustine converted to Christianity. Ambrose baptized the convert, who, after his mother's death, returned to North Africa where he lived the remaining decades of his life with other religious brethren. When he was about forty years old, Augustine penned the *Confessions*.

The *Confessions* recounts Augustine's life from childhood to middle age, tells the story of his conversion, and then, seeking to explain its significance, provides a detailed discussion of memory and time. Concerned to explain the origins of personal and human sin, he portrayed in detail his birth, infancy, and youth, some of which he recalled, but most of which he recreated by observing the behavior of other children. He argued that from birth, humans have unfulfilled material needs that impose on their spiritual development. Augustine assumed that from the beginning humans sin, which draws them away from God and leads them to misery. Happiness comes by denying their own wills and accepting God's will. The human journey through life is taken in stages of sin, resistance, self-deception, awareness, denial, acceptance, happiness. To prove his assertion he called upon his theories of knowledge and time.

Augustine conceived of knowledge as the universal transcendent phenomenon represented at particular times and places by the individual knower. Augustine knew this relationship between himself, the knower, and God (knowledge) because of an internal voice. This personal, temporal realization of God is the logos, long recognized in Greek thought as the transcendent creative force of thought and knowledge.

Time fascinated Augustine even as a youth. As he traced his own passing, he became aware that neither the past nor the future exist, only the fleeting present of no duration. Augustine discovered the human quandary of how to achieve knowledge in the passing moments of fluid experience. Augustine concluded that time is the experience of each individual's mind as it recalls the past by memory, awaits the future by expectation, and gauges the present by momentary awareness.

Augustine believed that even the most humble example taken from any random moment of a person's experience can provide an explanation for human history itself, since all humans share the same pattern of experiencing time and relying on memory, present awareness, and anticipation of the future to make sense of life and self. Time, the movement from future to present to past, hence history, is completely personal, in the mind, an individual's fleeting recollection of events experienced either vicariously or actually.

The *Confessions* portrays Augustine's experience of time as the human experience of time. Birth and death, creation and judgment, were the beginning and the end of Augustine's life span of seventy-six years. His life was one of infancy and childhood, rather like the creation of Adam and Eve and the age of the Patriarchs. His teen years were similar to the Hebrew sufferings in Egypt and the wanderings in the wilderness. His twenties were like the years of the kings of Israel and Judah and the captivity in Babylon. The first millennium BCE was centuries of expectation of the Messiah, and likewise Augustine's young adult years were in expectation of the truth. Then truth came in an *Incarnation,* a moment in time when God became known to man. Subsequent years were filled with memories of the grand event—Christians recalled the life and death of Jesus and tried to use memory to confront their own individual presents and futures as they approached, collectively, the end. Augustine used memory to recall the single most important event of his life, which irrevocably altered him and prepared him for death.

Augustine represents the transition from the ancient to the medieval worlds. He used the best of ancient philosophy and advanced it further under the umbrella of Christianity. He was the last great thinker of antiquity and the first great thinker of Medieval Europe. His ideas on human psychology and time have never really been surpassed, and they set the stage for later philosophers and scientists—

René Descartes, Francesco Petrarca, Martin Luther, Michel de Montaigne, Jonathan Edwards, Immanuel Kant, Sigmund Freud, William James, and Albert Einstein.

See also Later Roman Empire; Neoplatonism; Psychology; Stoicism; Time

References

Brown, Peter. *Augustine of Hippo.* Berkeley: University of California Press, 1967.

Chadwick, Henry. *Augustine.* Oxford: Oxford University Press, 1986.

Meagher, Robert. *Augustine: An Introduction.* New York: Harper and Row, 1978.

St. Augustine. *Confessions.* Translated by R. S. Pine-Coffin. Harmondsworth, Middlesex: Penguin Books, 1961.

Wilcox, Donald. *The Measure of Time's Past: Pre-Newtonian Chronologies and the Rhetoric of Relative Time.* Chicago: University of Chicago Press, 1987.

Wippel, John, and Allan Wolter, eds. *Medieval Philosophy.* New York: Free Press, 1969.

B

Babylon

Babylon was for thousands of years the symbol of worldliness, grandeur, magic, and astrology. An old Mesopotamian city, it emerged to political and cultural prominence at the beginning of the second millennium BCE. The city, situated at the lower Euphrates River, reputedly had walls sixty miles in circumference, two hundred feet high, and fifty feet wide. Babylon, which the Elder Pliny called the headquarters of the Chaldeans, the infamous astrologers of the ancient world, was the capital of the First Dynasty, which began in 1894. The most famous king of early Babylon was Hammurapi (1792–1750 BCE). Indeed, the Code of Hammurapi, one of the first law codes in the history of humankind, records a society where law has overcome brute force and blood vengeance in the settling of disputes. Under Hammurapi, laws were codified to deal with agriculture; water rights; the use of metal as a means of exchange; relations among master and slave and among equals; builders who built weak houses or leaky boats; and thieves of the *shaduf* and water wheel (used in irrigation).

The Code of Hammurapi reveals that Babylon had a dynamic medical community. Indeed, Mesopotamians were the first great practitioners of medical science. As early as the third millennium BCE, extensive materia medica existed indicating what medicines were useful for individual illnesses. Many of the laws of the Code deal with payments to physicians and penalties for malpractice. Physicians performed surgery, drained tumors, and set bones; veterinarians performed surgery on draft animals. Physicians, one gathers, were jack-of-all-trades scientists and astrologers. Of course magic and omens tempered the scientific efficacy of Babylonian medicine. Early documents indicate that the magician *(ashipu)* was often the same as the physician *(asu)*. Nevertheless, medical observations gave the Babylonians a keen awareness of many diseases and suggestions for how to treat them.

Astrology and Astronomy

The Babylonians of the second and first millennia BCE observed the heavens with the assumption that the movements of planets and stars and the phases of the moon had an impact on earthly events. The appearance of a new moon was greeted with wonder and gladness, as foreshadowing good things. The gradual appearance of the moon and its horns informed the prognosticator of the course of events. The moon lasting to the thirtieth day foreshadowed evil. Likewise other phenomena indicated good and evil according to the prognosticator's interpretation: eclipses;

halos; the simultaneous appearance of moon and sun; the conjunction of Jupiter and the moon; the appearance or disappearance and place on the horizon of Venus, Mercury, and Mars; the appearance of thunderstorms during certain celestial events; and earthquakes.

Beginning in the eighth century BCE, Babylonian astronomers kept ephemerides of lunar, planetary, and stellar phenomena. This included accurate lunar and solar eclipse charts from 450 BCE on. Pliny the Elder claimed that the Babylonian day began between sunrises and that earthquakes resulted when three planets (Mars, Jupiter, Saturn) were aligned with the sun. According to Epigenes, Babylonians recorded astronomical observations on clay tablets. The astronomer Ptolemy clearly knew of Babylonian mathematics and astronomy as well. Indeed Ptolemy's geocentric system relying on the inner planets Mercury and Venus orbiting the sun on epicycles as the sun orbited the earth was remarkably similar to Babylonian astronomical schemes. The most famous Babylonian astronomer was Berossus, a priest of Baal who lived at Cos in the Aegean Sea in the third century BCE.

Mathematics

The Babylonians were superb mathematicians. Place-value notation in numbers was developed by the Babylonians, who first used zero as a place notation toward the end of the first millennium BCE during the Hellenistic Age. Babylonian mathematicians divided the circle into 360 degrees. Babylonian algebra used quadratic equations, squares, cubes, square roots, coefficients, number progressions, and linear algebra. Babylonian mathematics, like Egyptian mathematics, was concerned largely with practical arithmetical problems and solutions. Cuneiform texts survive that indicate solutions to problems of engineering and building. Geometry, more abstract, was not as developed in Babylon. Nevertheless, the Pythagorean theorem was first used in Babylon as early as the first centuries of the second millennium BCE. Texts also indicate that the Babylonian mathematicians solved problems involving hexagons, triangles, trapezoids, and the radii of circles. Babylonians understood the principle that a line that extends from a right angle to the hypotenuse of a triangle creates two equal triangles. Geometry was also used in surveying. One of the oldest maps in the world, surviving on a clay tablet, is of the Euphrates flowing through the ancient city of Babylon.

See also Astronomy; Egypt; Mathematics; Mesopotamia

References
Neugebauer, O. *The Exact Sciences in Antiquity.* New York: Dover Books, 1969.
Oates, Joan. *Babylon.* London: Thames and Hudson, 1986.
O'Connor, J. J., and E. F. Robertson. *History of Mathematics:* http://www-history.mcs.st-andrews.ac.uk/history/References/Heron.html (website of School of Mathematics and Statistics, University of St. Andrew's Scotland).
Thompson, R. Campbell. *Assyrian and Babylonian Literature: Selected Transactions.* With a critical introduction by Robert Francis Harper. New York: D. Appleton and Company, 1901.

Biology/Botany
See Life Sciences

Bronze Age (3500–800 BCE)

Scientists categorize human development according to material culture, social and political institutions, sophistication of thought and culture, and level of technology. The latter is the traditional means by which scholars have designated the origins of civilization in Europe, Asia, Africa, and elsewhere. Precivilized societies did not practice metallurgy, and thus tools and weapons were limited and very primitive. Paleolithic (Old Stone Age) peoples relied on stone, wood, bone, and ivory for tools; metals, if used at all, were for decorative purposes. Some aspects of precivilized culture were anything but primitive. Art and sculpture from Paleolithic Europe, for example, shows that these people had a keen eye for nature, conceived and portrayed gods and goddesses, and even began to execute portraits of other humans. Social organization allowed for successful hunts, a rudimentary social hierarchy, and basic rituals and taboos by which to set rules of proper behavior. Paleolithic tools were often astonishingly beautiful and very effective. Some anthropologists have defined humans as tool users, which indeed fits the skill and success at adapting to the natural environment of Paleolithic peoples.

The Neolithic (New Stone Age) differed from previous times in that humans made revolutionary advances in thought, social organization, and adaptation to the environment. One of the greatest scientific discoveries in human history occurred at an unknown time by unknown individuals. Some person or group of people living at or near the Tigris and Euphrates river valleys in Asia (a place subsequently known to the Greeks as Mesopotamia) around 10,000 BCE used observation and hypothesis to perform an experiment. Perhaps they had noticed places where the land, previously barren of food, all of a sudden, during spring, produced wild barley or wild oats, which caused them to ponder how this occurred. It would have been obvious to such people that animals give birth to young in the spring, that trees rejuvenate and flower in the spring, that berries become plentiful on vines and bushes when the days grow longer and sun becomes hotter. How does the plant emerge from the soil, the egg appear in the nest, the woman become pregnant with new life? These appeared to be questions linked by a common miracle of newness, of birth, of growth. Ancient fertility cults devoted to plentiful foodstuffs, animal procreation, and human fertility reveal that long before civilization humans had discovered the idea of fertility, that of providing an environment suitable for growth, of the relationship of male and female to conception, pregnancy, and birth. Could there be a connection between male semen being implanted in a healthy, fertile female and a seed from a plant being planted in rich soil?

Agriculture, although rudimentary and haphazard at first, nevertheless involved a scientific process of planning, implementing, controlling, and producing results. As harvests became plentiful, and surplus food was produced and stored, Neolithic humans gained a basic understanding and experienced a general control over their environment, which is the essence of science. Surplus allowed for a break from day-to-day survival; it allowed for a conception of the future based on planning the necessary foodstuffs for a coming winter or period of drought. With more food, there was no longer the need for yearly migrations in search of food. Neolithic peoples were no longer nomads, like their forebears. Neolithic towns emerged in particularly productive areas. The earliest were in an area that scholars call the Fertile Crescent. These small towns, such as Jericho, supported a population of well over one thousand people, who lived in sun-dried-mud brick homes that looked out upon narrow avenues that crisscrossed at right angles. Mud brick walls surrounded the town. Townspeople developed a sense of commonality, a sense of community, which also implied a sense of the foreign. Restrictions, exclusiveness, control over property, struggle for more territory, and the beginnings of trade all characterized Neolithic society.

Bronze

Mesopotamians were the first to use bronze tools and weapons. Ancient Sumerian craftsmen had sufficient skill in metallurgy to combine the native copper of Mesopotamia with tin from the mountains of Turkey in forges that could reach sufficient temperatures to heat the metals, pour the molten metal into casts, and produce bronze, which was far superior to copper, stone, bone, ivory, or wood tools and weapons. Work with copper without heating it had occurred millennia earlier in Mesopotamia. Technology had advanced sufficiently by 6000 BCE that lead and copper were heated and combined. The advance of the Mesopotamian economy, the accumulation of surplus, and the demand for better tools and weapons over the course of centuries resulted in the discovery that one part tin to seven parts copper yielded bronze. The bronze industry helped stimulate a growing tool and weapon industry for agriculture and warfare. In Egypt, meanwhile, advances in metallurgy included the use of stone crucibles to host fire heated by air blown through reeds. Besides bronze, Egyptian metallurgists used copper and copper alloys for a variety of purposes, one example being materials for plumbing. A variety of different types of bellows and pipes to force air into the forge heating the fire were developed in Mesopotamia as well as in Egypt. Also by the end of the second millennium BCE, Bronze Age technology was emerging in Iran, China, and along the Indus River valley. Shang bronze workers produced strikingly beautiful and sophisticated objects.

Minoan Age

The ancient Mediterranean afforded many examples of Bronze Age society and culture. One of the most fascinating and least known was centered on the island of Crete during the third and second millennia BCE. Sir Arthur Evans, who performed the first archeological digs at Knossos and other Cretan cities, named the forgotten civilization Minoan, after Minos, the mythical king of Crete and son of Zeus. Minoan culture was sophisticated for its time, partly derivative of Near Eastern civilizations. There was a distinct social structure that included a royal house, aristocratic priests, middle class craftsmen, merchants, sailors, and professionals, farmers, and slaves. The remains of the palace at Knossos shows an intricate, well-decorated structure with enough rooms and halls to make it seem like a labyrinth to later generations. The Minoans had a thalassocracy, an empire built on the sea, on trade, and on a fleet of wooden triremes imposing the will of King Minos and his successors on surrounding subject states. They were devoted to the worship of the mother goddess, and the bull was sacred. Sculpture, art, met-

allurgy, and pottery were well developed at Crete. The highpoint of Minoan civilization was the development of a written script, which scholars call Linear A.

Archeologists have discovered a similar culture at Santorini, a small island sixty miles north of Crete. A massive volcanic eruption in the fifteenth century BCE partially destroyed the island, called Thera in antiquity, and ended a beautiful culture of sophisticated stone work, metallurgy, multistoried buildings, trade, and art. The ancient Therans built a town (Akrotiri) that included colonnaded homes decorated with bright colors and beautiful murals of sea creatures and simple pleasures. Lead pipes brought water to some homes and served as part of an elaborate sewage system that included drains below slabs of stone that made up roads and alleys.

Mycenaean Age

Greece and the islands of the Aegean were initially subject to the empire of Crete before gaining independence by the mid-second millennium BCE. This civilization, centered at the Greek Peloponnesus, was unknown until its discovery by Heinrich Schliemann in the nineteenth century. Schliemann had already discovered the ancient site of Troy in northwest Turkey. He claimed to have discovered the homeland of King Priam and Prince Hector of Troy and the kingdoms of Menelaus and Agamemnon, brothers and kings of Sparta and Mycenae and Argos. Schliemann referred to the Bronze Age cultures of the Aegean and Greece as the Mycenaean civilization, whereas modern scholars often refer to it as Helladic.

The Mycenaeans were similar to the Minoans in their sophisticated metallurgy, shipbuilding, trade, military, and fortresses. They possessed a form of writing, perhaps derived from the Minoan civilization, which scholars call Linear B. Kings and aristocrats ruled, and most people were farmers and herders, but there was also a middle class of craftsmen, scribes, physicians, and merchants. The Mycenaean civilization was patriarchal, as reflected in their deities, dominated by the male god Zeus. The people of Greece, like those of Crete, tried to explain the workings of nature but could do no better than to imagine supernatural forces at work behind the immensity of the sky, the depths of the sea, the thunderbolt, the fertility of soil and humans, human emotions, and illness and death. The Greek gods, ruling from Mount Olympus, personified the forces of nature for these Bronze Age people.

Dorian Invasions

At the beginning of the twelfth century BCE, a cataclysmic event occurred that forever altered the civilizations of the eastern Mediterranean. Invaders from northern Europe wielding iron weapons migrated into the Balkans and Asia Minor and south to Palestine and Egypt. Nomadic and primitive, illiterate and violent, but somehow discovering the secret to smelting iron, they were largely unstoppable. The Greeks called the invaders Dorians; they destroyed the Mycenaean civilization and took control especially of western Greece and the Peloponnesus. Perhaps they had a role in the fall of Troy. These same invaders conquered the Hittite Empire of Asia Minor, threatened (as the Philistines) the Hebrews in Palestine, and attacked the Egyptians. Though repulsed from Egypt, the Egyptians were nevertheless terrified of these people from the sea. The invaders are sometimes referred to as the "sea peoples."

The Ionians

The inhabitants of Mycenaean towns and cities fled at the Dorian approach, migrating east to the extreme peninsulas of the mainland, the islands of the Aegean, and the western coast of Turkey. These people, subsequently called the Ionians, founded Ionian city-states such as Athens, Miletus, Chios, Samos, Halicarnassus, Cos, Colophon, and Ephesus. The Ionians and Dorians in coming centuries always considered themselves different. They had similar traditions and language and worshipped similar gods and goddesses, but the level and sophistication of their respective cultures differed. The Dorians were more militaristic, and their cities focused on war and defense rather than art, poetry, and science. The Ionians, on the other hand, were devoted to thought, culture, investigating nature, and expressing their ideas. The Ionians in time became the leaders of Greek science during the Archaic, Classical, and Hellenistic ages of Greece. The cities of Athens, Miletus, Cos, and Chios became centers of philosophy and science. Homer, Thales, Anaxagoras, Anaximander, Hippocrates, Socrates, and Plato were representative of Ionian philosophers, scientists, and physicians.

See also Agriculture; Ionians; Irrigation Techniques; Mesopotamia

References

Botsford, George, and Charles A. Robinson. *Hellenic History.* Revised by Donald Kagan. New York: Macmillan Publishing, 1969.

Doumas, Christos G. *Thera: Pompeii of the Ancient Aegean.* London: Thames and Hudson, 1983.

Finley, M. I. *The World of Odysseus.* Harmondsworth, Middlesex: Penguin Books, 1972.

Oxford History of the Classical World. Oxford: Oxford University Press, 1986.

Pliny the Elder. *Natural History.* Translated by John F. Healy. London: Penguin Books, 1991.

Sandars, N. K. *The Sea Peoples.* London: Thames and Hudson, 1985.

C

Caesar, Julius (100–44 BCE)

Julius Caesar, best known for his military conquest of Gaul and civil war against the Roman Senate and its champion Gnaeus Pompey, was not only a man of action and political affairs but a superb writer who provided excellent descriptions of the lands in which he fought, in particular Gaul and Britain. Caesar reputedly wrote treatises on language and astronomy, but these have not survived. His *Civil War* and *Gallic War* do, however, survive, and provide us with insights into the lands and people of ancient northern Europe.

Gallic War allowed Caesar to write as an anthropologist, describing objectively and tersely his opponents the Gauls. Modern scholars rely heavily on Caesar's observations of the customs and groupings of these early Celtic and Germanic peoples. Caesar's account, for example, of Britain is revealing. Part of his discussion, especially of the extent of the island and Ireland as well, was based on hearsay. Yet he recorded information that the native Celts provided him. They claimed that during the winter solstice there were several days of complete darkness. Caesar, who was in Britain during warmer months, used the Roman water clock to measure the extent of darkness and found nights to be shorter than in Gaul and Italy, thereby contradicting the report. The Britons were warlike, primitive toward women, and very superstitious. Warriors dyed their bodies blue with woad to appear more fierce. Women had few rights, were shared by men, and had the reputation among Romans as being almost as courageous and warlike as the men. Caesar described the Celts of Britain and Gaul as having a primitive form of government, based on tribal and family loyalties. The masses were subject to the powerful few, led by the Druids, a religious caste of priests who maintained an oral tradition and teachings by word of mouth to retain secrecy and hence power. Caesar wrote that the Druids officiated at human sacrifice. War captives were offered to the gods as substitutes (in death) for the Celts. Celtic deities and the powers and actions they symbolized were very similar to the Greeks and Romans. They worshipped Mercury (Hermes), the patron of trade and inventions; Minerva (Athena), the patroness of crafts; Jupiter (Zeus), the king; Mars (Ares), the war god; and Apollo, the god of healing. The Druids, according to Caesar, attempted to understand the heavens, and conversed on astronomy, meteorology, geodesy, and geography. The Druids measured time according to nights rather than days.

Time was, indeed, an object of inquiry that fascinated Caesar. After becoming dictator in

The Roman conqueror, Julius Caesar, author of Gallic War. *Sculpted by Maradan, between 1850 and 1900. Right profile. (Library of Congress)*

45 BCE, he instituted a reform of the calendar. The old Roman calendar was based on a 355-day year, which over the years had made the months out of sync with the seasons. Caesar introduced a 365-day year, and added one day every fourth year. He added an initial two months to match the seasons with the calendar. According to the biographer Suetonius, Caesar revealed his scientific ability in other ways as well. He granted citizenship to physicians, scientists, and other intellectuals to keep them in Rome. He proposed a massive public works agenda that included the building of canals and draining of marshes. He supported the building of libraries and the ordering of Greek and Latin manuscripts. But, as Suetonius noted, many of his plans came to naught because of his assassination on the Ides of March, 44 BCE.

See also Calendars and Dating Systems; Geography/Geodesy; Military Science

References
Caesar. *The Civil War.* Translated by Jane F. Gardner. Harmondsworth, Middlesex: Penguin Books, 1976.
———. *The Conquest of Gaul.* Translated by S. A. Handford. Harmondsworth, Middlesex: Penguin Books, 1951.
Chadwick, Nora. *The Celts.* Harmondsworth, Middlesex: Penguin Books, 1970.
Suetonius. *The Twelve Caesars.* Translated by Robert Graves. Harmondsworth, Middlesex: Penguin Books, 1957.

Calendars and Dating Systems

The daily movement of the sun and nightly phases of the moon gave early humans a sense of passing, of human affairs being somehow linked to celestial phenomena. The female reproductive cycle was remarkably similar to the period from new moon to new moon, and thus ancient societies believed that the moon must have feminine characteristics. Religious festivals in honor of the moon goddess came to be as important as festivals tracing the solar year and the passing seasons. As agriculture developed, calendars became extremely important for tracking the time for planting and harvesting. Festivals built around the equinoxes and solstices were a natural consequence of coordinating humans affairs with solar and lunar movements. The Mesopotamians and Egyptians, the first two civilizations to develop agriculture and a sophisticated society based on the repetitive phenomena of the seasons, created the first calendars. The Babylonians had lunar calendars in which the month began on the evening of the appearance of the crescent moon. The Babylonian calendar required thirteen months in a year. Egyptians had lunar calendars only for festivals but otherwise relied on solar calendars. Egyptian solar calendars were based on 360 days, with five days added on at year's end. The Egyptian calendar coordinated the three farm seasons in four-month segments. The Egyptian new year began in July with the rising of the Nile River and the appearance of Sirius, the Dog Star. Chinese astronomers developed a solar calendar also, as early as 1300 BCE.

The Greeks made the greatest advances in measuring the lunar and solar years. Plutarch wrote that Solon introduced to the Athenians a lunar calendar. According to this calendar, on the one day per month when the moon and sun conjoin, the day would be called "the old and the new." Solon began on this day counting days to twenty. The last ten days were counted in descending order, conforming to the waning moon. That the lunar calendar was short of the solar calendar by 11½ days over the course of the year resulted in much confusion for the religious and thoughtful Greeks, which led mathematicians and astronomers to develop a variety of unique calculating techniques.

Octaëteris and Metonic Cycle

The remarkable lack of coordination of the solar and lunar years occupied the minds of ancient thinkers. What could be done to devise a calendar that would at the same time keep accurate track of the moon's phases and the sun's daily path? How could religious festivals based on the moon and those based on the sun not become completely confusing? The ancients developed the technique of inserting intercalary days to periodically keep the solar calendar reflecting the observed phenomena. The adding of a day every four years, the leap year, is a modern intercalary method. Greek astronomers and mathematicians were very creative in their attempts to use intercalary years with the least inconvenience and most efficiency.

Geminus, the Roman Stoic and astronomer of the first century CE, wrote in his *Introduction to Astronomy* that the Greeks of the Archaic Age developed the *octaëteris*: an eight-year cycle in which intercalary months could be added in the least confusing way. Since the lunar year lags behind the solar year by 11½ days, the Greeks discovered that the first point at which we find a reasonable

method to calculate intercalary months is at eight years (11½ times 8 equals roughly 90 days), when three months can be added to the lunar calendar to make it conform to the solar calendar. Geminus said that the Greeks decided to break this up in the *octaëteris* by inserting one month at intervals during the eight-year period. The *octaëteris* was still off by 1½ days, which led to the calculation of 16- and 160-year cycles, but most significantly, to the development of the Metonic Cycle of 19 years.

The Metonic Cycle was the creation of Meton of Athens, who lived in the fifth century BCE. He devised a calendar for use at Athens that showed the months, years, festivals, and ephemerides. Meton realized that 19 solar years equaled exactly 235 lunar months. Greeks knew, therefore, that every 19 years the cycle would begin again of the moon repeating the same phases on the same days of the solar calendar. With Meton's scheme, which still relied on intercalary months, mathematicians could coordinate lunar and solar calendar systems. The Metonic Cycle would in time be used to calculate the annual date of Easter. This was advocated by Anatolius, an Aristotelian philosopher, in the third century CE.

A contemporary of Meton, Oenopides of Chios, discovered the Great Year recurring every 59 years, which is the same as 730 complete lunar months. Oenopides calculated the year to a very accurate 365 days and 9 hours. The fourth-century mathematician Callippus of Cyzicus extended the Metonic Cycle to four periods, 76 years (the reason being that no matter what the Greeks tried to do, the cycles of solar and lunar years would always be a few minutes or hours off). The astronomer Hipparchus used an extended cycle of 304 years (four of Callippus's cycles) and developed a system that was highly accurate with respect to solar and lunar years, the latter being off only by one second per month. Hipparchus's estimate for the year was 365 days, five hours, fifty-five minutes, and fifteen seconds.

Rome

The calendar of early Rome, according to tradition and Plutarch, contained ten months, December being the tenth. The months were of varying numbers of days but totaled 360 days. The Romans had adopted this calendar from another source, perhaps the Etruscans, but did not understand its use, at least according to Plutarch. Then Numa Pompilius became king, succeeding Romulus. Plutarch, who had a balanced approach to history and legend, reported that Numa was a Pythagorean and scientist who reformed the calendar, adding two months, January and February, and making the Roman year begin not in March but in January. He was the first to show the Romans that the cycles of the moon and sun are different by eleven days per year, and that an intercalary month, called Mercedinus, must be occasionally added. This same calendar continued during the Republic until the time of Julius Caesar. Upon assuming dictatorial powers he embarked upon a series of reforms, one of which was the calendar. The Alexandrian astronomer Sosigenes influenced Caesar's calendar reform, which introduced the solar year of 365 days rather than the old lunar year of 355 days. Caesar introduced the 365-day year and a leap day every fourth year. He added an initial two months to bring the seasons and calendar together.

Timekeeping

The Babylonians developed the sexagesimal system of base 60, so that hours, minutes, and seconds could be determined as a fraction of 60 or its multiples. The Greeks used the Babylonian hexadecimal system combined with the Egyptian twenty-four-hour day. Time was kept in the Greco-Roman world by means of the sundial or gnomon and the water clock. The Greeks borrowed the idea of the gnomon from Egyptian and Babylonian scientists. Meton of Athens, the developer of the Metonic Cycle, erected a solar clock in fifth-century Athens. Aristarchus of Samos created a sundial that had "a concave hemi-spherical surface, with a pointer erected vertically in the middle throwing shadows and so enabling the direction of the height of the sun to be read off by means of lines marked on the surface of the hemisphere" (Heath 1913). The Hellenistic engineer Andronicus of Cyrrhus created a marble sundial on the island of Tinos and a water clock in Athens in a large octagonal structure with a bronze wind gauge at the top. Both Pliny the Younger and Julius Caesar described water clocks that marked the passing of time. Caesar remarked in the Gallic War that he determined the length of the British day using a water clock.

Dating Systems

Eratosthenes and Apollodorus dated events according to Spartan kings, the ephors; Thucydides dated events in his *Peloponnesian War* according to Sparton ephors but also Athenian archons. The historian Polybius used the Olympic games, occurring every four years beginning in 776 BCE, as his guide to constructing a regular chronology of historical events. Polybius relied on the work of Eratosthenes, who created a systematic rendering of the Olympiads, which was the basis for his *Chronography*. This system used the Olympiads as the means to measure time in the distant past, before 776, as well as for more contemporary events. According to historian Donald Wilcox (1987), Eratosthenes conceived of chronology in abstract terms, measuring events that are no longer felt or seen, events that have no existence except in the minds of those who recall them and the scratchings on parchment and stone that purport to record them. Plutarch, for one, thought that dating according to Olympiads was uncertain. Perhaps this explains why historians such as Polybius used other dating systems as well, such as the annual term of office of the Roman consul. Nevertheless Polybius showed the benefits of using one standard dating system to try to order the occurrence of all human events over time. Roman writers, such as the historians Livy and Tacitus, relied on the tried and true Olympiads and consulships but also dated events according to the hypothetical date of the founding of Rome (753 BCE). Hence Julius Caesar's assassination occurred in 709 (meaning 709 years since the founding of the city).

Christian Chronology

Christian scholars, of course, had to rely on the chronologies produced by their forebears. Hence Eusebius of Caesarea (260–339 CE), in *Ecclesiastical History,* dated the birth of Christ according to the year of Augustus's rule, the years since the Battle of Actium, and the reign of the governor of Syria, Quirinius. Eusebius published the *Chronological Canons,* in which he dated Christian, especially Apostolic, events of the first four centuries CE. Eusebius provided chronological tables of pagan and sacred events to provide comparisons with the past. He relied on some of the chronological estimates of the Hebrew historian Josephus. Eusebius dated Hebrew events from the birth of Abraham. Some Christian writers, such as Gregory of Tours and Paulus Orosius, used the creation of Adam as the logical starting point for chronicling human affairs. Even so, Orosius found it more convenient to rely for practical purposes on the years since the founding of Rome. St. Augustine, the greatest classical thinker on the subject of time, dated the passing of events in personal terms, according to the significance of one's life in relation to the coming of Christ, the Incarnation. Victorius of Aquitaine, meanwhile, devised a table with which to calculate the proper date of Easter, the Christian celebration of Christ's Resurrection. Victorius decided to date his Easter table beginning with the first Easter. Such a chronology, however, was not useful in the Roman world, where the year began not in the spring but after the winter solstice. Dionysius Exiguus in 525 CE drew up an Easter table that began with Christ's birth (December 25), traditionally celebrated by early Christians just a few days after the winter solstice at a time when the Romans had for centuries celebrated the Saturnalia.

Dionysius's Easter table eventually became the basis for dating events in yearly sequence from the birth of Christ, each year marking how many had passed since "the year of our Lord," *anno domini,* AD.

See also Astronomy; Aurelius Augustine; Easter; Hipparchus; Polybius; Time

References

Abell, George O. *Exploration of the Universe.* 3d ed. New York: Holt, Rinehart Winston, 1975.

Heath, Sir Thomas. *Aristarchus of Samos.* 1913; reprint ed., New York: Dover Books, 1982.

Neugebauer, O. *The Exact Sciences in Antiquity.* New York: Dover Books, 1969.

O'Connor, J. J., and E. F. Robertson. *History of Mathematics:* http://www-history.mcs.st-andrews.ac.uk/history/References/Heron.html (website of School of Mathematics and Statistics, University of St. Andrew's Scotland).

Plutarch. *The Lives of the Noble Grecians and Romans.* Translated by John Dryden; revised by Arthur Hugh Clough. 1864; reprint ed., New York: Random House, 1992.

Suetonius. *The Twelve Caesars.* Translated by Robert Graves. Harmondsworth, Middlesex: Penguin Books, 1957.

Wilcox, Donald. *The Measure of Time's Past: Pre-Newtonian Chronologies and the Rhetoric of Relative Time.* Chicago: University of Chicago Press, 1987.

Cato, Marcus Porcius (Elder) (234–149 BCE)

The Elder Cato was a philosopher, statesman, historian, and agricultural writer. His *On Agriculture* was written in Latin, Cato being very opposed to the growing Greek intellectual influence in Roman republican society. Cato's audience was the large landowner who was creating *latifundia,* the infamous plantations dedicated to wine and olive production, rather than the small freeholder who was, by the second century BCE, becoming a thing of the past.

Cato influenced many subsequent writers on agricultural topics, such as Columella, Varro, Palladius, and the Elder Pliny. The latter praised Cato for his expertise in viticulture—in olive growing and production of oil; in the purchase of farm property and deciding for what the land is best suited; and in particular crops and their medical efficacy. Cato, for example, praised cabbage as important in combating hypochondria, sleeplessness, and nightmares. Eating hare was also a sure remedy for insomnia. Pliny also relied on Cato for his comments on materia medica and veterinary medicine.

Cato believed that the Roman moral strength could be sapped by too heavy reliance upon other cultures. In an extant letter to his son he warned him to avoid Greek sophists and physicians; Greek learning can be useful, but not at the expense of Roman dignity, piety, courage, and honor.

See also Agriculture; Columella; Palladius; Pliny the Elder; Varro

References

Ogilvie, R. M. *Roman Literature and Society.* Harmondsworth, Middlesex: Penguin Books, 1980.

Pliny the Elder. *Natural History.* Translated by John F. Healy. London: Penguin Books, 1991.

Plutarch. *The Lives of the Noble Grecians and Romans.* Translated by John Dryden; revised by Arthur Hugh Clough. 1864; reprint ed., New York: Random House, 1992.

Celsus (floruit 25 CE)

Aurelius Cornelius Celsus was a Roman physician from Spain who lived and worked at the beginning of the Roman Principate. Celsus was a polymath who wrote a variety of works on topics such as agriculture, oratory, warfare, and medical science. His greatest work was *On Medicine,* written in Latin, in eight books. Celsus relied on his predecessors Hippocrates, Erasistratus, and Asclepiades. He was particularly indebted to Greek medical science. His was an encyclopedic work that encompassed all aspects of medicine, ranging from surgery to materia medica, to hearsay and superstition, to concrete discoveries in medicine and practical advice on good diet and health. Book One, for example, of *On Medicine,* discusses in detail the daily regimen of diet, exercise, purging the system, and so on to arrive at good health. Book Two discusses in Hippocratic fashion the impact of the environment upon good health.

The Roman physician Celsus. G. Engelmann Vigneron. (Courtesy of the National Library of Medicine)

Book Three includes an interesting assessment of mental illness.

Scholars disagree on whether or not Celsus was an interested observer or a practicing physician. He did refer to actual patients and seems to have practiced much of what he preached. His *On Medicine,* on the other hand, is a descriptive work focusing on observation, symptoms, diagnosis, and prevention rather than direct intervention to cure disease. Celsus's comments on medical practice relied chiefly on the traditional methods of purging the system and blood-letting. Even so, examining Celsus's achievements, one realizes that Roman medical science in the Augustan Age was sophisticated. Roman physicians and surgeons knew about dentistry, urology, obstetrics, ophthalmology, anesthesia, plastic surgery, and diseases of the ears and throat.

See also Agriculture; Asclepiades; Erasistratus; Galen; Hippocrates; Medicine; Roman Principate

References

Celsus, A. Cornelius. *On Medicine.* Translated by W. G. Spencer. Cambridge: Harvard University Press, 1938.

Durant, Will. *Caesar and Christ.* New York: Simon and Schuster, 1944.

Ogilvie, R. M. *Roman Literature and Society.* Harmondsworth, Middlesex: Penguin Books, 1980.

Chemistry
See Physical Sciences

China
See Asia, East and South

Cicero (106–43 BCE)

Marcus Tullius Cicero was one of the most well known of the Roman Stoic philosophers. He lived during the time of internal discord that destroyed the Roman Republic. Cicero translated his uncertainty about the state and corporeal matters into uncertainty about the nature and end of life. He was not quite sure what to make of religion, but he certainly doubted the traditional Roman pantheon of gods and goddesses. Cicero was a theorist about government and morality, though his own politics and ethics were sometimes questionable. He wrote a variety of dialogues and orations, most notably *On The Republic, On the Laws, Divination, On the Nature of the Gods,* and *On the Character of the Orator.*

Greek philosophy had a profound impact on Cicero. Two leaders of the Academy, Philo and Antiochus, were among his teachers. The Stoics Posidonius and Diodotus were his friends and mentors. Philodemus and Phaedrus were his Epicurean mentors. Indeed *On the Nature of the Gods* is an imaginary dialogue between an Epicurean, a Stoic, and an Academician. This dialogue provides an interesting analysis of the scientific and religious arguments for belief or disbelief in the divine.

Cicero's *On the Character of the Orator* presents the view that the successful orator must have broad knowledge, including of natural history and philosophy and political science, but especially knowledge of humans. The orator understands the individual and group feelings and expectations of his listeners. Cicero's psychology introduces the idea that em-

First-century BCE bust of the Roman Stoic and orator Cicero (106–43 BCE). (Araldo de Luca / Corbis)

pathy is required from the orator if he is to reach and influence his audience.

His imaginative essay "Scipio's Dream," found in Book 6 of Cicero's *Republic,* presents a cosmic, geographical, and psychological worldview. Cicero, like many geographers of his time, conceived of continents in different hemispheres of the earth separated by the oceans. For example, at the opposite side of the world from Italy were people whose feet imprinted the ground opposite to the Romans— these were the *antipodes.* Cicero agreed with most ancient geographers that there were five zones on the earth, two polar, two temperate, and a zone of fire at the equator.

Cicero is best remembered for his role in trying to halt the disintegration of the Roman Republic at the hands of military tyrants such as Catiline, Caesar, and Octavian. Cicero looked to an earlier time when the Senate ruled benevolently over a people content with public service and dedication to the Senate and people of Rome.

See also Academy; Epicureanism; Psychology; Social Sciences; Stoicism

References

Cicero. *Basic Works.* Edited by Moses Hadas. New York: Modern Library, 1951.

Ogilvie, R. M. *Roman Literature and Society.* Harmondsworth, Middlesex: Penguin Books, 1980.

Columella (5 BCE–60 CE)

Lucius Junius Moderatus Columella, a native of Cadiz, Spain, was a Roman agricultural writer, the author of *On Agriculture, On Trees,* and the lost *Against the Astrologers.* His books reveal the Roman concern for practical techniques of applied science. Columella wrote on aviculture (raising birds) and viticulture (cultivation of grapes, making of wine), so important to the Roman economy. He particularly emphasized viticulture as the best means to make land profitable. Columella's practical advice included that wheat does well in a field that has lain fallow for a year and that birds bathe in dust and ash and hence that the poultry man should line henhouses with such matter. Columella also advised crop rotation. Columella's writings had a significant impact on the work of later Latin scientists and agriculturalists, such as Pliny and Palladius.

See also Agriculture; Cato, Marcus Porcius; Palladius; Roman Principate; Varro

References

Columella. *On Agriculture.* Translated by Edward H. Heffner. Cambridge: Harvard University Press, 1989.

Ogilvie, R. M. *Roman Literature and Society.* Harmondsworth, Middlesex: Penguin Books, 1980.

Commentators

During late antiquity the Roman Empire was disintegrating, the barbarian kingdoms of Western Europe were being created, and the Byzantine Empire was emerging from the Eastern Roman Empire. There were few original thinkers and scientists during these centuries—most surviving works of science and philosophy were by commentators who examined the thinking of the greats of the past, such as Aristotle, and wrote extensive commentaries to preserve their teachings. Much of what we know about early Greek scientists comes from the work of the commentators of late antiquity. The most important of these commentators included Clement of Alexandria (150–215 CE), Hippolytus (180–235 CE), Pappas (floruit late third century CE), Macrobius (floruit fifth century CE), Proclus (412–485 CE), and Simplicius (500–540 CE).

Clement of Alexandria was a Christian and author of *Miscellanies,* in which he provided commentary on ancient Greek and Roman philosophers and scientists. Clement's purpose was the support of Christianity. He was one of the ancient sources for information on the Seven Sages of antiquity.

Hippolytus, a Christian theologian, wrote *Refutation of All Heresies,* in which he condemned pagan philosophy and science while offering commentary and excerpts. As a result, Hippolytus's *Refutation* becomes an important source for the writings and thought of Anaximander, Anaximenes, Empedocles, Xenophanes, Heraclitus, and Archelaus.

Pappas, who lived at the end of the third century CE and who was the author of *Mathematical Collection,* was a Late Roman commentator on the works of Archimedes, Euclid, and Ptolemy and also a geographer. His *Collection* included discussions of plane geometry, solid geometry, squaring the circle, the Pythagorean Theorem, volume, astronomy, conics (commenting on Apollonius of Perga), analytical geometry, and mechanics. Pappus preserved a discussion of the thirteen solids discovered by Archimedes.

Macrobius was a Late Roman author of the *Saturnalia,* in which he provided information and commentary on ancient science and philosophy. Macrobius's geography told of four continents in the four sections of a spherical earth—northern and southern latitudes were separated by an equatorial sea. The varied seas separating the continents flowed into each other, causing the tides.

Proclus of Lydia was a Late Roman mathematician and Neoplatonist philosopher who wrote the *Commentary on Euclid*. He studied at Athens and Alexandria. He attempted to measure the sun's diameter using a water clock. Proclus wrote commentaries on Aristotle and on astronomers such as Hipparchus. He studied eclipses, spheres of planets, and the distances between planets.

A Late Roman Neoplatonist, Simplicius wrote *Commentary on the Physics* and *Commentary on the Heavens,* two works that provide much information on otherwise unknown works by scientists and philosophers such as Hippo, Hippasus, Diogenes of Apollonia, Zeno of Elea, Parmenides, Melissus, Xenophanes, and Thales.

See also Aristotle; Diogenes Laertius; Later
   Roman Empire; Neoplatonism, Porphyry
Reference
Barnes, Jonathan, trans. *Early Greek Philosophy.*
   London: Penguin Books, 1987.

Constantinople

The Greek city of Byzantion was founded as a colony in the eighth century BCE by Dorian settlers. Byzantion possessed a wonderful site situated on a peninsula jutting into deep water overlooking the Bosphorus and the Sea of Marmara. The city of Byzantion lay astride sea lanes passing from the Black (Euxine) to the Aegean seas and land trade routes from western Asia to Eastern Europe. Byzantion thrived as a Greek polis, and then, after the birth of Christ, as the Greco-Roman city of Byzantium. The city, as a crossroads of trade, became a cosmopolitan place of cultures, institutions, and ideas. In the fourth century CE the emperor Constantine (who ruled from 306 to 337 CE) transformed the city into the capital of the Christian Roman Empire. Constantinople became the leading center of thought and culture for centuries to come.

The historical record is scant regarding the progress of science and philosophy in Greek Byzantion and Roman Byzantium. One reads of the Platonic philosopher Leon leading the defense of the city against Philip of Macedon in the mid-fourth century BCE. Perhaps Leon was leader because so few of his type resided in the city, which became a well-known center for astrologers, seers, and prognosticators. One of the most famous was Apollonius of Tyana, who practiced his miraculous arts at Byzantium in the second century CE, as recorded by the philosopher Philostratus in his biography of the wonder-worker. Shortly before Philostratus wrote his biography of Apollonius, Byzantium had been severely punished by the Roman emperor Septimius Severus for supporting a rival to the imperial purple. This was followed by years of stagnant trade and civil conflict. By the time that Constantine became emperor, Byzantium was an insignificant city in the Eastern Roman Empire.

The Emperor Constantine
Constantine was not a great intellect but instead a soldier who could see the strategic value of Byzantium. Seeking a new capital to glorify himself and his new devotion to Christ, Constantine decided in 324 to create a new city on the site of Byzantium. The City of Constantine was dedicated in 330, and quickly became the focus of the empire. Here was the palace of the emperor, the forum, the Hippodrome (where games were held), and the church of the holy wisdom, Hagia Sophia. Other churches, buildings, and statues surrounded the city's monumental core, which was located at the eastern end of the city, overlooking the Sea of Marmara. High cliffs and walls guarded the city on three sides; south was the Sea of Marmara, east was the Bosphorus, and north was the Golden Horn, a secure, deep harbor that was the basis for the city's extensive trade. The city could be accessed by land only to the European west, which Constantine fortified by a massive wall; his successors Theodosius and Justinian built walls, too.

Initially Constantinople was a military, administrative, and trade center rather than an intellectual center. Athens, Antioch, and Alexandria continued to take the lead in scientific and philosophical matters. Constantine, however, set the precedent for the emperor being the head of the church, which meant that he was the focal point of the ongoing theological debates centering upon the Christian Trinity, leadership in the church, and the accepted dogmas and canons of ecclesiastical rule. Christian philosophers and theologians therefore made Constantinople their home so that they could be near the emperor and, if possible, influence his decisions.

Constantine's successor Constantius II considered himself an enlightened Roman prince of an extensive, centralized republic. This facade of the old Roman princeps was believed by very few, except for the exceptionally credulous. Such men did not include the likes of Themistius, a pagan orator and philosopher whom Constantine accepted at the Christian court. Themistius played the game of pretending that the Rome of Constantius was akin to the Rome of Augustus. He was also a respected student of Greek Hellenism and a commentator of note on Aristotle. Other pagan philosophers, particularly Neoplatonists, were, like Themistius, tolerated at the imperial court. Notwithstanding the introduction and expansion of Christianity by Constantine and Constantius, the empire, especially in the eastern Mediterranean, was imbued with the centuries-old influence of Greek thought, literature, religion, and science.

The undercurrent of all things Greek in the Eastern Roman Empire was never more clearly seen at Constantinople than when Julian, the nephew of Constantine, came to the throne after the death of Constantius in 361. Julian considered himself a philosopher-king; he thought that the best and most trustworthy men were those who spent their lives in contemplation of Plato, Aristotle, Zeno, and Plotinus. He eulogized the Neoplatonist Iamblichus and supported his students, such as Maximus, and teachings, such as theurgy. His court at Constantinople was staffed with

Greeks who believed that the emperor was leading the empire to a new Hellenistic Age. Julian sought to spread his Hellenism to the Parthians, imitating Alexander's spread of Greek culture to Persia seven hundred years earlier. Julian was, however, not Alexander—he died in battle. So too did the dreams of the Hellenist philosophers and scientists.

Justinian

The glory days of Constantinople as the center of the Christian, Greek, and scientific culture of late antiquity occurred during the reign of the emperor Justinian (527–565 CE). Scholars today refer to Justinian as an emperor of the Byzantine Empire. Justinian considered himself a Roman emperor; the goal of his reign was to make concrete this perception by conquering the old Roman west, then in the hands of Germanic kings, and by resurrecting all things Roman, including thought, culture, and science. Justinian, like Constantine, was not an intellectual. Yet he patronized a host of thinkers—Aristotelian commentators, Christian theologians, Platonic thinkers, and some of the greatest legal minds of all time. It was under Justinian that the Digest of Roman Law and the Code of Justinian were compiled under the leadership of Tribonian, who, along with other legal scholars, such as Theophilus and Dorotheus, were scientists of law and government, forerunners of today's political scientists. They analyzed laws, hypothesized past situations, and deduced and induced the meaning and intention of past laws and their promulgators to gather the most significant laws and legal decisions and to create new standards of the Roman legal system that would last for centuries.

During Justinian's long reign, many public buildings and churches were built, the most notable being a new church dedicated to Holy Wisdom. Constantine's Hagia Sophia had burned early in Justinian's reign, and the emperor decided to build a new one on a much grander scale. He employed two of the most famous scientists of the day, Anthemius

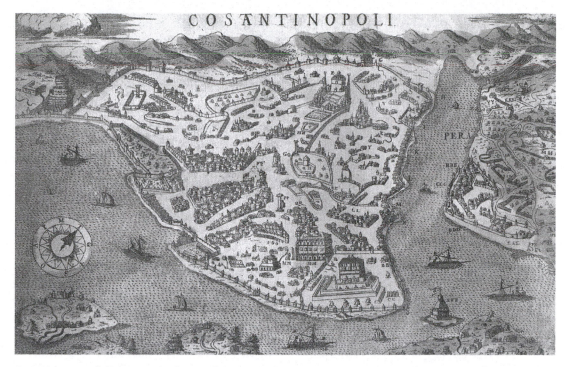

Renaissance map of Constantinople, the city of Constantine, which became an important intellectual center of the Later Roman Empire. Simon Pinargenti, "Isole che son da Venetia nella Dalmatia," 1573. (The Historic Cities Project, Hebrew University of Jerusalem and the Jewish National and University Libraries)

of Tralles and Isidorus of Miletus. These two mathematicians served as architects for the church. They planned and created a massive church with a central nave (for worship services) over which was a giant dome that Procopius, the historian of Justinian's reign, thought hung suspended from heaven. Indeed the natural forces weighing upon the dome seemed insignificant compared to the immaculate rising stone formed into countless arches, hemicycles, and smaller domes that countered the constant downward thrust. Isidorus and Anthemius were also the architects of the Church of the Holy Apostles in Constantinople.

Justinian sponsored the work of other Late Roman Byzantine scholars and scientists. The emperor threw his support behind the work of scholars at the University of Constantinople (originally founded during the reign of the emperor Theodosius II). Notable scientists included Cosmas Indicopleustes and Hierocles. The former was a traveler and perceptive geographer, author of *The Christian Topography,* in which he described many of the lands he had visited, such as Abyssinia and India. Strangely, Cosmas also believed that the earth (indeed, even the entire universe) was like a massive tabernacle, square rather than round. Hierocles' *A Fellow-Traveler of Hierocles* is a less ambitious, yet more descriptive and concrete analysis of the Byzantine Empire.

Justinian envisioned Constantinople as a promulgator of Greek culture in a thriving Roman Empire. If the latter goal was not entirely successful, the former goal was triumphantly accomplished. For almost a millennium after Justinian's death Constantinople served as a beacon of Greek culture and a repository of ancient documents, unsurpassed anywhere else in the world. Byzantines and Muslims alike shared an interest in the writings of such greats as Aristotle.

It was through Arab translations of many of Aristotle's works that Western Europeans in the thirteenth century became reacquainted with Aristotle, leading to an Aristotelian, scientific revival that culminated in the scientific achievements of the European Renaissance.

See also Aristotle; Julian; Later Roman Empire; Themistius

References

Cimok, Fatih. *Istanbul.* Istanbul: A Turizm Yayinlari Ltd., 1989.

Downey, Glanville. *Constantinople in the Age of Justinian.* Norman: University of Oklahoma Press, 1960.

Freeman, Kathleen. *Greek City-States.* New York: W. W. Norton, 1950.

Justinian. *The Digest of Roman Law.* Translated by C. F. Kolbert. Harmondsworth, Middlesex: Penguin Books, 1979.

Vasiliev, A. A. *History of the Byzantine Empire.* 2 vols. Madison: University of Wisconsin Press, 1958.

Constellations

The distant, ancient past is seen on every clear night by the person who peers into the starlit sky. The light of stars hundreds and thousands of light years away has arrived at the very moment one sees it. The position of the stars has hardly changed in the last several millennia; hence the patterns we see today are very much like those that Homer or Archimedes or Ptolemy saw. The wandering planets in the ancient night sky twinkled to the backdrop of the starry vault, the realm of fixed stars that changed slightly month by month but not with the dramatic movement of the sun, moon, and planets. A few astronomers, such as Hipparchus, understood the tremendous distance of the stars from our solar system; and Hipparchus seems also to have realized that, due to *parallax,* this distance meant that any movement of the stars would go generally undetected by humans on earth.

The seemingly unchanging *fixed* stars provided a stable, familiar phenomenon that a person could count on, like sunrise and the full moon, during the course of a long life. So familiar were the stars that early civilizations sought to identify them according to some apparent pattern or in honor of a particular deity or hero. Hence the ancients developed constellations, names for star patterns that were recognizable to young and old alike. Our constellations today are the same as they were two and three thousand years ago. Then as now, constellations provided bearings for sailors at sea, helped astronomers track the movement of planets and peculiar events such as comets and meteors, and helped storytellers along as they spun yarns for listeners over the centuries. Some constellations could be seen night after night throughout the year by ancient Mediterranean observers. Ursa Major and Ursa Minor, the tail of which forms the North Star, Polaris, were seen year-round in the northern horizon. Others came and went with the seasons. Orion the hunter, for example, appeared in late autumn and departed in the spring, spending his entire stay in the southern horizon. Following the same pattern were the twins Castor and Pollux, Gemini. The signs of the zodiac are, of course, twelve famous constellations that stay within the narrow path of the sun, the ecliptic. Other star formations or single stars were well known among the ancients. Sirius, the Dog Star, arrived after the winter solstice and departed after the spring equinox. The Pleiades, a cluster of stars almost directly above the Mediterranean observer, appeared after the autumn equinox and traveled slowly across the sky for the next six months, departing in the spring. The movement of the constellations, like that of the sun, moon, and planets, was east to west, matching the earth's eastward rotation.

See also Astronomy; Hipparchus

Reference

Abell, George O. *Exploration of the Universe.* 3d ed. New York: Holt, Rinehart Winston, 1975.

D

Democritus (460–370 BCE)

Ancient writers believed that Democritus was the student of Leucippus. They are associated together as the first philosophers to hypothesize that invisible material objects—atoms—make up the universe. Although, like Leucippus, little survives of Democritus's writings, the theory of atoms was widely discussed by ancient authors; hence much was known about Democritus and his theories even if only fragments of his writings survived. The breadth of his interests is astonishing. Diogenes Laertius in his brief biography lists Democritus's writings covering works on science such as *The Great World Ordering, On the Planets, On Nature, On Mind, On the Senses, On Images,* as well as works on meteorology, causation, zoology, botany, and mathematics, such as *On Different Shapes, On Changing Shapes,* and other works on angles, circles, spheres, numbers. Democritus's writings on medicine include *On the Nature of Man, On the Senses,* and other works on diet and fever. For geography there are such works as *On the Circumnavigation of the Ocean.* Democritus particularly made his mark in the application of his theories of the universe to everyday morality and the simple goal of living a good life.

Democritus, according to tradition, was born in northern Greece and later relocated to Athens. Like most philosophers of the time, he is said to have journeyed to Egypt. He was a contemporary of Socrates, which gives rise to some interesting speculations on what the discussions of these two men, holding such opposite beliefs, might have been. Socrates represented the school of thought that reality is immaterial, that thought is the essence of all things, and Democritus represented the school of thought that being is material, that invisible, irreducible particles compose existence, even what is normally considered the transcendent and ephemeral such as thoughts, the soul, and the divine. His lost works include *Pythagoras, Mind, Causes, Geometry,* and *Numbers,* which took issue with the Pythagorean hypotheses that abstractions represent reality, which can only be known by means of mathematical reasoning. If *number* dominates the universe, what is the role and significance of flesh and blood humans, or of a world composed of rock, dirt, plants, and animals? The Pythagoreans, argued Democritus, seek to reduce the universe to *one,* a singularity from which all else derives. But what does the universe really reveal to us? Multiplicity. There are infinite things, uncountable phenomena, multitudes of causes and effects leading to more causes and effects. How can an invisible, ephemeral number, a single being, be the sum of all things, the *cause* from which all else springs?

Democritus (460–370 BCE), polymath and scientific
visionary. Nineteenth-century portrait. (Archivo
Iconografico, S.A. / Corbis)

Democritus and his associate or teacher Leucippus argued that if being exists, it is material. All ideas, spirits, numbers, divinities, and souls, as well as the phenomena of nature, are formed by atoms (Greek *atomos*), irreducible substances of the four elements, earth, air, fire, and water, that are invisible yet universally present, in constant motion, undergoing continual change, combining and recombining into infinite forms. Atoms are distinct particles detached from an emptiness or void in which they move, combine, disintegrate, and recombine. How are atoms attached to each other? Rather like puzzle pieces, atoms have distinct and unique shapes, even "hooks" that allow an attachment, if not merging, of one to another. Aristotle, in *Metaphysics,* understandably condemned the atomist belief in the varied distinctions in types of atoms that form the bases of all reality.

The possibilities of "shape, order, and positions" are infinite, and thus infinity is the sine qua non of all things. Democritus thought that Creation and Destruction, if they exist, occur within the overall enduring pattern of infinite creations and destructions. Time is meaningless, if by time we mean the register of events in chronological, linear order from beginning to end. Neither *beginning* nor *end* have meaning in an infinite universe. There must then be infinite worlds, suns, stars, moons, men, cities, and so on. The implications are profound for a point of view that makes our solar system part of a vast whole and not alone and singular. If the heavenly bodies are not unique, they can potentially hold a lesser status, be brought down from the realm of the divine. Thus, for Democritus, the planets, stars, and sun are material, differing in heat and size. Anticipating Galileo's discoveries, Democritus argued (as did Anaxagoras before him) that the moon had mountains and valleys and was not a shining deity. And the geocentric view of the solar system is absurd in an infinite universe.

One wonders, What does have meaning in a material universe of constant motion and apparently random circumstances? Democritus's response was that one must find one's particular place in the universe: this is the means of individual contentment. He counseled acceptance of the contrariness and suffering of life—and acceptance of the joys and pleasures of life as well. Extremes in behavior, thought, and feelings lead to discontentment. One must discover the middle, where resides the greatest chance of peace. The universe is amoral, which requires humans to fashion their own moral system, which is personal and limited to one's time on earth. Death, and the release of one's atoms into oblivion, will come soon enough.

Democritus was a geographer as well. He wrote on the size and shape of the earth, the possibility of circumnavigating continents, the causes of terrestrial phenomena, history, and meteorology.

Democritus had a profound impact on subsequent thinkers. The ancient world had enough strife, pain, and bitterness to encourage a withdrawal to self and the circumscription of truth and morality to one's own life, thoughts, and feelings. The philosophy of Epicurus and his disciples, such as Lucretius, and Zeno and his fellow Stoics owed much to Democritus.

See also Astronomy; Atoms; Epicureanism; Greek Classical Age; Leucippus; Physical Sciences; Stoicism

References

Barnes, Jonathan, trans. *Early Greek Philosophy.* London: Penguin Books, 1987.

Heath, Sir Thomas. *Aristarchus of Samos.* New York: Dover Books, 1913.

Laertius, Diogenes. *Lives of the Philosophers.* Translated by R. D. Hicks. 2 vols. Cambridge: Harvard University Press, 1931, 1938.

Leicester, Henry M. *The Historical Background of Chemistry.* New York: Dover Books, 1971.

Diogenes Laertius (floruit third century CE)

Diogenes Laertius is an important source for the study of the history of ancient science. His *Lives and Opinions of Eminent Philosophers in Ten Books* examines the lives of ancient thinkers, beginning with the Ionian Thales and ending with the skeptic Saturninus. Diogenes divided Greek philosophy into the Ionian and Italian schools; the former was highlighted by Anaximander, Socrates, Plato, Aristotle, and Zeno, the founders of the Academy, Peripatetics, and Stoics; the latter featured Pythagoras, Xenophanes, Parmenides, and Epicurus, the founders of the Pythagorean and Epicurean schools.

Little is known of Diogenes' life. Besides the *Lives,* he wrote *Epigrams in Various Metres,* known today only in fragments. The selection of his topics in the *Lives* indicates he wrote after 200 CE. Diogenes was a Greek philosopher interested in the development of Hellenic thought as it expanded throughout the Mediterranean world. It is possible that he was one of the many philosophers (such as Philostratus) who were sponsored by the empress Julia Domna in the early third century.

Greek thought by 200 CE lacked creativity and dynamism—Diogenes' *Lives* reflects this malaise. Diogenes was a storyteller who delighted in the well-placed anecdote. He was not usually critical of his sources and perceived his role as an antiquarian collector of the relics of thought. Diogenes provided little historical, political, and geographic information in which to place the lives of his heroes. His are temporally disjointed lives *(bios)* in the same style as other biographers, such as Plutarch. He was rarely skeptical, being generally credulous about gods, prophecy, and magic. Diogenes was also not too particular about whom he classified as a philosopher. In his *Lives* we find a wide range of thinkers, natural scientists, mathematicians, metaphysicians, and biologists, all collectively considered lovers of wisdom *(sophia),* seekers of knowledge *(episteme),* and thus scientists.

Diogenes Laertius's *Lives of the Philosophers* is valuable in several ways. His is one of the few relatively complete collections of ancient thinkers written by an ancient, if mediocre, thinker. Many of his "facts," anecdotes, conversations, and letters are unique to his book, not found elsewhere in surviving sources. Diogenes, moreover, provided an undiscriminating collection of authors and commentators that are otherwise unknown, or whose works are lost except for the bits and pieces literary collectors such as Diogenes Laertius have passed down to modern times.

See also Later Roman Empire; Philosophy; Seven Sages; Theophrastus

References

Barnes, Jonathan, trans. *Early Greek Philosophy.* London: Penguin Books, 1987.

Laertius, Diogenes. *Lives of the Philosophers.* Translated by R. D. Hicks. 2 vols. Cambridge: Harvard University Press, 1931, 1938.

Diogenes of Apollonia (floruit late fifth century BCE)

Diogenes of Apollonia is a shadowy figure in the history of science, in part because nothing is known about his life, but also because his philosophy and science are obscure. We only know of his ideas from later commentators. His most well-known book, now lost, was *On Nature.* Diogenes argued that air is the fundamental element upon which all else depends. He believed that to understand the role of air in nature is to understand the distinct characteristics of animals, plants, and humans.

Diogenes accepted in principle the existence of the four elements—earth, air, fire, and water—but so tied are they one to another that a single element must be the source and essence of the other three. This single element is air, which Diogenes believed was the root of life and thought (for without air one dies and does not think). Air forms the soul *(psyche)* of each animal, particularly man. But the anatomies of humans, animals, and plants differ, and thus their respective use of air differs, as does their intelligence and souls.

Aristotle and his student Theophrastus discussed Diogenes' anatomical and psychological ideas at length. The keys to human intelligence, Diogenes argued, are the blood vessels that are the conduits for the movement of air throughout the human body. Diogenes had a clear if superficial knowledge about the extent and location of vessels (veins and arteries). The origins of the two central vessels are in the spleen and liver. The physician, seeking to correct an imbalance of the body's humors, will typically lance the spleen or liver vessel to bleed the patient. According to Theophrastus, Diogenes argued that the quantity and movement of air determines pain and pleasure, intelligence and dullness, courage and fear. An intelligent person, as opposed to a brute animal, dumb plant, stupid louse, or ignorant infant, has great quantities of light, fresh, dry air circulating throughout the body, inhabiting the mind, generating quick thoughts and clear judgments.

Diogenes was clearly a man of his times, echoing the materialist theories of Leucippus and Democritus and the developing notion of the four humors of the Hippocratic school. His influence on subsequent thought was limited, however, because of questionable theories described in confusing prose.

See also Democritus; Leucippus; Medicine; Psychology
Reference
Barnes, Jonathan, trans. *Early Greek Philosophy.* London: Penguin Books, 1987.

Dissection
See Medicine

Dreams
Until the work of Sigmund Freud, Carl Jung, and their successors, scientists gave scant attention to dreams as a proper object of inquiry. Dreams were stuff for the mystic, perhaps, but not for the scientist. The ancients, of course, did not analyze dreams as the working out of daily experience and as a necessary and healthy activity during sleep. They did not see dreams, as does the modern psychoanalyst, as reflections of the unconscious mind. Ancient thinkers did, however, recognize the significance of dreams, even if understanding was elusive.

The cultures of ancient Mesopotamia, Egypt, and the Mediterranean gave full credit to the soothsayer, prognosticator, fortune-teller, and astrologist who claimed to use natural phenomena to predict the future. One such phenomenon was the dream. Ancient humans could not conceive of dreams as anything other than a divine message hinting of what will be. There came to be a class of pseudoscientists who made their living predicting the future by means of the interpretation of dreams. Ancient literature is filled with such stories. In the *Old Testament,* in the Book of Genesis, Joseph interprets the dreams of the pharaoh and so gains a preeminent position in the kingdom. In the Book of Daniel, the Hebrew prophet Daniel interprets the dreams of the Babylonian king Nebuchadnezzar. Homer's poems are filled with accounts of dreams sent by the gods to inform humans of future possibilities. Typically, the Homeric world personified a natural occurrence by deifying it; hence Oneiros was the god of dreams. Common to all of these peoples of the ancient Mediterranean was the belief that dreams reflect natural or supernatural phenomena and that it takes reason and the analytical mind to correctly interpret them.

The Greek scientist Aristotle was sufficiently skeptical of dreams to wonder about their cause and significance. In his treatise *On Prophesying by Dreams,* he provided a balanced view of dreams, wondering why God would speak to humans through dreams, yet realizing that at times dreams do seem to reflect reality. One possibility he explored was that, since dreams often recall some of the details of the previous waking hours, likewise dreams might foretell actions of the next day insofar as the dreamer might (unconsciously) perform certain actions he had dreamed about the preceding night—hence the dream comes true. Carl Jung, the great modern student of dreams, clearly had the same understanding and lived his life in accordance with what his dreams predicted for the coming day. Aristotle recognized also that, among the host of dreams, a few might by coincidence end up occurring, which lacks a supernatural or scientific significance. Animals dream, as do slaves and other inferior (in Aristotle's mind) humans, and thus are more a product of nature rather than being sent by a god. But nature is itself divine, Aristotle argued: in this sense dreams are divine as well. Although Aristotle did not agree with the interpretation of dreams of materialists such as Democritus, that dreams are caused by the emanation of atoms that present images upon the brain, he did agree with their point of view that such an atomic rendering of dreams could in no way be prophetic of the future.

There were several important students of dreams during the Later Roman Empire. The most famous was the physician Galen, who believed that dreams helped direct him in diagnosis and healing in general. Galen, who was physician to the emperor Marcus Aurelius, imparted this respect for the teaching significance of dreams to the Stoic Aurelius. A fourth-century CE physician, Gennadius, learned of the soul's immortality by means of a dream. The most significant students of dreams were Artemidorus of Daldis and Aelius Aristides, both of the second century CE. Artemidorus wrote *Oneirocritica,* a book on dreams and their meanings. He took a scientific approach to dream prognostication. He assiduously recorded every aspect of dreams, compiling a precise record of this peculiar human activity. Similar was Aelius Aristides, a priest of Asclepius, the Greek god of healing. Aristides kept a full account of his many dreams over the space of several decades. He believed that Asclepius healed or gave advice on healing through dreams.

See also Aristotle; Asclepius / Asclepiads; Egypt; Medicine; Old Testament; Psychology

References

Aristotle. *On Sleep and Sleeplessness; On Prophesying by Dreams; On Memory and Reminiscence.* Translated by J. I. Beare. In *The Parva Naturalia.* Oxford: Clarendon Press, 1908.

Bowersock, G. W. *Fiction as History: Nero to Julian.* Berkeley: University of California Press, 1994.

Dodds, E. R. *Pagan and Christian in an Age of Anxiety.* New York: W. W. Norton, 1965.

Jung, Carl. *Man and His Symbols.* New York: Doubleday, 1964.

E

Easter

Easter, the day of the celebration of Christ's Resurrection, occurs every year on the first Sunday after a full moon from March 21 to April 21. The holiday is a holdover from pagan festivals, is named for the ancient Mesopotamian goddess Astarte, and is based on the lunar as well as the solar calendar. The debate over the yearly date of Easter has been longstanding and frequently acrimonious. The Council of Nicaea, a meeting of Christian bishops during the reign of the emperor Constantine, agreed in 325 CE on the formula for determining the date of Easter. It was decided that Easter would always fall on a Sunday in the spring after the vernal (spring) equinox (March 21). It was left to church mathematicians and astronomers to figure the dates of Easter for coming centuries according to the cycles of the phases of the moon. One of these scientists was Dionysius Exiguus, who during the sixth century CE, while working out his table, devised a dating system based on the Incarnation, the supposed date of Christ's birth. Although Dionysius made an error in his choice for the year of the birth, he established the dating system of years proceeding from Christ's birth. This is the modern chronological system of BC, Before Christ, and AD, *Anno Domini* (in the year of our Lord). The solar Julian calendar was slightly irregular, which over the centuries altered the calendar date for the vernal equinox; the Gregorian calendar, adopted in Europe in the sixteenth century and in the American colonies two hundred years later, corrected the irregularity, making Easter once again during the month after the vernal equinox.

See also Calendars and Dating Systems; Time
References
Boorstin, Daniel. *The Discoverers.* New York: Random House, 1983.
Wilcox, Donald. *The Measure of Time's Past: Pre-Newtonian Chronologies and the Rhetoric of Relative Time.* Chicago: University of Chicago Press, 1987.

Eclipses
See Astronomy

Egypt

Sun worship and the concern for understanding the environment were natural in a land wherein the people were dependent upon nature and its natural rhythms for their survival. The archaic and classical Greeks hailed Egyptian civilization as a prime source for Greek cultural and scientific achievements. Founders of Greek thought such as Thales and Pythagoras were thought to have visited

Egypt. Plutarch wrote that Solon learned of Atlantis from Pseuophis of Heliopolis and Sonchis of Sais. Others such as Herodotus and Plato later made the same pilgrimage to discover the secrets of Egypt. Even after its repeated conquest by the Assyrians, Persians, Greeks, and Romans, Egypt remained an important center of thought and culture. In later years the city of Alexandria was the premier center of science in the Mediterranean world.

Pyramids

Imhotep was the legendary builder of the first Egyptian step-pyramid (ziggurat), as well as a physician who was so honored by the Egyptians that he became the deity of learning and giver of science, rather like the Greek Prometheus. The Egyptians credited Imhotep with the development of mathematics, the calendar, architecture, and medicine. In time, Imhotep's shrine became a place where the sick went to be healed. Historically, Imhotep's pyramid, built around 2700 BCE at Saqqara in the third dynasty, was a series of mastabas (six in all) built up to form a hierarchical pyramid. Imhotep's ziggurat became a model for the building of more sophisticated pyramids as time passed.

The historian and geographer Herodotus, who visited Egypt in the mid fifth century BCE, provided in Book 2 of his *Histories* a concise account of the building of the Great Pyramid during the reign of Cheops (also known as Khufu) in the twenty-sixth century BCE. The pharaoh used one hundred thousand men to drag limestone blocks from distant quarries; for part of the way, the blocks were transported by barge on the Nile. Indeed Cheops had a canal dug that flooded with the rising Nile, allowing the barges to bring the limestone blocks right to the building site. The Great Pyramid took twenty years to build. It was built in stages by layers, like a step pyramid, the laborers using complicated levers to raise the blocks up each level. The massive limestone blocks were fitted exactly, then polished. The height of the pyramid is equal to each of its four sides at the base. According to Herodotus, the laborers of this astonishing work lived on a simple vegetarian diet.

Medicine

The Egyptians developed an extensive materia medica. Even in Homer's time they were known for their drugs and medicines. Herodotus claimed they were a race of doctors, there being a physician for every type of illness. Their knowledge of medicine was based on folklore more than empirical observation. The Egyptian practice of medicine relied on healthy doses of magic. Here, in medicine as well as in other branches of science, the Egyptians believed in a clear connection between the natural and the supernatural. According to Herodotus, Egyptians believed that good health required a monthly purging, using strong emetics.

Papyrus of Ani (Egyptian Book of the Dead)

The Egyptians had a deep belief in the power of amulets and magical sayings to help them achieve a blessed afterlife. A priest of the New Kingdom of the second millennium BCE, one Ani, recorded hymns and prayers and his beliefs about life and death in the *Book of the Dead*. Ani assumed that deities such as Osiris, Isis, and Ra personified natural phenomena. In a paean to Osiris, for example, Ani defined the god as he who is lord of the stars that never change. In the *Book of the Dead*, Osiris is the sun and Isis is the moon; the world is created and will perish. The universe is spherical, and the stars are on fire. The bright lights of the heavens determine human destiny.

Embalming

Herodotus observed on his visit to Egypt the different practices of mummification. The most extensive, done for the wealthy, involved removing the brain through the nostrils and clearing out the intestines through an incision made in the abdomen. The body

The Egyptian god of mummification Anubis, overseeing the final preparations of the dead. Wall relief from the nineteenth dynasty (thirteenth century BCE). (Corel Corporation)

was filled then with spices, particularly myrrh, and then soaked or "pickled" in natron (an embalming fluid made of sodium carbonate) for seventy days, after which the body was wrapped in white linen, with gum used as the adhesive. The less wealthy had "oil of cedar" injected through the anus into the intestinal cavity, after which they were soaked in natron as well. The very poor had the intestines cleaned with a strong emetic, after which they too were kept in natron for seventy days. The practice of mummification indicated the Egyptian belief in the afterlife. Herodotus heard from Egyptian priests that they believed in a cycle of reincarnation that lasted for three millennia, during which the soul migrated from one animal to another, up the chain of being, before returning to inhabit the human body again.

Astronomy and Mathematics

The Egyptians, living in a land of the distant horizon, the black night of countless stars, the hot summer days with the sun high overhead, made a host of astronomical observations, though most of them were done for simplistic purposes. They were particularly concerned with tracing the rising of Sirius, the Dog Star, which indicated the rise of the Nile—in July, when the Egyptians began their new year. Indeed Egyptian astronomers devised an accurate 360-day solar calendar, which was later adapted by the Greeks. Herodotus heard directly from priests, who were the astronomers, about their calendar and astronomical observations. Herodotus declared that the Egyptian technique of adding five intercalary days every year was the most efficient technique. The motions of other stars and planets indicated other meteorological events. According to Diogenes Laertius, Egyptian astronomers understood lunar and solar eclipses, counting 373 solar and 832 lunar eclipses. Herodotus claimed that the Egyptians were the first people to develop the pseudoscience of astrology.

Egyptian mathematics concentrated on arithmetic and fractions, although the Egyptians were not as sophisticated as the Babylonians. Egyptian mathematics was very practical. They conceived of numbers as concrete amounts, not as conceptual symbols. In geometry, the Egyptians engaged in simple calculations and measurements of shapes such as isosceles triangles, the circle, and varied rectangular shapes such as the trapezoid. Scholars are unsure whether Egyptian mathematicians calculated the value of pi (π). One wonders how the massive exactness of the pyramids could have been made without the knowledge that comes from a clear understanding of geometry.

See also Astronomy; Engineering and Technology; Herodotus of Halicarnassus; Irrigation Techniques; Mathematics; Mesopotamia

References

Budge, E. A. Wallis, trans. Papyrus of Ani: Egyptian Book of the Dead. New York: Dover Books, 1967.

Herodotus. The Histories. Translated by Aubrey de Selincourt. Harmondsworth, Middlesex: Penguin Books, 1972.

Neugebauer, O. The Exact Sciences in Antiquity. New York: Dover Books, 1969.

O'Connor, J. J., and E. F. Robertson. History of Mathematics: http://www-history.mcs.st-andrews.ac.uk/history/References/Heron.html (website of School of Mathematics and Statistics, University of St. Andrew's Scotland).

Riefstahl, Elizabeth. Thebes in the Time of Amunhotep III. Norman: University of Oklahoma Press, 1964.

Scholz, Piotr O. Ancient Egypt: An Illustrated Historical Overview. Hauppauge, N.Y.: Barron's Education Press, 1997.

White, Jon Manchip. Everyday Life in Ancient Egypt. New York: Capricorn Press, 1967.

Eleatic School

The Eleatic school of philosophy featured three great philosophers of the fifth century BCE: Parmenides and Zeno of Elea and Melissus of Samos. Parmenides, the founder of this style of thought, was from Elea in Magna Graecia. He was a student of Xenophanes, according to Diogenes Laertius, as well as an associate of the Pythagorean school. His sole work, Poem, survives only in fragments. In it Parmenides vaguely subscribes to the view of a universe directed by Being, which is the totality of all things, not created, eternal and infinite. Zeno, also from Elea, was a follower of Parmenides and was chiefly known for his paradoxes. For example, he tried to show that even emptiness has being, and motion is at rest. This is true only if one realizes that at each singular moment (the many parts of which make up the whole of movement), time, hence motion, are indeed still, as in still photography. Melissus of Samos (fifth century BCE) was a man of affairs, a statesman and general, who was also a philosopher. A follower of Parmenides, Melissus wrote On Nature or On What Exists, which survives only in fragments preserved by the Late Roman commentator Simplicius. Like Parmenides, Melissus concerned himself with arguments to prove that being is without cause, not created, infinite and eternal.

See also Greek Archaic Age; Magna Graecia; Plato; Physical Sciences; Pythagorus; Xenophanes of Colophon

References

Barnes, Jonathan, trans. Early Greek Philosophy. London: Penguin Books, 1987.

Laertius, Diogenes. Lives of the Philosophers. Translated by R. D. Hicks. 2 vols. Cambridge: Harvard University Press, 1931, 1938.

Elements

Knowledge of who first proposed the idea of fundamental material elements making up all existence is lost in time. One tradition has it that the Egyptians conceived of four elements as the basis of all things, which inspired Greek thinkers to enlarge on the theory. The earliest Greek scientists conceived of earth, air, fire, and water as being the fundamental elements of the universe. Thales argued for water being the primal element; Anaximenes thought it was air. Empedocles thought that love and strife defined and moved the four elements.

Aristotle conceived of a ranking of the elements in the universe: earth has a downward movement because it is heaviest; water is next in weight; air is third, being much lighter; fire is fourth, having an inherent upward movement. Aristotle argued for a fifth element, ether (aether) to provide the quintessence (fifth essence). Ether did not partake of the material nature of the other four, nor did it experience condensation and rarefaction. Since ether was the epitome of perfection, it had a circular motion and was the stuff through which the heavenly bodies roamed.

Later scientists, such as Leucippus, Democritus, and Epicurus, conceived of a more fundamental source of the material four elements: atoms. Each element, they thought, is composed of atoms, invisible, constantly moving, material foundations of all things.

See also Aristotle; Atoms; Physical Sciences
References
Heath, Sir Thomas. *Aristarchus of Samos.* New York: Dover Books, 1913.
Leicester, Henry M. *The Historical Background of Chemistry.* New York: Dover Books, 1971.

Engraving of the Greek philosopher and scientist Empedocles (495–435 BCE). (Courtesy of the National Library of Medicine)

Embalming
See Egypt

Empedocles (495–435 BCE)

Empedocles was one of the greatest pre-Socratic Greek scientists. A native of Acragas on the isle of Sicily, he was a philosopher, physician, mystic, and materialist. His work survives only in fragments, and his life is not well known. The best source for Empedocles' life, notwithstanding the plentiful anecdotes, is Diogenes Laertius.

A proponent of the four elements—earth, air, water, fire—Empedocles believed that from these are things generated and to these things are destroyed through the two affective forces, love and strife: the former attracts, the latter repulses. Empedocles, anticipating Aurelius Augustine's dualism of the City of God and City of Man, conceived of a transcendent realm dominated by love and a physical realm dominated by strife. Every-

thing, even the truth, is in a process of becoming that never ends. He hypothesized a materialist foundation to the universe that was built upon by Leucippus and Democritus. His books, in particular *On Nature* and *Purifications,* were written in obscure verse that tended to hide rather than reveal. In these works he dealt with the divine; the origins of humans; a basic astronomy of the relation of sun, earth, and moon; the nature of the earth; biology and zoology; the means of sensory perception; and medicine. His astronomy was primitive, advocating the notion that the universe is a crystal sphere within which is a dark hemisphere of air and a light hemisphere of fire, which gives us the phenomenon of day and night. Aristotle (according to Heath 1913) attributed to Empedocles the original theory that light travels from one point to the next over a certain period of time. He also studied the attraction and repulsion of magnets and the nature of sound and vision. As a physician, Empedocles established a medical school at Magna Graecia that was the counterpart to the more famous Hippocratic school at Cos in the Aegean.

See also Astronomy; Atoms; Elements; Greek Archaic Age; Medicine

References

Barnes, Jonathan, trans. *Early Greek Philosophy.* London: Penguin Books, 1987.

Heath, Sir Thomas. *Aristarchus of Samos.* New York: Dover Books, 1913.

Laertius, Diogenes. *Lives of the Philosophers.* Translated by R. D. Hicks. 2 vols. Cambridge: Harvard University Press, 1931, 1938.

Engineering and Technology

Mesopotamia

The first great advances in human technology were in the use of stone, bone, ivory, and wood that occurred in the Paleolithic Age. The development of fire and of human communication were two other fundamental technological developments whose origins are obscured by the distant past. The Neolithic Revolution after 10,000 BCE led to signal developments in agriculture and early attempts to construct shelters of mud brick. The fire drill, a means of creating fire artificially by friction, was developed perhaps initially in ancient India. The Mesopotamians, discovering that clay is vastly more workable than stone, developed pottery as early as 6000 BCE. The kind of pottery produced required kilns hosting temperatures up to 1,000 degrees centigrade. In the same area of Mesopotamia, the potter's wheel was invented by unknown craftsmen about 4000 BCE. Mesopotamia was the region where two other technological and engineering discoveries were made. Remains of buildings dating back to 2100 BCE show a pitched-brick vault of sun-dried bricks narrowing in to form a conical enclosure. The Mesopotamians were perhaps also responsible for the first monumental architecture: the ziggurat at Ur, dedicated to the moon god Sin, which had four stories or huge platforms built one upon another leading to a pinnacle and a rectangular enclosure.

Writing

At some point in the distant past, early humans developed the means by which they communicated concepts, ideas, facts, and simple observations by spoken words. Scholars think that the development of language was an invention of a form of technology, a tool that could be used to generate ideas, reflect upon the past, and anticipate the future. Language was the means to conquer isolation of time and place. Names of things—natural, human, physical—allowed for systematization and categorization of ideas. Cuneiform symbols made with a stylus in wet clay developed in third millennium Mesopotamia in response to the need to record agricultural surplus. In Egypt, pictograph and ideogram hieroglyphics similarly allowed for human communication, an analysis of the divine, and stories of men and gods to be not just told but also recorded. Toward the end of the second millennium BCE, the Phoenicians of the eastern Mediterranean developed a simple twenty-two-letter alphabet that became the basis for the Greek and Latin alphabets. The Phoenician alphabet allowed Greek philosophers and scientists to begin to develop their conceptions of existence and analyses of reality.

Pyramids

Some scholars believe that the Sumerians of Mesopotamia learned from the Egyptians how to make their step pyramids. The Egyptians most certainly were the master pyramid builders. Pyramids were constructed in several stages using ramps on which the large limestone blocks would be dragged up to the level of building activity. The higher the pyramid got, the wider the ramp had to be and the greater the number of ramps needed to accommodate the increasing structural pressure. Ramps would doubtless have been built along the sides of the pyramid. A step pyramid structure would have formed the inside of the outer pyramid to bolster it. Pyramids like the Great Pyramid of Cheops were built in the summer with the rising of the Nile so that water would bring barges close to the construction sight. Some scholars hypothesize that the Egyptians developed a working knowledge of pi (π) in building the pyramids.

Greco-Roman Developments

The Greeks were responsible for some astonishing inventions, for example, the massive lighthouse on the island of Pharos at Alexandria, steam power, and the still astonishing Greek temple, in particular, the Parthenon. The Parthenon, named for the maiden or virgin *(parthenos)* goddess Athena, was designed by Callicrates and built from 447 to 438 BCE under the authority of Pericles. Phidias was in charge of the artistic rendering of the Parthenon as well as other temples on the Athenian Acropolis.

Roman building accomplishments were no less significant. The Romans developed cement from volcanic ash combined with lime, sand or gravel, and water. Cement upheld the structural integrity of some of the most astonishing Roman works, such as the aqueducts. Roman engineers did not use cement in building the long-lasting roads of the empire. Rather basalt or limestone laid into a bed built using gravel and heated sand formed the road. Roman surveyors used the *groma,* a surveying instrument that relied on plumb lines, to build the road with a slight incline from the center to allow for good drainage. Roman engineers were able to solve some of the structural difficulties inherent in bridge building. Some Roman bridges and aqueducts used cement; others were built with huge blocks of stones rigorously and carefully fitted together. One of the great Roman bridge builders was Apollodorus of Damascus, who bridged the Danube and built the Alcántara in Spain and Trajan's column in Rome. Roman roads and bridges lasted for centuries; some are still in use. During the reign of the emperor Valens, when the empire was in the process of a slow disintegration, a huge aqueduct was built covering 150 miles across the Balkans to Constantinople; it lasted 800 years.

Other Roman building successes included the Pantheon and the Coliseum, both of which relied on the Roman technique of fashioning a vault or an arch by building a brick structural frame into which concrete was poured. The thrust of huge structures was balanced so that no buttresses were needed on walls. A case in point is the Pantheon, begun during the reign of the emperor Hadrian (117–138 CE) to honor all the world's deities. The diameter and height of the Pantheon are precisely the same, forming a perfect circle. The cupola at the extreme height of the ceiling is the only source of light. The dome relies on panels of concrete and other materials, built lighter at the top, heavier in descent. The panels of concrete on the dome also grow larger in descent, each supporting the one above. The Coliseum, begun during the reign of Nero (54–68 CE), was built of stone without the use of cement. Upon completion it could seat as many as fifty thousand spectators, who watched gladiatorial contests, mock battles, and wild animal hunts. Of particular note was the *velarium,* a partial covering to keep the audience protected from sun and the elements. The velarium was vastly complicated, requiring hundreds of seamen to operate the miles of rope, pulleys, and winches.

See also Egypt; Greek Classical Age; Mesopotamia; Roman Principate; Roman Roads and Bridges

References

Barrow, R. H. *The Romans.* Harmondsworth, Middlesex: Penguin Books, 1949.

Childe, Gordon. *What Happened in History.* Harmondsworth, Middlesex: Penguin Books, 1946.

Dal Maso, Leonard B. *Rome of the Caesars.* Translated by Michael Hollingsworth. Florence: Bonechi-Edizioni, 1974.

Hawkes, Jacquetta. *Prehistory: History of Mankind: Cultural and Scientific Developments,* vol. 1, pt. 1. New York: Mentor Books, 1965.

Pliny the Elder. *Natural History.* Translated by John F. Healy. London: Penguin Books, 1991.

Von Hagen, Victor W. *Roman Roads.* London: Werdenfeld and Nicholson, 1966.

Epictetus (55–135 CE)

Epictetus was a Greek slave who became a leading voice of Stoicism during the Roman Principate. He was a student of Musonius Rufus, a Roman Stoic philosopher. After being freed by his master Epaphroditus and then banished from Rome by the emperor Domitian, Epictetus set up a school in western Greece on the Adriatic, at Nicopolis. There he had great influence on Greek and Roman Stoics, his most famous student being the historian and biographer of Alexander the Great, Flavius Arrianus, Arrian (89–180 CE). Arrian recorded Epictetus's teachings in the *Discourses,* which he claimed were his own notes taken during the philosopher's lectures. Arrian also published the *Enchiridion,* a handbook of Epictetus's Stoic teachings.

Epictetus contributed to the development of the science of psychology in antiquity. Much of his moral philosophy dealt with the search for happiness and contentment; the path to coming to know oneself; and the ways to cope with anxiety. Epictetus's answer to all of these issues was to accept oneself, one's situation in life, one's surroundings, and the workings of time. He believed correct thinking about life and self could help in the healing process of body and mind. His focus on reason led him to discount the typical Roman reliance upon soothsayers and diviners; one should divine one's future based on awareness of self, Epictetus argued. He counseled acceptance of sickness, rather than resistance and the endless search for doctors and cures. Ultimately the individual has free choice to respond appropriately or not to the contingencies of life. Always one's "moral purpose" *(prohairesis)* must guide the response to peculiar situations and the manifold events of life.

Epictetus's *Discourses* were so curt and direct that his readers, particularly those of a similar mind-set, could scarcely disagree with his approach to life and thought. He deeply influenced Marcus Aurelius, and much later, Michel de Montaigne, who saw in Epictetus a philosopher who could address man's most essential limitations: fear of the future and fear of death.

See also Arrian; Aurelius, Marcus; Roman Principate; Stoicism

References

Epictetus. *The Discourses.* Edited by Christopher Gill. Everyman's Library. Rutland, Vt.: Tuttle Publishing, 2001.

Sandbach, F. H. *The Stoics.* New York: W. W. Norton, 1975.

Epicureanism

The Epicurean philosophy was a largely moral system of thought that influenced Greece and Rome particularly in the last several centuries BCE. Epicurus (371–271 BCE) gave his name to a philosophy built upon several assumptions that were radical at the time. Epicureans adopted the theories of Leucippus and Democritus that atoms—indestructible, irreducible, infinitely moving material particles—composed all things. Mind, soul, gods, love—anything emotional and spiritual—had an atomic basis. Atoms were, however, insentient, and thus impersonal and amoral. Assuming such a universe without apparent purpose, first Democritus and then Epicurus developed a moral philosophy in response. There was no need to fear anything if the phenomenon causing the most fear, death, was irrelevant. One died without knowing the result, as the body, mind, and soul disintegrated into multitudinous atoms that would eventually go to form some other material item. Why fear the retribution of the gods when the gods were impotent (if they did exist) and could not reward or punish?

Epicurus taught that one must focus exclusively on the self and the ability of the self to find meaning, purpose, and happiness. He argued that it was easier to find happiness without death and retribution hanging over a person. Time became, in a sense, irrelevant, as the duration of life hardly mattered when disintegration and nonexistence awaited the culmination of human life and endeavor. Epicurus sought peace of mind (Greek *ataraxia*), a stable, passive, almost emotionless state of lack of pain. Pleasure, the key to happiness, is simply the lack of pain, when emotionless peace becomes the sum of life.

Epicurus and many of his followers did not stray from philosophy to science, except when, under the influence of Rome, the philosophy acquired the scientific perspective of a materialistic universe. Epicurean philosophy made its way to Rome by means of Philodemus of Gadara, a writer and philosopher who influenced many first century Romans—Julius Caesar, Horace, Virgil, and Lucretius. Titus Lucretius Carus became the greatest exponent of Epicurean philosophy. Lucretius embraced the philosophy's potential to provide scientific explanations. Lucretius's *On the Nature of Things* is a detailed verse portrait of the universe and natural phenomena. Lucretius provided a complete description of atoms: constantly moving, infinite, indestructible, of varying shapes but otherwise indistinguishable—and invisible to humans. But the scientist is able to observe their effects. Lucretius explained the senses according to the movement of atoms; he described the atomic theory of the mind and soul; he developed a theory of human development and relations over time according to the absence of purpose and sentience in the universe; and he wrote a fascinating discussion of the meteorology of a materialistic universe and of how disease spreads through the agency of atoms.

See also Atoms; Democritus; Epicurus; Greek
    Classical Age; Hellenism; Leucippus; Lucretius
References
Grant, Michael. *From Alexander to Cleopatra: The
    Hellenistic World.* New York: History Book Club,
    2000.
Laertius, Diogenes. *Lives of the Philosophers.*
    Translated by R. D. Hicks. 2 vols. Cambridge:
    Harvard University Press, 1931, 1938.
Lucretius. *The Nature of the Universe.* Translated by
    R. E. Latham. Harmondsworth, Middlesex:
    Penguin Books, 1951.
Russell, Bertrand. *A History of Western Philosophy.*
    New York: Simon and Schuster, 1945.

Epicurus (341–271 BCE)

Epicurus gave his name to Epicureanism, a Greek philosophy that gained tremendous popularity in Rome. Epicurus was an Ionian Greek who lived part of his life in Athens. His teachers, according to Diogenes Laertius, were Nausiphanes and Naucydes. Epicurus gained his own followers upon developing a system of thought based on the atomism of Leucippus and Democritus. Epicurus taught that the universe was materialistic, formed exclusively by indestructible, irreducible particles (atoms) that are infinite and in constant motion. Since all is dominated by an impersonal anonymous force of matter, humans must respond with the search for individual peace of mind (Greek *ataraxia*).

Diogenes Laertius, in his extensive biography of Epicurus in *Lives of Eminent Philosophers,* claimed that Epicurus pursued his own path of learning when his teachers could not explain to him the concept of chaos. Not that the idea of chaos necessarily bothered him—what did bother him was being unprepared to meet the varied contingencies of life with a calm and disinterested passivity. Epicurus taught that the pursuit of pleasure—meaning the absence of pain—was what mattered in life. Death was inevitable, but since there was no sentience after life, only disintegration into atoms, death should cause no fear. The gods existed, but they were impotent in a materialistic universe; humans need have no fear of retribution for offending the powers of the universe—an atom simply could not be offended.

Epicurus was not a scientist, but rather a philosopher who formed a pattern of life in response to a particular scientific paradigm popular in Greece toward the end of the Classical Age and the beginning of the Hellenistic Age. Such were the conflicts and uncertainty of these last few centuries, BCE, that Epicurus's teachings continued to influence other thoughtful individuals looking for a way out of the conundrum of trying to explain self in what appeared to be an

Epicurus (341–271 BCE), the Greek atomist and founder of Epicurean philosophy. Roman copy of Greek original (ca. 270 BCE). (Kathleen Cohen / Pergamom Museum, Berlin)

increasingly cold and impersonal universe. His most famous disciple was the Roman poet Lucretius.

See also Atoms; Democritus; Epicureanism; Greek Classical Age; Hellenism; Leucippus; Lucretius; Philosophy

References
Grant, Michael. *From Alexander to Cleopatra: The Hellenistic World.* New York: History Book Club, 2000.
Laertius, Diogenes. *Lives of the Philosophers.* Translated by R. D. Hicks. 2 vols. Cambridge: Harvard University Press, 1931, 1938.
Russell, Bertrand. *A History of Western Philosophy.* New York: Simon and Schuster, 1945.

Erasistratus (275–194 BCE)

A Greek physician and physiologist and student of Herophilus of Chalcedon, Erasistratus worked in Alexandria (as did his teacher), performing observations, experiments, and even dissections to uncover some of the secrets of the workings of the human body. He studied the heart and hypothesized about the veins and arteries. As a practicing physician, Erasistratus believed that holistic living was the means to prevent illness. He discarded the four humors of the Hippocratic school in favor of relying upon the pulse to make diagnoses—his was a methodical approach to medicine, as was the Roman Asclepiades several centuries later. Influenced by Aristotle and his followers of the Peripatetic school, Erasistratus tried to find cause and effect relationships in medicine.

Erasistratus was unique in his ability to connect mind and body. He studied the brain and nervous system, identifying the cerebrum and cerebellum and discovering that the nerves are not airy tunnels. He explored illnesses of the mind *(psyche)* and nervous system, thereby beginning the field of study that today we call psychiatry.

See also Alexandria; Hellenism; Herophilus of Chalcedon; Hippocrates; Medicine

References
"Antiqua Medicina: Aspects in Ancient Medicine." http://www.med.virginia.edu/hs-library/historical/antiqua/anthome.html.
Boardman, John, Jasper Griffin, and Oswyn Murray. *Oxford History of the Classical World.* Oxford: Oxford University Press, 1986.
Durant, Will. *The Life of Greece.* New York: Simon and Schuster, 1939.
Grant, Michael. *From Alexander to Cleopatra: The Hellenistic World.* New York: History Book Club, 2000.
Pliny the Elder. *Natural History.* Translated by John F. Healy. London: Penguin Books, 1991.

Eratosthenes (276–195 BCE)

Eratosthenes of Cyrene was the Librarian at Alexandria and a geographer of note. Author of the *Geographica,* Eratosthenes mapped the world and estimated the earth's circumference, providing one of the most accurate assessments of the ancient world. He flourished at a time when Alexandria was becoming the premier center of science in the ancient world. He influenced many other thinkers, such as Polybius, Strabo, Hipparchus, and Ptolemy of Alexandria.

Eratosthenes provided some of the most accurate estimates of land surface measurements of his time. The geographer Strabo praised him for being more realistic than other geographers, such as Polybius, who allowed fancy to take hold of reason. Eratosthenes divided the earth into climatic zones—the poles, arctic, temperate, tropics (Cancer, Capricorn), equator. He believed that the tropics, where the solstices occur, have more extreme heat than the equator, which is higher in elevation and has more rain. He doubted Homer's geographic knowledge, even if others, such as Strabo, were more credulous.

Eratosthenes was the first scientist to map the earth according to latitude and longitude, profoundly influencing Hipparchus and Ptolemy. He devised the idea of the meridian, the abstract focal point from which all geographic measurements can proceed. In his *Chronography,* Eratosthenes devised a system of abstract chronology as well, basing the measure of passing years according to the Olympic games occurring every four years beginning in 776 BCE.

Eratosthenes' most famous experiment was his measurement of the shadow at Alexandria on the same date and time of day as when the rays of the sun were (he believed) directly overhead at Syrene, Egypt. According to the story (preserved by the first-century CE scientist Cleomedes), he determined this phenomenon at Syrene by observing the rays of the sun shining directly on the bottom of a well. Using a gnomon he determined the angle of the noon shadow at Alexandria to be 7.2 degrees, one-fiftieth of a circle, the spherical earth. The distance from Syrene to Alexandria was 5,000 stadia (about 2.5 million feet), which if multiplied by 50 gives the

result of the circumference of the earth, 250,000 stadia, or 23,300 miles, an estimate that was off by only 2,000 miles. (The way to accurately determine the earth's circumference is to multiply the diameter by pi. Part of the significance of Eratosthenes' experiment was his realization that the rays of the sun strike the varied places of the earth in parallel (not divergent) lines.

Eratosthenes, who believed that the landmass of Europe, Asia, and Africa was exclusive to the northern hemisphere, estimated the extent of Europe, Asia, and Africa to be 77,000 stadia. The unknown southern hemisphere must be inhabited, though by whom Eratosthenes was uncertain. It is possible that Eratosthenes, who advocated the theory of a greater ratio of water to land, believed that a western voyage across the Atlantic would return the voyager to Asia.

See also Alexandria; Geography/Geodesy; Polybius; Pytheas of Massilia; Strabo

References

Heath, Thomas. *Aristarchus of Samos: The Ancient Copernicus.* New York: Dover Books, 1981.

Polybius. *The Histories.* Translated by W. R. Paton. 6 vols. Cambridge: Harvard University Press, 1922–27.

Tillinghast, William H. "The Geographical Knowledge of the Ancients Considered in Relation to the Discovery of America." In *Narrative and Critical History of America,* vol. 1, ed. Justin Winsor. Boston: Houghton, Mifflin, 1889.

Ether (Aether)

See Elements

Euclid (floruit 300 BCE)

Euclid was arguably the ancient world's most important mathematician. His *Elements of Geometry* has influenced students of philosophy, science, and mathematics even to the present. The chief source for the scant details of the life of Euclid was the Late Roman writer Proclus (412–485 CE), who claimed that Euclid was a student of Plato's academy.

Copper engraving of the Alexandrian mathematician Euclid (floruit 300 BCE), author of Elements. *(Bettmann/Corbis)*

Besides this and the strong literary tradition that he was an Alexandrian mathematician, little else is known about Euclid. He was recognized as the authority on mathematics, even more than Apollonius of Perga and Archimedes, so that teachers warned prospective students, such as at the Academy, that one must know Euclid above all else. Besides *The Elements,* Euclid wrote *The Pseudaria,* a book on geometry that distinguished true from false theorems; *The Data,* another basic geometrical text that covered various propositions (if . . . , then . . .); *On Divisions,* examining geometric figures and derivatives; *Surface-loci,* covering geometric shapes such as cones and spheres; *Conics,* in four books, to which his disciple Apollonius added four more; *Phaenomena,* a work of astronomy; and *Optics, Porisms,* and *Elements of Music.*

The Elements is a mathematical treatise in thirteen books. Elements are initial, *a priori* principles that must be accepted as true before further analysis in the form of *postulates, axioms,* and *hypotheses* can be suggested. An element is an undoubted first principle of reality. Thus, Euclid began his book with the first principles of geometry dealing with the nature of lines and points on a line. From initial principles he derived postulates and axioms that provided for the student basic rules of geometry and measurement.

For the ancients of Euclid's time, before and after, who like Euclid were under the spell of Plato and Aristotle, the deduction of postulates and axioms from initial first principles was the means by which thinkers could deduce the reality of the universe from the initial causes and state of things. Euclid's statements in Book 1 of the *Elements* were not mere statements of geometry and mathematics but were statements of the basic truths of the universe.

> *See also* Apollonius of Perga; Archimedes; Commentators; Hellenism; Mathematics
>
> **Reference**
> Euclid. *The Thirteen Books of The Elements.* Translated by Sir Thomas Heath. New York: Dover Books, 1925.

Eudoxus of Cnidus (408–352 BCE)

Eudoxus, Pythagorean and student of Plato, was an astronomer, mathematician, and physicist. He wrote *Phaenomena,* one of the seminal statements from the ancient world on astronomy. Although the book was filled with erroneous information, arguing for the geocentric universe composed of twenty-seven spheres, Eudoxus believed in a completely rational approach devoid of superstition and mysticism. He had his own school at Athens, where he taught his students his geometric ideas on proportion, volume, the circle, pyramids, and cones. According to Diogenes Laertius, he wrote *Voyage round the World.* A mathematician of note, he anticipated some of Euclid's ideas in geometry, in particular the theory of proportion. He anticipated Archimedes in his development of the method of exhaustion.

According to Strabo, Eudoxus established an astronomical observatory at Heliopolis, Egypt; he also built one at his hometown of Cnidus. From these observatories he tracked stellar phenomena and was particularly intrigued by the star Canopus. His observations and theories were recorded in two books, *Mirror* and *Phaenomena;* the latter book was partially preserved in verse in Aratus's *Phaenomena.*

Eudoxus developed the theory of concentric spheres to attempt to fit together his assumptions of the spherical nature of the earth and the planets, sun and moon, and heavens, as well as his own observations on the movements of the night sky. The theory postulates a series of spheres of different sizes, all perfect circles, moving about the earth. The fixed stars have a sphere by which they move. The sun and moon each require three spheres; each planet has a sphere, but also a larger sphere centered at its poles. Eudoxus even required two more spheres for each planet in order to exactly replicate what he observed in the night sky. In all, there were twenty-seven spheres of varying sizes and movements in Eudoxus's complicated universe. He did not worry about the composition of the spheres, nor even their reality. His was a theoretical construct only, intended to predict astronomical phenomena, and nothing more.

Eudoxus's theories were carried forth by his students Menaechmus, Polemarchus, and particularly Callippus of Cyzicus. Aristotle relied on the work of Eudoxus and Callippus in creating his own scheme of the heavenly spheres. Eventually Ptolemy would take up the cause of Eudoxus's concentric spheres and try to correct some of its errors while still attempting to preserve the conceptual whole.

See also Aristotle; Astronomy; Euclid; Greek
    Classical Age; Mathematics
References
Durant, Will. *The Life of Greece.* New York: Simon
    and Schuster, 1939.
Heath, Sir Thomas. *Aristarchus of Samos.* New York:
    Dover Books, 1913.
Russell, Bertrand. *A History of Western Philosophy.*
    New York: Simon and Schuster, 1945.

Eunapius (floruit fifth century CE)

Eunapius was the pagan author of *Lives of the Sophists,* an important source of information on the lives of Late Roman philosophers and scientists of the third and fourth centuries CE. Eunapius's *Lives* is not a critical source, as much of his work deals with Neoplatonism and its fourth-century expression dominated by theurgists such as Iamblichus and Maximus of Ephesus. Theurgy was the work of charlatans who used magic to play upon the superstitions of their followers, even those with apparently incredulous minds such as the emperor Julian. This period of the Later Roman Empire was one of confusion and anxiety, the decline of paganism and rise of Christianity. Christians were uncertain as they sought to explain their basic doctrines, such as of the Trinity. Pagans were similarly unsure about what role ancient beliefs played in a changing society. Pythagorean and Platonic philosophers tried to bring back the Hellenic past. Eunapius was a faithful follower of these efforts, though they were ultimately doomed to failure.

See also Julian; Later Roman Empire; Plotinus;
    Porphyry; Maximus of Ephesus; Neoplatonism;
    Pythagoras
References
Brown, Peter. *The Making of Late Antiquity.*
    Cambridge: Harvard University Press, 1978.
Dodds, E. R. *Pagan and Christian in an Age of
    Anxiety.* New York: W. W. Norton, 1965.
Eunapius. *The Lives of the Sophists.* Translated by
    W. C. Wright. Cambridge: Harvard University
    Press, 1968.

F

Frontinus, Sextus Julius (floruit late first century and early second century CE)

Frontinus was the water commissioner in charge of the upkeep of the aqueducts that brought fresh water to the city of Rome during the reigns of Nerva (96–98 CE) and Trajan (98–117 CE). His treatise *On the Water-Management of the City of Rome* provides a detailed description of the origins, number, placement, upkeep, and utility of the Roman aqueducts. Rome's first aqueduct was the Aqua Appian, named for Appius Claudius Crassus, an old senator who was also responsible for the construction of the Appian Way. Frontinus systematically described such aqueducts as the Old Anio, Marcia, Tepula, Julia, Virgo, Augusta, Claudia, and New Anio. He laid out their extent in paces and distinguished those parts that were subterranean or aboveground upon a series of arches. Frontinus carefully described the bases of measurements (in digits and inches) of the varied pipes used to convey water. He estimated the amount of water delivered by each aqueduct in *quinaria,* a unit of measure developed by the Romans that was $5/4$ of a digit (which was $1/16$ of a foot). The *quinaria* measured not only length but volume as well. Frontinus proclaimed that the aqueducts brought health to the city: fresh pure water for drinking and bathing and water to cleanse the city streets and sewers. Work gangs of slaves maintained the aqueducts. Frontinus thought that the Roman aqueducts were Rome's great symbol, like the Egyptian pyramids were to Egypt; yet the pyramids accomplished nothing, while the Roman aqueducts were not only awesome and beautiful but pragmatic as well.

See also Engineering and Technology; Hydraulics; Roman Principate; Roman Roads and Bridges

Reference

Frontinus. *On the Water-Management of the City of Rome.* Translated by R. H. Rodgers. 2003. http://www.uvm.edu/~rrodgers/Frontinus.html.

G

Galen (130–200 CE)

Galen was a Greek physician from Asia Minor who was a master of medical science and physician to the Roman emperor Marcus Aurelius. Galen's first love was philosophy—the ongoing influence of Aristotle is clear in his writings. While still in his teens he began the study of medicine, traveling to many of the major centers of learning, particularly Alexandria, where he came to know the writings of Asclepiades, Erasistratus, Herophilus, and Hippocrates. Accepting the latter as his literary and scientific mentor, Galen was a physician to gladiators and then had a successful medical practice at Rome. There was much vitriol in Galen's writings, and apparently in his lectures and conversation as well. He was unafraid of offending others by challenging their beliefs and advocating his own as the only true way. He was forced to flee Rome for a time but returned to be physician and tutor to Commodus, the son of Marcus Aurelius and future emperor. His literary output was immense. In his works we find a physician and scientist who studied the brain and nervous system, the digestive and circulatory systems, anatomy, skeletal structure, the function of the organs, and materia medica. Although a rationalist, Galen still sometimes relied on the workings of the divine to understand the intricate ways of the human body. Nature, he believed, was the wise creator of the human body, which was an image of the rational and good rather than a mere organism or machinelike substance. He believed dreams could be used in prognosis and that the moon could affect the human body. Generally, however, Galen believed in experiment and observation by which to arrive at medical theories and diagnoses. He was a methodical, logical thinker, who, like Aristotle, could overpower his readers and encourage belief by the relentless force and sophistication of his arguments.

Influenced by Hippocrates, the great medical thinker of the fifth century BCE, Galen argued that the human body is made up of four humors: black bile, yellow bile, phlegm, and blood. Health depends on maintaining a balance of the humors by means of proper food, regular exercise, adequate sleep—in short, a temperate lifestyle. An overabundance of black bile, for example, can lead to cancer. Galen accepted the Hippocratic view that one must treat illness with opposites to reestablish the humoral balance. Hence wetness must act upon dryness; what is hot must be cooled. Blood is warm and moist, which is countered by black bile, which is cold and dry. Phlegm, which is cold and moist, is countered by yellow bile, which is warm and dry. Galen argued that drugs and foods influ-

Engraving of the Roman physician Galen (130–200 CE), by Vigneron. (Courtesy of the National Library of Medicine)

ence the humoral balance in the body: too much food can produce sickness, followed by disease. Galen's writings on food and nutrition include *On the Powers of Foods,* in which he experimented with the impact of fruit, such as apples and pears, on bowel movements, *On Barley Soup,* and *On the Causes of Disease.*

In the five centuries that separated the work of Hippocrates and the work of Galen, medicine had been heavily influenced by the materialist strain of Epicurean writers who believed that the mechanistic movement of atoms in the body has the greatest impact upon health. Galen was particularly incensed

at Asclepiades, a Greek physician of the first century BCE who refused to believe that a holistic approach to medicine was important, but rather that most illness was due to the constriction of tissues and vessels. One of Galen's extant works, *On the Natural Faculties,* is a sustained attack against the teachings of his predecessors except Hippocrates. Galen thought it absurd to assume that the human body has no living, spiritual component— that the body is but atoms in motion in varied combinations. How can one diagnose illness without considering the will and vitality of the human being?

The power of Galen's thought and his many writings influenced medical thought and practice during subsequent centuries. Galen was read by Christians and Muslims alike, who saw in him an Aristotelian thinker who also believed in the "vital spirit" present in each individual. The pagan Galen could therefore be adopted by monotheists looking for a physician who accepted the will and presence of the divine in human existence. Galen also argued that the human body acts like a system in which all parts work toward the functioning of the whole. Each part is intertwined, attracting and expelling like positive and negative forces—not in isolation, but in unison.

See also Asclepiades; Aurelius, Marcus; Celsus; Erasistratus; Hippocrates; Medicine; Oribasius; Roman Principate

References
Durant, Will. *Caesar and Christ*. New York: Simon and Schuster, 1944.
Galen. *On the Natural Faculties*. Translated by A. J. Brock. Cambridge: Harvard University Press, 1916.
Grant, Mark, ed. and trans. *Galen on Food and Diet*. New York: Routledge, 2000.

Gaza

Gaza was the ancient Philistine city at the southern edge of Palestine on the roads to Phoenicia, Petra, Egypt, and Alexandria. A Semitic city for most of its past, Gaza was nominally Phoenician in the fourth century BCE when Alexander the Great laid siege to it. At that time the city was forbidding, built on a hill surrounded by high walls and deep sand.

Hellenistic and Roman influence made Gaza during the Later Roman Empire a Semitic city with a predominant Greek culture; the inhabitants spoke Greek and Aramaic. During the fifth century CE, Gaza became a Christian city. Like any Greek city, Gaza had a hippodrome and amphitheater, temples and churches. The city, with streets in a grid dominated by right angles, was patterned after the ideas of the Milesian city designer Hippo-

damus. In the centuries after the foundation of Constantinople, Gaza increased in importance as one of the intellectual centers of the Eastern Roman (Byzantine) Empire along with the imperial city, Athens, and Alexandria.

Sixth-century Gaza looked less to Constantinople than to the Greek city of Alexandria in Egypt for scientific and intellectual leadership. Procopius of Gaza, for example, one of the well-known intellectuals of sixth-century Gaza, studied at Alexandria—he was famous for his panegyrics and literary descriptions. One, of a complicated clock, still survives. Another sixth-century writer, John of Gaza, produced a literary account of the universe based on a painting on display at the city. Aeneas of Gaza at the same time wrote an imaginary account of the Peripatetic school and its leader Theophrastus. In good Aristotelian fashion, Timothy of Gaza penned a scientific description of the animal kingdom. The schools of Gaza were considered of the same rank as those of Alexandria and Constantinople. Students at Gaza received a traditional Greek education *(paideia)* along with a sufficient grounding in Christian theology. The two approaches combined to produce Christian humanistic thinkers.

Choricius, one of the leading intellectuals of sixth-century Gaza, is a good example of the Christian scholar. He combined Christian theology with allusions to classical mythology in his writings, the most famous of which were detailed portrayals of Gaza churches. His description of the Basilica of St. Stephen combined myth, faith, and mathematics in one literary tour de force.

Science at the end of the ancient world, in the sixth century CE, was elementary compared to the great accomplishments of the past during the time of Aristotle and Ptolemy. Yet cities such as Gaza, by relating the concepts and writings of past thinkers, were able to bring this thought forward to later ages, to the Renaissance, and to the present.

See also Alexandria; Constantinople; Later Roman Empire

References

Arrian. *The Campaigns of Alexander.* Translated by Aubrey de Selincourt. Harmondsworth, Middlesex: Penguin Books, 1971.

Downey, Glanville. *Gaza in the Early Sixth Century.* Norman: University of Oklahoma Press, 1963.

Geminus (floruit first century CE)

Geminus was an astronomer and mathematician of the first century CE known for *Introduction to Astronomy* (*Isagoge*) and *Theory of Mathematics.* A Stoic influenced by Posidonius of Rhodes, Geminus possibly lived in Rhodes as well, an important center of science during the Hellenistic Age. Geminus focused on solar and lunar events and phases; the coordination of solar and lunar calendars; eclipses; the distances of the stars from the earth; constellations; and the zodiac. In *Introduction to Astronomy,* as well as in *Theory of Mathematics,* Geminus provided an interesting historical perspective, telling his readers that mathematics had changed over time: Pythagoras's concern for theory, and mathematics as an abstract source of truth, gave way to a more practical application of mathematics, represented by Geminus himself.

Geminus continues to be an important source for understanding the development of ancient calendars and dating systems. His *Introduction to Astronomy* tells us of the *octaëteris,* an eight-year cycle at the end of which three intercalary months were added in the ancient Greek lunar calendar to make months and dates conform to the phenomena of the seasons.

See also Astronomy; Calendars and Dating Systems; Mathematics; Posidonius of Rhodes

References

Heath, Sir Thomas. *Aristarchus of Samos.* New York: Dover Books, 1913.

O'Connor, J. J., and E. F. Robertson. *History of Mathematics:* http://www-history.mcs.st-andrews.ac.uk/history/References/Heron.html (website of School of Mathematics and Statistics, University of St. Andrew's Scotland).

Geocentric Universe

See Astronomy

Geography/Geodesy

The ancient Greeks invented the sciences of geography and geodesy. The search to make sense of space and one's place in it is clearly an essential human activity. Earlier civilizations had, it is true, engaged in geographic activities. For example, from ancient Babylon comes the earliest map of the world, with the Euphrates River at the center on a clay tablet with a legend inscribed in cuneiform. But the Greeks were the first to systematize the search to understand the nature of the world. The Greeks were wanderers who explored the entire Mediterranean region, the Black (Euxine) Sea, Asia from the Aegean to the Indus, the Arabian Sea, North Africa, Western Europe, the North Atlantic, and the Atlantic coasts of Europe and Africa. Although certainly naïve, especially regarding traditional myths and legends, the Greeks were the first to develop critical thought based on experience, observation, and logic respecting the extent and shape of the earth and its landscapes and cultures. The Greeks were ignorant of much: they maintained the limited view of three continents and two oceans; and they never knew of the Pacific or the Americas. Yet their great accomplishment was the development of an idea and a spirit of scientific exploration that later Europeans and Americans used as the basis for their own explorations of distant lands and peoples.

The First Explorers

Greek geography begins with Homer. The *Odyssey* records the peregrinations of Odysseus, who, driven by the gods, fate, and his own will to survive, wandered the Mediterranean for years seeking the way home to Ithaca, his kingdom, and his faithful wife, Penelope. According to Homer, Odysseus's travels took him from the Aegean Sea to the northern coasts of Africa, on to

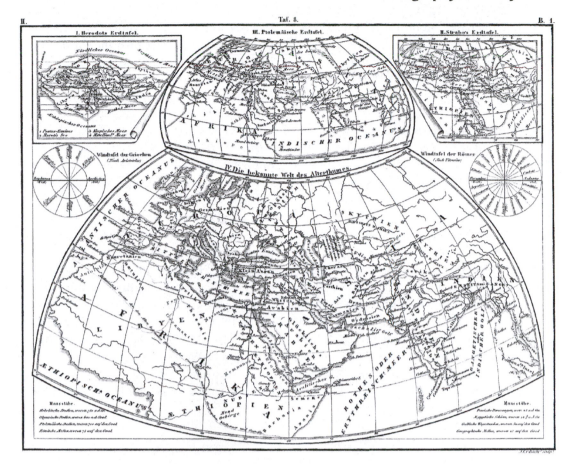

Renaissance map portraying the geographic conceptions of Herodotus, Strabo, and Ptolemy and the wind charts of Aristotle and Vitruvius. In Johann G. Heck, Iconographic Encyclopaedia of Science, Literature, and Art *(New York: Rudolph Garrigue, 1851, vol. 1, division 3, pl. 8). (Library of Congress)*

Sicily and the Strait of Messina, and as far as the "Ocean stream," the Atlantic.

Homer, of course, was a poet rather than a geographer. Yet the Homeric worldview was formed by myth and legend, which usually contain a kernel of truth. Odysseus's journey was one many Phoenician mariners made during the early centuries of the first millennium BCE. The Phoenicians left behind few records of their voyages to North Africa, Sicily, southern Spain, and beyond the Strait of Gibraltar to the Atlantic Ocean. Tales of Phoenician adventures became part of the epic cycle of Mediterranean bards, which ex-

plained how Homer borrowed so much from the Phoenician experience to mold the character and exploits of Odysseus. Odysseus's journey was longer, more daring, and more fantastic than that of his earlier counterpart, Jason, who with his Argonauts explored the Black Sea to its eastern limit at Colchis in quest of the golden fleece. That Greeks were by 800 BCE making voyages from the Aegean Sea to the Black Sea by way of the Hellespont and Bosphorus made the story of Jason, which featured mythological rendering of real places and peoples, all the more believable. Writings (*graphia*) about the world (*geo*) were initially based on tales of historical voyages made by anonymous explorers, who nevertheless acquired knowledge of the Mediterranean world and passed it on, however fancifully.

Homer and His Successors

Homer's *Iliad* and *Odyssey,* written during the eighth century BCE, provide plentiful if often erroneous information about the world. The poems describe a round disk, the earth, composed of three ambiguous continents, Europe, Asia, and Africa (Libya), surrounded by the river Ocean. The world-encircling ocean stretches from the waters west of the Pillars of Heracles to the Euxine (Black) Sea in the east. Homer's knowledge of the extent of the Mediterranean, from Gibraltar to the Dardanelles and beyond to the Atlantic and Black Sea, derived from the sailors of Egypt, Phoenicia, Carthage, Crete, and Greece. Homer's contemporary Hesiod wrote of similar mythic places, such as the Elysian Fields, an island in the Ocean west of the Pillars of Heracles. Homer and Hesiod both conceived of the land of the dead far to the west, on the verge of Ocean.

The *Iliad* and *Odyssey* as well as other poems of the Homeric Cycle inspired later writers to attempt recreations of possible Greek voyages of discovery. Notable in this regard was Apollonius of Rhodes, the author of the third century BCE poem *Argonautica.* The *Argonautica* recounts the Greek heroic quest for the Golden Fleece. Apollonius used myths going back millennia to tell the story of the voyage of *Argo.* The Argonauts sailed across the Aegean Sea to the Hellespont, north through the Bosphorus to the Black (Euxine) Sea, east to Colchis, then back across the Black Sea to the Danube River. They ascended the Danube to its source, descended the Rhone River to the Mediterranean Sea, and paralleled western Italy to Sicily. Near western Greece they were driven off course to North Africa. They finally returned to Greece by way of Crete and the islands of the Aegean Sea. It was a fantastic journey retold many times over the centuries. Apollonius provided the third-century BCE Greek version.

The Greeks gained greater knowledge and experienced new cultures when, in the eighth and seventh centuries, city-states sent colonizing expeditions to Anatolia, North Africa, Spain, southern France, Italy, and the shores of the Black Sea. By the seventh century BCE, the Greeks had explored and colonized the Atlantic and Mediterranean shores of the Iberian peninsula. Herodotus of Halicarnassus reported that colonists from Thera colonized Cyrene in North Africa. Herodotus, along with Hecataeus of Miletus and Hellanicus of Lesbos, made the first attempts to provide factual information divorced from myth of the lands and peoples, geography, and history of the Mediterranean. These historians and geographers based their accounts on their own travels, as well as on travelers' tales of distant lands provided by Phoenician, Cyrenian, Egyptian, Byzantion, and Massilian traders and sailors.

Pytheas of Massilia (floruit 300 BCE)

The seafaring colony of Massilia (Marseilles), for example, located at the mouth of the Rhone River, produced many adventurers and explorers. One was Euthymenes, who sailed south along the west African coast in about 500 BCE. He claimed to have reached the Senegal River, about 15 degrees north latitude. The most famous Massilian discoverer was Pytheas, whose account of his voyage is lost. The geographer Eratosthenes used Pytheas's account, which was condemned by the geographer Strabo as full of lies. The voyage, if it took place, occurred about 300 BCE and covered perhaps seven thousand miles. Pytheas circumnavigated the British Isles. His immediate object was tin, but he appears to have broadened his quest into a full-scale exploring expedition. Subsequent explorers journeyed to the "tin islands" visited by Pytheas. There are also anecdotal reports in the ancient literature that Ionian Greeks from Caria, in southwestern Turkey, made important voyages of discovery. The travel writer Pausanius described the voyage of Euphemus the Carian, who was caught in a storm, or the trade winds, off the coast of North Africa and blown west to an island in the Atlantic with unique inhabitants he had never before seen. Another Carian, Scylax, explored the route, from the Indus to the Tigris rivers, that Nearchus was to take in 325 BCE.

The Shape of the Earth

The Greeks speculated on the shape of the earth, the science of geodesy. The Ionian Greeks of western Anatolia (Turkey) were the first to hypothesize that the earth was not a flat disk: Anaximander of Miletus during the sixth century BCE, who reputedly drew the first map of the world, believed that the earth was a cylinder. Parmenides, a century later, speculated that the earth must have zones of heat and cold: torrid, frigid, and temperate zones. The Athenian Plato, in his dialogue *Phaedo,* followed the Pythagoreans in arguing that since the sphere is the most perfect form, this must be the earth's shape. Plato's student, the greatest scientist of classical Greece, Aristotle, provided empirical proof of the earth's sphericity by observing the earth's shadow cast upon the surface of the moon during a lunar eclipse. However, Aristotle still had a limited view of earth, underestimating the extent of Asia, believing that the Caspian Sea flows into the outer Ocean, and conceiving that India marks the eastern extreme of the continent. Aristotle had the genius to conceive of a hemispheric world, north and south, perhaps basing his ideas on the reports of Phoenician and Carthaginian sailors.

The speculative Greeks, and later the Romans, wondered what lay to the west, across the Atlantic. The fifth-century historian Herodotus's report that the Phoenicians circumnavigated Africa in about 600 BCE, sailing from the Indian to the Atlantic oceans, was believed by few, who were beholden to the myth of the ring of fire encircling earth's equator. There circulated other vague reports that the Carthaginians explored the North Atlantic to the British Isles, the Azores in the North Atlantic, and the west African coastline almost to the equator. Diodorus Siculus, the Greek historian of the first century BCE and author of *Universal History,* reported that the Carthaginians discovered a vast, fruitful, and temperate island with large rivers in the Atlantic Ocean. So wonderful were these isles that upon returning to Carthage all who knew of them were murdered so as to keep the islands secret and prevent a mass migration from Carthage.

The Greek biographer and scientist Plutarch, ever on the lookout to substantiate myth with fact, studied the nature and origin of stories about the Isles of the Blessed and Calypso's island of Ogygia. This island is featured in Homer's *Odyssey.* Homer placed the island, where Calypso held Odysseus against his will for seven years, somewhere in the west, which made sense since Calypso was the daughter of Atlas. Later legends placed Ogygia in the Atlantic, where Cronos, a god of Phoenician origin, held sway. In his dialogue "Concerning the Face Which Appears in the Orb of the Moon," Plutarch discussed in detail the myth, trying to put the best face on what might be true about it. He hypothesized that Ogygia lies to the west of Britain; the route is difficult going, in part because the sea is of a cold thickness and it is a land of the midnight sun. Pytheas discovered such conditions on his voyage, and it is possible that Plutarch used Pytheas's account as evidence for his discussion of Ogygia. Pytheas claimed to have visited Thule, which the Stoic Seneca also briefly mentioned in his play *Medea.* Likewise Ferdinando Columbus, in his biography of his father Christopher, claimed that the young Columbus in the 1470s sailed to the North Atlantic and visited Thule.

Plutarch, in his *Life of Sertorius,* also reported the legend of the Isles of the Blessed. Sertorius, a Roman general who was in Spain around 80 BCE, met with mariners who claimed to have just returned from islands twelve hundred miles off the coast of Spain. Why they left such a wonderful place of abundant fruits and continuous mild breezes is a mystery, but they convinced Sertorius (and Plutarch) of their reality, and made the Roman long to sail there to live his life in perfect repose.

The Elder Pliny also provided detailed descriptions of these isles in a failed attempt to make fiction fact. The daughters of the setting sun, he wrote, inhabited the Hesperides. He also discussed uncritically the island of Atlantis. Plato wrote of Atlantis in the *Timaeus*. The Athenian lawgiver Solon on his travels heard from the Egyptians about Atlantis, a large island hosting an advanced civilization that was destroyed by a tidal wave. From Plato's account it is not clear whether Atlantis, a vast island civilization that mysteriously vanished, was an actual place, the legends of which Plato had read, or merely the product of his (or another's) fertile imagination.

Hellenistic Geography

Aristotle's student Alexander the Great set off in 334 BCE to conquer and explore the Persian Empire, in part because of Aristotle's teachings that made the young king yearn (*pothos*) to know more. The student sent specimens to the teacher, penetrated the remoteness of Bactria (Afghanistan) and the Gedrosian Desert (Pakistan), descended the Indus River to its mouth, sent his admiral Nearchus to explore the Arabian Sea and Persian Gulf, and planned future journeys south and west before his death in 323.

Alexander opened up a whole new world for Greek scientists. The scientific center of Alexandria in Egypt, founded by Alexander in 331, sponsored a host of geographers during the ensuing Hellenistic Age. Eratosthenes, for example, the author of *Geographica*, developed the science of geodesy by hypothesizing earth's circumference to be 31,300 miles, which was remarkably accurate. He inspired many other geographers, such as Strabo, Posidonius of Rhodes, and Marinus of Tyre, to perform similar measurements. Working

from the library at Alexandria, Eratosthenes first used latitude and longitude to chart the globe. Inspired by the voyages of Nearchus, he believed in the possibilities of sailing west across the Atlantic to India. Hipparchus, a scientist from Nicaea in northwestern Turkey, created a grid pattern on maps that measured earth at precise arcs on a 360-degree scale. The geographer Strabo, a Greek who flourished during the reign of Augustus, wrote a multivolume *Geography* that encompassed the "known" world from the Atlantic Ocean to Arabia to India. Strabo relied heavily on other literary sources to create his encyclopedic account. Likewise, the Elder Pliny relied extensively on previous writers to pen his vast *Natural History*, which included much on world geography from a narrow Roman perspective. Pliny and Strabo both, for example, wrote at length about India, relying heavily on the works of Nearchus of Crete, Onesicritus of Astypalaea, and Aristobulus of Cassandrea, all of whom accompanied Alexander on his expedition and journey to India. On the other hand Julius Caesar, in the *Gallic War*, described the peoples, landscapes, and rivers of Gaul and Britain based in part on firsthand observations. Pomponius Mela, a Spaniard who authored the Latin *Chorographia*, provided a general overview of the geography of the Roman Empire during the first century CE. His contemporary, Theodosius of Tripolis, developed mathematical geography, in which he calculated the amount of time in terms of daylight and darkness for various places at different seasons at particular latitudes. He was thought by Vitruvius, the architect, to have invented a forerunner of the sextant to determine latitude.

Continents, Zones, and Seas

Greek geographers developed various theories to explain the relation of continents to oceans and different climatic zones. The first Greek scientists, such as Pythagoras, upon determining that the earth is spherical, hypothesized the existence of five climatic zones on the earth's surface: the two poles, two temperate zones, and the equator, which legend and imagination told them was an impassable zone of fire. Time and experience taught scientists like Polybius that such a zone of fire was absurd. Greek geographers had different conceptions about the relation of ocean and land on the earth. Aristotle and others, such as Strabo, Pliny, Crates, and Pomponius Mela, argued that there was a world-encircling ocean surrounding the three joined continents Europe, Asia, and Africa. Herodotus, Plato, Hipparchus, and Ptolemy believed the opposite, that land dominated seas on the earth's surface. Ptolemy, inspired by Marinus of Tyre, argued that the Indian Ocean was an inland sea and that Asia extended south and then west to join with Africa. Crates of Mallus, whom the ancients claimed invented a working globe, hypothesized four continents in four sections of the earth. Indeed many geographers argued for the presence of geographic sections; Pythagoras believed that an opposite realm, the antipodes, existed far to the south, mirroring the north. Others, such as Pomponius Mela, author of the *Chorographica,* conceived of the existence of a southern hemisphere that was impassable because of the ring of fire. He called such a land the *other world,* "Ora Australis." Cicero's imaginative "Scipio's Dream," in the *Republic,* presented a similar idea. Still others argued that the earth's landmass and peoples lived only in the northern hemisphere, the hypothetical south being uninhabitable. Obscure geographers such as Geminus, Cleomedes, and Achilles Tatius spent much time and thought on these theories. Another, Macrobius, in the fifth century CE, called the four continents "terra quadrifiga"; the north and south were separated by an equatorial sea, he believed, agreeing with Crates.

Ptolemy

The greatest geographer of the Roman Empire was Claudius Ptolemy, who lived during the second century CE at Alexandria. Ptolemy was an astronomer as well as a geographer. He developed standard directions (north, south, east, west) but made big errors, overestimating the size of Asia, underestimating the circumference of earth, and hypothesizing a landmass, the *terra incognita,* connecting Africa to Asia, making the Indian Ocean a landlocked sea.

Ptolemy's *Geography* became the standard during the Later Roman Empire and throughout the European Middle Ages. The Renaissance explorer Christopher Columbus relied on Ptolemy's geographical scheme to plan his "Enterprise of the Indies." Ptolemy's errors helped Columbus convince himself that a voyage from Spain west across the Atlantic to China was possible. He did not realize that America, unknown to the ancients, lay in between.

The journeys of ancient humans into the spatial unknown yielded more questions than answers. What is the earth's circumference, shape, limits? Can Africa be circumnavigated? How vast is the Ocean? Although ancient geographers did not find exact answers, they set the stage for those who would.

See also Alexander of Macedon; Aristotle; Caesar, Julius; Cicero; Eratosthenes; Herodotus of Halicarnassus; Hipparchus; Homer; Nearchus of Crete; Phoenicians; Plato; Pliny the Elder; Ptolemaeus, Claudius; Pytheas of Massilia

References

Apollonius of Rhodes. *The Voyage of Argo.* Translated by E. V. Rieu. Harmondsworth, Middlesex: Penguin Books, 1971.

Barnes, Jonathan, trans. *Early Greek Philosophy.* London: Penguin Books, 1987.

Boorstin, Daniel. *The Discoverers.* New York: Random House, 1983.

Cary, M. *The Geographical Background of Greek and Roman History.* Oxford: Clarendon Press, 1949.

Pliny the Elder. *Natural History: A Selection.* Translated by John F. Healy. London: Penguin Books, 1991.

Plutarch. *Moralia.* 15 vols. Cambridge: Harvard University Press, 1968–1976.

Polybius. *The Histories.* Translated by W. R. Paton. 6 vols. Cambridge: Harvard University Press, 1922–27.

Tillinghast, William H. "The Geographical Knowledge of the Ancients Considered in Relation to the Discovery of America." In *Narrative and Critical History of America,* vol. 1, ed. Justin Winsor. Boston: Houghton, Mifflin, 1889.

Warmington, E. H. *Greek Geography.* London: J. M. Dent, 1934.

Greek Archaic Age (800–500 BCE)

The history of ancient Greece is typically divided into three chronological divisions: Archaic (800–500 BCE), Classical (500–323 BCE), and Hellenistic (323–31 BCE). The Archaic Age was a time of new beginnings. Hitherto Greece had a violent and primitive past. At the beginning of the Archaic Age, Greece was emerging from a period of cultural, social, and economic darkness. The so-called Dark Ages occurred after centuries of Mycenaean domination of the Balkan peninsula and Peloponnesus. Mycenaean kings such as Agamemnon, Menelaus, Nestor, and Odysseus (as identified in Homer's *Iliad* and *Odyssey*) dominated society by means of the sword. The Mycenaean Age was a time of unending war. Invasions of Greece by an even more warlike people, the Dorians, destroyed Mycenaean dominance and forced the vanquished to strongholds in eastern Greece, the Aegean islands, and the Aegean shores of Asia Minor. These people of the Aegean region, as opposed to the mainland Greeks of the west and south, were the Ionians. The intervening centuries were dark—literate, urban culture disappeared. Few records survive from the Dark Ages, and those that do, like the *Iliad* and the *Odyssey,* were initially composed orally and not recorded in written script until centuries later.

The Greek Dark Ages ended at the beginning of the eighth century BCE when the historical record reveals that literacy, cities, trade, and sophisticated institutions returned to Greece. Such civilized attributes included scientific thought. By the eighth century, the Greek polis (the city-state) spread throughout Greece, the Aegean, and elsewhere. Greek poleis were independent regional urban powers that dotted Greece and fiercely promoted and defended their respective interests. The city of Athens controlled the region of Attica, for example, and competed with other city-states, Ionian and Dorian, such as Thebes, Corinth, and Sparta. The Greek polis was dynamic and wealthy, actively engaged in trade and in developing vibrant new institutions, and sought to extend its economic and political power throughout the Mediterranean. At the dawn of the Archaic Age, the Greek poleis were sufficiently populated that they sent groups of citizens on expeditions to discover and settle regions in other lands where a healthy trade could be guaranteed. This phenomenon of Greek colonization resulted in Greek poleis being spread west to Spain, France, Sicily, and Italy, south to North Africa, southeast to Egypt, east to Anatolia and Palestine, and northeast to the Black Sea region. Greek colonization led to the spread of Greek culture and ideas into Asia, Africa, and Eastern and Western Europe. Most important, the Greeks gained a greater awareness of geography and other peoples—new experiences and new ideas stimulated thought and led to the first scientific revolution in human history.

Historians of science refer to the Archaic Age philosophers and scientists of the seventh and sixth centuries BCE as the Pre-Socratics, that is, those who preceded the great Athenian philosopher Socrates. The number of Pre-Socratic philosophers and scientists is astonishing. Many were Ionians who came from western Asia Minor on the eastern shores of the Aegean Sea. Thales of Miletus, his student Anaximander, Anaximenes of Miletus, and Xenophanes of Colophon were the first Ionian thinkers. They sought to explain the universe by imposing the structure of the human mind upon it, to conceptualize it so as to understand it. They broke from the primitive anthropomorphism of their forebears to conceive of a universe of cause and effect relationships, of infinite existence and movement, of a primary universal cause. At the same time they sought the essence of all things in water, air, fire, or mind. Anaxagoras, who moved to Athens and influenced Pericles, advocated the latter idea, that mind *(nous)* is the infinite and universal, the cause of all that exists. Melissus of Samos, an island off the coast of Turkey near Miletus, argued that the universe is ungenerated, that "nothing" cannot exist.

Melissus adopted the theories of several philosophers who, in response to Persian aggression in Asia Minor, fled to the southern coasts of Italy, to what the colonists of the region called "Greater Greece" (Magna Graecia). The most famous of these philosopher-scientists were Parmenides and Pythagoras. Parmenides of Elea wrote in verse; in one poem, *On Nature,* he presented his views on the ungenerated *being,* the cause and essence of all things. Diogenes Laertius, in *Lives of the Philosophers,* claimed that Parmenides was the first to hypothesize the spherical nature of the earth. Parmenides possibly got the idea from Pythagoras, who was born in Samos but migrated to southern Italy, where he collected many disciples who influenced the development of philosophy, mathematics, and science for centuries to come. Pythagoras believed in the transmigration of souls and that *number* forms the basis of the universe. This theory of the mathematical foundations of reality would influence such important Greek philosophers as Plato and the mathematician Euclid.

Other Pre-Socratic philosophers developed theories about the material basis of existence. Heraclitus of Ephesus believed that fire forms all things, that opposites compose the universe, and that motion and change explain natural phenomena. Empedocles, one of the giants of the fifth century, advocated theories on the plurality of being. Four primary elements form all things: earth, air, fire, and water. Likewise Leucippus, who had connections to the philosophers of Ionia and Magna Graecia, hypothesized that substance rather than ideas forms existence: he developed the theory of invisible atoms combining and recombining to form all matter.

Alcmaeon, one of Pythagoras's associates, is the best example of the development of medicine during the Archaic Age. Hailing from Croton in southern Italy, Alcmaeon was possibly the first Greek to conceive of the indivisible eternity (rather than transmigration) of the human soul. He studied the human senses and argued that all existence is explained by opposites—in so doing he anticipated the physics of Heraclitus and Empedocles and the medical theories of Hippocrates, the contemporary of Socrates.

During the Archaic Age the Greeks also approached the mastery of the arts, crafts, and sciences of historical writing, verse, architecture, sculpture, pottery, metallurgy, and shipbuilding. It was left to the subsequent Classical Age to see these developments come together to form one of the most dynamic and creative times in human history.

See also Alcmaeon; Anaximander of Miletus; Anaximenes of Miletus; Astronomy; Eleatic School; Empedocles; Heraclitus of Ephesus; Hippocrates; Leucippus; Medicine; Miletus; Thales; Xenophanes of Colophon

References
Barnes, Jonathan, trans. *Early Greek Philosophy.* London: Penguin Books, 1987.
Boardman, John, Jasper Griffin, and Oswyn Murray. *Oxford History of the Classical World.* Oxford: Oxford University Press, 1986.
Burn, A. R. *The Pelican History of Greece.* Harmondsworth, Middlesex: Penguin Books, 1974.
Laertius, Diogenes. *Lives of the Philosophers.* Translated by R. D. Hicks. 2 vols. Cambridge: Harvard University Press, 1931, 1938.

Greek Classical Age (500–323 BCE)

The Greek Classical Age was a period of supreme intellectual achievement that occurred over the space of two hundred years during the fifth and fourth centuries BCE. The Classical Age was epitomized by the city-state of Athens and by the three most significant philosophers and scientists of the ancient world, Socrates (469–399), Plato (425–346), and Aristotle (384–322). Independent poleis (city-states) characterized

Greek civilization. They were competitive and aggressive, and thus war was common among the Greeks. Yet this competitiveness was expressed not only in war but in trade and thought as well. Herodotus, in the *Histories,* described the Greeks as a free people who showed what freedom can accomplish among humans if given the chance. Athens was the most democratic of the Greek city-states, which might explain why the Athenians produced such outstanding work in science and philosophy.

Sophists

Socrates, like his predecessor Pythagoras, either did not write anything or it has not survived time. What we know of Socrates comes from his students Plato and Xenophon. Plato wrote in dialogue form featuring the highly sophisticated conversations of Socrates and his students and sometimes his opponents, particularly the Sophists. The Sophists were paid teachers of wisdom who often focused less on the pursuit of truth and more on ways to contrive a good argument. Many, such as Protagoras, were humanists, that is, restricting knowledge to human experience, which was the opposite of what Socrates and Plato believed. Nor did Socrates and his students agree with the theories of the atomists, such as Leucippus and Democritus, who tried to explain nature according to physical substances rather than ideas.

Plato

In today's terms, Socrates and Plato were philosophers more than scientists. They built a philosophy around a conception of the divine attributes of the universe, what Socrates called *ideal forms.* These ideas, such as justice, beauty, and the good, resembled the Pre-Socratic notions of the mind, being, and logos. Truth is hidden from humans, who see only the shadows of what is real. The search for reality is therefore worthwhile, though it requires intense contemplation and intuition, years of study, and mastery of the theories of

music, logic, mathematics, justice, and epistemology. Socrates and Plato speculated on the nature of the universe, the shape of the world, the soul and its immortality, human thought, psychology, and politics, but they lacked the empirical focus that usually defines science. Nevertheless Platonic thinking influenced the philosophers and scientists of the ancient world, particularly the Neoplatonists, and scores of others in Europe and America for centuries.

Aristotle

Unlike Plato, his pupil Aristotle was a scientist interested in experimentation, observation, collection and categorization of data, and inductive and deductive reasoning. He used these tools of reason and analysis to master the topics of metaphysics, physics, logic, statecraft, biology, botany, and astronomy. Aristotle was a prolific writer. His *Metaphysics, Politics, Poetics, Physics,* and *Nichomachean Ethics* were and have remained classic treatises on those subjects. His school, the Lyceum, and his followers, the Peripatetics, beginning with Theophrastus, continued to influence Greek and European science for years to come. First the Romans, then the Byzantines, the Arabs, and Medieval European churchmen found inspiration and knowledge in Aristotle's writings.

Historia

Other, less metaphysical thinkers of fifth-century Greece included historians, physicians, architects, and engineers. Herodotus of Halicarnassus wrote *Histories (Historia),* a highly descriptive and entertaining account of the eastern Mediterranean. Herodotus was not terribly discriminating in his information. Yet he was an explorer who collected the information himself on long journeys in which the indefatigable inquirer asked numerous questions and took countless side trips, observing and recording as he went. During the latter half of the fifth century Thucydides the Athenian wrote *The Peloponnesian War,* a systematic chronological account of the war between the Ionians and the Dorians. Historians have long lauded Thucydides for using objective, seemingly scientific techniques of gathering and recording his information. Xenophon, the student of Socrates, wrote philosophical dialogues, history, and *Anabasis,* the story of ten thousand Greek mercenaries who fought for Cyrus, a Persian seeking to establish himself as Great King of Persia. Upon failing in this attempt and upon the death of Cyrus, the Greeks were forced to journey back to Greece through unknown territory. Xenophon became the leader, and the chronicler of their journey as well, providing a fascinating geographical account of Asia Minor and the southern coast of the Black Sea.

Age of Pericles

During the Classical Age, the Ionian Greeks of Asia Minor, the Aegean, and Attica continued to have a leading role in science and medicine. A native of the island of Cos, Hippocrates, dominated medical thinking. Hippocrates tried to understand how the environment—climate, weather, dietary habits—affected health. He studied the symptoms of disease without really understanding the cure. His was a holistic approach of general good health. Anaxagoras, a native of Clazomenae on the eastern shores of the Aegean, was one of the most accomplished scientists of the fifth century. He believed that mind *(nous)* is the infinite, creative force of the universe. His *Physics,* since lost, outlined his ideas. Anaxagoras crossed the Aegean to Athens and became friends with Pericles, the Athenian general and leader of Athens during the mid-fifth century. Pericles and his mistress Aspasia, herself a philosopher, gathered around them the leading minds of Athens and Ionia to create one of the most dynamic expressions of civilization ever seen in human history. It was Pericles who executed the plan to rebuild the Athenian Acropolis, which was the religious center of the city. The Persian

Eighteenth-century engraving of a bust of the Athenian Pericles (490–429 BCE) at the British Museum. (Library of Congress)

invasions of the early fifth century had destroyed many of the buildings. After the Greek defeat of the king of Persia, Xerxes, and the establishment of Greek freedom, Athens took the lead in forming the Delian League, designed to be an alliance of Ionian Greek city-states to protect western Turkey and the Aegean from Persian attack. Under Pericles' leadership, Athens took the lead in the Delian League and demanded tribute from subject Greek city-states in return for Athenian military and naval protection. These funds, acquired by means of the Athenian Empire, were used to rebuild the Acropolis.

Even so, the architectural, engineering, and artistic genius that went into the construction of the temples of the Athenian Acropolis continue to inspire and generate awe. The grandest, of course, is the Parthenon, named for Athena the virgin (*parthenos*) goddess and patroness of Athens. Even after twenty-four hundred years, the Parthenon continues to dominate the Acropolis. The architects were Ictinus and Callicrates, and Phidias oversaw the whole. The Parthenon is a monument to grace and beauty. One hardly thinks of the tons of marble sculpted, molded, and set in just the right way. The design is sophisticated and intricate; the quality of its construction and engineering is a marvel.

> *See also* Aristotle; Athens; Herodotus of
>   Halicarnassus; Hippocrates; History;
>   Peripatetic School; Plato; Socrates;
>   Theophrastus; Women and Science; Xenophon
> **References**
> Botsford, George, and Charles A. Robinson.
>   *Hellenic History.* Revised by Donald Kagan.
>   New York: Macmillan Publishing, 1969.
> Durant, Will. *The Life of Greece.* New York: Simon
>   and Schuster, 1939.
> Robinson, Charles A., Jr. *Athens in the Age of*
>   *Pericles.* Norman: University of Oklahoma
>   Press, 1959.

Greek Hellenistic Age (323–31 BCE)

Alexander the Great

The Hellenistic Age began with the conquests of Alexander the Great. From 334–324 BCE, Alexander, son of Philip, King of Macedonia, led a coalition of Greek and Macedonian forces into Asia. During a ten-year period, Alexander conquered Asia Minor, Phoenicia, Palestine, Egypt, Iraq, Iran, Bactria and Sogdiana (Afghanistan), and the Indus River valley (Pakistan). Greek culture and ideas, including Greek religious beliefs and institutions, met and merged with African and Asian culture and religious traditions. Although Alexander died shortly after the conclusion of his military campaign, Greek generals and kings continued to control and influence the vast region spreading from Macedonia to Egypt to the Indus River. Three

Greek kingdoms emerged in the wake of Alexander's death: the Macedonian, Ptolemaic, and Seleucid. The resulting interaction of Hellenism—Greek culture, institutions, and government—with the traditions of Persia, Egypt, India, Palestine, Mesopotamia, and Anatolia created a volatile, dynamic, creative period of three centuries that historians have labeled the Hellenistic Age. The Hellenistic Age came to an end with the fall of the three Hellenistic Kingdoms to the Romans during the second and first centuries BCE.

Alexander, student of Aristotle, brought with him on his journey to Asia a number of sophists, seers, writers, and scientists. Notable in this group was Callisthenes of Olynth, the grandnephew of Aristotle. As knowledgeable as Aristotle and his followers were, they nevertheless retained the narrow Greek views toward non-Greeks—"barbarians." Callisthenes agreed with his greatuncle that the Persians were barbarians—and that they were fit to be conquered by the Greeks. But when Alexander surprised everyone with his epiphany that the Persians and Greeks were one people, Callisthenes was too stubborn to go along with the king and was open and arrogant in his disagreement. Alexander grew impatient with the philosopher and was all too ready to believe accusations leveled at Callisthenes that he conspired against the king. After his death, the connection between Alexander and Aristotle ended.

Zeno

This idea of Alexander's that peoples of the world (other than Alexander) were inherently equal was his most important legacy. Philosophers of varying backgrounds at the leading Hellenistic capitals celebrated the diversity that Alexander's conquests had inspired: the mixture of peoples, ideas, beliefs, customs, and ways of life. A Semite from Cyprus, Zeno, who arrived at Athens in 311, started a school of philosophy based on

Alexander's concept of universal brotherhood. The Stoics studied natural history and human behavior to discover the presence of a universal reason, the logos, that ordered all things. The goal of the thoughtful human was to imitate the reason and order of the cosmos so as to find contentment within himself or herself. Similar to Zeno's Stoicism were the ideas of another teacher at Athens, Epicurus, who taught that the universe is completely material, formed of atoms in varying forms and combinations. Athens also hosted skeptics and cynics, as well as followers of Plato, the Academicians, and followers of Aristotle, the Peripatetics, notably Theophrastus and Strato.

Alexandria

Alexandria, the city that Alexander founded in 331, quickly eclipsed Athens and other Hellenistic cities such as Antioch and Pergamon as the premier center of science during the Hellenistic Age and after. Greco-Egyptian scientists and philosophers under the sponsorship of the Ptolemaic pharaohs working with Greeks throughout the Hellenistic world made significant advances in the study of mathematics, astronomy, and geography. The five-hundred-thousand-volume library at Alexandria, in conjunction with the Alexandrian museum, was a multicultural research center. Some of the greatest scientists of all time were at Alexandria, such as Euclid, author of *The Elements,* which remained the standard work of mathematics for centuries. Euclid's approach owed much to the Platonic effort to discover the hidden reality of the universe by means of mathematics. A mathematician who turned his attention to geography, in particular the measurement of the earth's circumference, was Eratosthenes of Alexandria. Eratosthenes was the second librarian at Alexandria, Callimachus being the first. Other noteworthy Alexandrian scientists included Ctesibius, an inventor and engineer, who made advances in understanding air pressure and hydraulics, and Philo of

Byzantium, his student, who identified and wrote *Seven Wonders of the World.* Alexandria became the center of medical discoveries as well in anatomy and physiology. Herophilus of Chalcedon researched the brain and nervous system, and Erasistratus studied the digestive and vascular systems.

Hellenistic Creativity

The leading minds of the Hellenistic Age, however, worked in other cities throughout the Mediterranean. Archimedes, although he studied at Alexandria, moved to Syracuse in Sicily, where he was an inventor, engineer, and mathematician of note. Much of his engineering talent went to devising means of defense against Roman attacks during the Second Punic War. Archimedes discovered pi, invented the "Archimedes' screw," researched the nature of volume, and made advancements in geometry. Posidonius of Apamea worked as an astronomer and geographer on the Aegean island of Rhodes. He measured the circumference of the earth and tried to gauge the distance to the sun; he was very interested in the study of meteorology. Aristarchus of Samos, also an astronomer and mathematician, discovered the heliocentric (sun-centered) universe, although he was alone in this knowledge since the idea contradicted sensory experience. Hipparchus of Nicaea, for example, could not doubt what his senses told him, that the sun circled the earth. Nevertheless Hipparchus cataloged the stars and discovered the precession of the equinoxes. The Hellenistic philosopher Aratus preserved (in *Phaenomena*) the theory of Eudoxus of Cnidus that the earth is spherical because the altitude of the stars changes as the latitude of the observer changes.

The Hellenistic Age set the stage for subsequent centuries of scientific inquiry. The Roman conquest of the Hellenistic world during the last two centuries BCE involved political unification under Roman government and the Roman legions. Yet the Hellenistic Greeks conquered the Romans in terms of science, philosophy, art, culture, and religion. The great thinkers and scientists of the later Roman Republic and Roman Principate were heavily dependent upon their predecessors, particularly the scientists, astronomers, mathematicians, and geographers of the Greek Hellenistic Age.

See also Alexander of Macedon; Alexandria; Archimedes; Aristarchus of Samos; Aristotle; Astronomy; Erasistratus; Eratosthenes; Euclid; Hipparchus; Peripatetic School; Posidonius of Rhodes; Roman Principate

References

Boorstin, Daniel. *The Discoverers.* New York: Random House, 1983.

Botsford, George, and Charles A. Robinson. *Hellenic History.* Revised by Donald Kagan. New York: Macmillan Publishing, 1969.

Grant, Michael. *From Alexander to Cleopatra: The Hellenistic World.* New York: History Book Club, 2000.

Heath, Sir Thomas. *Aristarchus of Samos.* New York: Dover Books, 1913.

H

Hebrews

See Old Testament

Hecataeus of Miletus (floruit 500 BCE)

Hecataeus of Miletus, the son of Hegesander, was an Ionian Greek and a contemporary of Xenophanes who, like Xenophanes, wrote one of the first works critical of traditional Greek mythology. This was his *Genealogies,* in which Hecataeus tried to provide a rational account of myth and legend, including an account of his own supposed descent (after sixteen generations) from a god. The gods are not eternal, but created, he argued. Hecataeus also wrote a book that he titled *Periegesis,* journeys. The *Periegesis* was an account of the world, which Hecataeus divided into two continents, Europe and Asia (Africa being an extension of the latter). It was a historical and geographical account of Europe and Asia based loosely on the map of the world drawn by Anaximander around 550 BCE.

Hecataeus's works do not survive. Herodotus, who wrote his *Histories* about fifty years after Hecataeus, paraphrased a few passages from Hecataeus and clearly relied on him for information on history and geography. Herodotus related that Hecataeus went to Egypt and talked to the priests of Amen at Thebes about their land, its people, and history. Like Herodotus, Hecataeus, lacking documents and the convenience of libraries, had to travel about interviewing people to arrive at the bases of his knowledge with which to write an account of the human journey *(Periegesis)* based on his own journeys. According to Diogenes Laertius, Hecataeus also wrote a treatise, *On the Egyptian Philosophy.*

See also Geography/Geodesy; Greek Archaic
    Age; Herodotus of Halicarnassus; History
References
Boardman, John, Jasper Griffin, and Oswyn
    Murray. *Oxford History of the Classical World.*
    Oxford: Oxford University Press, 1986.
Grant, Michael. *Readings in the Classical Historians.*
    New York: Scribner's, 1992.

Heliocentric Universe

See Astronomy

Hellanicus of Lesbos (floruit fifth century BCE)

Little is known of Hellanicus's life. He came from the city of Mytilene on the island of Lesbos in the Aegean Sea. He was an Ionian Greek. His many works have not survived. Dionysius of Halicarnassus, a historian of the first century BCE, paraphrased a few of

Hellanicus's comments from his books on the Etruscans and Italy. Thucydides, in Book 1 of the *Peloponnesian War,* commented on Hellanicus's *Attic History,* deriding it as inaccurate and incomplete. Hellanicus was apparently a scholar of note, penning dozens of books, mostly chronologies of earlier times. He was one of the first historians to try to make sense of human events according to a temporal process. Yet he was still bound to a mythological past, assuming that the likes of Heracles founded some of the first cities throughout the Mediterranean region.

See also Greek Archaic Age; Herodotus of
    Halicarnassus; History; Thucydides; Time
References
Boardman, John, Jasper Griffin, and Oswyn
    Murray. *Oxford History of the Classical World.*
    Oxford: Oxford University Press, 1986.
Grant, Michael. *Readings in the Classical Historians.*
    New York: Scribner's, 1992.

Hellenism

Ideas drive science. The initial hypothesis, which leads to investigation, experiment, and an attempt to answer, derives from a question that is formed through a thoughtful response to nature and experience. Questions and hypotheses are generated by a society's worldview, the collection of fundamental assumptions about existence. Answers, scientific knowledge, likewise generate the worldview. The single most important idea that drove science in the ancient world was Hellenism.

Homer, in the *Iliad* and *Odyssey,* typically referred to the Greeks as the Achaeans, Argives, and Danaans. Yet in a few instances he referred to the whole of Greece as *Hellas,* and to the Greeks as a people, *Hellenes.* The idea of a common people and land had roots in mythology. The hero Hellen, the son of Deucalion, the Noah of the Greeks and son of Prometheus and Pyrrha, the daughter of Pandora, was the first Greek, the founder of the Hellenes.

Homer's poems describe the characteristics and beliefs that made the Hellenes unique. The poems portray a single world culture of Achaeans (Europeans) and Trojans (Asians). They speak the same language, worship the same deities, have the same customs, live and die by the same code of honor. The heroes of the two poems are "godlike"; the gods are humanlike. The anthropomorphism of Homer's poems does not so much denigrate the divine as elevate what is human. Human struggles, wars, life, and death are beautiful, universal, divine. Scholars refer to Homer's brilliant portrayal of the common humanness of the Achaeans, Trojans, even the gods, as humanism. But Homer's humanism derived from a more fundamental idea—Hellenism.

The idea of Hellenism was fully developed in fifth-century Athens. Classical Athens was a unique moment in human history. The Greek mind, its creativity, wonder, pursuit of knowledge, and expression of truth, soared to a pinnacle of human achievement. Phidias and Praxiteles designed and built the Parthenon on the Athenian acropolis. The playwrights Aeschylus, Euripides, and Sophocles wrote masterpieces of tragedy. Thucydides wrote one of the great histories of all time. Socrates questioned and taught and pursued wisdom. Pericles molded Athenian politics into the first and perhaps greatest democracy. Pericles referred to Athens as "the school of Hellas," a comment that gave praise not only to the Athenians but to the Hellenes as a whole. Protagoras, an Athenian philosopher, described Athenian society, as well as the fundamental assumptions of Hellenism, when he proclaimed that man is the ultimate concern of man.

During the fourth century BCE, Alexander the Great epitomized the ideals and behavior of a Hellenistic thinker. Alexander was born and raised in Macedon, north of Greece, a land that the Hellenes considered a cultural backwater. Alexander, when he became king of Macedon, ruler of Greece, and leader of the Hellenes against the Persian Empire, embraced Hellenic thought and culture. Alexander conquered Persia not only politically but culturally as well. He purposefully established Greek cities, such as Alexandria in Egypt, and encouraged a mix of Greek culture and ideas with those of the Egyptians, Persians, and Indians. Historians refer to the period after Alexander's conquests and the subsequent three centuries (323–31 BCE) as the Hellenistic Age, designating these three centuries in the Mediterranean and Asia as one of dynamic growth, cultural accomplishment, and scientific achievement.

Hellenism was the inspiration of the Hellenistic Age. Greek questioning, the pursuit of answers using the mind, the focus on human reason and expression, the emphasis on individual accomplishment, and the stress on a common human culture defined Hellenism. The Greeks spoke of this time as the *ecumene*, the common world culture, with a common Greek language, *koine*, spoken Greek. The *ecumene* encouraged and hosted not only a common lingua franca but also common beliefs, institutions, and culture. Peripatetic philosophy and science, modeled on Aristotle, was widespread throughout the Mediterranean. Stoicism, a philosophy of reason and human universality, became the dominant philosophy of the Hellenistic Age and after, when Greek culture was embraced by the Romans. The Roman Empire made the *ecumene*, the basic ideas of Hellenism, a concrete reality. During the Pax Romana from 31 BCE to 180 CE, this common Greco-Roman culture encompassed parts of three continents and included up to one hundred million people. Scientists such as Pliny the Elder and Strabo wrote massive compendia of knowledge, befitting an ecumenical society. The Roman orator Cicero proclaimed himself a "citizen of the world"; the theologian Augustine spoke of a universal "city of man" countered by a transcendent "city of God." The emperor Julian, when he came to power in 361, after fifty years of imperial support for Christianity, blamed Rome's increasing troubles on the rejection of Hellenism. Julian believed that a society devoted to the traditional gods and the traditional values of virtue, honor, human experience, and individual greatness would rectify Rome's downward trend.

Julian enjoyed only a brief reign of less than two years. But his was a lasting legacy. Julian and other Hellenists, particularly Greek philosophers, scientists, artists, and writers, spoke to future generations searching for similar ecumenical, secular, humanistic ideals. Thinkers of the European Renaissance called themselves humanists, by which they meant an approach to life based on the thought of the Greeks—on Hellenism.

See also Alexander of Macedon; Athens; Greek Classical Age; Homer; Julian

References

Finley, M. I. *The World of Odysseus*. Harmondsworth, Middlesex: Penguin Books, 1972.

Hadas, Moses. *Humanism: The Greek Ideal and Its Survival*. New York: Mentor Books, 1972.

Wright, W. C., trans. *The Works of the Emperor Julian*. Cambridge: Harvard University Press, 1962, 1969.

Zimmerman, J. E. *Dictionary of Classical Mythology*. New York: Harper and Row, 1971.

Heraclides of Pontus (floruit fourth century BCE)

Heraclides was an astronomer of note and the first known to speculate that at least some planets orbit the sun. He was a student of the Academy and was influenced by both Plato and Aristotle. A polymath, he wrote on a variety of subjects. Ancient commentators claimed that Heraclides wrote books on history, playwrights, ethics, the mind, music, poetry, grammar, and nature. He made his mark in astronomy with two startling theories. First, Heraclides argued that the earth spins on its own axis. Second, analyzing the phenomena of Mercury and Venus never traversing the zodiac like the other planets but rather remaining near the horizon as morning and evening planets, Heraclides argued that Mercury and Venus orbit the sun rather than the earth. He combined, therefore, the geocentric and heliocentric theories of the solar system, anticipating the theory of Tycho Brahe some eighteen hundred years later.

Heraclides also believed that the heavenly bodies are deities, that comets are on fire, and that each star is its own universe with planets and moons.

See also Astronomy; Hellenism
Reference
Heath, Sir Thomas. *Aristarchus of Samos.* New York: Dover Books, 1913.

Heraclitus of Ephesus (540–480 BCE)

Heraclitus had the reputation among ancients of being one of the most difficult philosophers to comprehend, either because of brilliant or muddled thinking. He was perhaps more than any other thinker almost modern in his emphasis on the contradictions and absurdities of existence out of which emerges a sort of truth. Sextus Empiricus, the skeptic, could respect such vagaries and inconsistencies, and approved of some of Heraclitus's comments in *On Nature*. Aristotle, however, was not as approving, and condemned Heraclitus's "childish" astronomy, which included the view that the sun is as we see it, only about a foot in diameter (Heath 1913). Hippolytus, the Late Roman commentator, quoted long excerpts from Heraclitus's writings, in which we find ideas of an eternal fire that is the ultimate reality. Fire is the creator and destroyer, and through it all change occurs. Fire condenses into water and then into earth and vice versa. Fire is the source for the lights of the sky—the sun, moon, planets, and stars being concave repositories of this divine fire. The repository in which lies the sun's fire is extinguished every evening and kindled again in the morning; how the repository moves from west to east unseen over the course of the night to begin a new day is unclear.

Heraclitus put an emphasis on change, on things becoming one thing then another. There was a lot of the Stoic and the skeptic in Heraclitus, who inspired a host of

Engraving of a bust of the ancient scientist and philosopher Heraclitus (540–480 BCE). (Courtesy of the National Library of Medicine)

philosophers and scientists to question, to doubt, to search, to seek answers in nature and in self.

See also Greek Archaic Age; Philosophy; Stoicism
References
Barnes, Jonathan, trans. *Early Greek Philosophy.* London: Penguin Books, 1987.
Heath, Sir Thomas. *Aristarchus of Samos.* New York: Dover Books, 1913.

Hero (62–152 CE)

The Alexandrian inventor, physicist, and mathematician Hero was a creative mind of the second century CE. Hero lived, worked, and taught at Alexandria. Influenced by Aristotle and the atomists, he also built on the work of the mechanical engineer Ctesibius. Hero wrote *Pneumatica* and *Automatapoeica,* which described his ideas on physical forces and mechanisms to displace weight, water, and air. He was interested in land measurement, wrote on surveying, and invented a forerunner of the theodolite, a surveyor's instrument for measuring angles.

Hero was fascinated by actions upon air and water. He argued that air is a material substance that exists within an apparently empty container. He analyzed the displacement of air by pouring water into a jar. He experimented with compression and argued for the presence of vacuums in nature. He was one of the founders of theories of kinetic energy. He explained the action of fire on substances according to the Aristotelian theory that heavy objects fall toward the center while lighter objects ascend toward the heavens. Hero invented a steam mechanism that featured a cauldron of boiling water that released steam through a small tube entering a sphere with two pipes at right angles. As the steam was forced through the pipes the sphere rotated. Another device heated air that filled a container of oil; the oil was forced by the air into tubes held within statues; the oil dripped from the stone hands holding cups for libations. Hero also experimented with pistons, valves, pneumatics, and hydraulics. Most of his inventions were, however, used as toys or for tricks to amuse the rich. For example, Hero contrived a device that, by forcing air through small valves, would produce the appearance and sound of bird's singing. Another device used principles of heat and air pressure: it was a device made of an iron cauldron filled with water that was heated by a fire. Steam was forced through a small opening at the top of the device, which provided sufficient force to cause a small ball to hang and dance just above the opening.

Hero's devices were built at a time of slavery when there was no demand for such labor-saving machines. Hero, like most ancient engineers, also turned his skills to military science, working on siege engines, slings, missiles and other ballistics. He also invented an odometer and designed "An Altar Organ blown by the agency of a Wind-mill."

See also Alexandria; Archimedes; Philo of Byzantium; Physical Sciences; Ptolemaeus, Claudius

References

Boardman, John, Jasper Griffin, and Oswyn Murray. *Oxford History of the Classical World.* Oxford: Oxford University Press, 1986.

Hero of Alexandria. *The Pneumatics.* Translated by Bennet Woodcroft. London: C. Whittingham, 1851.

Leicester, Henry M. *The Historical Background of Chemistry.* New York: Dover Books, 1971.

Technology Museum of Thessaloniki website: www.tmth.edu.

Herodotus of Halicarnassus (490–430 BCE)

Herodotus is often called the father of history, but he could as well be given the epitaphs father of geography and father of anthropology. Herodotus sought to write a complete history of the world in which he intertwined natural history and human history. The result was *The Histories,* one of the first professed factual accounts of human experience.

Herodotus was a boy living in his native Halicarnassus when the Greeks defeated the invading Persians at Salamis and Plataea in 480 and 479 BCE. The war began in part because the Greek cities of western Turkey—Ionian Greek city-states such as Halicarnassus—revolted from Persian control. Darius I, king of Persia, put down the rebellion and decided to punish Greece as a whole. After he failed, his successor Xerxes tried and failed as well. Herodotus set himself the task of explaining the improbable Greek success. The Persians had a massive empire stretching from the Aegean Sea to the Indus River, from the Caspian Sea to Egypt. They vastly outnumbered the Greeks, perhaps ten to one. And yet the Greeks defeated the Persians on several occasions. How? Herodotus spent years searching for an answer, traveling throughout the Persian Empire, going to Phrygia (in central Turkey), the Black Sea, the Tigris and Euphrates river valleys, the Persian Gulf, Palestine, and Egypt. He studied the Persians, Phrygians, Phoenicians, Egyptians, Arabians, Indians, and Scythians. Lacking

Herodotus of Halicarnassus (490–430 BCE), the "father of history" and author of Histories, *a political, cultural, and geographical portrait of the ancient Mediterranean. (Library of Congress)*

many literary sources, he acquired information by personal observation and oral interviews. He called his work "histories" (Greek, *historia*), meaning "researches, inquiries." Herodotus's *Histories* involves past kings, politics, and war. But more, Herodotus described the culture, society, institutions, beliefs, and legends of the peoples of Europe, Asia, and Africa—the world as he knew it. He portrayed human experience in light of natural history, in particular geography: landscape, climate, flora, fauna, rivers, deserts, mountains. In the course of *The Histories,* Herodotus had much to say about science.

Herodotus related information about the origins, extent, and characteristics of the Nile River in Africa. The Nile rose year after year at the summer solstice, when the rays of the sun are directly over the Tropic of Cancer. At the solstice, the Nile inundates lower Egypt, leaving behind rich soil upon receding and

constantly altering the landscape of the delta, the silt mouth of the river. Herodotus, fascinated by the Nile delta, theorized that Egypt north of Memphis was comparatively new. The Nile was in a sense annually creating an altogether different Egypt.

Herodotus's experience was that most rivers rise in the spring. It was perplexing to discover that the Nile rises at the summer solstice, the beginning of summer. What causes this unusual summer flood? Herodotus disagreed with the three most prevalent theories. The first was that north winds blow against the northern flowing waters, backing up the current and causing the river to spill over its banks. The second theory, advocated by Hecataeus, a geographer and historian, was that the Nile's source is the "river Ocean" encircling the earth, south of Africa; the Nile's behavior is therefore dependent on the ocean. The third theory, that the Nile's rise is caused by melting snow, seemed absurd to Herodotus—for the further south one goes toward the source of the Nile the hotter it gets. Where, then is the snow? Herodotus's own view reflected the limitations of his astronomy. He believed that strong winds drive the sun before them, moving it away from the Nile's source and depriving the river of its heat, therefore limiting evaporation and resulting in a rising river.

Herodotus described the geography of all three (known) continents: Europe, Asia, and Africa. He argued that those countries at the earth's extremes, India, Arabia, Ethiopia, and the Tin Islands (Britain), produce the biggest, most fragrant, richest items; animals are larger, men are gigantic, gold is profuse, and spices cause a general fragrance in the air. At the western extreme of the earth, Libya, a land of sun and sand, Mount Atlas rises from the parched earth. Locals reported that Atlas was so high that its summit was never seen. Yet Atlas was not as high as the Caucasus of the east. The Caucasus bounds the western shores of the Caspian Sea. Unlike the Mediterranean, which flows into the outer ocean of the world, the Caspian is an inland sea—self-contained. The world-encircling ocean marks the circumference of a disk-shaped earth that is dominated more by land than by water.

The Histories is encyclopedic in its description of the peoples that made up Herodotus's immediate past, the fifth century BCE. Perhaps because he was a traveler, a tourist in faraway countries, his reports of distant peoples and their strange customs have the tone of fascination, not condescension. Many Greeks of Herodotus's time, and after, referred to any non-Greek as a barbarian. But one does not find such bigotry in Herodotus. He was credulous, to be sure, but objective in his way, too. An anthropologist (student of *anthropos,* man), Herodotus observed without preconception and recorded what he heard, saw, and felt. He did not purposefully mislead, even if his information was fanciful and often inaccurate. He sought to understand the Egyptians, Persians, Scythians, and others on their terms, not his own.

Herodotus provided fascinating information on Egyptian astronomy and medicine; on the exotic creatures, such as the crocodile and hippopotamus, of Africa; on the remote Scythians of northern Asia; and on the flora and fauna of the diverse regions of the world. In the history of science, Herodotus made his mark in the study of the earth (geography), in the study of human culture (anthropology), and in inquiries into the human experience (history).

See also Egypt; Geography/Geodesy; Greek Archaic Age; Hecataeus of Miletus; History

References

Boardman, John, Jasper Griffin, and Oswyn Murray. *Oxford History of the Classical World.* Oxford: Oxford University Press, 1986.

Herodotus. *The Histories.* Translated by Aubrey de Selincourt. Harmondsworth, Middlesex: Penguin Books, 1972.

Herophilus of Chalcedon (floruit third century BCE)

Herophilus, a native of Chalcedon, spent his professional life as a physician and anatomist at Alexandria. A student of Praxagoras, who identified the pulse as an important diagnostic tool, Herophilus discovered that the pulse was not inherent to the arteries, but instead derived from the pumping of the heart. He tried to describe the pulse according to the theory of music. Herophilus's understanding of human physiology was informed by experiments, dissections, and autopsies (of executed criminals). He explored the nervous system and the circulation of the blood. Herophilus discovered the duodenum, which is a part of the small intestine. He defended the Hippocratic method, seeing the physician as an artist. Health is the foundation for all individual accomplishments, he thought. The environment is especially important in causes of disease, and diet, rest, and exercise are important in its prevention. Herophilus was nevertheless often skeptical of the human presumption of knowledge. Herophilus's most famous student was Erasistratus.

See also Alexandria; Erasistratus; Hellenism; Hippocrates; Medicine

References

"Antiqua Medicina: Aspects in Ancient Medicine." http://www.med.virginia.edu/hs-library/historical/antiqua/anthome.html.

Boardman, John, Jasper Griffin, and Oswyn Murray. *Oxford History of the Classical World.* Oxford: Oxford University Press, 1986.

Durant, Will. *The Life of Greece.* New York: Simon and Schuster, 1939.

Grant, Michael. *From Alexander to Cleopatra: The Hellenistic World.* New York: History Book Club, 2000.

Hesiod (floruit late eighth century BCE)

Hesiod was a theogonist. In his attempt to understand the origins of the divine, he explored as well the beginnings of humankind. Hesiod's *Works and Days,* an account of the pastoral life, and *Theogony,* an account of the gods, are poetry rather than science. At times, however, poetry and science mix. Often it takes the poet to imagine the possibilities inherent in life and nature.

Hesiod claimed legitimacy from the inspiration coming to him as he tended sheep at the foot of Mount Helicon in Boeotia, in eastern Greece. The daughters of Zeus, the Muses, particularly Calliope, the muse of poetry, paid a visit to the shepherd, inspiring in him divine song of the purposes and ways of humankind. Hesiod sought the origins of human crafts such as metallurgy and agriculture and found an answer in the story of Prometheus, the titan who rebelled against Zeus and gave civilizing fire to humankind. Hesiod explained suffering and evil with the story of Pandora, the wife of Prometheus's brother Epimetheus. Pandora, and women in general, unleashed troubles on man, according to Hesiod.

Hesiod's *Theogony* provided an account of the origins and powers of the divine. Uranos, the sky, and Gaia, the earth, bore the titans, including Cronos (time), Prometheus (foresight), and Epimetheus (hindsight). Cronos rebelled against his father, Uranos, to establish his own rule, only to lose it to the wielder of the thunderbolt, Zeus. Zeus thereafter ruled gods and humans from his throne atop Mount Olympus. Stories of Cronos and Prometheus probably derived from the Phoenicians. Greek legends of Cronos living on an island in the Atlantic were similarly inspired by voyages beyond the Strait of Gibraltar. Hesiod's poem also revealed a geodesic view of a disk-like earth: "The plane earth cut the cosmos sphere like a diaphragm shutting the light from Tartarus" (Tillinghast 1889).

Hesiod revealed the farmer's reliance upon astronomical sightings and natural signs for when to plant and harvest. The agricultural year began two months after the winter solstice with the rising of the star Arcturus, as well as the setting of the Pleiades and the appearance of the swallow and the snail and the cries of the crane. The winnowing of winter grain occurred with the appearance of Orion in the night sky.

Hesiod's works illustrate how the ancient mind anthropomorphized the divine and personified natural phenomena. Human behavior was understandable if the gods themselves engaged in slander, theft, rape, murder, adultery, violence, jealousy, and so on. The gods personified human emotions such as love and anger, propensities such as rumor and indolence, and behavior such as war and creativity. If such anthropomorphism lessened human responsibility for one's own actions, it nevertheless did not avoid or whitewash the issues of human psychology, but instead introduced them for debate, as it were, among contemporaries and later thinkers.

The gods personified, as well, natural phenomena. The myth of Persephone's capture by Hades, the god of the underworld, explained the changing seasons. Human and natural fertility were explained by the existence of Artemis, the goddess of childbirth and the fecundity of nature; Demeter, the goddess of the harvest and of grain; and Selene, the goddess of the monthly cycle of the moon. Parents explained thunderstorms to their children by noting Zeus's frequent anger. Plague occurred when sent by the god of rats, Apollo.

The Greeks were not alone among ancient peoples in wrestling with the mysteries and complexities of nature and human behavior. Nor were they unique in using what appear to be childish stories to explain things. Hesiod was among the best at providing such explanations. He had the curiosity and propensity of a scientist during a time, the eighth century BCE, of poets, centaurs, nymphs, heroes, and gods.

See also Greek Archaic Age; Homer; Myth; Prometheus

References

Burkert, Walter. *Structure and History in Greek Mythology and Ritual*. Berkeley: University of California Press, 1979.

Burn, A. R. *The World of Hesiod*. Harmondsworth, Middlesex: Penguin Books, 1936.

Griffin, Jaspar. "Greek Myth and Hesiod." In *Oxford History of the Classical World*. Oxford: Oxford University Press, 1986.

Hesiod. *Theogony and Works and Days*. Translated by Richard Lattimore. Ann Arbor: University of Michigan Press, 1959.

Tillinghast, William H. "The Geographical Knowledge of the Ancients Considered in Relation to the Discovery of America." In *Narrative and Critical History of America,* vol. 1, ed. Justin Winsor. Boston: Houghton, Mifflin, 1889.

Hipparchus (190–120 BCE)

Hipparchus was the most important astronomer of the Hellenistic Age after Aristarchus of Samos. Unlike Aristarchus, Hipparchus believed in the spherical, geocentric universe of Aristotle. A noted mathematician, Hipparchus relied on the work of his predecessor Apollonius of Perga. Hipparchus, for example, gauged the movement of the sun and the moon using a deferent-epicycle system devised by Apollonius. In his geographical work, Hipparchus was influenced by Eratosthenes.

Hipparchus, who was from Nicaea in northwest Asia Minor, lived and worked at Rhodes and Alexandria. At Rhodes he set up an observatory, identifying 850 stars and charting their movements and relative brightness. Hipparchus studied the precession of the equinoxes, the circuit that the earth makes over thousands of years as it rotates on its axis (a length of time known as the Great Year). Following Eratosthenes, Hipparchus knew that measurements could be made by calculating the angle of the rays of the sun at Alexandria at the summer solstice. Using observations of a solar eclipse taken from Alexandria, where the eclipse was partial, and the northern Aegean, where it was total, Hipparchus worked out an estimate of the distance of the moon from the earth.

As a geodesist, Hipparchus used latitude and longitude in a grid pattern at precise intervals to measure the surface of the earth. He also established a set of coordinates based on a 360-degree spherical globe. Hipparchus was influenced by what he could learn from Babylonian astronomers, particularly Babylonian ephemerides.

In his use of the deferent-epicycle system of the geocentric universe and cartographical coordinates to measure the earth, Hipparchus had a profound influence on other astronomers and geographers—notably Claudius Ptolemaeus.

See also Apollonius of Perga; Aristarchus of Samos; Astronomy; Greek Hellenistic Age; Ptolemaeus, Claudius; Eratosthenes

References

Crowe, Michael J. *Theories of the World from Antiquity to the Copernican Revolution.* New York: Dover Books, 1990.

Heath, Sir Thomas. *Aristarchus of Samos.* New York: Dover Books, 1913.

Hippo of Croton (floruit late fifth century BCE)

A Pythagorean philosopher who wrote on human health and the essential elements in nature, Hippo of Croton believed that moisture was the most important phenomenon, the excess or insufficiency of which caused ill health. A well person or animal has a good balance of moisture in the body. Animals acquire water from ponds, rivers, streams, and wells, all of which derive ultimately from the sea. The depth of the sea is greater than all else, and thus it is the source of all water.

Hippo was a contemporary of Socrates, though he was considered a mediocre thinker next to the great Athenian philosopher. One similarity he had with Socrates was that, right or wrong, he was accused of being an atheist.

See also Greek Archaic Age; Medicine; Pythagoras

Reference

Barnes, Jonathan, trans. *Early Greek Philosophy.* London: Penguin Books, 1987.

Hippocrates (460–377 BCE)

Hippocrates is generally recognized as the greatest physician in the history of the ancient world. An Asclepiad who lived on the Aegean island of Cos, Hippocrates brought medicine from its reliance upon superstition and faith-healing to a more empirical approach toward the study of the human body and illness. Hippocrates and his followers believed that dis-

Bust of Hippocrates of Cos (460–377 BCE), ancient Ionian Greek physician. (Courtesy of the National Library of Medicine)

ease resulted from an imbalance of nature, a disruption of the normal balance of the four humors. In the natural conflict between health and disease, the illness would typically reach a crisis point at which nature determined the future course of the illness—slow recovery or a critical phase usually resulting in death. Much of the Hippocratic writings that survive deal with observations of illness, the crisis point, and the resolution. In some sense Hippocrates was more of a medical observer and scientist than a healer. A good many of his patients died. Nevertheless it was his attempt to explain rationally what disease is, how it is caused, and what course it takes, that made Hippocrates the most significant physician of all time.

The Ionian Approach to Medicine

Cos was an island community that, like its Aegean neighbors Miletus, Halicarnassus, and Chios, was a center of Ionian culture during the Classical Age of Greek history. The scientific community at Cos featured a clan or guild of physicians that claimed descent either physically or symbolically from the mythical healer and god Asclepius. The Asclepiads of Cos developed the theory of the four humors that regulate health in the human body. If any of the four, phlegm, blood, yellow bile, and black bile, became more or less dominant than normal, compared to the others, illness was the result. The healthy body maintained this balance and thus avoided disease. Diet, rest, exercise, and climate helped to prevent imbalance and to correct the imbalance in case of illness.

Ionian medicine at Cos was similar to Ionian science in general during the sixth and fifth centuries BCE. Ionian scientists such as Thales, Anaximander, Anaximenes, and Anaxagoras were interested in explaining natural phenomena through physical or natural causes; they observed the effects of nature to help explain its causes and processes; they tried to understand by thought and observation the essence and patterns of nature. Likewise, Hippocrates and his fellow Asclepiads were interested in explaining disease according to cause and effect relationships, natural rather than supernatural forces.

Hippocratic Corpus

The *Hippocratic Corpus* is a collection of writings generally oriented around fifth-century Cos and is thought to reflect Hippocrates' thought and teachings, even if it is not exactly known whether Hippocrates actually wrote any of the treatises and case studies. A general theme of the writings, such as that argued in

Ancient Science, is that medicine is an art form, not part of the repertoire of the philosopher. Art and science frequently complement the other. Moreover, the *Hippocratic Corpus* emphasized the ability of the human body to heal itself. This holistic approach to medicine, and hence the Hippocratic approach to medicine, has seen a resurgence in the Western world in recent decades.

The *Hippocratic Corpus* emphasized the rational, scientific mind in the detection and analysis of illness. The *Prenotions of Cos* and *First Prorrhetic* reveal a scientific concern for prognosis. *Regime in Acute Diseases* discusses possible remedies for illness such as purgatives, emetics, baths, and potions of barley water, wine, honey water, or honey vinegar. The treatise *Ancient Medicine* describes the four humors as forces or powers inherent in the human body and not actual physical substances. Nevertheless, the humors represent the contrasts of hot and cold, moist and dry, aridity, fluidity, clarity, and dimness. The diseases cataloged in the *Hippocratic Corpus* include malaria and its consequences fever, ague, and delirium; consumption, asthma, and other pulmonary complaints; and diarrhea, dysentery, and other intestinal problems. *Airs, Waters, and Places* analyzes the impact of climate and meteorological conditions of heat, cold, wind, sun, moisture, and drought on disease. The change of seasons, particularly at the solstice and equinox, can have an impact on health. Asia, which has fewer climatic challenges, produces people who are less aggressive and warlike than the Europeans with their harsh and varied climate. The latter are hard men, contrasted with the soft, effeminate types of Asia. The environment of various regions, Hippocrates argued, helps to determine the varied physical, mental, and racial characteristics of different people.

On Epidemics

A large part of the *Hippocratic Corpus* is a detailed account of various epidemics at obscure times and places. In case after case, the physician observes disease in generally anonymous people. Typically the disease worsens to a crisis. Then either a slow recovery ensues or there is degeneration to death. Observations of the patient include bodily heat and moisture, lethargy, thirst, appetite, the color and smell of the urine and feces, and the consistency of the latter. At one point Hippocrates was very explicit as to what he looked for in making a diagnosis. He relied on observation and experience, trying to judge a particular illness according to general physical phenomena. Diagnosis was based on a long list of items to observe and record: the patient's habits and lifestyle, physical attributes, diet, frequency and description of urination, defecation, hiccups, and the like.

Sometimes the patient, after struggling through a painful illness, quickly reached a crisis and turned the corner toward health. Meton, for example, suffered from fever and headache, red, loose feces, and black urine. After several days he began to have nosebleeds, perspired profusely, and suffered from insomnia. Once the "crisis" was reached, the patient had come to a turning point at which he would decline, usually dying, or recover, even if slowly. Hippocrates recorded the experiences of a new mother who experienced intense pain and fever after giving birth. The pain spread throughout her body. She experienced abnormal bowel movements and insomnia. It took eighty days for her to reach a crisis; shortly thereafter she recovered.

The case of Crito, however, was different. He had a terrible throbbing in his toe and experienced fever and vomiting. Delirium took over shortly. The foot grew worse, as did the swelling, fever, and pain. After only two days he died after a short, brutal illness.

Legacy

Hippocrates' reach forward in time was extensive. The Hippocratic method of seeking physical causes for illness, making observation of symptoms, formulating prognoses, and prescribing medicine, rest, and healthy living continued to be practiced by physi-

cians for centuries. No less a physician than the Roman Galen practiced the Hippocratic approach to medicine. More than anything, however, Hippocrates influenced later medical practice by means of the Hippocratic Oath. The Oath is a fascinating testament to medical practice and concern for the patient. Hippocrates prayed to Asclepius and to the goddesses Hygeia and Panacea, and for help in his scientific observations and for good judgment to help those needing healing. He thought of his medical practice as an art that he wished to transmit to his sons and successors. He called upon his followers to refrain from deceiving and hurting patients; to not practice abortions; to not prescribe dangerous medications or force patients to undergo unnecessary surgery; and to respect the privacy of patients and keep patient information confidential. These are still the goals and guidelines of modern medical practice today.

See also Asclepiades; Asclepius/Asclepiads; Celsus; Galen; Greek Classical Age; Medicine
References
Galen. *On the Natural Faculties.* Translated by A. J. Brock. Cambridge: Harvard University Press, 1916.
Jones, W. H. S., trans. *Hippocrates.* Vol. 1. Cambridge: Harvard University Press, 1923.

History

History was science in the ancient world. Aristotle, in *Poetics,* contrasted the concern of poetry for the subjective and intuitive with the objective and factual account of past events found in the written discourse of history. Homer and Hesiod were poets, Aristotle argued, and hence described the general truth of human experience. Historians such as Thucydides described the factual basis of particular human events.

Historical study as much as scientific analysis is an attribute of civilization. The Sumerians and Egyptians, upon inventing cuneiform and hieroglyphic writing, used their invention to record crops and livestock, thus preserving a written record of past experience. The Hebrews of Israel and Judah early in the first millennium BCE wrote narratives of creation, the first humans, the migration of the Hebrews, the first prophets and lawgivers, the chronologies of kings and wars. Some of these narratives verge on myth; others are quite concrete and accurate. The Hebrew sense of history, as revealed in the Old Testament, derived from their incredible sense of consciousness as a chosen people, which required an understanding of the path of the chosen through time. Knowing from the Pentateuch and the first prophet Moses what God (Yahweh) intended for them, they looked to the known past for guidance—indeed the past was the future in a sense.

Herodotus

If the Hebrews were certain of their past and future, the Greeks of the first millennium BCE were not. Questioning all things, especially the past, characterized Greeks such as Herodotus, who referred to historical study as *historia,* which meant "arbiter" to Homer and "researches" or "inquiries" into human experience to Herodotus. Herodotus's inquiries were not exactly what Aristotle had in mind when he defined history in *Poetics.* Herodotus's *Histories* are wandering and anecdotal, recording stories of varying worth and historical accuracy based on his sources. Herodotus wandered the eastern Mediterranean during the mid-fifth century BCE, searching for answers to explain why the Persians under Darius I in 490 and Xerxes in 480 attacked the city-states of Greece and why against all apparent reason the Greeks won these two contests of the Persian Wars. Herodotus included ruminations on human nature, discussions of Asian and African culture, and detailed descriptions of natural phenomena, such as the flooding of the Nile and that odd creature, the hippopotamus. He sought information on the extent of continents and seas, the origins of rivers, and the differences in human customs. Herodotus was not a precise recorder of events but he was an inquisitive wanderer, a first-class geographer, and a tireless researcher.

Thucydides

Herodotus hardly fit the ideal of the objective inquirer, but the Athenian historian Thucydides, who lived a generation later, did. Thucydides (460–400 BCE) was an Athenian who served in the Peloponnesian War (431–404), the great war between the Dorians of southern and western Greece and the western Mediterranean, led by Sparta, and the Ionians of eastern Greece, the Aegean, and western Turkey, led by Athens. Thucydides wrote *The Peloponnesian War* based on the assumption that it would be one of the greatest conflicts in history. He used the pathos and drama of war to portray constant human emotions and characteristics. Thucydides was a precursor to modern social and behavioral scientists and their search for laws of human behavior. Thucydides, therefore, had an objective ideal. He criticized poets and storytellers for their proclivity to accept fancy and to indulge in subjective reporting of past events. Like Herodotus, Thucydides filled his account with numerous digressions. Unlike Herodotus, these digressions were not to entertain the reader with fascinating stories and legends. Rather, Thucydides digressed to correct false assumptions and incorrect accounts of past events. He was in other respects very much like the modern scientific scholar. Thucydides followed a strict chronological narrative. He rarely allowed himself to speculate on the events of the war. He did, to be sure, put speculative speeches into the mouths of the Dorian and Ionian statesmen. Clearly based on reports and rumors, these speeches nevertheless had the look and feel of authenticity. Thucydides knew the precise form—the thesis, arguments, exhortations, and conclusion—of these speeches and used this familiar pattern to recreate the essential characteristic of Greek political culture, namely rhetoric.

Polybius

Several centuries passed, and Greek power was eclipsed first by the Macedonians in the fourth century and then by the Romans in the second century. Polybius was a Greek historian captured by the Romans. Living in Italy, he took an interest in Rome's rise to power, and he traced Roman history in his multivolume *Historia*. Polybius merged the apparently competing techniques of Herodotus's storytelling and Thucydides' infatuation with a strict chronological narrative. Polybius wrote a precise account of history following a chronological pattern of Olympiads; yet he digressed and theorized, related fascinating stories, and described the geography, culture, customs, flora, and fauna of the regions, such as North Africa, conquered by the Romans. Polybius journeyed to the Alps, the great barrier to Italy that the Carthaginian general Hannibal crossed. Polybius believed that history was an expression of the truth of human experience. As in Book 12 of his *Histories,* he constantly raised the banner of an objective account of the past using a clear analysis of documents and firsthand knowledge of peoples and places.

Livy

Rome eventually came to rule up to one hundred million people from England to Mesopotamia to Morocco. The drama and grandeur of Rome's rise to power encouraged the thoughtful, the analytical, and the didactic to record Rome's history. Because of the historical writings of Sallust, Caesar, Livy, Appian, Tacitus, Suetonius, Plutarch, Dio Cassius, and Ammianus Marcellinus, the great Roman contribution to the history of thought was through the writing of history. A pervasive historical perspective and sense of time pervaded Rome's politics, customs, and beliefs. The spirit of Rome united past and present by means of the deep awareness of the individual Roman for his or her ancestors and descendants. The Roman worldview was molded by a state that was completely temporal: the account of conquest and con-

querors over time fascinated Romans. The greatest Roman narrator of historical events was the historian Titus Livius—Livy—whose account of the origins and rise to power of the city on the Tiber towered above other towering historical writers. Yet Livy claimed that his history had less to do with temporal affairs and more to do with transcendent morals. History has a didactic function, he wrote, teaching us right from wrong, behavior in others to imitate or avoid. Livy's didactic history was a narrative of past events to prepare those of the future for similar events. Livy was a masterly storyteller who sacrificed a strict accounting of detailed fact for a sometimes heavy reliance on legend and anecdote.

Tacitus

If Livy was not inclined toward a scientific viewpoint in his historical writing, the same cannot be said about Cornelius Tacitus, the best historian of the centuries after the birth of Christ. Tacitus authored the *Histories, Annals, Germania,* and *Agricola.* Even more than Thucydides, Tacitus sought legitimacy in his terse historical writing. To write Rome's history, Tacitus used whatever valid historical documents he could find, including memoirs, senate records, eyewitness accounts, letters from observant friends (such as Pliny the Younger), contemporary letters and speeches, historical narratives, and official journals. His accounts also included perceptive assessments of the natural environment. And if this were not enough, Tacitus was the first historian to write from what historians today would call a behavioral science approach. Tacitus sought to recreate the personalities, motives, emotional distresses, and bouts of insanity of the objects of his inquiry, particularly the emperors Tiberius, Caligula, and Nero.

Tacitus's *Germania* was an interesting ethnographic study of Rome's enemies—the German peoples of the Rhine River valley. Tacitus described the geography of the region, the customs and beliefs of the people, their form of government, and their varied disputes and wars. Although the Germans were the enemies of the Roman people, Tacitus employed empathy to try to understand these strange people. He found much to despise and condemn, yet much to admire as well.

Ammianus Marcellinus

Centuries passed, the Roman Empire went through political, social, economic, and moral crises, and the scope of history became confusing, not at all like the five centuries BCE, of Rome's rise to power. Nevertheless in the fourth century CE, one man attempted to write the history of the Roman people, taking up where Tacitus had left off. Ammianus Marcellinus's *History* was a multivolume work that encompassed the three centuries from 100 to 400 CE. Marcellinus modeled his work on Tacitus's style, method, and approach. He recorded the political and military events of the Later Roman Empire but also digressed to describe the customs, beliefs, institutions, and geography of surrounding peoples—the Gauls, Goths, Parthians, and others.

Ancient historical writing did not, of course, involve experiments, lab reports, and mathematics. But science involves more than the manipulation of nature in a controlled environment. The Greeks and Romans believed science to be the systematic acquisition of knowledge. The great historians among the Greeks and Romans believed historical study, along with geographical and anthropological study, was as much a science as the study of natural philosophy and natural history.

See also Ammianus Marcellinus; Greek Archaic Age; Greek Classical Age; Herodotus of Halicarnassus; Hesiod; Homer; Later Roman Empire; Old Testament; Polybius; Roman Principate; Tacitus

References

Breisach, Ernst. *Historiography: Ancient, Medieval and Modern.* Chicago: University of Chicago Press, 1983.

Herodotus. *The Histories.* Translated by Aubrey de Selincourt. Harmondsworth, Middlesex: Penguin Books, 1972.

Lawson, Russell. "Montaigne's Dialogue with the Past." *Journal of Unconventional History.* Volume 6, 1994.

Livy. *The Early History of Rome.* Translated by Aubrey de Selincourt. Harmondsworth, Middlesex: Penguin Books, 1971.

Polybius. *The Histories.* Translated by W. R. Paton. 6 vols. Cambridge: Harvard University Press, 1922–27.

Rolfe, John C., trans. *Ammianus Marcellinus.* 2 vols. Cambridge: Harvard University Press, 1950.

Starr, Chester. *The Awakening of the Greek Historical Spirit.* New York: Knopf, 1968.

Tacitus. *The Agricola and the Germania.* Translated by H. Mattingly. Harmondsworth, Middlesex: Penguin Books, 1970.

———. *The Histories.* Translated by Kenneth Wellesley. Harmondsworth, Middlesex: Penguin Books, 1972.

Thucydides. *The Peloponnesian War.* Translated by Rex Warner. Harmondsworth, Middlesex: Penguin Books, 1972.

Homer (floruit eighth century BCE)

To Homer, an anonymous Greek poet who lived sometime during the beginning of the first millennium BCE, man is a journeyer. Homer's *Iliad* and *Odyssey,* composed around 1000 BCE but penned during the eighth century, present the Greeks as wanderers, explorers, and discoverers. Greek history was built upon the words "in search of." Because of the Greek quest to know, the heritage of Western civilization during the past two millennia is an unending search for answers to inspired questions.

Who Was Homer?

One of the longstanding mysteries in ancient history involves Homer, who he was, when he lived, and whether or not his poems relate the episodes of real events. The word *Homer* in Greek means "one who is led," literally "blind." *Homer* might not refer to one person but rather to the frequent occurrence in the ancient world of bards who were blind. To the ancients, however, Homer was a real person who came from several possible places. The people of Smyrna, Chios, and Colophon all claimed Homer as a favorite son. The Roman

Homer (eighth century BCE), the blind bard from Chios in the Aegean and author of the Iliad *and the* Odyssey, *which provide an early poetic portrait of Greek life, culture, and geography. (Library of Congress)*

emperor Hadrian decided to settle the matter once and for all by submitting the question of Homer's origins to the Oracle of Apollo at Delphi. The oracle told Hadrian a nice fable, that Homer was the son of Telemachus and grandson of Odysseus and Nestor (through his daughter Epicasta).

Anthropos

Notwithstanding his uncertain origins, Homer's poems have been admired for thousands of years. The anthropomorphic portrait of the *Iliad* and *Odyssey* make Homer's work a pious testament to the wonder and beauty of the universe. Homer presented a moving portrait of universal human characteristics that was at the same time down-to-earth and majestically physical. The *numinous,* or tran-

scendent divine, in Homer is the pathos of death; the beauty of the human body; the anguish of war; the wondrous rhetoric of great heroes; the awesome human strength, will, and stubborn refusal to bend or to surrender; the elevation of humans to equality among natural phenomena; the treasure of love and life amid the unceasing roar of armies and cries of the vanquished; the endless human struggle against time and destiny; the elegant dignity of humankind.

The Mythological Past

Homer's *Iliad* and *Odyssey* are stories that describe a precivilized, protoscientific culture. Homer's story has no clear antecedent, no set time frame. It is an episodic, vaguely chronological account of a shadowy past time. The poet provides no clear explanation of the events of the past. Causation is directed by anonymous fate, an act of the faceless divine. The river Ocean surrounds the disk of the earth that is filled with mysterious forces, nymphs, satyrs, demons, and spirits of nature, rarely seen but present. Heaven's vault hosts the movement of the sun and stars, which emerge from the river Ocean in the east and submerge below its wine-dark waters in the west. Constellations associated with the mythological past move across the sky: the Pleiades, Hyades, the Great and Little Bear, the hunter Orion. In contrast, under the disk of earth to an uncertain distance is the unending gulf of Tartarus.

The Homeric poems describe a time of wealthy warriors and impoverished peasants, with few specialized workers. Seers, soothsayers, and healers form the rudiments of a middle class, along with bards, craftsmen who fashioned items from clay, wood, and stone, and metal workers. Homer's world was a Bronze Age world; the poet took great care to describe the beauty of bronze shields, weapons, and cauldrons. Also portrayed in the poems are the sleek black ships of the Greeks, powered by a single square sail, and the strength of the warriors who at sea became rowers. Greek mariners rarely crossed the sea out of sight of land, yet the poems imply that extended sea voyages were not improbable.

Iliad

The *Iliad* opens with an account of the god Apollo, who sent plague to the disobedient Greek host. Apollo was not only the god of plague, but also of healing and medicine, of music and crafts. Apollo sired Asclepius, who was taught the healing art by Chiron the Centaur. Asclepius in turn passed on his knowledge to his sons Podalirios and Machaon, who in the *Iliad* healed Menelaus from an arrow wound, by putting balm on the wound. Later, according to the Homeric Cycle of myth, the sons of Asclepius healed Heracles' son Philoctetes, considered the master of archery among the Greek host. The *Iliad* portrays human consciousness as the presence of the divine. But more, Homer described distinct humans, singular characters of a certain place and time. The Homeric heroes are individual actors forging their own destinies within the vague confines of fate. Heroes such as Achilles battle not only humans but also gods that personify natural forces. For example, Achilles fights the river Scamander to a draw. The *Iliad* presents a wonderful picture of the drama and pathos of humans and nature.

Odyssey

The *Odyssey* provides a narrative account of the adventures of Odysseus, king of Ithaca, as he spends years sailing the Mediterranean in search of a way home to his wife Penelope and son Telemachus. Odysseus reaches home because of fate, which plays a huge role in both of the Homeric poems. Fate is the ultimate dictator of all things, human, natural, and divine. Although the Greeks gave names to the trio of fates (Lachesis, Clotho, and Atropos), the operation of fate was an anonymous power not unlike the dominance of natural law in modern times.

Odysseus arrives home at Ithaca because of fate but also because of his intelligence—"wit," according to Homer, the ability to think oneself out of scrapes. Odysseus outthinks his opponents by weighing a given situation through observation and analysis, then giving a measured, common-sense response. He engages in on-the-spot reasoning. He uses his mind to corral his passions and emotions. Not a scientist, nevertheless Odysseus serves as a patron for all subsequent Greek thinkers who had the curiosity to go in search of knowledge.

See also Asclepius / Asclepiads; Astronomy; Geography / Geodesy; Greek Archaic Age; Hesiod; Myth

References

Finley, M. I. *The World of Odysseus.* Harmondsworth, Middlesex: Penguin Books, 1972.

Heath, Sir Thomas. *Aristarchus of Samos.* New York: Dover Books, 1913.

Hesiod. *Homeric Hymns, Epic Cycle, Homerica.* Translated by Hugh G. Evelyn-White. Cambridge: Harvard University Press, 1936.

Homer. *Iliad.* Translated by Robert Fitzgerald. New York: Doubleday, 1989.

———. *Odyssey.* Translated by Robert Fitzgerald. New York: Random House, 1990.

Taplin, Oliver. "Homer." In *Oxford History of the Classical World.* Oxford: Oxford University Press, 1986.

Zimmerman, J. E. *Dictionary of Classical Mythology.* New York: Harper and Row, 1971.

Hydraulics

Hydraulics, the science of the movement and force of water, was an important study for early civilizations, particularly those with the dry climate of the Near East and large cities, such as Rome, demanding a huge daily water supply. Ancient Egyptians, dependent on the rising and falling of the Nile River, had to organize their activities to utilize most efficiently the land's water resources. The spring rising of the Nile inundates the parched land of Egypt, actually swelling the soil and making drainage difficult but agriculture successful. During dry months the farmer used the *shaduf* or *sakia* to irrigate the land. The Egyptians of

Photograph of the remains of a Roman aqueduct at Aspendos, Turkey. (Corel Corporation)

the Old Dynasty of the third millennium BCE had basins made of stone and lavatories and copper pipes to eliminate water and waste. Egyptian metallurgists and craftsmen even devised copper pipes and pipe fittings, plugs, and drains. The city of Alexandria, planned by Alexander and immediately a booming settlement, yet built between the sea and lakes, required canals. Crates of Olynthus designed and built them.

The greatest hydraulic engineers of antiquity were the Romans. Aqueducts were not unknown to other cultures—reputedly one Eupalinus built an aqueduct through a mountain on the island of Samos in the sixth century BCE. But the Romans made the building of aqueducts a science and an art. Appius Claudius Crassus, the creator of the Via Appia, was also the force behind the construction of the first aqueduct built to provide fresh water for the city. Marcus Agrippa, the friend and associate of Octavian (Augustus) Caesar, brought Rome's hydraulics to its most efficient level, constructing and repairing aqueducts, cleaning sewers, and ensuring a continual flow of water for private and public use by means of public fountains, public and private baths, and water to flush latrines and sewers. Wealthy Romans could have water brought to their homes by means of lead pipes. There was much illegal tapping of water, which the authorities attempted to stop, usually in vain. One such authority was Frontinus, an expert on hydraulics.

By the first century CE, there were eleven aqueducts bringing water to the city. One of the last aqueducts built by the emperor Valens in the late fourth century lasted eight hundred years and extended one hundred fifty miles across the Balkans to Constantinople, the capital of the Eastern Roman Empire.

See also Engineering and Technology; Frontinus, Sextus Julius; Roman Roads and Bridges; Vitruvius

References

Dal Maso, Leonard B. *Rome of the Caesars*. Translated by Michael Hollingsworth. Florence: Bonechi-Edizioni, 1974.

Frontinus. *The Aqueducts of Rome*. Translated by Charles E. Bennett. Cambridge: Harvard University Press, 1925.

Pliny the Elder. *Natural History*. Translated by John F. Healy. London: Penguin Books, 1991.

Rowell, Henry Thompson. *Rome in the Augustan Age*. Norman: University of Oklahoma Press, 1962.

Vitruvius. *On Architecture*. Translated by Joseph Gwilt. London: Priestley and Weale, 1826.

Von Hagen, Victor W. *Roman Roads*. London: Werdenfeld and Nicholson, 1966.

Hypatia of Alexandria (370–415 CE)

Hypatia is one of the few ancient female scientists for whom we have clear information, owing to the tragic nature of her death, her accomplishments as a mathematician, and her many students. Hypatia was a pagan Neoplatonist in Christian Alexandria. She was an astronomer and mathematician and wrote several commentaries on her precursors, such as the second-century CE astronomer Ptolemy of Alexandria and the third-century BCE mathematicians Diophantus of Alexandria and Apollonius of Perga. Indeed, third- and fourth-century CE Alexandria was the most important center of science in the Later Roman Empire. Hypatia's predecessors in Alexandria included Diophantus, who wrote the *Arithmetica;* Pappas, who wrote on geometry; the Neoplatonist Proclus; Claudius Ptolemaeus, the astronomer and geographer; and Hypatia's father, Theon, who was head of the museum and library at Alexandria under the emperor Theodosius. Theon was a mathematician who wrote commentaries on Ptolemy, Euclid, and Archimedes, and a scientist who wrote other works on the flooding of the Nile, the rising of the Dog Star, Sirius, and divination. Hypatia was the teacher of the famous Christian bishop Synesius of Cyrene.

As Hypatia's writings are lost, it is difficult to reconstruct her work and its significance. She clearly was a student of Ptolemy's *Almagest,* as was her father. She also was a commentator on geometry, especially Archimedes' work on the circle and Apollonius's work on conic sections. She was interested in dreams, like her student Synesius. Hypatia and Synesius also corresponded about scientific apparati such as the astrolabe, used for measuring the positions of the stars in the heavens.

Alexandria was famous for its religious conflicts, and Hypatia ultimately fell victim to one of these. Christians accused Hypatia of practicing magic and astrology, which were illegal in late fourth- and early fifth-century Rome, although widespread among the populace. Apparently this undeserved reputation as a sorceress led to her terrible death at the hands of an Alexandrian mob. The Christian historian Socrates Scholasticus in the *Ecclesiastical History* noted that Hypatia was very confident in her bearing, wore the garb of a Greek philosopher, and associated with men as equals. Hypatia, reputedly a beautiful woman, was stripped, tortured, dismembered, and burned at the hands of angry Christians in 415.

See also Alexandria; Apollonius of Perga; Archimedes; Later Roman Empire; Mathematics; Neoplatonism; Ptolemaeus, Claudius

References

Jones, Tom B. *In the Twilight of Antiquity*. Minneapolis: University of Minnesota Press, 1978.

Socrates Scholasticus. *History of the Church*. London: Henry G. Bohn, 1853.

I

Iamblichus (250–325 CE)

Iamblichus was the leading Neoplatonist philosopher of the fourth century CE. A native of Syria, Iamblichus was a student of Porphyry and follower of Plotinus. Iamblichus broke from the ascetic and deeply intuitive and spiritual approach of his forebears to embrace magic and theurgy. He was closer in spirit to Pythagoras, whom Iamblichus admired sufficiently to write a treatise, *On the Pythagorean Way of Life*. As a theurgist, Iamblichus used magic to call upon the power of the gods. He could put his audience and disciples under a spell, some of whom were credulous enough to believe in such magic; others were incredulous, but recognized the power that such trickery could have over the simple-minded. Iamblichus died during the reign of Constantine, yet his teachings, writings, and example continued to influence later philosophers and theurgists such as Maximus of Ephesus and Julian, the Roman emperor, who compared Iamblichus to Plato and Pythagoras.

Iamblichus was one of quite a few holy men of the third and fourth centuries who attracted disciples and sycophants because of their unique skills at calling upon the divine. Eunapius, the biographer, recorded one instance in which Iamblichus was able to produce two youthful deities before his astonished (and credulous) followers. In *On the Mysteries,* Iamblichus wrote in detail about the varied techniques to call upon the gods and enjoy a mystical union. Gods might so change a person that he could withstand fire and knife wounds and other pain. Or a god might inhabit a person's body so as to allow elevation and other such gravity-defying tricks. There was a hierarchy of divine possession. Iamblichus claimed not only to be able to give himself to the god, or absorb the god in him, but also—the pinnacle of mystical joining—to become equal to the god and merge in a dual union. Mysticism required not just the willing mind but spells and incantations, even the power of numbers. He lauded Pythagoras for giving to men the source of knowledge and power found in the "tetrad," which was an order of the numbers 1, 2, 3, 4, that when arranged in accumulating order added to 10. The tetrad visually appears as a pyramid, rather like a set of bowling pins. To the ancients it was a symbol of Platonic truth.

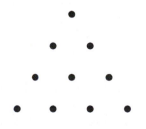

Besides *On the Mysteries* and *On the Pythagorean Way of Life,* Iamblichus wrote *On the Soul, Theological Arithmetic,* and *Commentary to Nichomachus' Introduction to Arithmetic.* Fragments of all of these works survive.

See also Julian; Later Roman Empire; Maximus of Ephesus; Neoplatonism; Plato; Plotinus; Porphyry; Pythagoras

References
Barnes, Jonathan, trans. *Early Greek Philosophy.* London: Penguin Books, 1987.
Brown, Peter. *The Making of Late Antiquity.* Cambridge: Harvard University Press, 1978.
Dodds, E. R. *Pagan and Christian in an Age of Anxiety.* New York: W. W. Norton, 1965.
Eunapius. *The Lives of the Sophists.* Translated by W. C. Wright. Cambridge: Harvard University Press, 1968.
Wright, W. C., trans. *The Works of the Emperor Julian.* Cambridge: Harvard University Press, 1962, 1969.

Imhotep
See Egypt

India
See Asia, East and South

Ionians
The Ionian school of thought featured the first great scientist-philosophers of the ancient world, most of whom hailed from Miletus or other small cities of western Turkey, which the Greeks called Ionia. Thales, Anaximander, and Anaximenes of Miletus and Anaxagoras of Clazomenae were the most famous of the Ionian scientists. Other significant Ionian thinkers included Hippocrates, Herodotus, Pythagoras, and Homer. It was the Homeric influence on the Ionian refugees from Greece that undoubtedly set in motion the pattern of thought central to this region of the Mediterranean. Homer's works, though epic poetry, create a worldview of an inhabitable world known by men who are thinkers, doers, creators, and individualists.

Ionian thinkers embraced Homer's subtle call to find explanations for all that *is.* They replaced Homer's explanation of natural and human phenomena according to fate, the will of the gods, and the human interaction with the divine with more realistic explanations of physical phenomena exclusive of direct divine action and intervention.

The Ionians sought the First Cause. Thales, for example, rejected supernatural cause and arbitrariness in the universe for universal physical causes. The initial element, he argued, is water, from which all else springs. Plutarch lauded Thales as the first analytical philosopher. Thales' student Anaximander elevated the level of inquiry even higher with his argument that the infinite is the essence of all things. His student Anaximenes sought the origins and nature of existence in air. Thales and Anaximenes were the first Greek students of chemistry.

Anaximenes' student Anaxagoras, Anaxagoras's student Archelaus, and Archelaus's student Socrates brought Ionian thought to Athens in the fifth century BCE. Anaxagoras believed that the First Cause and ongoing universal providence was Mind *(nous),* which is incorporeal and transcendent. Socrates apparently came to these beliefs by means of Archelaus. The Ionian philosophers at Athens countered Sophists such as Protagoras who advocated a completely human-centered view. The more speculative Ionians believed that reality is not necessarily what humans perceive nor how they perceive it. Our individual minds allow us to peer through the window of the soul to Mind, though the window is often cloudy and our observations inexact. It takes rigorous years of thought and study to train the individual mind to be able to perceive qualities of Mind, or Good as Socrates and Plato called the ultimate reality.

Ionian thought reached fruition through the efforts of Plato and Aristotle. Though the former was a speculative philosopher and the latter was an analytical scientist, Plato and

Aristotle agreed in the essential spiritual core of the universe, that *being* acting through the mind and soul unites humans together into a great whole, that the First Cause is an unknown unmoved mover that transcends all human thoughts and actions.

See also Anaxagoras of Clazomenae; Anaximander of Miletus; Anaximenes of Miletus; Archelaus of Athens; Aristotle; Athens; Greek Archaic Age; Greek Classical Age; Miletus; Plato; Socrates; Thales

References

Barnes, Jonathan, trans. *Early Greek Philosophy.* London: Penguin Books, 1987.

Heath, Sir Thomas. *Aristarchus of Samos.* New York: Dover Books, 1913.

Laertius, Diogenes. *Lives of the Philosophers.* Translated by R. D. Hicks. 2 vols. Cambridge: Harvard University Press, 1931, 1938.

Plutarch. *The Lives of the Noble Grecians and Romans.* Translated by John Dryden; revised by Arthur Hugh Clough. 1864; reprint ed., New York: Random House, 1992.

Iron Age

A revolution in metallurgy that led to the dissemination of power and wealth and the rise of more widespread tools for farmers and weapons for soldiers occurred at the end of the second millennium BCE in Asia Minor. This was the development of the process of digging iron ore from the ground and heating it to such high temperatures that finished iron could be wrought, using the anvil and hammer; sufficient carburization of the iron produced steel. After the millennia of bronze tools and weapons, which were difficult to make and expensive and thus limited to aristocrats, iron signaled the coming power of the middle-class merchant and farmer of the first millennium BCE. The spread of literacy and coinage also helped in the movement of the masses toward economic and social power and influence compared to the old landed aristocracy. And then, increasingly, philosophy and science became an activity that others besides the privileged few could participate in.

The first iron users were the Hittites of eastern Anatolia, who relied on the expertise of iron-working Armenians. These people had apparently discovered the means to heat iron in the same fashion as copper was heated to drive out the impurities; the metalworker could then hammer the wrought iron into shape. Wrought iron was not useful as a weapon and was essentially decorative. The Egyptians—who borrowed the use of iron from the Hittites, at first using meteoric iron, calling it the "iron of heaven"—used wrought iron. The process of turning iron into steel probably occurred for the first time toward the end of the second millennium BCE in Anatolia. It involved the use of the forge and bellows. The charcoal was heated to extreme temperatures—white hot, over 2,000 degrees Fahrenheit—and then the iron was smelted to a point that impurities were removed. This process of *carburization* of the iron is what produced steel.

The first peoples to use iron weapons with a steel edge—the Hittites of Turkey, the Dorians who invaded Greece and destroyed the Mycenaean civilization, and the Sea Peoples such as the Philistines who swept through the eastern Mediterranean ravaging and conquering—were not noted for their cultural advances. Yet these seemingly primitive peoples conquered more sophisticated peoples who still used bronze weapons. Particularly after 1000 BCE in the Mediterranean region, warriors turned to iron as the weapon of choice. During the first millennium BCE, bronze weapons were still used, but iron was preferred.

See also Bronze Age; Physical Sciences

References

Childe, Gordon. *What Happened in History.* Harmondsworth, Middlesex: Penguin Books, 1946.

Leicester, Henry M. *The Historical Background of Chemistry.* New York: Dover Books, 1971.

Woolley, Leonard. *The Beginnings of Civilization: History of Mankind: Cultural and Scientific Developments,* vol. 1, pt. 2. New York: Mentor Books, 1965.

Irrigation Techniques

Irrigation of land to produce surplus crops has been a driving force in the history of civilization. The agricultural revolution that began in the Fertile Crescent of western Asia began because early agriculturalists realized that dry soil did not support plants. Where the climate is such that the land is parched, humans must artificially water or flood the land to ensure moisture for the growing plants. Irrigation probably first took place along the banks of the Tigris and Euphrates rivers in Mesopotamia (Iraq). The Tigris and Euphrates flood in the spring, bringing the water from melting snow of the mountains in eastern Turkey. These rivers have low banks, and thus rising water often escapes the river bed and floods the land. Such flooding is unpredictable. Near the mouths of the Tigris and Euphrates rivers there was swampy land with a high saline content; draining the moisture and channeling fresh water into the soil

was imperative for successful agriculture. The early inhabitants of Mesopotamia decided to exercise human will over the flooding waters and marshy lands, building an intricate series of dikes and canals to channel the water in the direction of fields requiring extra moisture. These dikes and canals also were useful during the dry and hot seasons of the year; farmers would purposely channel water from the rivers into their dry fields, providing the moisture necessary for crops to grow.

The Nile River of Egypt floods in the spring when the snow of the highlands of Ethiopia melts and the Nile rises, overflowing its low banks to inundate the land of upper (southern) and lower (northern) Egypt. This land in low-lying areas received sufficient moisture as well as a fertile layer of silt from the flooding Nile. Land at higher elevations surrounding the Nile required artificial watering. The Egyptians used an irrigation tool called a *shaduf,* which was a simple machine

Irrigation canals along the Nile River have changed very little over five thousand years. (Corel Corporation)

operated by the farmer. The *shaduf* had a pail tied to a rotating pole, connected to a stationary pole, that acted as a lever to raise the pail filled with water, rotate it to a waiting pool or channel, empty it, and then return it to the river to retrieve more water. Similar was the *sakia,* a rotating water wheel fitted with cups that would scoop up water as the wheel rotated, driven by a chain and lever. Upon reaching the pinnacle and beginning the descent, the cups deposited the water in a waiting canal.

One of the more famous irrigation devices was reputedly invented by the Hellenistic mathematician and scientist Archimedes, who was an expert in hydraulics. Archimedes' Screw was a simple machine that resembled a large screw enclosed by a cylindrical frame. When set in the water and rotated manually, the device would wind about bringing water to the top, which was above ground, where it would be emptied into a waiting pool.

See also Agriculture; Archimedes; Egypt; Mesopotamia

References

Erman, Adolf. *Life in Ancient Egypt.* Translated by H. M. Tirard. New York: Dover Books, 1894.

"Irrigation." *Encyclopedia Britannica,* vol. 12 (1962).

J

Julian (331–363 CE)

Julian, the emperor of the Roman Empire from 361 to 363 CE, was a self-perceived philosopher-king and student of ancient science who sought to promote Hellenism—Greek thought and learning—during a time dominated by Christianity. Julian was the nephew of the emperor Constantine. When Constantine's son Constantius came to power upon his father's death in 337, his supporters eliminated rivals to his power, including Julian's family. Julian himself was spared because of his youth; but he was subsequently kept under a sort of house arrest. He rejected the Christian teachings of his tutors by the time he was in his teens and sought to study under the great philosophers and scientists of the Greeks. Constantius allowed this, seeing nothing very harmful in Julian's search for learning. Julian became a studious and intelligent neophyte philosopher hungry for knowledge of Greek philosophy and science. He became attracted to Neoplatonism and Stoicism and became friends with clear-headed thinkers such as Themistius the philosopher, Libanius the orator, and Oribasius the physician. Julian also succumbed to the fascination of his age with magic and superstition and became a disciple of the theurgist Maximus. Nevertheless Julian was an important patron of science and philosophy during his brief reign.

Julian's surviving letters reveal the scope of his scientific interests and the network of fourth-century science and philosophy. Julian surrounded himself with Neoplatonists and Aristotelians, pagans as well as Christians. He was a student while in Athens of the Christian philosopher Prohaeresius and had a long-standing friendship with the Aristotelian Aëtius, who became a Christian bishop. Julian thanked the philosopher Priscus for introducing him to the study of Aristotle. Indeed Julian claimed that Aristotle and Plato form the basis for all inquiry. His correspondence with the Aristotelian commentator Themistius focused on the contemplative side of Aristotle's philosophy. But Julian was clearly more attracted to Platonism, particularly the watered-down version practiced by Iamblichus and his followers. Julian sacrificed reason for fantasy when he became a follower of Maximus, the theurgist and miracle worker.

Nevertheless Julian was interested in more serious science. Music fascinated him, and he enjoyed studying the purported founder, the philosopher Amphion, whom Julian claimed was responsible for developing the science of harmony. In letters to Ecdicius, an official in

Egypt, Julian requested that, since the temple to the Egyptian god Serapis was being restored, the "Nilometer," a device used to measure the rising and lowering of the Nile River, be activated again. Perhaps because of the influence of his friend Oribasius, Julian was very interested in the study of medicine. He wrote to Zeno, an Alexandrian physician, praising the importance of physicians to society. Julian supported the study of medicine and work of physicians by imperial decree in 362, proclaiming that physicians be exempted from otherwise compulsory military and civil service. Indeed, one might conclude that the most important legacy of Julian's reign as emperor of Rome was his encouragement of the study of science and medicine, especially his support of his friend Oribasius, who produced the important *Synopsis* of the work of Galen.

See also Iamblichus; Later Roman Empire; Maximus of Ephesus; Neoplatonism; Oribasius; Themistius

References

Bowersock, G. W. *Julian the Apostate.* Cambridge: Harvard University Press, 1978.

Browning, Robert. *The Emperor Julian.* Berkeley: University of California Press, 1976.

Wright, W. C., trans. *The Works of the Emperor Julian.* Cambridge: Harvard University Press, 1962, 1969.

L

Later Roman Empire (180–565 CE)

After 200 CE there was little scientific creativity in the ancient Mediterranean world. The achievements of Aristotle, Ptolemy, Euclid, and Galen would set the standard for the understanding of the universe, the world, mathematics, and medicine in the coming centuries. Not until 1500, during the Renaissance in Europe, would there be similar accomplishments so fundamental to scientific theory and practice. Scientists from the third to the sixth centuries, and after, tended to be synthesizers and proselytizers, pedagogues repeating the same theories to students, commentators making the same comments in books and lectures. The fall of Rome occurred in a long process from 200 to 500 CE. Edward Gibbon, the great historian of Rome's fall, traced the decline of ancient civilization, the loss of past greatness, the military, political, and intellectual weakness of the time. Theurgists, magicians, and sophists dominated what passed for science. Neoplatonists and Aristotelians subjected science to the realm of philosophy. The practice of medicine became too often the realm of the charlatan and astrologer. The great debate between pagan-humanists and Christian intellectuals distracted thinkers from the general decline in political stability, economic health, artistic and literary creativity, and scientific accomplishment. By 500, scientific thought and practice in the Western Roman Empire was buried under the suffering, poverty, famine, and sickness of petty Germanic warlords competing for control of what was left of Rome. In the Eastern Roman (Byzantine) Empire, it was a different story, not so much decline as business as usual, as students of Aristotle, Euclid, Ptolemy, and Galen carried upon their intellectual shoulders the scientific legacy of the ancient world.

Superstition has often been a strange bedfellow of science over the course of human history. The ancient world, notwithstanding its huge accomplishments in science, hosted an amazing variety of magicians, soothsayers, prognosticators, astrologers, theurgists, and the like. Even during the Principate of the first and second centuries CE, when Roman culture was at its height, superstition typically dwarfed scientific inquiry. This imbalance of fantasy and reality grew during the third century and after, as the empire fell victim to civil conflict and its usual consequences of moral and intellectual malaise. Hence, after 200 CE there was very little good philosophy and even less good science. Yet humans still yearned to observe nature and exercise power over their environment. Unwilling or unable to engage in clear observation of natural phenomena and the systematic ordering of data, intellectuals of the third and fourth centuries turned more to pseudoscience, superstition, and the fabulous and remarkable.

The scientific centers of the Later Roman Empire continued to be Athens, Alexandria, Pergamum, and Antioch. The city of Rome was sometimes important, too, especially under the patronage of the emperors and their families. Julia Domna, the consort of Septimius Severus, patronized Philostratus, the compiler of the *Lives of the Sophists.* Philostratus was himself a sophist, a paid teacher of "wisdom"—rhetoric and philosophy. It should not surprise us that compilations of past science, books that told the story of great philosophers and sophists of the past, should be popular and widespread during years when there was little intellectual creativity. Besides Philostratus, there were Eunapius's *Lives of the Sophists* and Diogenes Laertius's *Lives of the Philosophers.* These works, typical for a time of intellectual malaise, tended to be anecdotal accounts of great thinkers of mythic quality. Whereas Philostratus wrote accounts of philosophers of the Principate, Diogenes wrote of the great ones of the past, the early Ionian masters of science such as Thales and Anaximander and the Athenians Plato and Aristotle. Eunapius, on the other hand, centered his efforts on the Neoplatonic heroes of the fourth century, his own time, and their champion, the emperor Julian.

Thinkers during the Later Roman Empire continued the tendency begun during the Hellenistic Age and continuing into the Roman Principate of dividing scientific and philosophic theories and methods into two schools of thought: the Platonic and the Aristotelian. The former, with its focus on the metaphysical, gained new strength with the teachings of Plotinus and his followers Porphyry and Iamblichus. The scientific thought of these Neoplatonists was limited by their distrust of the senses and belief that reality is rarely seen or experienced in human existence. Yet their counterparts the Aristotelians (Peripatetic philosophers) were hardly more successful at science, being so heavily dependent upon the teachings of Aristotle and expending most of their intellectual energy on the task of passing on what the Master said. The leading Aristotelians were Themistius and Boethius.

Exceptions to the dominance of the two schools of thought included Ammianus Marcellinus, a retired soldier who sought to imitate the historian Tacitus and bring forward his chronicle of the Roman Empire to Ammianus's own time, the late fourth century. Ammianus's history of Rome included some thoughtful ruminations on the manners and customs of various peoples and the geography of unfamiliar lands. Another exceptional Late Roman thinker was Zosimus of Panopolis, a fourth-century chemist from Egypt and a student of Porphyry. Zosimus distinguished chemistry from physics and wrote treatises on yeasts, mercury, lime, and distillation apparatuses. He collected an encyclopedia of alchemical processes and terminology.

Upon the collapse of the Roman Empire in the West during the fifth century, most intellectual concerns, including science, fell subject to the violence and chaos of war and the primitive urge to survive in a time of declining trade and agriculture. The Eastern Roman Empire, subsequently called the Byzantine Empire, continued to thrive under energetic emperors as well as thinkers trying to carry the Aristotelian and Platonic torches forward into the future. The legacy of ancient science was seen most dramatically during the period of Byzantine dominance in Eastern Europe during the Middle Ages.

See also Ammianus Marcellinus; Julian; Magic; Neoplatonism; Themistius

References

Dodds, E. R. *Pagan and Christian in an Age of Anxiety.* New York: W. W. Norton, 1965.

Gibbon, Edward. *The Decline and Fall of the Roman Empire.* New York: Modern Library, 1932.

Grant, Michael. *The Climax of Rome.* Boston: Little, Brown, 1968.

Philostratus. *Lives of the Sophists.* Translated by W. C. Wright. Cambridge: Harvard University Press, 1921.

Leucippus (floruit fifth century BCE)

The first scientist to develop a complete theory for a universe based on the existence of an infinite number of atoms, Leucippus influenced generations of physicists and chemists in their search to understand the basic structure, the infinitesimal particles, of the universe. He did not have sophisticated equipment, nor did he practice empirical science. He relied on the teaching of his predecessors, made logical assumptions, and arrived at a theory to explain the structure of matter. Over two millennia later, physicists such as Ernst Rutherford and Niels Bohr confirmed the existence of atoms, which vindicated Leucippus's initial theoretical stab in the dark.

Leucippus was an Ionian Greek, born sometime after 500 BCE somewhere in western Turkey or the islands of the Aegean Sea. Nothing really is known about his life, except that he was influenced by the materialist philosopher Empedocles and the idealists Parmenides and Anaxagoras. Only one line survives from his writings. In *On Mind,* he argued that all things happen by necessity. To the ongoing debate in classical Greece about the nature of the universe, whether it is finite or infinite, fundamentally material or spiritual, created or uncreated, Leucippus contributed his view that the universe is infinite, uncreated, and in constant motion and change. In this he agreed with Empedocles. Beyond the growth and decay that one witnesses in nature and everyday life, Leucippus posited the existence of invisible material bodies, atoms (Greek *atomos*), that are always moving, changing, combining and recombining, and of varying shapes and sizes. Atoms are small enough that we cannot see them, but we feel their presence. How else, Leucippus wondered, can we explain matter, its changes, its variety, unless we realize the existence of atoms? What separates a tree from a stone, a fish from a human, if not the underlying differences in these invisible particles? To speak of particles moving and changing implies some substance or arena in which they move and change. Leucippus argued for the presence of a void or space devoid of particles, of anything. Nevertheless, the void exists. It does not represent "being," the basic fundamental of existence, but rather "nonbeing," the opposite of existence, the opposite of anything. *Nothing* therefore exists, Leucippus argued. Being cannot exist without nonbeing; atoms cannot exist without the void in which they move and act.

He naturally used his atomic theory to explain the origins and extent of the universe. According to Diogenes Laertius, Leucippus argued that atoms of like form are attracted to the center of a "vortex," a swirling mass; unlike atoms are thrust outside the vortex. The vortex eventually forms a central spherical body, such as the earth; other atoms form the stars and other planets. Leucippus believed that such a process occurs infinitely, leading to a host of other worlds and stars. The planets orbit the earth, which is at the center of a solar system. The sun orbits at the extreme. The brightness of the sun, stars, and moon derives from their movement, the friction of which, one gathers, induces fire. Leucippus hypothesized that the earth is broad in the middle, like a drum or, as Thomas Heath (1913) says, tambourine. The earth swirls around at the center on an axis that tilts toward the south. The northern regions of the earth are damp and frozen; the southern regions hot and on fire.

Leucippus initiated a school of thought that would have a major impact on subsequent science and philosophy, not only in the ancient world, but through all centuries to the present. His most famous disciples were Democritus, Epicurus, and Zeno. From Leucippus's basic supposition, the philosophies of Epicureanism and Stoicism would spring. His would be a philosophy in constant opposition to the idealism of Plato and Christian philosophers. Leucippus's atomic theory would be resurrected two thousand years later by scientists such as Robert Boyle, who called atoms "corpuscles." Boyle's corpuscular theories went a long way toward sustaining the scientific revolution of the sixteenth, seventeenth, and eighteenth centuries. Ironically, over these past two millennia, knowledge of Leucippus has dwindled to almost nothing, while knowledge of his theory has come to dominate the world of science.

See also Astronomy; Atoms; Democritus; Epicureanism; Greek Classical Age; Physical Sciences

References
Barnes, Jonathan, trans. *Early Greek Philosophy.* London: Penguin Books, 1987.
Heath, Sir Thomas. *Aristarchus of Samos.* New York: Dover Books, 1913.
Laertius, Diogenes. *Lives of the Philosophers.* Translated by R. D. Hicks. 2 vols. Cambridge: Harvard University Press, 1931, 1938.
Leicester, Henry M. *The Historical Background of Chemistry.* New York: Dover Books, 1971.

Life Sciences

The beginnings of life sciences in the ancient world were associated with interest in magic and the belief that the divine often used natural phenomena such as animals to prophesy and fulfill what has been fated to occur. The first botanists were scientists interested in creating a materia medica of plants and herbs that could be used in healing, especially in association with incantations and spells. The first biologists studied life in relation to the divine, seeing in the natural the supernatural, assuming that humans have a direct link with the gods. The first zoologists were soothsayers who examined sacrificial animals to determine the future and priests who conceived of deities with animal characteristics. In time the supernatural and magic became dissociated from the natural and real, and a true life science was born.

According to Plutarch *(Natural Questions),* some of the first Greek scientists, such as Anaxagoras, Plato, and Democritus, believed that plants were but animals riveted to the soil. Anaxagoras claimed that humans are superior to animals because of their use of analytical and conceptual thought. Herodotus,

during the fifth century BCE, reported after a trip to Egypt that the Egyptians had a complete materia medica and were knowledgeable about many plants. The Egyptians had discovered the qualities of the lotus plant: they harvested it, ate the root, which was a sweet like a fruit, and dried the head, a poppy, and made bread out of it. They also collected a plant called kiki, which produced something like castor oil, which they used like olive oil, though Herodotus found the smell annoying. The papyrus plant was harvested to make paper and used in constructing reed boats but was also good for eating when baked. Herodotus also observed or heard about crocodiles, the ibis, hippopotami, and elephants. He correctly reported on the characteristics of the crocodile, pointing out how its lower jaw is stationary while the upper jaw opens wide to gorge itself on food. Always in search of the remarkable, Herodotus claimed that the crocodile allowed the sandpiper to pick leeches out of its open mouth. Herodotus was fascinated by fowl and provided an interesting description of the ibis. He was also credulous enough to report on the phoenix, though confessing that he had never seen one himself. He reported on the reproductive cycle of fish. Bolos of Mende, a contemporary of Herodotus, wrote *On Sympathies and Antipathies,* in which he classified flora and fauna based on the four elements. He also penned *On Natural Drugs.*

Aristotle was very interested in plant and animal life and relied on his student Alexander for specimens of the flora and fauna of Asia. Aristotle was a collector and cataloger of flora and fauna. Aristotle's *Description of Animals, Parts of Animals,* and *Generation of Animals* compared humans with animals, assuming that the latter, like the former, participated in Being and had similar behavior and physical attributes. Aristotle, like his teacher Plato, conceived of a chain of being that allowed for the categorization of animals according to their physical and spiritual characteristics. Aristotle's student Theophrastus,

Ancient peoples relied on herbal medicine, including concoctions made from squeezing animal skins filled with herbs. In this image from Egypt, two women skilled in materia medica produce liquid medicine from herbs. (Bettmann/Corbis)

the Greek Peripatetic and master of the Lyceum, produced an encyclopedic *Enquiry into Plants* in which he provided a system of classifying plants according to type, function, usefulness, and healing qualities. Another important Hellenistic life scientist was Nicander of Colophon, a physician, who, during the second century BCE, wrote on agriculture, beekeeping, and poisonous plants and reptiles.

Roman thinkers continued to speculate on the distinctions between animals and humans. Pliny, a typical Roman thinker, echoed Aristotle's comments comparing beasts and humans. Humans are at the pinnacle of the animal scale of being and the only creature to exhibit consistent rational thought and behav-

ior. Pliny did, however, conceive of animals showing remarkable humanlike characteristics, such as pity, logical (if rudimentary) thought, piety, empathy, a sense of duty. The honeybee had social and behavioral characteristics similar to Rome under the Republic. Pliny was naïve in many respects about human and animal life, assuming that in the far reaches of Asia and Africa strange creatures and humans with odd characteristics existed. Many Roman biologists were polymaths like Pliny. Another was Plutarch, whose vast corpus of writings included the *Natural Questions,* in which he explored remarkable phenomena, such as the ability of the octopus to change color to deceive prey and predators.

Pliny's contemporaries Crateus and Dioscorides were herbalists and botanists who created an extensive pharmacology. Dioscorides traveled with Roman armies as a physician—he collected specimens of flora and fauna, and he published a complete materia medica. In some respects Dioscorides was the first real Roman pharmacist—he wrote a pharmacology that listed hundreds of floral remedies. One of the last famous Roman life scientists was Aelian, who penned *On the Characteristics of Animals* at the beginning of the third century. Aelian was a credulous rather than a critical observer and filled his *Characteristics of Animals* with anecdotes and the miraculous.

See also Aelian, Claudius; Aristotle; Herodotus of
    Halicarnassus; Pliny the Elder; Theophrastus
References
Aelian. *On the Characteristics of Animals.* 3 vols.
    Translated by A. F. Scholfield. Cambridge:
    Harvard University Press, 1971.
Herodotus. *The Histories.* Translated by Aubrey de
    Selincourt. Harmondsworth, Middlesex:
    Penguin Books, 1972.
Pliny the Elder. *Natural History.* Translated by John
    F. Healy. London: Penguin Books, 1991.
Technology Museum of Thessaloniki website:
    www.tmth.edu.

Logic
See Aristotle

Logos

Logos is one of the few Greek ideas that continues to be argued among intellectuals and scientists as the third millennium CE begins. The great debate among Greek scientists during the first millennium BCE involved the question, What is the creative force, the underlying reality, of the universe? Philosophers by the time of Thales and his successors had abandoned the simplistic belief in the Greek gods—but what was to replace Zeus, the Fates, Hades, the nymphs, the great mother goddess Cybele, and Athena? What else, but the "logos." Logos, the *word,* represented to ancient thinkers the universal transcendence, the creative expression of the universal mind.

Logos derives from the Greek verb *legein,* meaning "to say, tell, count." It had a variety of different meanings in the ancient world. The first poets and historians, such as Herodotus, referred to the spirit of truth guiding their work as the logos. Aristotle referred to the logos as a principle of scientific or philosophic language or a principle of existence, of being. This latter view was adopted by the philosopher Zeno of Alexandria, who lived at the beginning of the third century BCE. Zeno argued that logos is the eternal idea or word, the source of all being. Humans derive from the logos and return to the logos. Human behavior and society that imitates the harmony of the universal logos will achieve happiness. This happiness, however, is limited to the duration of human existence. Zeno tried to bridge the gap between the idealist philosophers such as Plato and Parmenides, who believed being was a force of mind, of spirit, and the materialists Heraclitus and Democritus, who believed that being was material rather than spiritual—being is a substance. Zeno's theory was that logos is material and spiritual, a substance and an idea.

Zeno founded the philosophy of Stoicism, which along with Epicureanism was the route that the logos generally took from 300 BCE to 200 CE. Stoic and Epicurean philosophers were attracted to a concept that combines in one phenomenon thought and action, body and soul, time and eternity, creation and destruction. Marcus Aurelius, the most famous Stoic philosopher, interpreted the logos as the holy spirit, the divine fire. Logos created and destroyed—gave life, then took it. Logos made up all existence, each and every thing, each individual. The Stoics put a new twist on the dualism of body and soul, matter and spirit, arguing that the soul is invisible, spiritual, yet also material. All ideas, all truth, are material. One's soul consists of atoms, which will be rearranged upon one's death. The soul lasts only as long as the body does. The logos is in each human even as it transcends each human. Philo, a Jewish writer who lived in Alexandria at the end of the first century BCE and the beginning of the first century CE, adapted Platonic and Stoic thinking about the logos to Hebrew thought. Philo argued that the logos is something like the mind of the eternal, unknowable God; the logos is knowable since it is knowledge itself.

The Epicurean and Stoic logos was an impersonal, anonymous force of creation and destruction. Other thinkers of the ancient world sought a more personal force of creation, a being who encompassed and transcended each individual, who brought about life and then embraced us at death. John, the disciple of Jesus of Nazareth, conceived of Jesus as the logos, the timeless word, the eternal transcendence that encompassed body and soul, life and death, truth, God. "In the beginning was the word," wrote John, "the word was with God, and the word was God." According to the Gospel of John, "the word was made flesh, and dwelt among us" as Jesus, the Christ. "All things were made by" the word. He is the being that unites and transcends all being. (King James Version)

The concept of logos, and the debate surrounding it, is not only ancient, but very modern, very real. Scientists still wonder about the origins of life, of the universe, of being. Philosophers still wonder whether being is material or spiritual. Christians still argue that Christ was and is the logos, the "defining principle" of Aristotle, the "word" of Zeno, the "holy spirit" of Marcus Aurelius.

See also Aurelius, Marcus; Epicureanism; Epicurus; Hellenism; New Testament; Stoicism

References

Aurelius, Marcus. *Meditations.* Translated by Maxwell Staniforth. Harmondsworth, Middlesex: Penguin Books, 1964.

Barnes, Jonathan, trans. *Early Greek Philosophy.* London: Penguin Books, 1987.

Boardman, John, Jasper Griffin, and Oswyn Murray. *Oxford History of the Classical World.* Oxford: Oxford University Press, 1986.

New Oxford Annotated Bible with the Apocrypha. Oxford: Oxford University Press, 1977.

Lucretius (floruit first century BCE)

Titus Lucretius Carus was the most famous disciple, as well as the greatest exponent, of the teachings of the Greek philosopher Epicurus. Lucretius's poem, *On the Nature of Things,* is an account of the structure of the universe, written in verse according to Epicurean philosophy. *On the Nature of Things* is the work of a polymath who used the Epicurean philosophy of materialism to describe and explain matter, motion, mind, soul, body, society, and natural phenomena. The essence of all things, he argued, is found in constantly moving, indestructible yet invisible objects: atoms.

Lucretius lived during the first half of the first century BCE. Romans of the second and first centuries actively embraced Greek culture and philosophy in the wake of the Roman political conquest of the Greek world in the decades after 200 BCE. Scientists, philosophers, physicians, and teachers were typically Greeks writing in Greek. Lucretius, like his contemporary Cicero, was an exception: Lucretius was a Latin poet and a Roman writing Greek philosophy. His philosophy was formed by the fourth-century BCE Greek atomist Epicurus who, along with his forebears Leucippus and Democritus, advocated a materialist philosophy that shunned the spiritual and metaphysical, branding as superstitions such beliefs.

Leucippus, Democritus, and Epicurus, the atomists, hypothesized that atoms were the fundamental structures of existence. All life, spiritual as well as material, as well as the world, planets, the stars and sun, were made of invisible particles constantly in motion. Gods may or may not exist—in any case, they are irrelevant. Perhaps mind, beauty, the good, the word, being exist; if so atoms are the components of what other philosophers considered to be grand metaphysical, spiritual forces. Nothing could be further from the thought of Parmenides, Socrates, and Plato than atoms. The atomists believed that speculation on the spiritual world can be unending and unsubstantiated by the senses and experience. They demanded that explanations of existence be reduced to common sense and the evidence of the senses. This radical empiricism required a disbelief in anything that could not be seen, heard, smelled, touched, or tasted. Everything else must be the products of overactive imaginations. The atomists allowed themselves one general supposition. There must be a force that causes the movement in things detected by humans. This force must be the basis of cause, of *the nature of things,* hence the fundamental causative force in the universe. But cause, like all of existence, must result from a thing—something material, composed of matter—not an idea.

Lucretius, in support of the empirical arguments of the atomists, used the example of wind. The senses allow humans to detect the presence of the hot winds of summer and the cool breezes of winter. The phenomenon itself is invisible to the eye, but humans can trace it in blowing leaves, the dust being hurled about in a storm, the waves being whipped up, and the billowing sails of a ship at sea. Something that is invisible yet sensed by taste, smell, touch, and hearing clearly exists, and clearly has a material basis. But it is so small that the sense of sight cannot detect it. It is so small it cannot be made smaller, cannot be cut (Greek, *atomos*). The irreducible form of matter that makes up the essence of all things is the atom.

In *On the Nature of Things,* Lucretius took many pains to hypothesize the qualities and characteristics of the atom. Since nothing cannot exist, the atom must be indestructible, eternal, and infinite. Atoms clearly move and cause motion and thus cannot be packed together without space in between. There must be vacuity, a vacuum, in which atoms move. Atoms make up all that is. They are of different sizes, colors, combinations, and patterns. One thing differs from another because of atomic structure. Lucretius and the atomists did not hypothesize the presence of the electron, proton, and neutron. That discovery awaited the atomists of the twentieth century.

Rather, Lucretius realized that there must be at least a part that is irreducible—that this atom must be infinite in number and composition because otherwise there must exist a limit on things, and he could not envision such a limit. Limitless atoms meant a limitless universe.

This notion of the limitless universe, which had its origins with Greek philosophers such as Parmenides and was later embraced by the atomists, was a true revolution in thought. The limitless universe frees humans from impositions on their power and free will. It frees creation from limits posed on its extent, quantity, and reproductivity. A limitless universe can host limitless time, limitless motion, limitless types of living beings, limitless stars and planets, limitless universes.

Limitless was the anonymous power and impersonal will exercised by atoms in their capacity as building blocks of the four elements. Like Democritus and before him Empedocles, Lucretius assumed that earth, air, fire, and water made up all things—and making up the four elements were atoms. Without mind, or will, or fate, atoms determined the universe, even if the particulars were never clear. But one knew that from atoms one was born, and to the atoms one would go upon death. There was no escape.

Lucretius believed humans had a limited power in their ability to grasp the infiniteness in scope, power, and duration of atoms. Once one knew the simple truth, everything could be understood. This was clearly the goal of *On the Nature of Things,* which was unfinished at Lucretius's early and untimely death. He was prepared to take on all topics that had occupied the minds of past philosophers. His atomic theory allowed an explanation of reality, of birth and death, of the mind and soul, of the senses, of emotions, of thought and imagination, of sex and conception. Lucretius conceived of the universe evolving over time from a massive disjointed mixture of atoms at the beginning of time to their subsequent coagulation into distinct forms—the stars, planets, sun, moon, and earth. The earth itself was initially water, but the deep was heated by the fire of the sun and slowly dried to reveal earth. Above and surrounding the earth is the air, and beyond that, ether. The heavenly bodies are buoyed by the air in the ether and rotate around the solid earth, the most substantial, heaviest, and central unmoved body. The sun, a ball of fire, daily crosses from horizon to horizon, only to sink below the earth and then be regenerated again in the morning. For regeneration from the countless atoms is the nature of things. More convincing was Lucretius's argument that the moon reflects the light of the sun and becomes full or wanes according to its position respecting the sun's rays.

When considering the origins of humans, Lucretius found himself in a dilemma. The Greeks and Romans, like most peoples, assumed a divine role in the astonishing creation of man. Lucretius, however, was obliged by his atomic theory to conclude that humans and animals simply emerged from the atomic mix. Earth, like a young mother, bore her children, but not consciously, not purposefully. In an attempt to reconcile myth and science, Lucretius hypothesized that the earth also generated monsters of every sort. Anticipating Darwin, Lucretius proposed that such monsters became extinct because they were unable to find sufficient food and adapt to the environment. Lucretius stuck to the old assumption of Homer and Hesiod that the first humans were strong and heroic, yet primitive and savage. His portrait of early man had an interesting evolutionary tint to it. The first humans were primitive, without laws or morals, living according to the naked laws of nature. In time, mutual survival brought humans together into society. Fire tamed their savagery. Civilization emerged—social structure, laws, cities, trade, metallurgy, and organized religion. This latter development Lucretius blamed on human ignorance. The human mind assigns to mysterious phenomena the agency of the divine. Lucretius, in short, composed an anthropology of humans struggling to survive, lifting themselves from

the simple struggle of life, developing agriculture to sustain a growing population and to generate wealth, and creating the arts and sciences to make life comfortable, to express joy in song, and to recover the past in verse and prose. It was not Prometheus who gave fire and civilizing arts and sciences to humans. Rather, the generations of men struggling against time and nature developed a unique, sophisticated society.

Lucretius concluded *On the Nature of Things* with a fascinating scientific potpourri. He began with meteorology. Thunder, he argued, occurs because of the clash of clouds, wind blowing through them, and the rupture of clouds, like the burst of a bladder filled with air. Thunder, of course, follows close on the heels of lightning, which is produced with atoms of fire, inherent in clouds, which are forced to emerge from clouds by the wind. Mountaintops are often cloudy due to the force of the wind driving condensed "cloudlets" up craggy slopes to the summits.

The wind, the agent of causation in Lucretius's meteorology, skims the surfaces of rivers and seas, collecting atoms of moisture, which form eventually in clouds. Moisture-swollen clouds release rain. Sunlight reflects on raindrops to produce the rainbow. The wind is also responsible for earthquakes. The largely hollow earth serves as a pathway for violent winds that, along with raging seas and massive caverns, sometimes topple mountains and collapse caves—an earthquake on the surface of the earth is the result. Winds soar through hollow mountains, collecting atoms of fire and producing volcanic eruptions.

Last, Lucretius considered magnets and epidemics. The strange power of attraction and repulsion exhibited by magnetic stones was due, once again, to the unusual behavior of atoms. Air is found among atoms in all things. When the atoms from a magnet stone emerge outward toward a piece of iron, the air is scattered, creating a vacuum, which forces the iron to move toward the magnet. Lucretius concluded *On the Nature of Things* with a description of plague. Some atoms are destructive to humans and animals. The quality of air varies from place to place; the air of one country that is healthy to its inhabitants is dangerous to the foreigner. Unfortunately, one does not have to travel to a foreign country to be infected by the plague-ridden atoms of dangerous air. Air masses move about the world; some arrive in neighborhoods from distant places carrying their dangerous atomic cargo. Thus epidemics and plagues result.

The concluding pages of Lucretius's *On the Nature of Things* provides a brutally real description of plague—the suffering, torture, horror, fear, and death. Strangely, this was a fit conclusion to the book. The Epicurean philosophy had little room for happiness, salvation, grace, and redemption. Life is slow death. Pain is ubiquitous. The universe is morally and emotionally dead, an anonymous and unfeeling force. One must have low expectations, seek the path of least resistance, avoid pain, accept the few and simple pleasures life has to offer. Death cannot be avoided, nor must it be feared. Death brings annihilation—a lack of knowing, an end of feeling, which, in Lucretius's world, is not altogether bad.

See also Atoms; Epicureanism; Epicurus; Roman Principate; Stoicism

References
Lucretius. *The Nature of the Universe.* Translated by R. E. Latham. Harmondsworth, Middlesex: Penguin Books, 1951.
Ogilvie, R. M. *Roman Literature and Society.* Harmondsworth, Middlesex: Penguin Books, 1980.

Lyceum

The Lyceum was founded by Aristotle after his return to Athens in 334 BCE. Upon Plato's death in 347, Speusippus, rather than Aristotle, took over as head of Plato's school, the Academy; Aristotle left Athens and went to the small kingdom in the Troad ruled by Hermias, a former student at the Academy. There the philosopher stayed, marrying the king's niece, until King Philip of Macedon, an old acquaintance, invited the philosopher to be tutor to the prince Alexander. After Alexander's accession to power and invasion of the Persian Empire, Aristotle returned to Athens, where he established his own school, the Lyceum, its curricula and methodology contrasting to the Academy. The Lyceum was named for a grove in Athens sacred to Apollo.

The Lyceum was famous for its Peripatetic approach to teaching: Aristotle enjoyed strolling about the groves of the park, discoursing to his students—rather like Socrates did a century before, and Aristotle himself did with Alexander and other select students at Macedon ten years before. Aristotle also gave public lectures of his philosophy and science, which were taken down by students and eventually published in a similar format.

Upon the death of Alexander in 323, Aristotle retired from the Lyceum, and his student Theophrastus took over leadership of the school. Theophrastus was a polymath like his teacher and the organizer (perhaps) of Aristotle's papers. Theophrastus himself taught in the Peripatetic fashion, and his students took down his lectures and had them published. The garden of the Lyceum was not only where Theophrastus experimented with his floral studies, but also where he was buried, just as his teacher Aristotle had been.

See also Academy; Aristotle; Athens; Greek Classical Age; Peripatetic School; Theophrastus

Reference
Wheelwright, Philip, ed. and trans. *Aristotle.* New York: Odyssey Press, 1951.

M

Magi

The Magi were the wise men, identified in the New Testament book of Matthew, who followed an eastern star from Anatolia to Judaea where they found the Christ child lying in a manger beneath it. Mediterranean writers who wrote extensively on the magi, such as Hermippus, Eudemius, Xanthus, and Theopompus, typically identified them as followers of Zoroaster, the Persian mystic who explained the world according to an eternal battle between Good (Ahura Mazda) and Evil (Ahriman). For Zoroastrians, as well as for the magi, astrology was extremely important, for by identifying the stars and knowing their movements, even predicting their movements, one might know, predict, the future. According to Diogenes Laertius, the magi believed that they had the ability to pull shapes from the air, hence to see what others cannot. The historian Dinon claimed that Zoroaster means literally "star worshipper," which fits the worldview of the astrologer and the magician. Matthew 2:10–11 describes how the Magi followed the star until it stopped over a house in Bethlehem, wherein was the newborn Jesus—the Magi brought gifts and worshipped him whom they associated with the star. Some Asian goddesses, such as As-

tarte and Ishtar, were identified with astral phenomena—one wonders whether or not the Magi stopped to worship the Virgin Mary as well. Other Mediterranean writers associated magi with Chaldeans, who were astrologers and soothsayers of Babylon, and gymnosophists, who were the wise men of India. Clearchus of Soli, according to Diogenes Laertius, claimed that gymnosophists were latter-day magi.

Pliny the Elder, who could be very superstitious, nevertheless condemned the magi for ridiculous magical tricks and fantasies. He believed that the magi, and their leader Zoroaster, originated the use of magic in Asia, from which it spread to Greece. The magi employed their dark arts in reputed healings, poisonings, and fortune-telling. Pliny recalled a magus he had once known, who claimed that a certain herb *(cynocephalia)* was useful to prevent black magic from being employed against oneself, but if one pulled it from the ground, roots and all, it was lethal. Pliny, nevertheless, did not doubt that the magi knew the use of magic. To block their spells he advised the use of asbestos.

The magi most likely were religious leaders under the Achaeminian dynasty of Persian kings initiated by Cyrus in the sixth century

Portrait of the Magi worshipping the Christ child by sixteenth-century Renaissance artist Quentin Massys. New York Metropolitan Museum of Art. (Kathleen Cohen)

BCE. Zoroaster himself might date from this time. Some scholars believe that Zoroaster was a Mede, and that the magi as a whole were derived from a Median caste of religious leaders.

See also Babylon; Diogenes Laertius; Magic; Mesopotamia; New Testament

References
Ghirshman, R. *Iran: From the Earliest Times to the Islamic Conquest.* Harmondsworth, Middlesex: Penguin Books, 1954.
Laertius, Diogenes. *Lives of the Philosophers.* Translated by R. D. Hicks. 2 vols. Cambridge: Harvard University Press, 1931, 1938.
Oxford Companion to the Bible. Oxford: Oxford University Press, 1993.
Pliny the Elder. *Natural History.* Translated by John F. Healy. London: Penguin Books, 1991.
The Holy Bible, Containing the Old and New Testaments. New York: American Bible Society, 1865.

Magic

Magic was widely used in the ancient world as a means of manipulating or bringing about forces of nature. Magic involved astrology, soothsaying, the reliance upon omens, sacrifice, spells, and incantations. Magic is a word derived by the Greeks from the class of holy and wise men of Persia and the East, the magi, and their founder Zoroaster. Diogenes Laertius, the author of *Lives of the Philosophers,* claimed that Zoroaster was the first magician. The Roman scientist Pliny likewise blamed magic on the magi, specifically Zoroaster. Pliny condemned magic (and the magi) not because it was false, but because it was wrong and sometimes led people to believe in nonsensical potions and spells. Pliny indicated that a Persian who accompanied Xerxes on his expedition against the Greeks in 480 BCE, Othanes, wrote a book on magic that had a profound impact on the Greeks.

Magic, of course, developed in Paleolithic and Neolithic times when ancient humans sought to feel the spiritual forces inherent in nature and to encourage their presence and their benevolence. The shaman in primitive societies is the religious leader who practices his magical arts to bring about the good harvest, the successful hunt, the safety of the tribe, and the healing of the sick. The shaman's work is protoscientific, as is magic itself. Hence, in ancient civilized societies, such as Mesopotamia and Egypt, soothsayers and diviners had the important role of divining what fate had in store for a person or the community at large. There was much empathy in this science—feeling what nature might bring, hoping to see a sign, observing nature, and practicing sacrifice to discover what the predetermined future held.

Magic was often associated with influencing the divine in respect to the afterlife. Egypt, the first society to develop a clear sense of a blessed afterlife, often relied on magical incantations (as prescribed in the Egyptian *Book of the Dead*) to influence the judge Osiris by altering the weight of the heart, making it lighter and not weighed down with sin. Soothsayers and diviners were especially prevalent throughout the ancient world and in ancient literature. The *Iliad* begins with the advice of the diviner skilled in reading the hidden message of fate inherent in the flight of birds. According to Plutarch, Roman diviners used a staff called a *lituus* to mark the sky conceptually for ease in watching the flight of birds. The gods spoke as well through the organs of sacrificial animals, particularly the livers of goats or bulls. The soothsayer was an expert at reading what the liver had to tell a people. Many ancient leaders, warriors, and kings had their minds changed and their actions altered by the shape of a liver.

The Chaldeans, the wise men of ancient Babylon, were infamous practitioners of magic who grew legendary among ancient historians and commentators. They were known to be experts at foretelling the future because of their expertise in astrology. They were practitioners of medicine and were often identified as physicians in early law codes. The Chaldeans and magi are good examples of the close association of magic and science in the ancient world.

See also Astronomy; Babylon; Magi; Paganism
References
Cassirer, Ernst. *An Essay on Man.* New Haven: Yale University Press, 1944.
Neugebauer, O. *The Exact Sciences in Antiquity.* New York: Dover Books, 1969.

Magna Graecia

Magna Graecia, "Greater Greece," was a region in southern Italy settled by Greek colonists in the eighth and seventh centuries BCE. This area of the foot of Italy, along with neighboring Greek states across the Strait of Messina in Sicily, became the leading center of scientific culture in the western Mediterranean during the first millennium BCE. Acragas and Syracuse in Sicily and Thourioi, Croton, Elea, and Tarentum in Italy were cities founded originally as colonies of the more established Greek city-states of Corinth, Athens, and Rhodes. Magna Graecia was the home of some of the greatest philosophers and scientists of the ancient world, such as Pythagoras of Croton, Empedocles of Acragas, Parmenides of Elea, and Herodotus of Thourioi.

Diogenes Laertius, the Late Roman biographer of philosophers and scientists, distinguished between the Italian school of Pythagoras, Xenophanes, and Democritus and the Ionian school of Thales, Anaximander, and Anaximenes. Not everyone in the Italian school lived in Italy. Diogenes used a geographic convenience to separate the philosophers of "becoming" from the philosophers of "being." The founder of the Italian school, Pythagoras, was more of a thinker who focused on "being"; yet it was from his home in Croton that Pythagoras founded a school of thought that would produce many of the greatest philosophers of the ancient world, most of whom focused on "becoming," change and movement, rather than "being," which is the stable and transcendent counter to change.

Alcmaeon was a student of Pythagoras from Croton in southern Italy. He was a thorough Pythagorean in thought and inclination, a physician, and an astronomer. Other natives of Croton who were Pythagoreans included Hippo and Philolaus. Another of Pythagoras's disciples was Empedocles, from Acragas in southern Sicily. Empedocles, like most Pythagoreans, was interested in Orphism (a mystery religion dedicated to the cult of Orpheus). Empedocles wrote on natural phenomena, biology, and medicine. Acragans were also devoted to the worship of Asclepius, and we can assume the same for Empedocles. Thurii (Thourioi) was another important town of Magna Graecia. An Athenian colony, Thurii claimed to be a town where Pythagoras had lived at one point in his life. Perhaps this explains why Thurii had a school of seers. Hippodamus, the Ionian city designer from Miletus, was said to have designed Thurii. Thurii was also the place where the great historian and geographer Herodotus rested after his long life of travel. Timaeus, a philosopher of Locri in southern Italy, was a Pythagorean, mathematician, and astronomer and a central character in Plato's book of the same name. Another town in Magna Graecia, Elea, became home to the Eleatic school of philosophers, the most famous of whom were Parmenides and Zeno.

See also Alcmaeon; Diogenes Laertius; Eleatic School; Empedocles; Hippo of Croton; Philolaus; Pythagoras
References
Barnes, Jonathan, trans. *Early Greek Philosophy.* London: Penguin Books, 1987.
Freeman, Kathleen. *Greek City-States.* New York: W. W. Norton, 1950.
Laertius, Diogenes. *Lives of the Philosophers.* Translated by R. D. Hicks. 2 vols. Cambridge: Harvard University Press, 1931, 1938.

Marine Science

The mysteries of seas and oceans intrigued ancient humans, even as they tried to penetrate the vastness of the earth's waters and conquer their intuitive fear of what lay hidden beneath the "wine dark sea." The Hebrews believed that God formed the waters of the deep stocked with sea creatures and monsters during the first three days of creation. Noah became the first shipbuilder and navigator when called upon by God to build an ark—one of fantastic dimensions to withstand the forty days and nights of rain that resulted in the inundation of the earth and the death of all animals and humans except those on the ark. Gilgamesh found the key to ageless youth on the ocean floor after visiting the Sumerian Noah, Upnashitim. Homer placed Hades in the river Ocean west of the Pillars of Heracles, the Strait of Gibraltar. Odysseus was driven by the angry god of the sea, Poseidon, all around the mysterious Mediterranean. The sea came closest to defeating the most resourceful man in Homer's poems. The Greeks were so certain that the ocean was a place of mystery—like the dark forests and the high mountains—that they populated it

with countless Nereides, maidens of the sea, as well as varied sea monsters—such as Charybdis, the whirlpool that engulfed many of Odysseus's men, and the clashing rocks that met Jason's *Argo*.

The modern student looks mostly in vain for the beginnings of oceanography in the ancient world. The mysteries of the ocean remained mostly mysteries, the stuff of fantasy and legend. Among the Greeks there were a few thinkers who tried to move from fantasy to fact regarding the ocean. Thales thought that water was the basic element of all things. His student Anaximander went further, declaring that humans evolved from the sea. The third-century CE Roman writer Censorinus declared that Anaximander thought that humans derived from fish. Plutarch wrote that some Greeks revered Poseidon because they believed that humans originally came from the sea. Xenophanes argued that the oceans produced meteorological events such as the wind and rain. He recognized fossils of sea creatures for what they were and speculated on the inundation of the earth that had occurred in the past and would occur again to destroy humankind.

The science of navigation was primitive in the ancient world. Even the best Phoenician and Greek navigators hugged the coasts, venturing out into the open sea only on starlit nights and clear days when they could use Polaris, the Pleiades, Sirius, and constellations or the position of the sun to indicate latitude.

By and large, ancient marine science was focused on navigation and shipbuilding. The earliest boats were primitive rafts and canoes made of reeds, wood, and skin. Early Mesopotamians fashioned coracles from skin stretched over wooden frames. Canoes were made of dugout trunks and buoyant bark. The Polynesians rigged canoes with sails to explore the South Pacific. Ancient Incas of South America, according to Thor Heyerdahl, built balsa rafts that allowed them to sail west to Easter Island, Micronesia, and Polynesia.

Larger ships were made from the acacia tree and papyrus reeds. The Ark, according to the book of Genesis, was made of these materials, as were Egyptian boats. Herodotus described boats of the Nile as made of acacia wood cut into planks for the hull and decking. No ribs were used, which made the boats useful only for river navigation. The Egyptians used the papyrus plant to caulk the ships and to make sails. Rather than building the ship first by laying the keel and joining ribs to it, Mesopotamian and Egyptian shipbuilders fashioned the hull of the ship to the keel without ribs, using mortise-and-tenon joints to join planks to keel. Papyrus rope bound through mortises helped provide stability otherwise provided by the ribs of the ship. Because of this shell mode of construction, such ships were hardly seaworthy, and ancient Mesopotamian and Egyptian shipbuilders devised a method of constructing seaworthy ships from papyrus reeds. Thor Heyerdahl, the foremost archeologist and historian of the ancient reed ship, has described (1980) the strong possibility of ancient reed ships being able to navigate the Mediterranean, Red, and Arabian seas, and perhaps others as well. Shipbuilders set two massive bundles of reeds side by side, then roped them together, using papyrus rope as well to make a crescent design by hoisting the bow and stern, fore and aft. A single wooden mast with a papyrus sail propelled the ship. Heyerdahl discovered that papyrus bundles swell in seawater, becoming incredibly buoyant and airtight.

Phoenician and Greek shipbuilders advanced merchant and warship construction by basing the construction of the ship on a keel and rib design. Apollonius of Rhodes, who described the *Argo,* claimed that the shipbuilders bound a strong rope about the sides to provide additional holding power to the planks to withstand being battered by the swells of the sea. The single mast was secured in a mast-box and pulled taut by ropes secured fore and aft. Greek and Phoenician ships relied heavily on rowers—the Phoenicians developed the two-row system of oars, the bireme; the Greeks added a third row, the trireme. According to Herodotus, Phoenician

Phoenician trading ship of the first century CE. (Gianni Dagli Orti / Corbis)

ships were sufficiently seaworthy to circumnavigate Africa, negotiating the strong winds and currents off the Cape of Good Hope and the Horn of Africa. Roman merchant vessels were even more seaworthy. Roman shipbuilders constructed their boats with deeper drafts, though they still were heavily reliant on oars to complement the single mast and sail.

See also Anaximander of Miletus; Apollonius of Perga; Phoenicians, Xenophanes of Colophon

References

Apollonius of Rhodes. *The Voyage of Argo.* Translated by E. V. Rieu. Harmondsworth, Middlesex: Penguin Books, 1971.

Barnes, Jonathan, trans. *Early Greek Philosophy.* London: Penguin Books, 1987.

Bass, George F. "Sea and River Craft in the Ancient Near East." Vol. 3, in *Civilizations of the Ancient Near East.* 4 vols., ed. Jack Sasson et al. New York: Charles Scribner's Sons, 1995.

Casson, Lionel. *Ships and Seamanship in the Ancient World.* Princeton: Princeton University Press, 1971.

Herodotus. *The Histories.* Translated by Aubrey de Selincourt. Harmondsworth, Middlesex: Penguin Books, 1972.

Heyerdahl, Thor. *Early Man and the Ocean: A Search for the Beginning of Navigation and Seaborne Civilizations.* New York: Vintage Books, 1980.

"Ship." *Encyclopedia Britannica,* vol. 20 (1962).

Mathematics

Mathematics as an activity of abstract science began with the early human fascination for number, and not only as the amount of items, but number as an abstract concept as well. The ancients conceived of *one,* a singularity, the whole of all things; *two,* a dualism, the counterpart of one thing with another, such as good and evil; *three,* the additional substance or idea that includes what is not either the one or the other, but in between, a third. Ancient mathematicians also arrived at the concept of place value (of tens, hundreds, thousands, et cetera) in denoting numbers.

Asia

Babylonian mathematicians developed many of the initial ideas and techniques that would characterize Greek mathematics of the first century BCE. Babylonian mathematics, clearly meant for practical rather than merely theoretical purposes, included algebra and simple geometry. They developed quadratic equations and solutions to geometric problems such as the Pythagorean theorem (long before Pythagoras). They worked with coefficients, squares, cubes, and the radii of circles. They were the first to use zero (ca. 400 BCE) as a place-value notation, and the first to divide the circle into 360 degrees. Egyptian mathematicians were not as sophisticated as their Babylonian counterparts. Egyptians used basic arithmetic and fractions largely for practical purposes. The Egyptians did, however, approximate the value of pi (π), the ratio of the circumference of a circle to its diameter. Chinese mathematicians, in the first few centuries of the common era (Liu Hui in the third century CE), gained an approximate

knowledge of π. Later mathematicians such as Archimedes, Vitruvius, and Ptolemy engaged in more intricate studies of π. Some scholars believe that Chinese mathematicians developed an independent knowledge of the Pythagorean theorem. During the first millennium BCE, the use of counting boards and a decimal system developed in China.

The Greeks

Greeks journeying to Iraq in the wake of Alexander's conquests came into contact with Babylonian mathematicians. They adopted the use of zero as a place notation from Babylonians, although the Greeks were the first to use the sign 0, the Babylonians having only a cuneiform symbol. Hellenistic mathematicians discovered irrational numbers and geometric algebra. Greeks combined Babylonian quadratic equations with irrational numbers to form, in Otto Neugebauer's (1957) words, a geometry of algebra.

Hellenistic mathematicians made some of the great discoveries in mathematics. Conic sections, discovered at the beginning of the Hellenistic Age, were studied using algebra by Apollonius in the third century BCE. Eudemus of Rhodes (350–290 BCE), a student of Aristotle who opened an Aristotelian school at Rhodes, wrote a history of mathematics and treatises on arithmetic, astrology, geometry, physics, and angles. Another Rhodian, Geminus, who was heavily influenced by Posidonius's work at Rhodes, wrote a history of mathematics and treatises on geometry and arithmetic. Hypsicles of Alexandria, who was a mathematician and astronomer of the second century CE, wrote in the wake of Euclid a book *On Polyhedrons.* Menelaus, also of Alexandria, in the late first century CE, used trigonometry and geometry in astronomy and to make detailed studies of the sphere. According to the historian of mathematics Reviel Netz, Greek mathematics used very esoteric yet not symbolic language to express mathematical concepts.

See also Apollonius of Perga; Asia, East and South; Egypt; Euclid; Hellenism; Hypatia of Alexandria; Mesopotamia

References

Heath, Sir Thomas. *Aristarchus of Samos.* New York: Dover Books, 1913.

Netz, Reviel. *The Shaping of Deduction in Greek Mathematics.* Cambridge: Cambridge University Press, 2003.

Neugebauer, O. *The Exact Sciences in Antiquity.* New York: Dover Books, 1969.

O'Connor, J. J., and E. F. Robertson. *History of Mathematics:* http://www-history.mcs.st-andrews.ac.uk/history/References/Heron.html (website of School of Mathematics and Statistics, University of St. Andrew's Scotland).

Maximus of Ephesus (floruit fourth century CE)

Maximus is a good example of the degeneration of Greco-Roman thought during the fourth century CE. He was a native of Ephesus in western Turkey and a follower of the Neoplatonist Plotinus and his disciple Iamblichus. Plotinus's esoteric and metaphysical Neoplatonic thought had been watered down a century after his death to become the province of magicians and astrologers. One of these was Maximus, who used magic and divination and the formulaic incantations of the *Chaldaean Oracles* to convince the gullible of his power and influence over nature and the gods. Maximus's most famous pupil was the emperor Julian the Apostate, who ruled Rome from 361–363 CE.

With the decline of civilization in the Roman Empire after 200 CE, there was very little good philosophy and even less good science. Yet men still yearned to observe nature and exercise power over their environment. Unwilling or unable to engage in clear observation of natural phenomena and engage in systematic ordering of data, intellectuals of the third and fourth centuries turned to pseudoscience, superstition, and the fabulous and remarkable. Julian, the nephew of the emperor Constantine, was a studious and intelligent sort who studied Neoplatonism and Stoicism. He became friends with clearheaded thinkers such as Themistius the philosopher and Libanius the orator. But something in Julian, something about his culture, demanded more than the simple tasks of contemplation and recording of observations.

When Constantine's son Constantius came to power upon his father's death in 337, he and his supporters eliminated rivals to his power, including Julian's family. Julian himself was spared because of his youth—but he was kept under a sort of house arrest. He rejected the Christian teachings of his tutors by the time he was in his teens and sought to study under the great philosophers and scientists of the Greeks. Constantius allowed this, seeing nothing harmful in Julian's search for learning. Julian eventually attached himself to a group of Sophists who were disciples of the aged philosopher Aidesios. Julian studied under one of these men, Eusebius, who was a miracle-worker. One anecdote, described by the biographer Eunapius, has Eusebius criticizing Maximus of Ephesus for his tricks that astonished his observers: he could make the statue of the goddess Hekate smile, and the torches that she held, as well as the hair on her head, would burst into flames at the commands of Maximus. Julian, rather than being incited against Maximus for his theatrics, declared that he wanted to become Maximus's disciple.

Maximus taught a corrupt form of Neoplatonism. The philosophy of Plotinus focused on the unity of all reality in the One, which was too great for human observation or comprehension. Hence Neoplatonists such as Plotinus taught that there were sometimes visible manifestations of the One. Julian was a worshipper of the god Helios, the sun, believed to be a visible representative of the one truth. Maximus taught that the Greek goddess Hekate was a manifestation of the great mother of nature, the warmth and love of the One. Maximus was a theurgist—part theologian, part philosopher, part charlatan, and part magician. Perhaps he believed that his magic was the go-between between humans and the divine. Other scientists of the past and present have believed as much. He and his time of the fourth century CE are good examples of an era when magic was considered science, and science was thought to be magic.

See also Julian; Later Roman Empire; Magic; Neoplatonism

References

Bowersock, G. W. *Julian the Apostate.* Cambridge: Harvard University Press, 1978.

Browning, Robert. *The Emperor Julian.* Berkeley: University of California Press, 1976.

Eunapius. *The Lives of the Sophists.* Translated by W. C. Wright. Cambridge: Harvard University Press, 1968.

Medicine

The most significant figure in the history of medicine was Hippocrates, a Greek of the fifth century BCE who gathered about him a school of thought that detached the study of the human body and disease from the philosophers, astrologers, magicians, and priests. The history of the Mesopotamians and Egyptians includes little evidence that the peoples of the ancient Near East developed the science of medicine much beyond the practices and precepts of their precivilized, Neolithic ancestors. The ancient Sumerians did have a materia medica (pharmaceutical knowledge) of basic salves and analgesics for injuries and pain, but they probably did not develop the sophisticated observation and diagnosis of disease. The Babylonians of Hammurapi's time had surgeons and physicians who could drain tumors, set broken bones, and assist in the healing of other injuries. Likewise Egyptian dentists and physicians could pull teeth, deliver babies, set bones, and prescribe medicine for healing. Their knowledge of anatomy and physiology was rudimentary, though there are records of physicians examining patients and making diagnoses. The Egyptians had an extensive materia medica; the most able physicians were knowledgeable about botany. In Egypt, as elsewhere in the ancient Near East, religious concerns and rituals came before the practice of medicine.

The Semitic Hebrews of the eastern Mediterranean were generally suspicious of healers who advocated cures divorced from the healing power of God (Yahweh). The Old Testament mentions a materia medica that included balsam for wounds and mandrake for infertility. However, healing was entirely up to God and his prophets. For example, in the second book of Kings of the Old Testament, the prophet Elisha heals the Aramaean Naaman through the agency of God, so as to show the power of God. The Temple in Jerusalem was a place where the sick could go for divine healing, though at the time of Jesus of Nazareth, the sick, who were considered unclean by the Pharisees, were restricted from the Temple. The Old Testament and the New Testament identify mental illnesses as caused by demons. The most prevalent physical illness was leprosy, which was loosely used by Hebrew and Christian writers alike to mean a variety of illnesses, chiefly of the skin. The New Testament, like the Old Testament, rarely discusses physicians and medical practice, the few exceptions being to treat them with suspicion.

Greek Medicine

The Greeks of the first millennium BCE had, like their predecessors of the Near East, a superstitious approach to healing. Asclepius was the Greek god of healing. Priests of Asclepius practiced his healing arts; the sick slept in the god's temples to be visited by Asclepius during the night so that they could greet the morning free of illness. Homer's *Iliad* mentions two sons of Asclepius who were active in healing wounded warriors. Indeed Hippocrates was an Asclepiad, a member of a clan or order of physicians that served the god on the island of Cos in the Aegean Sea. The first Greek physician who put aside superstition to approach medicine in realistic, if philosophical, terms was Alcmaeon of Croton in Italy. Alcmaeon was a Pythagorean who developed theories on the nature of disease. Whether or not he was a practicing physician is not clear. Empedocles also had a reputation as a physician, though he was more the seer than the healer. The Asclepiads of Cos also preceded Hippocrates in practicing medicine. How distinct was the "father of medicine" from his fellow Asclepiads is not clear, nor is it certain what of the *Hippocratic Corpus* came from his pen as opposed to others of his association.

Nevertheless, by 400 BCE there existed a body of medical writings that modern scholars consider to be by Hippocrates or from the Hippocratic school of thought. These varied works, called the *Hippocratic Corpus,* propound the theory of the four humors, discuss the impact of the environment on disease and health, prescribe remedies for disease, and describe varied diseases using specific case studies. The Hippocratic approach assumed that the body had a precise balance and that disease reflected an imbalance. Let nature alone, Hippocrates advised, and let disease run its course. The physician sought evidence that one of the four humors—blood, phlegm, black bile, yellow bile—was dominant in the system. The job of the physician was primarily to diagnose the illness and to observe the progress of the patient as the disease took its course, reached a crisis, and then culminated in death or recovery. Near contemporaries of Hippocrates had different approaches to medicine. Petron believed that disease derived from improper diet. Hippon thought moisture was the key to health. Philolaus determined that there were three rather than four humors—bile, blood, phlegm. Thrasymachus focused on an excess of heat or cold. Menerates sought a balance of blood, bile, phlegm, and breath. Largely because of the influence of Hippocrates, the physician became less of an itinerant healer and more a stable member of a community. Some city-states employed physicians for healing the poor. Women physicians specializing in women's health became more prevalent as well.

During the Hellenistic Age Alexandria dominated medical studies chiefly because of the work of Herophilus of Chalcedon and Erasistratus of Ceos, both of whom were concerned with discovering the precise structure and function of the organs and circulatory system. They engaged in empirical study and dissection, discovering much about the brain and nervous system, the eyes, stomach, liver, reproductive systems, blood, and heart. The kings of Egypt, the Ptolemies, supported Herophilus and his students by giving them the corpses of condemned criminals to dissect and study. Unlike Herophilus, Erasistratus rejected Hippocratic theories and focused on diagnosis instead of the prevention of illness. Other important Hellenistic scientists were the female physician Aspasia of Athens and Philistion of Locri, who argued that the soul is located in the heart. Theophrastus, Aristotle's successor at the Lyceum, wrote an extensive study of plants, including some of their medicinal properties.

Roman Medicine

Asclepiades in the first century BCE and Celsus in the first century CE were the leading Roman physicians before Galen. The Epicurean Asclepiades believed that physical health and disease were the product of the movement and combinations of invisible atoms; his was a "mechanistic" view of medicine. He was nevertheless tireless in treating malarial patients, the mentally disturbed, and those with arthritic complaints. Celsus, on the other hand, was a polymath who wrote on medicine, a compendium of Hippocratic teachings and Greek medical techniques and terminology. By the beginning of the second century CE, Roman medicine, based on Greek models, particularly Hippocrates, became specialized into varying fields of expertise: gynecology, urology, ophthalmology, surgery, dentistry. Women physicians specialized in obstetrics and herbal medicine, including a variety of herbs used in birth control and abortion.

Galen of Pergamum was a follower of Hippocrates, yet his originality and medical expertise made him much more than an imitator. Galen was physician to gladiators as well as to emperors over the course of his long life. He believed in the unity of the living organism, in the wonderful creativity of nature (*techne*) in forming the human, and in the vital principle (*pneuma*) that is the spiritual center of the human being. Galen summarized his thought in *On the Natural Faculties,* in which he attacked his opponents past and present and discussed his theories of the operation of the kidneys in producing urine, the role of the liver in storing food, and the action of the veins in the flow of blood. Building on the theories of Hippocrates, Galen's forceful approach to medicine had an overwhelming impact on subsequent centuries until the dawn of modern medical science after 1500 CE. During the Later Roman Empire, Galen's followers, such as Oribasius, recorded the master's teachings in books such as the *Synopsis,* which allowed the continued study of Galen's theories and observations in the Eastern Roman Empire, Byzantine Empire, and among Arab scholars of the Middle Ages. Another Roman writer of medicine who had a significant impact on Medieval Europe was the polymath Pliny the Elder, whose *Natural History* provided a compendium of medical tidbits, information on materia medica, and a discussion of magic and medicine.

See also Alexandria; Asclepiades; Celsus; Erasistratus; Galen; Greek Archaic Age; Greek Classical Age; Hellenism; Herophilus of Chalcedon; Hippocrates; Later Roman Empire; Oribasius; Pliny the Elder; Roman Principate; Women and Science

References

Durant, Will. *Caesar and Christ.* New York: Simon and Schuster, 1944.

———. *The Life of Greece.* New York: Simon and Schuster, 1939.

Erman, Adolf. *Life in Ancient Egypt.* Translated by H. M. Tirard. New York: Dover Books, 1894.

Galen. *On the Natural Faculties.* Translated by A. J. Brock. Cambridge: Harvard University Press, 1916.

Grant, Michael. *From Alexander to Cleopatra: The Hellenistic World.* New York: History Book Club, 2000.

Jones, W. H. S., trans. *Hippocrates.* Vol. 1. Cambridge: Harvard University Press, 1923.

Pliny the Elder. *Natural History.* Translated by John F. Healy. London: Penguin Books, 1991.

Thatcher, Oliver J., ed. *The Library of Original Sources.* Vol. 3, *The Roman World,* pp. 286–292. Milwaukee: University Research Extension, 1907.

Melissus of Samos

See Eleatic School

Mesopotamia (3500–550 BCE)

Neolithic Age

Archeologists tell us that the first towns appeared in the Near East perhaps ten thousand years ago in what is known as the fertile crescent. Jericho, near the Dead Sea, and Catal Huyuk, in eastern Anatolia, were small walled communities with ordered streets, whose economy depended upon agriculture. Such Neolithic villages ensured much more stability for the inhabitants than the previous hunting and gathering way of life. Slowly, with hard work and an accommodating climate, agricultural surplus led to population increase and a higher standard of living. Surplus meant wealth, some of which was available for trade. Agricultural surplus and trade yielded a nascent class system: farmers and merchants, laborers and landowners. As the few acquired more rights for less work and suffering, they engaged in intellectual pursuits: a class of priests emerged who associated the success of the community with a patron (or patroness) deity. As the mediators of humans to the gods, the priests achieved tremendous power. This, and the need for an organized system to ensure that fields were irrigated, led to government. The desire to record laws and the reigns of kings as well as more mundane administrative and trade data led to a primitive form of writing, cuneiform, used for record-keeping and, in time, to the creation of such heroic epics as the *Epic of Gilgamesh*. By the end of the fourth millennium BCE, the people of the Tigris and Euphrates river valleys had developed the first civilization.

Civilization

The English word *civilization* derives from the Latin root of the word, *civis*: "citizen." A citizen implies one who resides in an urban area; hence "civilization" generally refers to a level of society that includes cities. This is natural because cities are the product of a settled existence, which itself relies on the domestication of agriculture and livestock and the consequent trade.

The Sumerians

Indeed, the first sophisticated society based on cities, surplus wealth, and trade—Sumer, in the land of Mesopotamia—is usually considered the first civilization in world history. The scattered city-states of Sumer during the fourth and third millennia BCE were the first in a great many human accomplishments. Cities such as Ur, Eridu, Kish, Lagash, and Nippur had tens of thousands of people at their peak. They were busy metropolises surrounded by thick walls and ramparts; the "Seven Sages" laid the foundations for the walls of Uruk, according to the *Epic of Gilgamesh*. There existed extensive trade, the production of crafts, specialization of labor, and a multilayered social structure. The government was as organized as the economy; priests served as conduits for divine instructions from patron deities; scribes recorded the decisions of gods and men. Writing, created to account for surplus wealth and trade, developed into an expression of human hopes, fears, and aspirations. Once humans had gained the capacity to guarantee a surplus of food year after year—to gain greater control over life and ensure survival—they were free to speculate on human existence and the mysteries of nature.

Gilgamesh

Works such as the *Epic of Gilgamesh* reveal the growing awareness of humans detached from nature and an emerging sense of confidence that humans can explain natural phenomena. Sumerian literature not only conceptualizes the forces of nature with a set and identifiable pantheon of gods and goddesses but also elevates the stature of humans to semidivine status; hence Gilgamesh was two-thirds divine and one-third human, although fully mortal in regard to death. The gods themselves had human traits, which shows that the Sumerians were sufficiently confident to bring nature and the divine down to a human level (since the reverse was impossible). Rather than humans being a small insignificant part of the cosmos, human concerns gauged the significance of the cosmos. Gilgamesh, who traveled to the ends of the earth seeking the secret of eternal life and to join the gods, failed but became wise in failure. He realized that if he could not be like the gods, then he should be gloriously human and build great cities and accomplish great things and even spurn the gods if need be.

Yet the *Epic of Gilgamesh* revealed the belief that an anonymous, mysterious fate spun the fabric of life. Each person had a destiny, but all that one could understand of life and nature came from vague, sporadic hints provided by the gods or were inherent in the order of things. Fate bound the gods themselves, who had more knowledge than humans about the fated course of existence but just as little power to alter them. Humans might cajole or persuade the gods to act on their behalf in various matters; but once an event was fated, nothing could change it.

Fate

Not surprisingly, then, the Mesopotamians and other peoples of the ancient Near East looked at the divine and the universe with astonishment and fear—if piety was a result so too was curiosity and the quest to know. Clues for the inquiring Sumerians were found in the apparent operation of natural phenomena. Fate had its own inherent inner laws that captivated and puzzled humans. There is nothing a scientist likes better than a puzzle. Fate seemed less bewildering once the Sumerians realized that nature provided hints of future events. The gods, too, knew the future even if they could not change it. A goal of religious rites was to appeal to the gods for direction as to the course of future events. The first scientists—soothsayers, diviners, astrologers, prognosticators, and as Homer wrote, those "skilled in the flight of birds"—examined natural phenomena looking for clues as to the way of things. The task of Sumerian and Babylonian astrologers was to scan the sky, studying at night the cycles of the moon and the movements of planets and during the day the constantly changing position of the sun, searching for omens to indicate the future of nature and man. Thunderstorms, earthquakes, floods, drought, pestilence, war, sudden death, the random occurrence, and the slip of the tongue all held a hidden meaning for prophets and seers.

The First Scientists

The worldview of the astrologer and soothsayer, that by observing nature one can prepare for what is to come, is not very different from the worldview of the scientist, that by observing nature one can understand natural phenomena, which allows one to be better prepared for what is to come. The ancient Sumerians of the Tigris and Euphrates river valleys were the first scientists in world history because they were the first to take this intellectual leap from the superstitious to the scientific worldview. The earliest accounts of science were necessarily attached to mythical stories. One story identifies a gardener named Shukallituda whose crops were repeatedly destroyed by heat and wind. He prayed to heaven for help. Receiving help in the form of a new idea, he determined to plant his garden under shade trees. The idea worked—the shade helped the vegetables survive in the hot climate. Shukallituda iden-

tified a problem, conceived of a hypothetical solution, tested it, and achieved a desirable result that could be repeated again elsewhere. Other clay cuneiform documents that survive from Iraq indicate that, four thousand years ago, Sumerian farmers had an empirical approach to farming and used almanacs to record data and give advice. The Babylonian Code of Hammurapi indicates the use in Mesopotamia of the *shaduf* for irrigation.

Medicine

The Sumerians of the third millennium BCE also collected herbs and substances thought to aid in the healing of the body, and at one point a physician recorded this data on a clay tablet. The tablet describes what medicine to take for what illness. It does not record results, and is more a manual than a text of clinical observations. The physician used salt and sodium nitrate and the oils of plants and teas made from boiling herbs such as myrtle and thyme. Some medicines were salves used externally. Others were taken internally, washed down with beer. This feat of preparing a materia medica was notable in that no magical spells or incantations reinforced the use of medicine. The physician's scientific approach used various materials to achieve a physical result, the healing of the human body.

Significance

The Mesopotamians made some notable discoveries in the hard sciences and mathematics. Sumerian chemists discovered a technique to smelt copper and tin to produce bronze, which revolutionized tool use and warfare. The people of Sumeria also developed a sexagesimal system of arithmetic that became the basis for the earliest mode of keeping daily time: sixty seconds is one minute, sixty minutes is one hour. The initial interest in astrology became a more practical interest in astronomy—the Mesopotamians became adept at tracing the movement of the planets, identifying the constellations of the night sky, and predicting the phases of the moon. Astronom-

Marble relief plaque of the Babylonian king Hammurapi (1792–1750 BCE). By Thomas H. Jones, early twentieth century. (Library of Congress)

ical observations led the Babylonians to remarkably accurate lunar calendars.

The ancient Mesopotamians developed the first explanations of the origins and make-up of the earth, gods, and humans. These were not expressed scientifically, but rather as myths. The Sumerians were the first to build ocean-going vessels and to sail the seas. Their ideas spread to Egypt, India, the Mediterranean, and the Aegean. Mesopotamian science had a clear impact on the development of Greek science during the first millennium BCE. The Mesopotamians anticipated the mathematical theorems of Pythagoras and Euclid. Babylonian astronomy and mathematics influenced Thales, the first notable Greek scientist. His notion that the primal element is water was derived from Sumerians of an earlier millennium. Ancient cultures adopted the Mesopotamian system of time-keeping and figuring the yearly calendar. Mesopotamian astronomy and astrology came to be represented by the Chaldeans and magi of the ancient Near East.

See also Agriculture; Astronomy; Bronze Age;
   Euclid; Irrigation Techniques; Marine Science;
   Mathematics; Pythagoras; Thales; Time

References

Hallo, William, and William Simpson. *The Ancient
   Near East.* New York: Harcourt Brace
   Jovanovich, 1971.

Kramer, Samuel Noah. *History Begins at Sumer.*
   Philadelphia: University of Pennsylvania Press,
   1980.

Neugebauer, O. *The Exact Sciences in Antiquity.* New
   York: Dover Books, 1969.

Sandars, N. K., trans. *Epic of Gilgamesh.* London:
   Penguin Books, 1972.

Sasson, Jack, et al., eds. *Civilizations of the Ancient
   Near East.* 4 vols. New York: Charles Scribner's
   Sons, 1995.

Metallurgy

See Bronze Age; Iron Age

Meteorology

Ancient humans as agrarian peoples were
weather-watchers, concerned about climate
and rainfall, when to plant, and when to harvest. From the beginning of writing in
Mesopotamia, weather forecasting was part
of the creation of the almanac. Myth and superstition, of course, formed the bases of
early meteorology. Ancient peoples personalized meteorological phenomena by means of
gods of winds, rain, and thunderstorms. The
anger of storm gods such as Enlil and Zeus
seemed the only explanation for the violence
of the sudden thunderstorm.

According to Diogenes Laertius, Egyptian
meteorologists understood the cause of rain
to be an atmospheric change. The geographer
Herodotus's notion of the meteorology of
Egypt, which he doubtless got from Egyptian
priests, was extremely primitive: He believed
that the strong African winds blew the sun off
course along the upper Nile Valley, making it
very dry and affecting the level of the Nile
downstream in Egypt.

The climate of the Aegean Sea influenced
Greek views of the gods and nature. Boreas
was the source of the prevailing north

winds—the Etesian winds—that blew from
May to October. The Zephyr, the west wind
that blew in like a stampeding horse, was husband to the goddess Iris, the rainbow. The
Greek western shores of the Aegean were
drier than the Turkish eastern shores of the
Aegean; the north Aegean was cooler than
the south Aegean. The first Greeks to try to
explain meteorological phenomena included
the Ionians Anaximander, Anaximenes, and
Anaxagoras. Anaximander believed that wind
blowing against clouds caused lightning; the
winds themselves derived from air. Rainbows, notwithstanding that they are caused
by vapor in sunlight, were considered a clear
sign of a coming storm.

Anaximander's student Anaximenes had a
more advanced view: He explained hail and
snow as rainwater cooling and solidifying as it
falls to earth and rainbows as caused by sunlight hitting water vapor. Anaxagoras said that
Egyptians and Greeks planted according to
the appearance of the Dog Star, Sirius, in the
early spring.

Herodotus learned from Egyptian priests
that the weather had a direct connection to
health and illness. Hippocrates, the greatest
Greek physician, agreed, discussing meteorology and human health in his treatise *Airs, Waters,
and Places.* The winds and climate of a place, the
prevalence of heat or cold, the season of the
year—all determined wellness or illness. For
example, a community that received the hot
winds of the south tended to have inhabitants
with excess phlegm dripping from their si-
nuses, men who were weak and fat, women
who were subject to constant bleeding and diarrhea, children who suffered from asthma.

Aristotle and his student Theophrastus
wrote seminal accounts on meteorology in
which they ascribed to astronomical phenomena the causes of meteorological phenomena. The rising of the Pleiades, the phases
of the moon, the appearance of the moon
upon rising, and the appearance of the horizon upon sunrise and sunset all have an impact on, and give warning about, the weather.
Theophrastus thought that animal behavior

indicated weather changes. The quacking of a duck, the calling of a crow, the preening of a hawk forecast the weather. Flies biting reveal that rain is nigh. High winds accompany a dog rolling about on the ground. Theophrastus agreed with Aristotle (in the *Meteorologica*) about the eight principle winds observed at Athens.

Plutarch, in his *Natural Questions,* had many common questions about meteorological events, such as what produces thunder and lightning, which he explained according to the combination of cold and heat. He pondered the causes of dew and the differences between sea and fresh water and its impact on plants and animals, including humans and wellness or sickness. Following Homer, Plutarch considered the cold west wind the swifter of the winds. Lightning evaporates sweet, clear water, producing salty scum where it strikes the sea.

> **See also** Anaxagoras of Clazomenae; Anaximander of Miletus; Anaximenes of Miletus; Aristotle; Herodotus of Halicarnassus; Hippocrates; Ionians; Plutarch; Theophrastus

References

Barnes, Jonathan, trans. *Early Greek Philosophy.* London: Penguin Books, 1987.

Herodotus. *The Histories.* Translated by Aubrey de Selincourt. Harmondsworth, Middlesex: Penguin Books, 1972.

Jones, W. H. S., trans. *Hippocrates.* Vol. 1. Cambridge: Harvard University Press, 1923.

Plutarch, *Moralia,* trans. Lionel Pearson and F. H. Sandbach, vol. 11. Cambridge: Harvard University Press, 1920.

Theophrastus. *Enquiry into Plants and Minor Works on Odours and Weather Signs.* Translated by Arthur Hort. Vol. 2. Cambridge: Harvard University Press, 1916.

Miletus

Sixth-century BCE Miletus was one of the most dynamic centers of speculative and scientific thought in the history of humankind. Diogenes Laertius's *Lives of the Philosophers* identifies the Ionian school of thought, which in the sixth century was really the Milesian school. The first great scientists and philosophers of ancient Greece came from Miletus. These included Thales, Anaximander, Anaximenes, and Hecataeus. Tradition has it that the original inhabitants of Miletus were Carians, the natives of Anatolia or Asia Minor (present western Turkey). Invaders from Athens, however, themselves responding to invasions of the Dorians farther west, crossed the Aegean Sea and attacked the Carians of Miletus. The victorious Athenians established Miletus as one of twelve cities of this region inhabited by the Greeks from eastern Greece and the Aegean. These twelve Ionian cities were collectively called Ionia. Ionian Greek city-states had a reputation throughout the ancient world for thought and culture, as opposed to the Dorian states of western Greece. Among Ionian city-states, Miletus was the early leader.

It is perhaps not surprising that theoretical physics should have begun at Ionia, which was a crossroads of east and west. The first notable Milesian scientist, Thales, learned from the Chaldeans of Mesopotamia as well as Egyptian scientists; some sources say that he was an Egyptian emigrant from Phoenicia in the eastern Mediterranean. Ionians such as Thales combined Babylonian and Egyptian knowledge of astronomy and mathematics with the Greek speculative habit of questioning. The Milesians Thales, Anaximander, and Anaximenes were more significant for the questions that they asked than for the answers they attempted. All three speculated on the ultimate cause in a temporal sense and the limitless being in the transcendent sense. Each man assumed that an ultimate reality must exist, but they differed on its nature and substance. Thales thought that water forms the essence; for Anaximander it is the infinite; for Anaximenes it is air. Such explanations appear simplistic today. But the questions that produce the search for answers are far from simple. What is the cause of all things? Whence comes the cause? What is its nature? Is there existence prior to the cause? Is time limited? Why is there change and how does an effect yield a further cause? Are we humans brought forth by the cause? If so, how? The questions were unending; so too were the answers.

Miletus was a natural place for such questioning and answering to occur. Questioning is often a product of uncertainty. Sixth-century Miletus was a city often at war against outsiders such as the Lydians. It was a busy port city situated on the Meander River and the Gulf of Latmos. Milesian ships traveled about the Aegean and beyond, particularly north through Hellespont and Bosphorus to the Black (Euxine) Sea. Milesian trading colonies dotted the shores of the Black Sea. Miletus was also a restive place domestically, as economic classes fought for control. Tyrants ruled sixth-century Miletus.

About the time of the birth of Thales, Miletus began to mint coins made of electrum, which yielded efficient and increased trade. The Milesians got the idea from the Lydian city of Sardis, located about one hundred miles to the northeast. The Lydians were ruled by kings, the most notable being Croesus. According to Herodotus, Croesus made Sardis a center of philosophy—exactly how is not clear. It does not seem unreasonable, however, that Croesus would have employed the services of Milesian scientists. Croesus recruited Thales, according to Herodotus; the philosopher diverted the Halys River so the Lydian army could get across during a time of war. The Lydians themselves appear to have produced few scientists—a notable exception being Xanthus—hence Croesus's reliance upon Milesian scientists.

Perhaps it was Miletus's far-flung trade that led many townspeople to dream of faraway places. One such Milesian was Hecataeus, a mapmaker, historian, and geographer who traveled the Mediterranean. Anticipating Herodotus, Hecataeus journeyed to such places as Egypt, transmitting his wanderings to posterity in the *Periegesis.* Hecataeus was also involved in civic affairs, giving advice to the Milesians about their external affairs with the Persian Empire, the dominant force of the region about 500 BCE.

Miletus was just north of Didyma, a shrine to the god Apollo, Apollo Didymaeus. Apollo was the god of healing, wisdom, and learning. The Milesians clearly took to heart the influence of their divine neighbor. One anecdote from the life of Thales informs us of the special relationship of the city with Apollo. Once fishermen brought up a golden tripod from the sea. Not sure what to do with the miraculous treasure, they sent to the oracle at Delphi to ask Apollo who deserved such treasure. Apollo replied that it should be given "to the wisest." The fishermen assumed Apollo meant Thales, but Thales modestly disagreed. After going the rounds to all of the Seven Sages, the tripod returned to Thales, who wisely sent it to Delphi, for only god "is the wisest." This story is remarkably similar to Plato's *Apology,* in which Apollo calls Socrates the wisest, an honor that Socrates declines saying that he knows, on the contrary, that he does not know. Thales, in questioning and searching for answers, was a precursor to Socrates, just as Miletus the sixth-century center of science anticipated Athens, the dominant center of science in the fifth century BCE.

After the glory days of the sixth century, Miletus boasted few scientists. Exceptions included Hippodamus, an urban planner and early political scientist who redesigned the Athenian port city of Piraeus as well as planning the structure of the Athenian colony of Thourioi (Thurii) in southern Italy. Another famous Athenian who hailed from Miletus was Aspasia, the consort of Pericles and friend of Socrates who was exceptional among Athenian women in her freedom to move among men and express her own ideas. Later significant Milesian scientists included Isidorus of Miletus, a mathematician and architect who, along with Anthemius of Tralles, designed and oversaw construction of the Church of Hagia Sophia in Constantinople during the reign of Justinian in the sixth century CE. In short, Miletus was an exceptional city that shaped the foundations of science in the ancient Greek, Roman, and Byzantine worlds.

See also Anaximander of Miletus; Anaximenes of
Miletus; Constantinople; Greek Archaic Age;
Hecataeus of Miletus; Thales

References

Barnes, Jonathan, trans. *Early Greek Philosophy.*
London: Penguin Books, 1987.

Burnet, John, ed. and trans. *Early Greek Philosophy.*
London: Adam and C. Black, 1930.

Downey, Glanville. *Constantinople in the Age of
Justinian.* Norman: University of Oklahoma
Press, 1960.

Freeman, Kathleen. *Greek City-States.* New York:
W. W. Norton, 1950.

Herodotus. *The Histories.* Translated by Aubrey de
Selincourt. Harmondsworth, Middlesex:
Penguin Books, 1972.

Pedley, John G. *Sardis in the Age of Croesus.*
Norman: University of Oklahoma Press, 1968.

Military Science

Ancient Hoplites

Greek city-states of the Classical Age developed the best fighting force of the time, centered on hoplite foot soldiers. The hoplites were heavily armed infantrymen who marched in a phalanx formation. They were highly maneuverable and, when they locked shields together, appeared impregnable to their enemies. Greek hoplite armies successfully defeated Persian armies in the fifth and fourth centuries BCE and had some success against the Romans in the third century. Demetrius (337–283 BCE), son of Antigonus I, invented siege engines such as the turtle, a protective battering ram, and a large drill for boring. Similar kinds of military inventions came from Diodes of Pella, who accompanied Alexander on his Asian campaigns. Alexander's conquests introduced Greek scientists to the use of petroleum, sulphur, and arsenic in formulating weapons and poisons in warfare.

The Romans of the first millennium BCE used military science to build a vast empire that surrounded the Mediterranean Sea and encompassed three continents: Europe, western Asia, and North Africa. Roman soldiers were superb engineers. They knew the basic techniques of surveying, built stone roads that lasted for centuries, erected walls that tourists still explore, and devised a system of military camps that were impregnable to enemy attack. The Roman army evolved over centuries as the Romans constantly observed weaknesses in army units, learned from the techniques of their opponents, and implemented necessary changes. Commanders kept up with military technology as it developed in the ancient world and outfitted the Roman legions with the best siege engines, catapults, pikes, spears, helmets, shields, and swords. The Romans adopted Greek hoplite techniques and improved upon them. They also developed a superior system of logistics to maintain communications and ensure supplies. Yet the greatest accomplishment of the Roman army was, ironically, their system of encampment and defense.

Military Discipline

Roman military success was marked by superior organization, rigorous training, and attention to detail. The Roman legion formed the core of the army. The Greek historian Polybius reported that during his time (second century BCE) 4,200 men made up one legion. Each legion had ten maniples of 420 men that acted as a single unit. The maniples were grouped on the battlefield in a checkerboard fashion, to allow for utmost maneuverability in all directions to respond to superior enemy forces on the wings, front, or rear. Maniples were further divided into cohorts and centuries, commanded by a centurion. Centurions drilled new recruits and veteran legionnaires unceasingly, not just in war but in fortifications and encampment as well. Discipline was a high priority. Death was often the punishment for faltering at one's post. According to the historian Josephus, each soldier carried, in addition to his weapons, his own food as well as tools for constructing camp. In truth, the legionnaire spent more time shoveling and carrying dirt, building and taking down, than he did fighting.

The Castra

Polybius, a Greek captured by the Romans who recognized the military genius of his captors, penned a multivolume history of the Roman rise to power that provides the best description of the Roman military camp, the castra. Whenever marching, at day's end or under attack requiring defense, officers and surveyors reconnoitered a likely position for the camp. The ground had to be level and dry and an open space with a fresh water supply and good drainage; preferably the camp would not be surrounded by hills and thick woods. Surveyors, led by a master builder/surveyor, quickly formed the plan for the camp, measuring a 40,000-square-foot area formed as a square, everything at right angles, with fortifications, gates, and roads. Flags of varying colors designated where officers' tents, the tents of foot soldiers, the depots for supplies or booty, latrines, pits for rubbish, and corrals for pack animals and horses would be located. Surveyors ensured that the tents were set back two hundred feet from the fortifications. Streets were generally one hundred feet long. Three streets connected the four gates of the camp, and met at the central headquarters. One road was perpendicular to two parallel roads. Temporary camps were made of turf and timber; soldiers quickly erected skin tents that sheltered eight men. Permanent winter camps used stone; the soldiers' quarters were small snug huts with thatched roofs. Permanent camps included granaries, a hospital, a training area, and barracks. According to Polybius, the Roman legionnaires were so well trained that the layout of the camp and their own duties were obvious. Polybius compared the camp to a small city, and each man went to the location of his tent as he would go to the location of his home.

Josephus, who, like Polybius, was a Roman prisoner turned supporter and historian who had personal acquaintance with the Roman camp, reported that on military campaigns when at dawn it was time to break camp and march each soldier had specific duties in breaking camp. Heralds blowing horns would signal tasks to accomplish in precise order—first, to bring all tents down; second, to load baggage on the mules; third, to set fire to the encampment to prevent its use by the enemy. If they were under attack, the herald asked three times if the men were prepared to do battle to which the men shouted their assent three times with right arms raised. Josephus described the urban character of the camp, complete with marketplace (agora). The permanent camps he saw commanded by Vespasian and his son Titus in about 60 CE had towers on the walls at regular intervals and catapults positioned to hurl objects at the enemy. The Romans, unlike their enemies who built fortified camps, took the time to level the ground to ensure order and regularity. Josephus was impressed by the Roman discipline requiring that the camp be constructed before any battle was begun. This explains why the Romans experienced few major military disasters caused by ambush. The most famous, the destruction of Publius Quinctilius Varus's legions in 9 CE in the Teutoburg forest, was due to a lack of discipline and the inability of the commanders to organize the troops into forming the emergency camp. Julius Caesar's *Gallic War,* by contrast, shows that a Roman commander exercising strict control over his troops could protect them from unexpected disaster, even when surrounded and overwhelmed by the enemies' numbers. Caesar's military treatise reveals that his strategy for fighting the Gauls and other Germanic tribes of central and Western Europe relied heavily on the camp as a means of defense from which aggressive actions could begin and to which soldiers could go for aid, rest, and reinforcement.

Vegetius

The fourth-century CE Roman military scientist Flavius Vegetius Renatus, author of *Epitoma Rei Militari (Of Military Matters),* compared the Roman marching camp to a city, following Polybius. Vegetius's rules for build-

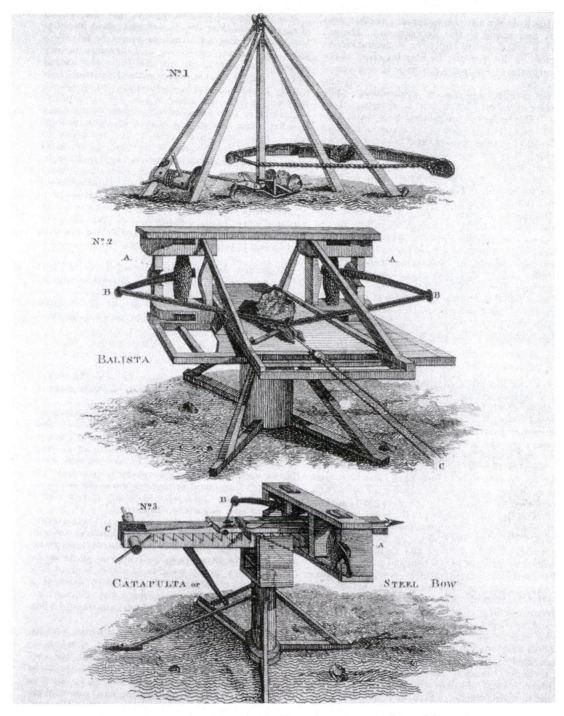

Ancient military machines for catapulting and launching boulders and giant arrows. (Library of Congress)

ing a camp were as follows: If there was no immediate threat, the Romans constructed a ditch that was three feet deep and four feet wide; a three foot earthen wall stood behind the ditch. Soldiers placed sharpened wooden stakes into the wall to repel possible enemy attack. If in enemy territory, where attack seemed inevitable, the ditch was expanded to nine feet wide and seven feet deep. If under attack, the legionnaires would nevertheless set to their task of constructing the camp, building a ditch twelve feet wide and nine feet deep, backed by a wall that was twelve feet high with stakes mounted on top.

> *See also* Caesar, Julius; Polybius; Roman
>   Principate; Roman Roads and Bridges; Tacitus
> *References*
> Caesar. *The Conquest of Gaul.* Translated by S. A.
>   Handford. Harmondsworth, Middlesex:
>   Penguin Books, 1951.
> Josephus. *The Jewish War.* Translated by G. A.
>   Williamson. Harmondsworth, Middlesex:
>   Penguin Books, 1969.
> Lawson, Russell. "The Roman Marching Camp."
>   *Calliope.* Volume 8, 1997.
> Polybius. *The Histories.* Translated by W. R. Paton.
>   6 vols. Cambridge: Harvard University Press,
>   1922–27.
> Technology Museum of Thessaloniki website:
>   www.tmth.edu.
> Vegetius. *Epitome of Military Science.* Translated by
>   N. P. Milner. Liverpool: Liverpool University
>   Press, 1993.

Moon
See Astronomy

Motion
See Physical Sciences

Mountains

Among ancient peoples, mountains were places of terror, dread, and mystery, in part because of their forbidding distances, shrouded summits, and thunderous noises, but also because mountains were the abodes of the gods. It is rare to find in ancient literature accounts of humans ascending mountains, except out of necessity. But mountains so fascinated humans that they sought to explain the strange phenomena associated with grand peaks. Early attempts at explanation were mythological and fantastic. But with time ancient thinkers began to ask sophisticated questions and seek realistic answers.

Mountains and Myths

Mythical accounts of mountains are found in many world cultures. Ancient Hindus were in awe of Meru, a legendary mountain north of the Himalaya range. Hindus and Buddhists throughout southern Asia built artificial mountains in imitation of Meru. Likewise, ancient Mesopotamians, Egyptians, and Americans built artificial mountains—ziggurats and pyramids—in symbolic attempts to approach the divine. Ancient societies of the Near East also had experiences with real mountains that are reflected in some of the world's oldest literature. The *Epic of Gilgamesh,* composed at the end of the third millennium BCE, describes the adventures of the hero Gilgamesh, who confronted the realm of the divine, mountains, and had the courage to ascend them in pursuit of glory. Mountains were associated with some of the most important gods of the Mesopotamian pantheon. Enlil, the leading deity, took control of a great heavenly mountain that contained the earth and air. A monster protected Mashu, twin peaks where the sun descended and ascended, and within which a hellish darkness reigned. Cedar Mountain, guarded by the monster Humbaba, was sacred to Ishtar, a fertility goddess associated with love and lust. Gilgamesh and his friend Enkidu ascended the Cedar Mountain, where they saw wild grain growing, blown by the wind, and experienced strange transcendental dreams indicating future events.

The Hebrews also had miraculous experiences upon mountains. The Old Testament book of Exodus, composed during the second millennium BCE, describes the prophet Moses receiving from God (Yahweh) the Decalogue, the Ten Commandments, on Mount Sinai, a 7,500-foot peak in the Sinai Peninsula. Sinai was terrifying, encompassed by "thunders and lightnings, and a thick cloud upon the mount, and the voice of the trumpet was exceeding loud; so that all the people who were in the camp trembled" (Exodus 19:16). Peals of thunder echoing from a mountain summit covered in dark clouds pierced by frequent strokes of lightning can sound like massive blasts of some otherworldly trumpet.

The Greeks

Greece has a landscape of undulating terrain—with mountains and valleys but few plains. This rocky peninsula jutting into the Mediterranean Sea, between the Ionian and Aegean seas, hosted the hunter and shepherd and the poet as well. Particularly the mountains of Greece astonished and inspired the Greeks to attempt explanations of their sublimity and a search by means of words to penetrate their mystery.

The great mountains in the neighborhood of Greece that held the Greek imagination for centuries were Parnassus, Nysa, Kyllene, Ida, Dindymum, and Olympus. The Greek world was hemmed in by two titans suffering the consequences of disobedience to Zeus. Atlas in the west held up the heavens, his shoulders appearing like massive peaks. In the east, at the extreme of the world were the Caucasus Mountains, where Prometheus was chained to a rock, daily enduring the torture of a vulture gnawing at his liver. Closer to home, Parnassus, at over 8,000 feet, loomed over Delphi, the Oracle sacred to the archer god Apollo; Parnassus was also the home to the twelve muses, the daughters of Zeus. Mount Nysa in Thrace was sacred to the god of wine Dionysus. At Nysa, mountain nymphs raised the young god. The ancient Hymn to Aphrodite had perhaps Mount Nysa in mind in proclaiming that the oaks and pines of mountains are sacred groves where the fairylike nymphs played. Mount Kyllene in Arcadia, the Greek Peloponnesus, was the birthplace of Hermes, the winged son of Zeus and Maia, the daughter of Atlas. On Mount Kyllene, Hermes invented the lyre from a tortoise shell. Mount Ida in Crete was sacred to Zeus, the king of the gods and wielder of the thunderbolt. Mount Ida (another mountain of the same name in northwest Asia Minor) was famous for hosting the rivers that watered the Troad, where stood ancient Troy and Ilios. On Mount Ida also, Aphrodite conceived Aeneas the great

Trojan warrior. Mount Dindymum in Cyzicus was sacred to an early fertility goddess, Rhea, mother of Zeus and wife of Cronos.

The most famous mountain was Olympus, which, as the highest mountain in Greece at 9,794 feet, was perfectly suited to be the home of the gods. The Greeks refused to climb the mountain because of its height and forbidding countenance and because of its holy stature. Clouds often hid the distant summit, a perfect cover for the gods' secret eternal lives. The frequent storms could be none other than Zeus nodding his great thunderous head and deities such as his daughter Athena darting to earth, lightning fast, to spread word of the father's will. From the perspective of Olympus the gods observed human behavior, heard their prayers and pleas, and made judgments based upon their awareness of the future in light of the present and the past. The mountain symbolically was raised above human ignorance and time, to provide the bright rays of timeless truth.

The searfaring Greeks were more familiar with the sea than the mountains. Both phenomena were astonishing and terrifying, but mountains were all the more so because they were nearby, always in sight, yet forbidding and ultimately unknown. Mountains served to explain perplexing phenomena such as lightning and thunder; the mysterious forested slopes; the quake of the earth; the frequent meteorological changes and displays on mountain summits; the sublime sense of the divine apparent in the unapproachable parts of nature; and the relationship of earth and sky.

Even during subsequent centuries when Mediterranean societies became more sophisticated and the Greek scientific mind awoke from slumber, mountains were still distant, daunting, and unapproachable. Polybius, who traveled through the Alps and saw Mount Atlas at a distance, allowed his amazement to take hold of his senses: he described the extent of the Alps as being over a million feet. The few recorded ascents of mountains were for military reasons. Thus Alexander of

Macedon in the fourth century BCE crossed the Taurus Mountains of southeastern Turkey and the Hindu Kush of Afghanistan. Hannibal of Carthage attacked Rome in 218 BCE after having crossed the Pyrenees and then the Alps. The Roman historian Livy recorded the ascent of Mount Hebrus in Thrace at the beginning of the second century BCE. King Philip of Macedon, at war with Rome, made the ascent to spy on Roman troop movements. It took three days for the mountaineers to journey through the foothills and ascend the summit. The subsequent descent took two days. The suffering the men experienced was immense, particularly because of the cold; the third night on the summit was awful in this regard. According to Livy, who obviously knew little about mountain climbing, the thick fog that enveloped Philip and his men at the summit was an unusual phenomenon.

The Romans

The Greeks, and after them the Romans, rarely attempted to explain mountain phenomena. Science requires not only observation but analysis based on direct experience and experiment. And the Greeks lacked the will to ascend the lofty peaks. Also, the mountains were considered sacred, associated with the supernatural and transcendent. Lucretius the Epicurean, who refused to believe in anything that could not be explained according to matter in motion, the perpetual movement of invisible atoms, not surprisingly was able to view mountain phenomena from an empirical point of view. Mountains are hollow, Lucretius believed, and volcanic eruptions occur when atoms of fire are forced out of the cone. Closer to the truth was his observation that clouds develop on mountain peaks because of warm air rushing up the slopes to the cool air at the summit.

The most famous Roman to investigate mountains was Gaius Plinius Secundus, the Elder Pliny. In 79 CE, Mount Vesuvius erupted, blasting ash and fire throughout the beautiful region of Campania. Pliny, who could see the volcano from his house at the Bay of Naples, ordered a boat in order to investigate the black plume of smoke rising from Vesuvius. He took notes of his observations as the boat reached the shores south of Pompeii and continued to observe the falling ash and pumice until his death from asphyxiation.

Christians

At the same time, in the first century CE, Christians continued the Jewish fascination with mountains. Jesus of Nazareth, as described in the Gospels of the New Testament, found meaning and transcendence on the small mountains surrounding Jerusalem. Aurelius Augustine, however, several centuries later, decried the human fascination with mountains at the expense of self-awareness. The subsequent Medieval European attitude toward such physical monuments to the Creator was to eschew concern for the sake of the incorporeal and spiritual. It was left to the Renaissance humanist and mountaineer Francesco Petrarca in the fourteenth century to call attention to the possibilities of self-discovery in the experience of ascending the distant peak.

See also Geography / Geodesy; Homer; Mesopotamia; Myth; New Testament; Pliny the Elder; Polybius; Vesuvius

References

Aeschylus. *Prometheus Bound.* Translated by Rex Warner. In *Ten Greek Plays.* Boston: Houghton Mifflin, 1957.

Apollonius of Rhodes. *The Voyage of Argo.* Translated by E. V. Rieu. Harmondsworth, Middlesex: Penguin Books, 1971.

Boorstin, Daniel. *The Discoverers.* New York: Random House, 1983.

Homer. *Odyssey.* Translated by Robert Fitzgerald. New York: Random House, 1990.

Livy. *Rome and the Mediterranean.* Translated by Henry Bettenson. Harmondsworth, Middlesex: Penguin Books, 1976.

New Oxford Annotated Bible with the Apocrypha. Oxford: Oxford University Press, 1977.

Pliny the Elder. *Natural History.* 2 vols. Translated by H. Rackham. Cambridge: Harvard University Press, 1938, 1947.

Pliny the Younger. *The Letters of the Younger Pliny.* Translated by Betty Radice. Harmondsworth, Middlesex: Penguin Books, 1963.

Polybius. *The Histories.* Translated by W. R. Paton. 6 vols. Cambridge: Harvard University Press, 1922–27.

Sandars, N. K., trans. *Epic of Gilgamesh.* London: Penguin Books, 1972.

Myth

Mythology is an expression of human existence, an ever-changing mirror of the perceptions of the human condition. Myths are based in a real past that is imprecise in time, a reality of human behavior that transcends a particular time and place. Science, too, has these attributes. The close association of myth and science is clearly seen when considering ancient science. The ancients struggled to explain the natural environment and their own humanness in respect to the divine. Initial explanations involved gods and heroes, fantastic occurrences and remarkable events. Beneath the fantastic and remarkable of the oral tradition, the poems sung by the ancient bard, was a real attempt to understand and portray nature and self.

Ancient Sumerian civilization was the result of the organization, labor, and engineering of dikes and canals that controlled the flood-prone Tigris and Euphrates and irrigated the parched land during the dry season. Sumerian culture owed its foundation to water and its uses. The Sumerian epic of creation, *Enuma Elish,* describes Apsu, the deified personification of the original waters of creation. Adad was the god of storms; Ea of waters; Ennugi of irrigation; Ningirsu, of the fertility of irrigated soil; Ninurta, of freshwater wells. The Sumerians clearly thought a lot about water. Rain and river water led to plentiful crops, watched over by Nisaba, the goddess of crops. Ninhursag, the mother goddess, also oversaw all plants and animals—all foodstuffs. Once the crops were harvested, Shulpae oversaw the happy feasting; Siduri joined in, as the goddess of wine. The miracles of water, food, plenty, drink, feasts, and full bellies had to be explained—how else, but because of the benevolence of the gods.

The Egyptians, likewise, were dependent upon the climate, particularly upon the Nile and its annual floods and the ever-present sun. Various gods had the sun as their domain of power: Amen, Re (the sun at noon), Aten (the sun's disk), Khepri (the sun in the east), Atum (the sun in the west). Other deities ruled various regions of Egypt according to the location of the Nile (upper or lower Egypt). Fertility gods and goddesses were frequently associated with the Nile: Hapy was the god of the Nile flooding during summer. Nun and Nefertem were deities of the waters of the deep that were present at the creation. Sobek was the god of the swamp. The Egyptians, devoted to understanding nature upon which they were so dependent, worshipped gods of science and learning. Imhotep, who was reputedly a builder during the age of the pyramids in the third millennium BCE, was in time a god of healing and magic. Selqet was his female counterpart, the goddess of healing. Seshat and Thoth were deities of learning, scribes, and wisdom.

Greece is a landscape of deep valleys, massive ridges, hidden forests, and daunting mountains. The gods of Greece were therefore those of the mountains, forests, rivers, the rocky coast of the sea, and the isles of the Aegean and Adriatic. Scholars believe that before the coming to power of the Mycenaean Greeks, the early Greeks and people of Crete and the islands worshipped nature deities dominated by fertility goddesses. Athena, Aphrodite, Hera, Artemis, Hestia, Demeter, and Rhea were once, in the mythical past, the primary objects of worship among the Greeks. Then Rhea's son Zeus took power from his father Cronos and brought to power as well his brothers Poseidon and Hades. Zeus ruled through the terrible thunderbolt, which only he controlled. It cast fear into gods and humans alike. Poseidon personified the sea; Hades ruled (became) the underworld. The fertility goddesses dwindled in power, or assumed

Odysseus and the Sirens. Greek sailors confronted the mysteries of the deep with supernatural explanations.
(Bettmann / Corbis)

different guises—for example, Athena became a manlike virgin; Hera became a powerless shrew and nag of her brother and husband Zeus; Aphrodite was the vixenish goddess of love always getting gods and humans into uncomfortable affairs of lust and adultery; Demeter retained her role as a fertility goddess of the grain.

The poems of Homer, Homeric hymns, and poems of Hesiod illustrate how the ancient bards personified natural and human phenomena by means of the gods and goddesses. Hesiod explained the presence of evil according to the female Pandora and her witless husband Epimetheus, who exercised hindsight but not foresight—that was the realm of his brother Prometheus. Lies and thievery are explained by the presence of Hermes, skilled at sleight of hand. Hesiod, believing in the age-old decline in culture from "the good old days," argued that his time was an Iron Age of evil and despair, unlike the previous ages of humankind: the Golden Age of men that were like gods; the Silver Age of hubris, when Zeus punished human arrogance; the Bronze Age, when humans were giants; and the Heroic Age of heroes, descended from the gods but destroyed by the Trojan War.

The Homeric hymns and the *Iliad* and *Odyssey* describe a worldview that is entirely anthropomorphic. Gods and goddesses mingle constantly with humans, so much so that humans never are entirely sure who is god and who is mortal. Perhaps the stranger at the door is a god sent to test man, as the characters of the *Iliad* and *Odyssey* constantly wonder and worry. The gods symbolize the conscious and the subconscious mind, so that when Achilles sought to destroy Agamemnon in Book 1 of the *Iliad,* Athena stilled his anger and brought reason and patience to him. The *Odyssey* describes the dichotomy of civilization (thought, personified by Odysseus) and savagery (the Cyclops). Odysseus repeatedly uses his wits, ruses, deceptions, and analytical thought to get himself out of scrapes. Odysseus has wisdom, that is, he exercises reason over passions, he has forethought and hindsight, he has patience when others are impulsive. Divinities of wisdom, thought, and wit logically aid Odysseus. Athena watches over him, as does Hermes (Odysseus's great-grandfather). Indeed we find in Greek mythology an emphasis on deities that personify human thought in one way or another. Besides Athena, Apollo is a god of wisdom, of the lyre, of dreams, of prophecy, of seers. Prometheus teaches humans creativity, analytical thinking, inventiveness, and healing. Asclepius, the son of Apollo, learns from Chiron the centaur; Asclepius becomes the principal god of healing. Some myths have Asclepius joining Jason and the crew of the *Argo* on their voyage to Colchis to steal the golden fleece. Perhaps this is because, besides Asclepius, Chiron was supposed to have taught Jason and Heracles as well. Apollo and Asclepius as healers were often called Paean. Myth also described a healer by the same name (Paeon) who cared for injured gods, like Ares and Aphrodite, who stupidly fought against the Achaeans at Troy.

See also Asclepius/Asclepiads; Bronze Age; Egypt; Hesiod; Homer; Magic; Mesopotamia; Prometheus

References
Hesiod. *Homeric Hymns, Epic Cycle, Homerica.* Translated by Hugh G. Evelyn-White. Cambridge: Harvard University Press, 1936.

Homer. *Iliad.* Translated by Robert Fitzgerald. New York: Doubleday, 1989.

_____. *Odyssey.* Translated by Robert Fitzgerald. New York: Random House, 1990.

Jacobsen, Thorkild. *The Treasures of Darkness: A History of Mesopotamian Religion.* New Haven: Yale University Press, 1976.

Sandars, N. K., trans. *Epic of Gilgamesh.* London: Penguin Books, 1972.

Sasson, Jack, et al., eds. *Civilizations of the Ancient Near East.* 4 vols. New York: Charles Scribner's Sons, 1995.

Zimmerman, J. E. *Dictionary of Classical Mythology.* New York: Harper and Row, 1971.

N

Navigation

See Marine Science

Nearchus of Crete (ca. 360–312 BCE)

Nearchus was Alexander the Great's admiral of an expedition that in 325 BCE explored the coastal waters of the Arabian Sea and Persian Gulf from the Indus River to the Tigris and Euphrates. The landscape and some of the peoples Nearchus encountered were hostile. The naval expedition paralleled a land expedition of Macedonian troops led by Alexander through the harsh Gedrosian Desert. Besides providing logistical support for Alexander's journey, Alexander ordered Nearchus to make observations of the landscape and seascape, the peoples along the way, the natural productions, and remarkable phenomena. Nearchus's observations became the basis for Arrian's *Indica,* appended to the account of Alexander's campaigns into the Persian Empire, the *Anabasis.* Nearchus was an ad hoc scientist, an explorer and adventurer who by the circumstances of time and place was confronted with a terra incognita, a land unknown to himself and his contemporaries. Mere survival required that he make accurate observations and quick judgments about the diverse and unexpected experiences he encountered.

Nearchus, the son of Androtimus, had come to the Macedonian court at Pella from Crete when Alexander was still a youth. Nearchus was several years older, yet the two became friends. He was one of Alexander's companions who went into exile in response to the break between Alexander and his father King Philip in 337. During the Persian campaign, Nearchus served as a satrap (governor) of Phrygia; later, having rejoined Alexander, he served as admiral of the Macedonian fleet. The ancient sources are vague on Nearchus and his life, but one assumes that as a Cretan he followed the tradition of his people in learning early how to sail the Mediterranean. Such experience was useful when Alexander ordered Nearchus to explore the Arabian Sea.

Arrian's *Indica* is wandering and inexact, the typical work of a geographer who relied heavily on the accounts of others as well as tradition and hearsay. Nearchus was the prime source for Arrian's account of the Indus River, Arabian Sea, and Persian Gulf. Arrian supplemented his information with other less useful sources, such as Nearchus's navigator, Onesicritus, and geographers such as Herodotus and Eratosthenes. The *Anabasis* as well as the *Indica* repeat the errors of geography taught by Aristotle and assumed without compelling contradictory evidence by Alexander and Nearchus. For example, Aristotle taught and Arrian records as fact, based on Nearchus, that the Taurus Mountains (of Asia Minor) extend east across Asia to India and beyond to the outer ocean that washes the eastern shores of India. Arrian used Nearchus's accounts of zoology to confirm or deny the legends promulgated by more fanciful authors such as Megasthenes. Nearchus claimed to have seen a tiger skin, but not a tiger, so he could not substantiate the story that they are more swift than a horse and can fell a single elephant on their own. Nearchus did observe a parrot, and its chattering like a human, of which Arrian was skeptical. And he reported on the snakes of India and of how the Greeks had no antidotes for the snake bite but the Indian physicians did, who also were useful healers for other physical complaints.

Nearchus also reported on the strange and unexpected position of the stars and the sun. As they made preparations for the voyage near the mouth of the Indus in the late summer, the men were amazed to find at noon not the slightest shadow. As they were near the Tropic of Cancer soon after the summer solstice, the rays of the sun at noon would appear almost directly overhead.

After negotiating the shoals, tides, and maze of channels at the mouth of the Indus River and waiting for favorable winds to carry them forth, they began their journey along the coast, in what the Greeks called the Erythraeum Sea. The forbidding coastline challenged the ability of the rowers aboard the barges and triremes of the flotilla. The men were preoccupied with finding food and fresh water and avoiding shipwreck in shoal water. Nearchus kept a precise account of the voyage, noting the islands, shape of the coast, and distances traveled in "stades" (stadia). Local pilots guided the Greeks and pointed out landmarks and provided histori-

cal and scientific tidbits. From such information, an accurate map could eventually be made. At the Tomerus River, on today's Pakistani coast, they confronted a native host who were extremely primitive. They were dirty and hairy, their untrimmed nails long and thick, rather like those of a wild animal. The people used their nails for digging and cutting—in short, as tools and weapons. Their clothing was made of fish skins, and their huts from fish bones. The pilots called these neolithic people the "fish-eaters," the Ichthyophagi. Shortly thereafter they met a band of friendly fish-eaters, who offered the Greeks mutton, which tasted like fish. Eventually coming to a harbor where fishermen used primitive boats to harvest the sea, they took on board a pilot who knew the coastline. His name was Hydraces. Near today's border of Pakistan and Iran, they raided a small village for food, which was mostly made from fish flour.

The fish-eaters made good use of the backbones of whales—forming large huts. Nearchus reported that whales much larger than those of the Mediterranean appeared around the ships, terrifying the sailors. Nearchus inspired them by leading them into naval combat against the whales. One of these sea mammals was twenty-five fathoms, about 150 feet. It was, perhaps, the blue whale. Locals informed the Greeks about another mystery of the deep—an island off the coast of Iran that was holy to Helios the sun; those who embarked on it disappeared.

When the fleet reached Cape Sharita at the Strait of Hormuz, the entrance to the Persian Gulf, Arrian claimed, based on Nearchus's authority, that they had a brief rendezvous with Alexander, in the region of Carmania, before setting forth and sailing along the eastern shore of the Persian Gulf. Nearchus's descriptions of this region were not as detailed as he desired, because there were few good harbors and beaches at which to make port. Eventually they reached the Euphrates River, up which they rowed to Babylon. Discovering that Alexander expected a rendezvous at the city of Susa, east of the Tigris, the fleet set sail once again, descended the Euphrates, ascended the Pasitigris River, and ended their voyage.

Nearchus's voyage opened a completely unknown region to Greek conquest, trade, and culture. His description of the South Asian coast was sufficiently accurate for other mariners to base their itineraries on. Later writers continued to rely on Nearchus. Other biographers of Alexander, such as Diodorus and Plutarch, relied on Nearchus. Scientists such as Strabo and Pliny the Elder did as well. Nearchus's fame was richly deserved. But one wonders about those nameless pilots, the local guides, who along with Hydraces were the true explorers, upon whose knowledge and experience Nearchus relied and could not do without.

See also Alexander of Macedon; Aristotle; Arrian; Asia, East and South; Geography/Geodesy; Hellenism; Strabo

References

Arrian. *Anabasis* and *Indica*. Translated by P. A. Brunt and E. Iliff Robson. 2 vols. Cambridge: Harvard University Press, 1933, 1976.

Fox, Robin Lane. *The Search for Alexander*. Boston: Little, Brown, 1979.

Neoplatonism

The Neoplatonic philosophy of the Later Roman Empire explained physical reality according to transcendent universals. Neoplatonists used reason, abstract thinking, mathematics, and intuitive thought to identify the intelligible world of the hidden essences of the divine, the intellectual world of the visible manifestations of the divine, the human realm of soul and body, and the material world of nature. Neoplatonism is a modern term used to distinguish followers of the philosophy of Plato during the Later Roman Empire from his earlier followers of the Academy. The leading Neoplatonists were Plotinus, Porphyry, Iamblichus, Maximus of Ephesus, and the Roman emperor Julian. Their thinking was in-

spired not only by Plato but by other Greek philosophers such as Pythagoras, Parmenides, Anaxagoras, and Aristotle.

Plotinus's *Enneads* is the chief source for Neoplatonist thought. Plotinus (205–270), following Plato, argued that the intelligible world is a trinity of sorts: One, Intelligence, and Soul. The One is the source of all being, the unmoved mover, the Good. The One encompasses all; it is the unity, the source of all reality, seen and unseen. Intelligence, begotten of the One, is the logos, the creative word that encompasses all things. The logos has its visible counterpart in light—the tremendous power and warmth of the sun. The soul is a world soul, for all existence is spiritual, and soul imbues all things. The planets and the stars have being, as do humans. Notwithstanding the body, the soul makes the man. The manifestations in the intellectual world of human existence that conform to the intelligible world of ideal forms are the individual sense of a unified reality, rational thought, and one's feeling of an individual unique soul.

Like Plato, Plotinus taught that the philosopher can achieve awareness of one's inner being, the world soul, universal intelligence, and ultimately the One by means of the study of mathematics and dialectical philosophy, the ability to synthesize through logic what appear to be contradictions (the thesis and antithesis). The Neoplatonists, like Pythagoras, believed that "Number" encompassed the universe, beginning of course with 1, the One. Geometry, in particular, was the route to understand the incorporeal forms that make up existence. Neoplatonist psychology involved the recognition of the duality of human existence, that the individual human is at the same time good and evil, soul and body, incorporeal and corporeal. The individual must recognize that bodily impulses drag one down to earth, as it were, preventing one from achieving awareness of the Good within oneself. The goal of philosophy is the greater recognition of the truth within oneself, which can yield to an understanding of reality and possible union with the One.

Plotinus's philosophy emerged during the third century CE when the Roman Empire was racked by civil unrest, war, poverty, and disease—in short, chaos and anarchy, which bred anxiety, alienation, despair, and a loss of hope. Philosophy was the means to rise above the conflicts and contradictions of earthly existence. Other philosophies and religions, too, gained strength during such turbulent times. Christianity was growing during the third century and competed with Neoplatonism for adherents. The commensurability of the Neoplatonist triad to the Christian concept of trinity (Godhead, Logos, Holy Spirit) is remarkable. Many Christians, such as the Roman emperor Julian (330–363), became Neoplatonists, and Neoplatonists such as Aurelius Augustine (354–430) often became Christians. Then there were those like the theologian Origen (184–254) who combined Neoplatonic and Christian thinking to form a belief based on reason seeking union with the logos, the word that is the expression of reason.

Fourth-century CE Neoplatonism succumbed to declining leadership and the weakening of Plotinus's original philosophical standards with a turn toward mysticism and fancy. After Plotinus's death in 270, his disciple Porphyry wrote of the master's life and teachings. Porphyry himself had disciples, such as Iamblichus, who became the leading Neoplatonist of the fourth century CE. Iamblichus made the unfortunate decision to see the Asian savior god Mithras as the manifestation of the logos, the source of the intellectual world. Mithras's followers identified their savior with the Good and the Sun. There was, in fact, a cult of the sun at the end of the third and beginning of the fourth centuries. *Sol Invictus,* the "Unconquered Sun," was popular with Roman soldiers and emperors, such as Aurelian and Constantine. Mithras became identified with the Unconquered Sun, and

with other cults as well. The ancient cult to the mother goddess Cybele featured a savior god, Attis, who became associated with Mithras and the sun. Out of this confusing mess emerged Helios.

The emperor Julian, at least, saw Helios, the sun, as the answer to the strange mixture of Greek and Asian philosophy and mysticism that went by the name of Neoplatonism. Julian was a Christian who apostatized himself to embrace the philosophy of Plotinus as it was represented by Iamblichus and other famous fourth-century Neoplatonists, such as the wonder-working theurgist Maximus of Ephesus. Julian, who wrote a hymn to Helios, explained that Helios is the mediator, the logos, between the Intelligible and Intellectual worlds. Helios is the visible manifestation of the One. And hence Helios is approachable, can be seen and felt, prayed to, unlike the unfathomable, distant, anonymous One. To Julian, Helios is the light, the truth, the father of men—rather like the logos, through whom all things were made. Seeing Greek myth as allegorical stories meant to represent a deeper truth, Julian saw this truth as Helios, who in a way encompassed the Greek and Roman pantheon of gods and goddesses.

Helios, hence Neoplatonism, at the hands of Julian was the means to explain what otherwise eluded explanation. The Neoplatonists sought the origins of nature, an explanation of the universe, an understanding of human personality and behavior. Their search for answers took them into the realm of philosophy and mathematics, which were the foremost outlets available to ancient scientists seeking the ultimate truth. In time, however, reflecting the overall degeneration of culture in the fourth century CE, Neoplatonism became a simplistic search for easy answers, a new form of sun worship, which symbolized the descent of science to the realm of magic during the Later Roman Empire.

Even so, there were some important if rare Neoplatonic thinkers who preserved the writings of classical science. Proclus (412–485 CE), for example, a Neoplatonist and mathematician, wrote a *Commentary on Euclid*. Philoponus, who flourished in the 6th century CE, was a Neoplatonist, Christian, and commentator, the author of *Commentary on the Physics*. Simplicius (500–540 CE) was a Neoplatonist and author of *Commentary on the Physics* and *Commentary on the Heavens*. All of these commentators provided extensive quotes from early philosophers and scientists, many of whom are otherwise scarcely known and their works lost.

See also Commentators; Iamblichus; Julian; Later Roman Empire; Magic; Maximus of Ephesus; Plato; Plotinus; Porphyry

References
Dodds, E. R. *Pagan and Christian in an Age of Anxiety.* New York: W. W. Norton, 1965.
Eunapius. *The Lives of the Sophists.* Translated by W. C. Wright. Cambridge: Harvard University Press, 1968.
Katz, Joseph, ed. *The Philosophy of Plotinus.* New York: Appleton Century Crofts: 1950.
Wright, W. C., trans. *The Works of the Emperor Julian.* Cambridge: Harvard University Press, 1962, 1969.

New Testament

The New Testament, the Greek writings that make up the second part of the Christian Bible, do not seem upon initial consideration to have anything to do with science. The New Testament is filled with miracles, prophecy, theology, revelation, and the acts of God. Yet the Gospels, history, epistles, and prophecy of the New Testament mirror the times in which they were written, during the first-century CE Roman Empire. The writers of the New Testament were Jews who had adopted the teachings of Jesus of Nazareth to become Christians. They came from the eastern Mediterranean, particularly the region of Palestine, and the Roman protectorates of Galilee and Judaea. Palestine at this time was a culturally diverse region, with many languages, customs, and religious beliefs. The land had been Hellenized, that is, imbued with Greek culture, in the wake of the fourth-century BCE conquests of Alexander the Great. The authors of the New Testament knew Hebrew and Aramaic, but they wrote in Greek. Thus some of their ideas inevitably involved Greek ideas, including the ideas of science and philosophy.

Dreams

The Gospel of Matthew sets the tone for how ancient science is portrayed throughout the New Testament. Joseph, the father of Jesus and husband of Mary, learns from a dream that he is to marry his betrothed, even though she is already pregnant. The Greeks typically thought that dreams reflected divine messages—the gods sometimes formed what appears in retrospect to have been a rudimentary conception of consciousness and the conscience. The psychoanalyst Carl Jung, a student of classical mythology and of early Christianity, argued that dreams reflect the psychic underpinnings of reality. Hence when Joseph dreamed that he must take his young child and wife to Egypt, it was a real answer to the daunting problem of the Judaean King Herod's vengeance. Likewise, the three wise men, the magi from the East, were told in a dream to depart for home, avoiding a return trip to Herod's court. Again, the dream provided a real solution to a perplexing issue.

The magi were influenced not only by dreams but by the stars as well. The Gospel of Matthew describes how the magi were led to Bethlehem by a majestic star that appeared in the East. Ancient magi were Mesopotamian (Chaldean) or Persian (Zoroastrian) astrologers and magicians who believed that the position of stars and planets indicated the course of things. It required tremendous faith in the stars to make a long and hazardous journey merely to follow a bright heavenly body. But, indeed, the ancient world usually considered stars and planets, the sun and the moon, to have a divine, spiritual presence.

Hence the names of the planets are the names of Roman gods.

Jesus the Logos

The Greco-Roman world was one of superstition and belief in the supernatural and magical. Jesus of Nazareth was not the first holy man to foretell the future, heal the sick, and command natural phenomena to suit his will. The ancient shaman, soothsayer, prognosticator, and the like claimed to know how to unlock, manipulate, and read the implicit spiritual powers contained in natural phenomena. That Jesus could calm the winds on the Sea of Galilee by a verbal command or walk on water at will was astonishing to the typical human who did not know the ways of magic. Jesus prophesied the future, such as the destruction of Jerusalem in 70 CE, like so many other seers of his time claimed to do. The Christian faithful believe that Jesus, as the logos, used such tricks to reveal his complete power over nature. The logos was a common idea in Greek and Roman philosophical and scientific circles. The logos was the "word," the transcendent idea of creation that linked the human mind to immortal, eternal truth. The Gospel of John specifically identifies Jesus as the logos, and hence identifies him with the same creative force understood by Plato, the Stoics, the Pythagoreans, and the Gnostics.

Medicine

Jesus was also a healer, and the New Testament gives wonderful insights into the practical medical techniques of the ancient Mediterranean. Ointments of varying types were used to treat illnesses of the skin, to relieve pain, or to soothe one's body and mind. Myrrh was not only an ointment used to prepare corpses for burial but was also a salve used for skin ailments or, when mixed with wine, as a general analgesic. The writer of the third Gospel, traditionally identified as Luke, a physician from Antioch, tells the story of the woman who anointed Jesus with an expensive ointment held in an alabaster container. Jesus reprimands the Pharisee who questions her act of love, pointing out that he had not welcomed Jesus to his home by anointing his hair with such ointment.

Besides the use of salves, oil made from olives or other seeds or fruits, and wine, the sick had few remedies to rely upon, except prayer or the intervention of a holy man or other such healer. Christianity focused on God the healer. Thus the ill must approach God through faith, fasting, and prayer. A physician trained in the ways of the Greeks, for example a follower of the Hippocratic school, would be looked upon with suspicion by the common folk who were healed by Jesus. For example, the Gospel of Mark gives the account of a woman healed of a hemorrhage by her merely touching the garment of Jesus. According to Mark she had been ill for years and had spent her money on the advice of physicians, to no avail. Others, with diseases for which there was no apparent cure, were similarly attracted to Jesus by the hope of instantaneous healing. Leprosy, a degenerative disease for which there was no cure, was a common complaint of the time. Leprosy was contagious, and lepers were pushed to the outskirts of society. As in the Old Testament, the writers of the New Testament used the word *lepros* indiscriminately to refer to a person with a variety of different skin diseases. In an age when degenerative illness was a sign of the consequences of sin, lepers were particularly shunned as unclean, both physically and spiritually. But Jesus touched and healed them nevertheless.

Jesus the Healer

Jesus of Nazareth, the son of a carpenter, was not the typical faith healer. The New Testament Gospels introduce a subtle and sophisticated approach to healing that bridges the gap between practical medical techniques on the one hand and healing magic on the other. The latter relied upon the manipulation of nature, in this case the diseased body. At first glance Jesus appears to be this kind of healer. On the other hand, the practical Hippocratic approach to healing involved a balanced approach to living, adopting the dictum of moderation in all things. Rest, exercise, and moderation in diet and drink had long-term healing qualities—these are called preventive medicine today. Hippocrates taught that the healthy person lives in harmony with nature. The Hippocratic Oath calls for the physician to respect the rights of the patient and to feel compassion and to sympathize with the patient's condition. In the first chapter of the Gospel of Mark, a leper approaches Jesus and begs him for healing. Jesus, "feeling sorry for him," heals the man. This sounds in part like the Hippocratic relationship of physician and patient, yet Hippocrates and his students never expected a miraculous disappearance of illness, especially such a terribly wasting disease as leprosy.

To the Christian faithful of the past and present, Jesus was a completely unique healer for his time in his method of healing through empathy. He did not use magical arts to heal, rather he had the ability to feel completely what the other person felt, whether anguish, depression, fatigue, or pain. His was a full expression of love and empathy revealed in the touch of his hand and the soft words of counsel and command. His healing required faith in the patient. Unless he or she could believe in Jesus and thus empathize with him, the healing would not occur. This kind of healing through faith, love, and empathy was new to the ancient world. Indeed, it is new to our world. Yet in recent years more students of the body and mind are understanding the incredible power of emotion, belief, and love in the eradication of disease.

See also Dreams; Hippocrates; Logos; Magi; Magic; Medicine; Old Testament; Psychology

References

Grant, Michael. *Jesus: An Historian's Review of the Gospels.* New York: Charles Scribner's Sons, 1977.

Kelsey, Morton. *Healing and Christianity.* New York: Harper and Row, 1973.

New Oxford Annotated Bible with the Apocrypha. Oxford: Oxford University Press, 1977.

The Holy Bible, Containing the Old and New Testaments. New York: American Bible Society, 1865.

Numerical Systems—Hexadecimal, Decimal

See Mathematics

O

Oceanography
See Marine Science

Old Testament (Hebrew Bible)

During the second millenium BCE, certain Mesopotamians of Semitic origin migrated west to a land that they called Canaan. The book of Genesis, the initial chapter of the Old Testament, describes the transformation of these Semites into Hebrews by focusing upon the story of a man, Abram, and his wife, Sarai, who embracing the God Yahweh became the ancestors of the people of Israel. The Hebrews were among the most creative and dynamic of the early peoples of the Near East. Their civilization, centered at Jerusalem, was oriented around an all-powerful, all-knowing God—the only God, the creator, father, protector, and judge of his children, the chosen people of Israel. In the second book of the Old Testament, Exodus, Moses discovered a God of law and deliverance who referred to himself as "I Am Who I Am"—YHWH (Yahweh).

Natural Theology

Although the Hebrews under the leadership of Moses continued to feel the terror of the unknown, their fear was mitigated by their realization that Yahweh cared for them, that he was Fate himself, that he controlled all things, and that he could circumvent the laws of nature should he so desire. The Hebrews as a result developed a sophisticated sense of natural theology, that is, a pious search to understand nature qua God's creation. The apocryphal book Wisdom of Solomon, for example, counters the supposed wisdom of the credulous pagan with the understanding of the nature of the pious Hebrew. The author of Wisdom, an Alexandrian Jew of the first century BCE, was clearly knowledgeable about Greek science—Empedocles' theory of the four elements, for example. The book of Wisdom honors God for giving men the ability to use science.

Diviners and Physicians

The focus of the Old Testament on God's chosen people can give the impression that the Hebrews were the only people. Genesis and Exodus do, however, describe the interaction of the Hebrews with other peoples of the ancient Near East such as the Egyptians and Mesopotamians. The culture of the Near East during the second and first millennia BCE was superstitious—priests and prophets being diviners of fate and the will of the gods as well as serving as healers and interpreters of dreams. Upon explaining the pharaoh's dreams, the prisoner and outcast Joseph grew to be the most powerful man in Egypt. Daniel was able to interpret the dreams of King Nebuchadnezzar when the host of "magicians," "enchanters," "sorcerers," and "Chaldeans" could not. In the apocryphal book of Tobit, the angel of God tells Tobias, a young man seeking to wed Sarah, that he can expel demons by using the heart and liver of a fish and make the blind see by anointing eyes with the gall of the fish. The Hebrews also believed in the magical, spiritual significance of numbers, such as 1, unity; 3, heaven; 4, the corners of the earth and directions of the winds; 7, the sum of 3 and 4 and the total number of the planets, sun, and moon orbiting the earth.

In the Old Testament, illness is often the result of sin, requiring spiritual cleansing as well as physical healing. The book of Leviticus, originally written in the early first millennium BCE, provides a detailed description of skin diseases (lumped under the vague diagnosis of leprosy). The priest inspected the rash or boils as would a physician, then pronounced his opinion not on how to cure the illness, but rather on whether the patient was unclean and therefore unable to enter the sanctuary of the temple in Jerusalem. Centuries later in the second century BCE in the apocryphal book Ecclesiasticus (Sirach), a hellenized Jew, clearly imbued with a healthy respect for physicians, characteristic of the Hellenistic Age, wrote of the honor due physicians who were the agents of God, who used the medicines and medical techniques given to man from Heaven above. Physicians in turn must praise God and call upon His help in the healing of patients.

Psychology

The Old Testament describes the identification of self with God. Yahweh has a direct interest in his people in general and each person in particular. This powerful sense of the divine nature of the human psyche grew more sophisticated with the passing centuries. Through the intimate interaction with God, humans develop a more clear sense of individual identity and all that life as a unique human entails: suffering, sin, and redemption; the struggle between God's will and individual free will; love and hate; trust and mistrust. The Old Testament, in short, provides a series of detailed individual and group psychological portraits that encompass the whole of human experience. The writings of the Psalmist David, for example, king of the united kingdom of Israel and Judah from 1000 to 961 BCE, reveals who God is and what his powers and interest in humans are, particularly in respect to one human, David. David was at the same time a warrior, murderer, adulterer, and conqueror, as well as a poet and a singer of extraordinary talent and sensitivity, whose Psalms express the epitome of piety and love. Psalm 139 reads, for example: "O Lord, thou hast searched me and known me! Thou knowest my downsitting down and mine uprising, thou understandest my thought afar off. Thou compassest my path and my lying down, and art acquainted with all my ways. For there is not a word in my tongue, but, lo, O Lord, thou knowest it altogether. Thou hast beset me behind and before, and laid thine hand upon me. Such knowledge is too wonderful for me; it is high, I cannot attain unto it."

Believing that Yahweh knew the Hebrews individually and collectively, and that they in turn knew Yahweh and his works, the Hebrews were confident in their religious beliefs but also in their scientific observations. The opening lines of Genesis betray this certainty that humans could, when inspired by God, know the nature of things, the origin of the universe and human existence. Every ancient civilization had stories of the origins and/or process of the universe. The Hebrew description was poetic, similar to those found in other cultures of the Near East and Mediterranean regions, and extremely sophisticated in its brevity, yet with a clarity in describing what should be indescribable. "In the beginning God created the heavens and the earth. And the earth was without form and void; and darkness was upon the face of the deep. And the Spirit of God moved upon the face of the waters" (Genesis 1:1–2).

> **See also** Dreams; History; Magic; Medicine; New Testament; Psychology
> **References**
> *New Oxford Annotated Bible with the Apocrypha.* Oxford: Oxford University Press, 1977.
> Orlinsky, Harry M. *Ancient Israel.* Ithaca: Cornell University Press, 1960.
> *Oxford Companion to the Bible.* Oxford: Oxford University Press, 1993.
> *The Holy Bible, Containing the Old and New Testaments.* New York: American Bible Society, 1865.

One
See Neoplatonism

Oribasius (floruit fourth century CE)

Oribasius, a Greek physician during the Later Roman Empire, was a confidant to the pagan emperor Julian and a synthesizer of the writings of the great Roman physician Galen. Galen's work had a tremendous impact on the European Middle Ages and Renaissance and among Arab scholars, partly because of Oribasius's *Synopsis,* which made the vast output of Galen understandable to scholars and practitioners of medicine. Oribasius was born a little over a century after Galen's death in Galen's hometown in Asia Minor. Pergamon was a center of Greek learning, culture, and science; and because of Galen and Oribasius, it was the leading center of medicine in late antiquity as well. According to the ancient biographer Eunapius, Oribasius was a precocious learner when growing up toward the end of Constantine's reign and the beginning of the reign of his son and successor, Constantius. Oribasius

studied with the Sophist Zeno of Cyprus at Alexandria. At some point Oribasius was studying or practicing medicine at Athens when he met the future emperor Julian, himself a student at Athens in the early 350s CE. The two became friends; Oribasius earned the right, even after Julian became Caesar and Augustus, to counsel and speak frankly to the emperor. Eunapius claimed that Oribasius taught the neophyte philosopher the bearing and patience necessary in an emperor. Julian in turn encouraged Oribasius to prepare the seventy-book *Synopsis* of Galen. After Julian died fighting against the Parthians in 363, subsequent Christian emperors exiled the pagan Oribasius. According to Eunapius, Oribasius became legendary even among the "barbarians" because of his healing arts. Eventually he was recalled from exile and was still living when Eunapius wrote his *Lives of the Philosophers* at the end of the fourth and beginning of the fifth centuries. Eunapius, also a pagan, called Oribasius a friend and relied on him heavily in the preparation of the *Lives.*

As a physician Oribasius modeled Galen's approach to medicine. In discussing the illness and death of the aged Chrysanthius, a fellow pagan Sophist, Eunapius described how initially physicians bled the old man, sick with a terrible stomachache; but the bleeding weakened and brought him near death. Oribasius finally arrived to help his friend Chrysanthius. Oribasius, like Galen, was devoted to the theories of Hippocrates. The Hippocratic physician believed that nature is a whole, as is the human organism. One must treat the whole organism rather than focus on isolated parts. The well person is a balanced whole, and the four *humors* of the body—blood, phlegm, black bile, yellow bile—must be in perfect accord. The sick person has an imbalance of the humors. The way to bring the body back into balance is to treat an excess of a humor with its opposite. Apply heat to cold and vice versa. Oribasius diagnosed Chrysanthius with a chill in his stomach and joints, and an excess of phlegm, so he applied heat to the affected areas. Chrysanthius, an old man weakened by the bleeding, never recovered. Oribasius, no doubt, did not despair on the loss of his patient, because a Hippocratic physician knew that death is part of the whole, in balance with the constant generation of new life.

See also Eunapius; Galen; Hippocrates; Julian; Later Roman Empire; Medicine

References

Eunapius. *The Lives of the Sophists*. Translated by W. C. Wright. Cambridge: Harvard University Press, 1968.

Galen. *On the Natural Faculties*. Translated by A. J. Brock. Cambridge: Harvard University Press, 1916.

P

Paganism

Ancient peoples were religious peoples. They were typically polytheistic, believing in many deities. Polytheism relies on an assumption that nature is infused with the divine. To recognize the divine in nature is to propitiate the gods, for by gaining their favor one will enjoy more happiness in this world and perhaps avoid disaster. To worship transcendent deities, to assume that supernatural beings cause and control nature, logically requires the study of nature. Hence ancient peoples were natural theologians as a result of their religious assumptions. The practice of religion (Latin, *religio*) meant a reverent response, a sense of awe and piety, toward the divine. Nature, directly controlled by the divine, continually reveals the character of the divine.

The earliest people to observe and study nature with an intent to acquire knowledge of natural (and supernatural) phenomena were soothsayers. Mopsus, for example, who journeyed with the Argonauts to Colchis, excelled all in interpreting the flight of birds. Gudea, a Sumerian king of the third millennium BCE, interpreted dreams and inspected livers of sacrificed animals to gain insights into the will of the gods. The fundamental assumption of the soothsayer and seer was that the gods spoke through natural phenomena: animal organs, bird habits, thunderstorms, earthquakes, and so on. The gods spoke through nature under different circumstances of time and place. The common universal law of nature, as it were, was that nature was a means of communication, a way for humans to discover the intent and will of the gods, and in particular Fate. One's fate could not be changed, but knowledge nevertheless gave the individual a sense of power, a slight control over his destiny. Apollonius of Rhodes tells the story of Idmon, the student of Apollo's art, who joined the voyage of the *Argo* even though the signs of birds told him he was fated to die soon.

Early Near East monotheists expressed a more sophisticated view of a similar idea. The Hebrews recognized that Yahweh expresses his will through natural law, yet he is not bound to the set order of the universe. The Egyptian pharaoh Akhenaten (Amenhotep IV, ruled 1379–1362 BCE) also conceived of a single god, Aten, the disk of the sun. In his "Hymn to the Aten" Akhenaten sang of Aten, the all knowing, the giver of life, the source of wisdom.

Greek religion of the second millennium at Crete and the Greek Peloponnesus was a primitive form of anthropomorphism: gods and nature both were organic and sentimental; life, nature, and the supernatural were

Osiris, the judge of the dead, and Atum, the Creator. Pagan religions conceived of multiple gods to explain the supernatural and natural. (Corel Corporation)

one. With the Archaic Age and the dawn of philosophy, some aspects of Greek religion became more sophisticated, as philosophers such as Xenophanes rejected the gods who acted so much like spoiled humans. Increasingly philosophers of *being* such as Thales, Anaximander, Parmenides, and Plato conceived of the divine in metaphysical terms. Theology (literally, the study of God) for these Greek scientists and philosophers was an intellectual study to understand nature insofar as nature is an extension of self, something from the collective past of humans and nature experienced in the present moment.

At the same time Greeks increasingly looked within to find God (*theos*). One might argue that the first great psychology occurred as the result of Greeks being initiated into the mysteries of the many fertility cults of the ancient Mediterranean. The mystical rites of the Gnostics, for example, involved the initiate finding the presence of god, hidden in nature, within themselves. The divine and supernatural lived within a person; the mystery cults helped the individual to discover the divine presence. In so discovering god within, the initiate found salvation (*salus*), a release from temporal cares, a guarantee of release upon death to a spiritual and metaphysical realm of being. Some of the more famous mysteries were the rites of Isis, the Egyptian goddess; Cybele, an Anatolian mother goddess; the savior gods Adonis and Serapis; Demeter, one of the ancient Olympians; and Mithras, an Asian import. By the time of the third and fourth centuries CE, during the declining centuries of the Roman Empire, Neoplatonic philosophers were worshipping natural phenomena, as did their ancestors of centuries past, but with a new twist. Julian the philosopher/emperor worshipped Helios the sun because Helios was the most visible manifestation for the unseen, unknowable, anonymous, and distant One. Studying natural phenomena was the means to find the truth.

See also Apollonius of Perga; Greek Archaic Age; Greek Classical Age; Hellenism; Julian; Magic; Mesopotamia; Myth; Philosophy

References

Apollonius of Rhodes. *The Voyage of Argo.* Translated by E. V. Rieu. Harmondsworth, Middlesex: Penguin Books, 1971.

Dodds, E. R. *Pagan and Christian in an Age of Anxiety.* New York: W. W. Norton, 1965.

Jacobsen, Thorkild. *The Treasures of Darkness: A History of Mesopotamian Religion.* New Haven: Yale University Press, 1976.

Pritchard, James B., ed. *Ancient Near Eastern Texts Relating to the Old Testament.* Princeton: Princeton University Press, 1969.

Steiner, Rudolph. *Christianity as a Mystical Fact.* New York: Anthroposophic Press, 1947.

Palladius (floruit mid-fourth century BCE)

Palladius was the Latin author of the book *On Husbandrie.* Very little is known about his life. He came from an important Roman family, the Aemiliani, and was a wealthy landowner in Italy. He lived sometime during the fourth century when the Roman economy had not yet ground to a halt in the western half of the empire but agriculture was clearly on the decline. Palladius appears to have been a pagan rather than a Christian. His fourteen-volume *On Husbandrie* became an important resource for landowners during the European Middle Ages. Palladius's sources included the early Roman agricultural writers Columella and Cato.

On Husbandrie is divided into books based on the seasons of the year. It reads rather like an almanac—it discusses the best times to engage in the various activities of husbandry. Palladius followed a lunar cycle to direct his agricultural planning. *On Husbandrie* gives advice on the use of manure—of different animals for different crops. He discussed ways to construct a warm stable for farm animals. He gave advice on beekeeping; on the proper tools to use for pruning, digging, plowing, and cutting; on when to plant asparagus, wheat, beets, lettuce, and radishes; on the planting of nuts and orchards; on the use of

prayers and the value of keeping faith in preparing for a good harvest. Palladius wrote in prose, though he had a poetic side to him. His writing reminds one of the pastoral literature of the Augustan Age.

See also Agriculture; Cato, Marcus Porcius; Celsus; Columella; Later Roman Empire

References

Jones, A. H. M. *The Decline of the Ancient World.* London: Longman, 1966.

Palladius. *On Husbandrie.* Translated by Barton Lodge. London: Early English Text Society, 1879.

Parmenides

See Eleatic School

Peripatetic School

The Peripatetics were followers of Aristotle who got their name from the habit of the teacher at the Lyceum walking about among disciples as he taught them the foundations of his philosophy. The Peripatetic school of thought was therefore associated with the Lyceum, Aristotle's school at Athens. Peripatetic philosophy as Aristotelian philosophy was focused on a concrete approach to the acquisition of knowledge, as opposed to the Academics, the followers of Plato, who believed that such knowledge was elusive and involved a spiritual, intuitive approach to discovering what is real. For the Peripatetics, observation, collection of data, analysis, and experimentation would provide the thinker with a good understanding of reality, which is present before us, not hidden in some ethereal realm of being.

Some of the more famous Peripatetic philosophers included Theophrastus, Aristotle's successor at the Lyceum, and Theophrastus's successor Strato. Theophrastus was a polymath, like his teacher devoted to philosophy and science to the exclusion of personal ambition and wealth. He is largely remembered today for his studies of plants. Strato was more an empiricist than Theophrastus and focused the studies of the Lyceum down this more experimental path. Eudemus of Rhodes (350–290 BCE) was a student of Aristotle who opened an Aristotelian school at Rhodes. He wrote a history of mathematics and treatises on arithmetic, astrology, geometry, and physics. Another Rhodian, Andronicus, during the first century CE published an edition of Aristotle's works, generating renewed interest in the philosopher among Romans. Anatolius was a third-century CE Aristotelian, the Christian bishop of Laodicea, and author of *Elements of Arithmetic*. He advocated the use of the Metonic Cycle in figuring Easter. The Peripatetic influence in philosophy and science had a long reach throughout antiquity, influencing Greeks and Romans, pagans and Christians.

See also Academy; Aristotle; Athens; Greek
   Classical Age; Theophrastus
References
Eusebius. *History of the Church*. Translated by G. A.
   Williamson. Harmondsworth, Middlesex:
   Penguin Books, 1965.
Grant, Michael. *From Alexander to Cleopatra: The
   Hellenistic World*. New York: History Book Club,
   2000.
Wheelwright, Philip, ed. and trans. *Aristotle*. New
   York: Odyssey Press, 1951.

Philo of Byzantium (260–180 BCE)

Philo was an engineer and inventor as well as the Greek author of *Seven Wonders of the Ancient World*. His specialty was pneumatics, and he wrote a book of that title, in which he developed a number of theories and a multitude of devices such as an air pump operating bellows, a chain pump, whistles and sirens, and pistons, all of which used principles of air expansion and contraction due to heat. His work, like that of Hero of Alexandria, foreshadowed modern steam power. Like Hero, however, Philo's inventions were used more for show or leisure than to perform work.

Philo's *Seven Wonders of the Ancient World* discusses those accomplishments of ancient culture that the modern world continues to look upon in astonishment. The seven wonders were the Temple of Artemis at Ephesus, the Temple of Zeus at Olympia, the Hanging Gardens of Babylon, the Great Pyramid of Egypt, the Lighthouse at Alexandria, the Colossus of Rhodes, and the Mausoleum at Halicarnassus.

See also Engineering and Technology; Hero;
   Hydraulics; Seven Wonders of the Ancient
   World
References
Technology Museum of Thessaloniki website:
   www.tmth.edu.
"The Seven Wonders of the Ancient World":
   http://ce.eng.usf.edu/pharos/wonders/index
   .html.

Philolaus (floruit fifth century BCE)

Philolaus of Croton in Italy was one of the leading Pythagorean philosophers of the ancient world. Indeed, many of the ideas attributed to Pythagoras might have originated with Philolaus. His writings, such as the *Bacchae* and *On the World,* exist only in fragments preserved by later commentators. Philolaus hypothesized the counter-world that brings to ten the number of heavenly bodies: Sun, moon, earth, five planets, and realm of fixed stars make nine. But as nine is a number less perfect than ten (the sum of 1, 2, 3, and 4), there must be another heavenly body, the counter-earth, hidden behind the sun, hence unseen to earthlings. Philolaus also advocated the idea of the central fire around which the heavenly bodies (even the earth) orbit—this was an early version of a heliocentric universe. Pythagoreans such as Philolaus hypothesized other contrasts in nature, such as the infinite and the finite, and even and odd numbers, as well as an even-odd number. Number is the most elevated of all truths; geometry is the form of thought that can conceive of the purity of mathematical forms. Proclus, the mathematician of the Late Roman Empire, wrote that Philolaus assigned geometric forms to the traditional Greek gods. Indeed the four elements also had their divine counterparts: Cronos, the Titan and father of Zeus, is water; Ares, the god of war, is fire; Hades, the god of the underworld, is earth; Dionysus, the god of wine, represents the warm moist nature of air.

Philolaus, like other Pythagoreans, was concerned with health, seeing good health as the product of a balance and believing that animal flesh is to be avoided. Iamblichus recorded Philolaus's belief that animals are defined by their brain, the source of thought; the heart, the seat of the soul; the navel, the basis of growth; and the genitals, the source of regeneration. Enjoining the principle of like attracts like, Philolaus argued that animals are conceived and live in heat, as semen is hot, the womb is hot, and whatever enters into the human body is expelled in a heated form: cool air is exhaled as warm breath; cool water is expelled as hot urine.

See also Astronomy; Greek Archaic Age; Magna Graecia; Mathematics; Medicine; Pythagoras
Reference
Barnes, Jonathan, trans. *Early Greek Philosophy.* London: Penguin Books, 1987.

Philosophy

Science and philosophy were more closely associated in the ancient world than at any other time in human history. The Greek word for science, *episteme,* means knowledge, while philosophy means love *(philo)* of wisdom *(sophia).* Both of these words, knowledge and wisdom, are pregnant with possibilities, contradictions, and questions. For example, how does one derive knowledge? Or wisdom? How does one recognize knowledge and wisdom in others? Can a person possess knowledge but not wisdom? Wisdom but not knowledge? Wisdom implies awareness of the timeless, yet science often seems very down to earth. To be wise one is removed from everyday concerns; a scientist has to be an expert in the ins and outs of the everyday. Wisdom is a product of age and experience. Is knowledge as well? Can one *know* and still be young and foolish?

The ancients, in particular the Greeks, answered these questions by making science devoted to the acquisition of wisdom, and

making philosophy rely on knowledge. Knowledge can be abstract as well as concrete. Today's scientist eschews the metaphysical (that which transcends the physical) for the physical, and tries as much as possible to divorce science from religion (the supernatural). The ancient scientist often could not distinguish between the physical and metaphysical, the natural and the supernatural. For example, the Greek scientist Aristotle sought the essence *(ousia)* in phenomena. An essence can of course be physical and concrete, perceived by the five senses. But Aristotle also believed essence can be ephemeral, transcendent, supernatural, and metaphysical.

The Greeks provided an interesting dichotomy with which to approach this question of science and philosophy. All of science and philosophy can be explained according to *being* and *becoming* (that is, *coming to be). Being* is the principle of staticity, of the unchanging, of existence that is eternal and absolute, neither generated nor regenerated. To be *(esse)* is to exist in a fundamental way that is uninterrupted by outside forces, change, time, anything that is becoming. That which is becoming is undergoing change and movement. It is generated and regenerated, and if absolute it is an absolute formed by alteration over time. Being implies the metaphysical; becoming implies the material. Philosophers tend to find being more attractive; scientists find becoming more attractive. Greek philosophers and scientists who focused on being more than becoming were those who emphasized the mind *(nous),* essence *(ousia),* and thought *(logos).* Those who focused on becoming more than being emphasized the primary substances, the four elements, the corporeal basis of all things.

Among the Greeks, we might include among the scientists of being Thales of Miletus, who was one of the first Greek thinkers to conceive of and seek an ultimate basis of reality. Thales' student Anaximander believed the fundamental reality was the *infinite.* Pythagoras tried to identify the ultimate reality with transcendent *number.* Xenophanes of Colophon and Anaxagoras of Clazomenae hypothesized that *mind* is the basis of all things. Parmenides of Elea, a Pythagorean, theorized about *the one* encompassing all reality.

Greek scientists looking at the basis of reality *coming to be* included Heraclitus of Ephesus, who believed that fire is the essential element. Empedocles of Acragas expanded the idea of basic material elements to include not only fire but air, water, and earth. It was left to Leucippus and Democritus to hypothesize an unending plurality of elements coming to be, atoms of constant movement and change.

Aristotle was the greatest philosopher/scientist of the ancient world because he was able to integrate these two points of view, being and becoming. Aristotle assumed a metaphysical being, an essence *(ousia)* to all things. Yet he was quite adamant that change is also fundamental to the universe. Unlike the pure metaphysician, Aristotle relied on experience, observation, and logic—the methods of science—to arrive at an understanding of being. At the same time he used the methods of the philosopher, logic and reason, to deduce universals from particulars and to induce particulars from universals.

The Stoics also bridged the two Greek approaches to knowledge. Stoic thinkers believed on the one hand in a divine fire, a universal being and creator who was unlike *mind* or *number,* unlike a metaphysical ultimate reality. The Stoic *logos* was physical, made of atoms like all else in a material universe, yet one and eternal.

Skeptics such as Pyrrho of Elis (365–270 BCE), who was one of the philosophers of Alexander's expedition, possibly came into contact with Indian philosophers such as Calanus who taught an extreme form of asceticism. His disciple Sextus Empiricus, an early third-century CE physician, wrote the *Outlines of Pyrrhonism* in defense of Pyrrho's thought and *Against the Mathematicians* to pour out his doubt and ire against scientists, mathematicians, and philosophers.

Over the course of Western thought, the distinction between science and philosophy is more apparent than real. The past holds many examples of the commensuration of objective and subjective thought, empiricism and idealism. The ideals and metaphysics of the teacher Plato were followed by the more concrete science of the student Aristotle. The theologian Thomas Aquinas was Aristotelian, the mathematician Copernicus a Platonist. Isaac Newton spent more time studying God and the Creation than he did mass, force, and acceleration. Twentieth-century physicists could at the same time speak of the godless Big Bang and the beauty and wonder of the Singularity that preceded it. Theorists of science have come to see logical positivism as a distant dream and posit the subjectivity of the most concrete and objective scientific discipline. Einstein reshaped our perception of the universe with mathematics stimulated by a creative imagination that refused to believe that "God plays dice." Thales or Anaximander, Anaxagoras or Parmenides could not have stated the relationship between science and philosophy any better.

See also Anaxagoras of Clazomenae; Anaximander of Miletus; Aristotle; Atoms; Empedocles; Heraclitus of Ephesus; Stoicism; Thales; Xenophanes of Colophon

References

Barnes, Jonathan, trans. *Early Greek Philosophy.* London: Penguin Books, 1987.

Davies, Paul. *God and the New Physics.* New York: Simon and Schuster, 1983.

Wheelwright, Philip, ed. and trans. *Aristotle.* New York: Odyssey Press, 1951.

Philostratus (170–250 CE)

Philostratus wrote the *Life of Apollonius* and *Lives of the Sophists.* He was active at the court of Septimius Severus, receiving the patronage of the empress Julia Domna, who brought together Sophists and astrologers and others involved in pseudoscience. Although limited, Philostratus's *Lives of the Sophists* provides some information about intellectual life during the chaotic third century of the Roman Empire. The *Life of Apollonius of Tyana* is even less valuable, being a somewhat imaginary account of the life of the wonder-worker Apollonius of Tyana.

Philostratus's brief biographies included lives of famous scientists such as Eudoxus of Cnidus; Favorinus, the geographer and historian; Protagoras, the sophist made famous by Plato in his dialogues; Hippias of Elia, the geographer and astronomer; Aelius Aristides, the analyzer of dreams and devotee of Asclepius; and Aelian, the zoologist.

See also Aelian, Claudius; Eudoxus of Cnidus; Later Roman Empire; Magic; Women and Science

References
Philostratus. *Life of Apollonius of Tyana.* Translated by F. C. Conybeare. Cambridge: Harvard University Press, 1912.
_____. *Lives of the Sophists.* Translated by W. C. Wright. Cambridge: Harvard University Press, 1921.

Phoenicians

The Phoenicians contributed much to ancient knowledge of geography and navigation. The Phoenicians were the great mariners of antiquity, sailing on trading expeditions out of their port cities of Tyre, Sidon, and Byblos in the eastern Mediterranean. They opened the entire Mediterranean region to trade, sailing beyond the Strait of Gibraltar (the Pillars of Heracles) at the end of the second millennium BCE. They founded the port cities of Carthage and Utica in North Africa and Cadiz in Spain and were thought by the Greeks to have founded the trading center of Tartessus on the Atlantic Coast of Spain. The Phoenicians of Carthage were responsible for creating a great trading empire that extended from North Africa to Sicily to Spain and in the Atlantic from the British Isles to the western coast of Africa. Homer's somewhat erratic understanding of geography in the *Odyssey* owes much to Phoenician exploration. The Greeks, emerging from their Dark Ages in the eighth century, borrowed the Phoenician alphabet. Ironically, however, few records survive from Phoenician city-states, even Carthage. The

sources for Phoenician exploration and science come from Greek and Roman writers.

Herodotus, writing in the mid fifth century, described in detail the peoples of the ancient Near East, recording stories in particular that he had heard about the Phoenicians. He was told, for example, that when the Persian king Xerxes was marching against the Greeks in 480, he ordered the Phoenicians to construct a bridge across the Hellespont (Dardanelles), the strait that separates Asia from Europe. Phoenician bridge builders lashed boats together, side by side across the strait, using thick ropes made of flax. They tied massive boards to the decks of the ships to allow the hundreds of thousands of Persian troops, camp followers, and animals to cross.

Herodotus also described one of the great exploring expeditions of all time. He learned from Egyptians, when he traveled to Egypt doing research for his book, that the pharaoh Necho II had, around 600 BCE, ordered Phoenician sailors to discover the extent and nature of Africa, called by the Greeks Libya. In Book 4 of *The Histories,* Herodotus narrated the voyage of the Phoenicians. They set sail from the northern tip of the Red Sea, exited into the Indian Ocean, and proceeded along the eastern coast of Africa. Their small wooden ships were sufficiently seaworthy to navigate the shoal waters along the coast. Herodotus claimed that they patiently made port in autumn, sowed seed, waited, harvested the crop, then pursued the journey rested and well supplied with food. It took them over two years to make the voyage, during which they observed and recorded their findings. Upon circumnavigating the continent, rounding the Cape of Good Hope sailing east to west, they entered Atlantic waters and sailed up the coast of Africa to the Gulf of Guinea. They then rounded the horn of Africa, battling contrary winds and currents, ultimately reaching the Pillars of Heracles and the Mediterranean. Once back to the Nile River, they reported to Necho a strange phenomenon. Sailing west from the Indian to the Atlantic oceans, rounding the Cape of

Good Hope, they noted the sun on the port (right hand) side of their ships. When Herodotus heard this he was incredulous, knowing from his experience that ships sailing west in the Mediterranean always had the sun on their starboard (left hand) side. He recorded the dubious story anyway, in so doing providing later observers with clear evidence that the Phoenicians had indeed crossed the Tropic of Capricorn into the southern hemisphere, where for travelers going east to west the rays of the sun are always to the north.

The Phoenician colony of Carthage in North Africa became the dominant city of the western Mediterranean. Carthage controlled the trade of the region, dominated Africa, Sicily, Sardinia, southern France, and Spain, and explored the Atlantic coast of Western Europe and western Africa. Because of the three Punic Wars between Rome and Carthage, in which Rome was victorious, and particularly the last war, in which Rome completely destroyed Carthage, few records of Carthaginian civilization survive. One of the few is the *Periplus* of Hanno.

The *Periplus* describes a Carthaginian expedition of the sixth century BCE, led by Hanno, a king of Carthage. Hanno led a fleet west through the Strait of Gibraltar, then south down the coast of Africa past the Tropic of Cancer to the region of the Cape Verde Islands, modern Senegal. The Carthaginians explored, recorded their observations, and took samples. Elephants, crocodiles, and hippopotamuses fascinated them. The native inhabitants were fascinating, too, and a bit terrifying. The Carthaginians made contact with a people they called the Troglodytes as well as with another savage people, whose women had shaggy bodies. The Carthaginians pursued the men without luck and contented themselves with flaying the women captives, the skins of which they took back to Carthage as a specimen of the inhabitants and strange lands.

Hanno's voyage was apparently just one of many carried out by the Carthaginians.

Roman and Greek writers periodically referred to Carthaginian exploits, such as the voyage of Himilco, a Carthaginian captain who possibly explored the North Atlantic to the British Isles, perhaps even the Sargasso Sea. Diodorus Siculus recounted the story of the Carthaginian discovery of large islands with vast rivers in the Atlantic, which has led some imaginative historians to assert the Carthaginian discovery of America.

In short, the Phoenicians and Carthaginians were an active, enterprising people rather like Americans—pragmatic explorers and observers of nature who were content less with grand theories than with exploring their environment and working to build powerful, long-lasting communities.

See also Geography/Geodesy; Greek Archaic Age; Herodotus of Halicarnassus; Marine Science

References
Cary, M., and E. H. Warmington. *The Ancient Explorers.* Harmondsworth, Middlesex: Penguin Books, 1963.
Herodotus. *The Histories.* Translated by Aubrey de Selincourt. Harmondsworth, Middlesex: Penguin Books, 1972.
Lipinski, Edward. "The Phoenicians." In *Civilizations of the Ancient Near East.* 4 vols., ed. Jack Sasson et al. New York: Charles Scribner's Sons, 1995.

Physical Sciences
Physics
The Greeks were the first great physicists of the ancient world because of their efforts to discover the sources of movement and change in nature. Thales, Anaximander, and Anaximenes, all of Miletus in Asia Minor, speculated on the ultimate cause and nature of things. Thales argued that movement and change came about through the agency of water. Anaximenes believed that air was the causal agent. Anaximander, more metaphysical, believed that the infinite (*apeiron*) was responsible for all movement. The infinite is unknowable, anonymous, absolute, without beginning or end.

PHYSICORVM

ARISTOTELIS
LIBRI,

IOACHIMO PERIONIO
interprete:nunc verò opera doctif-
simi Nicolai Grouchij inte-
grè restituti,limati,
& emendati.

QVORVM SERIEM
pagina sequens in-
dicabit.

IN VIRTVTE, ET FORTVNA.

LVGDVNI,
APVD GVLIEL. ROVILLIVM,
SVB SCVTO VENETO.
M. D. LXI.

Title page of the Latin edition (1561, Lyons, France) of Aristotle's Physics (Physicorum). *(Archivo Iconografico, S.A. / Corbis)*

The Infinite

The concept of the infinite perplexed Greek thinkers and inspired them to some of the most advanced thought of all time. Ionian, Pythagorean, and Eleatic philosophers of the Greek Archaic Age speculated on the nature of time, its extent and duration, and the nature of space, of physical boundaries, its extent and scope. The infinite is spatial and temporal. Zeno, the Eleatic philosopher, speculated on the infinite possibilities contained in each moment. In each moment of time a person recalls past experiences, is aware of persent experience, and can anticipate infinite experiences as well. The potential for action is seemingly infinite each and every moment because the imagination presents to the individual infinite possibilities.

Aristotle, less metaphysical than the pre-Socratic philosophers of Greece, wrote *Physics* to explore what are the fundamental principles of nature. Aristotle identified four natural causes of movement in nature: the material substance of an object; the class *(genos)* to which it belongs; the agent that moves the object; and the ultimate goal *(telos)* of said movement. Aristotle believed that most movement is finite since it is linear between different points. The four elements, earth, air, fire, and water, move in a linear path and thus are finite. Each element has its set, natural place. Earth moves toward the center, while fire tends upward. The only form of infinity in Aristotle's mind was the endlessness of the circle. He conceived of a fifth element, ether, as having a circular path. Thus it is in infinite motion.

Atomists

Stoic and Epicurean thinkers such as Leucippus, Democritus, Epicurus, Zeno, and Lucretius explained cause and motion according to atoms, invisible material objects that are infinite in number and cause and compose all things. The atomists not surprisingly rarely conceived of a direct divine agent in natural and human affairs and they usually conceived of the universe as infinite and eternal, forever in change and movement.

Chemistry

The origins of the study of chemistry in the ancient world occurred as an intellectual exercise of philosophers attempting to understand the fundamental bases of the universe as well as a more practical exercise of scientists and magicians attempting to uncover the uses of the substances of the earth. Of the former, the Greeks of the Archaic and Classical ages stand out; of the latter, the alchemists of the Hellenistic Age and of ancient China were chemistry's first practitioners.

The Ionian Greek philosophers Thales, Anaximander, Anaximenes, and Anaxagoras were the founders of chemical thinking in that they tried to undercover what are the basic substances of the universe. Their joint conclusion was that the universe is composed of several foundational substances: water, air, fire, earth, and ether, organized in perhaps infinite quantities (Anaximander) by a creative and sustaining mind (Anaxagoras) that is the essence of all being. The materialists and atomists Empedocles, Heraclitus, Leucippus, and Democritus, on the other hand, argued for the material rather than the metaphysical foundations of the universe—that change and conflict, matter in motion, and invisible particles, atoms, formed a universe that is always in the process of becoming.

Alchemists

Ancient humans, sensing the presence of the mysterious in nature, tried by magical means to assert control over the forces inherent in the natural environment. The attempt to understand material substances of the earth so as to contrive to alter their character, producing other, more valuable substances, marked the beginnings of chemistry in the ancient world. The first alchemists were Hellenistic chemists working with substances such as sulfur and metals in attempting to improve the appearance and qualities of metals to transform them into something else. They worked under the influence of Aristotle and the atomists, believing that the elements could be expressed in terms of solids, liquids, gases, and colors. They believed that a spiritual substance (pneuma) underlay all material substances, and they thought that by changing a substance the spiritual would be unleashed or changed as well. This change was called transmutation and involved reducing the substance to a fundamental mass of black material, and then acting upon it in successive stages to arrive at a white and then a yellow substance, the latter of which, if the alchemist had performed the work correctly, would be gold. The key to all of this was a manipulation of not only the material aspect of the metal but the spiritual aspect as well. In a sense the alchemist thought he was reducing the material to a state of death and then encouraging the seeds of life to regenerate the material into something else. Sulfur was used as a causal agent of such change. Another important material in the alchemist's repertoire was mercury, which seemed to be the ideal substance of change from liquid to metal and back. Its shiny, silver appearance made it particularly valuable. To produce changes to metals the alchemist developed a variety of apparatuses with which to heat materials and perform experiments. These included cauldrons, beakers, tubes, stills, furnaces, ovens, and so on.

The practice of alchemy in ancient China was similar to that of Alexandria in the Hellenistic Age in that the Chinese were concerned with bringing the spiritual qualities from metals and turning materials into the perfect and incorruptible substance of gold. They used many of the same apparatuses and experimented with similar substances, such as mercury made from the ore of cinnabar. The main difference between Hellenistic and Chinese alchemy was that the latter sought to make gold for ingestion, the idea being that gold had magical, curative properties that could lead to rejuvenation and eternal life. Often the opposite resulted when those ingesting materials like mercury for the sake of youth and eternity poisoned themselves.

See also Anaximander of Miletus; Anaximenes of Miletus; Aristotle; Asia, East and South; Atoms; Eleatic School; Elements; Hellenism; Thales

References
Leicester, Henry M. *The Historical Background of Chemistry.* New York: Dover Books, 1971.
Pliny the Elder. *Natural History.* Translated by John F. Healy. London: Penguin Books, 1991.
Plutarch. *Moralia.* 15 vols. Cambridge: Harvard University Press, 1968–1976.

Physics
See Physical Sciences

Planets
See Astronomy

Plato (427–347 BCE)
Greek thinkers of the sixth and fifth centuries BCE such as Thales, Pythagoras, Anaxagoras, Xenophanes, and Socrates sought to explain the universe by imposing the structure of the human mind upon it—to conceptualize it so as to understand it. They broke from the primitive anthropomorphism of their forebears to create a universe that resembled the human mind—a universe with a sound ethical structure, one with a logical, orderly, harmonious whole. The Greek philosopher Plato built a philosophy around his conception of the divine attributes of the universe, what he called *ideal forms.*

Plato was a product of aristocratic Athenian society naturally suspicious of democracy, which often appeared to be mob rule. This was his experience as a young man watching his friend and mentor Socrates stand trial for simply teaching the truth. Many of Plato's most famous dialogues feature Socrates teaching his students, confronting his enemies, defending himself, and preparing for death by drinking hemlock. Socrates died in 399 BCE, after which Plato traveled and learned more about Pythagoras and his teachings. When he returned to Athens after about

Roman marble copy of a bronze original of the Athenian philosopher Plato (427–347 BCE). (Kathleen Cohen / Victoria and Albert Museum, London)

ten years, he opened a school called the Academy. Students at the Academy studied philosophy, logic, music, astronomy, and mathematics. Plato believed that knowledge derived from intuition and reason. He eschewed empirical, scientific thinking, arguing that mere observation reveals only the shadows of reality. Plato was not a scientist, yet his thought was so broad and penetrating that he had a founding role in many disciplines of study that would become in time empirical sciences.

Plato, his mentor Socrates, and his student Aristotle could arguably be considered the founders of what today we call political science. They formed a systematic approach to government employing a methodology based on reason, logic, and observation. Most important, for Plato, was to consider what government *should be,* then to follow with implementation of ideas upon what *is.* Plato argued in his dialogue *Republic* that the principle of justice could be mirrored in human society by building a community wherein all members perform the task they are meant to do. Plato extended community justice to the self, arguing that the just individual achieves order and tranquility in his conduct by self-mastery and discipline, bringing oneself into tune with the universe and forming an inward musical harmony.

Plato's ideal society in the *Republic* has been oft-criticized for creating a totalitarian state based on the absolute control of the *guardians*—those who, like Socrates, approached knowledge of the ideal forms. Plato, a product of the Athenian democracy of the fifth century BCE, sought to free humans from the problems inherent in the free exchange of ideas, by forcing them to conform to the *truth,* the ideal forms as understood by the guardians. Plato thus erected something akin to an ideal city, one reflecting the truth. What would be the point of freedom in a society where the truth is known? Freedom only matters in a society where the truth is *not known*—hence comes the demand for the freedom to pursue it.

The truth, as Plato conceived it, is transcendent, invisible, generally unknown; material, corporeal existence hints at the truth, as the mind informed by the senses can only approximate an understanding of truth. Humans only experience the shadows of what is real. But the shadows provide a beginning for those exceptional thinkers, such as Socrates, who can bring the mind out of its inherent darkness to approach the light of truth. The technique to discovering reality first involves mathematics, understanding the principle of *number,* which is based on infinite individual units that are distinct wholes. Geometry, the shapes that represent transcendent forms, helps the mind to grasp abstract ideas, which sets the stage for dialectic. Socrates was the master of dialectic, the technique of question and answer, of drawing out the truth by a series of ever more penetrating interrogatives.

Through geometry and dialectic, for example, Plato discovered (after Pythagoras) that the earth is a sphere. The sphere is the most perfect shape, he wrote in *Phaedo,* and as the earth is the most perfect solid, the earth therefore is a sphere. Astronomy is important, but only insofar as mathematics and dialectic inform us of the true nature of the universe that we only dimly perceive with our senses.

Plato believed that the wisest persons in a society should rule it. In the *Republic,* these were the *guardians,* both male and female, who trained for years to recognize and know the truth, living in communal fashion, unconcerned with the material conditions of life. Plato also conceived of a society where the single ruler, the king, would be a philosopher as well, therefore ruling according to justice. This idea of the philosopher-king was one of Plato's greatest legacies. Alexander the Great, the student of Aristotle, sought to rule as a philosopher. Marcus Aurelius the Stoic was emperor of Rome. Many more Roman emperors thought of themselves as philosophers, even if the fact did not match the image. Julian (331–363 CE) was the ideal philosopher-king: he ruled according to philosophy (Neoplatonism), he modeled himself on the philosophers of past and present, and he exercised the wisdom of humility. Plato himself tried to put his ideas into action in the person of Dionysius II, tyrant of Syracuse. As in most such cases, however, power was more persuasive than philosophy, and Plato failed miserably.

Plato expected the philosopher, king or not, to have a clear awareness of the limitations of human thought. In *Theatetus,* Plato argued that a science of knowing is impossible, that the philosopher must rely on belief. In *The Sophist* Plato challenged the thinker to understand the nature of being as opposed to becoming, the former being an immutable presence in the universe, the core of truth, the latter being material and changing, based on faulty human perception. Arguing against Parmenides' concept of being, Plato argued that one must conceive of the possible being of nonbeing. In *Timaeus,* Plato discussed the One, which would have such influence on Neoplatonists of the Late Roman Empire. The One is the ultimate reality from which springs the Good.

Plato influenced subsequent Greek and Roman thought by means of his writings, which were widely circulated, as well as by means of the Academy. The Academy existed for centuries after Plato's death, sometimes exercising very little influence on philosophy, at other times being a center of thought in the Mediterranean world. The two most important leaders of the Academy after Plato were Xenocrates, who lived the life of a philosopher and whose behavior and motives were beyond reproach, and Carneades, who continued Plato's emphasis on the hazy understanding of reality in a physical world.

Plato's legacy of thought reaches forward two millennia to modern times. Neoplatonist philosophers and scientists dominated thought at the end of the Roman Empire. Medieval philosophers such as Augustine, Boethius, and Anselm were heavily influenced by Plato. During the European Renaissance, Platonic thought experienced a revival—the philosopher Ficino is an example. Platonic thought was an important inspiration to the nineteenth-century Romantics. Among scientists, Plato's impact has been more checkered. Science does not easily accommodate a philosophy that limits the reality of physical phenomena, that proclaims that all a scientist does in studying nature is to understand the mere shadows of what is real. And yet subjective thought is part of scientific thinking. Plato has had a major impact on science, even if it is not altogether clear.

See also Academy; Aristotle; Aurelius, Marcus; Greek Classical Age; Neoplatonism; Plotinus; Socrates

References

Hare, R. M. *Plato.* Oxford: Oxford University Press, 1982.

Jowett, Benjamin, trans. *The Portable Plato.* Harmondsworth, Middlesex: Penguin Books, 1976.

Plutarch. *The Lives of the Noble Grecians and Romans.* Translated by John Dryden; revised by Arthur Hugh Clough. 1864; reprint ed., New York: Random House, 1992.

Pliny the Elder (23–79 CE)

Pliny the Elder, Gaius Plinius Secundus, was a Roman polymath and author of *Natural History,* which is a diverse collection of anecdotes, history, geography, medical information of varying worth, discussions of astronomy and earth science, and a catalog of Roman knowledge on botany and zoology. Pliny's information varies in its quality; sometimes he seems amazingly credulous; at other times he appears a worthwhile scientist. *Natural History* is filled with interesting information and useful facts, which may explain why it was one of the most widely read books during the Late Roman Empire, Middle Ages, and Renaissance.

Pliny was born during the reign of the second Roman emperor Tiberius (14–37 CE); he died in the same year that the emperor Vespasian died and his son Titus, Pliny's friend, assumed the throne. Pliny was of the equestrian class, which the Roman emperors relied on for political support and to fill the many administrative positions in the far-flung Roman Empire. Pliny served in the military, as a provincial governor (procurator), and as head of the Roman fleet, a position he held at his death. Indeed, the fleet was moored at Misenum on the Bay of Naples up the coast from Pompeii and Herculaneum when Mount Vesuvius erupted in August, 79 CE. Pliny died when he responded to the eruption with a sense of duty to help those who were trying to flee the volcano as well as a sense of curiosity about the phenomenon of a volcanic eruption. A Stoic, he had a no-nonsense approach to life, approaching death fearlessly, doing his duty to the last, and not allowing emotions to overwhelm reason. Pliny believed in the Stoic concept of afterlife, that whatever it is, it will not involve conscious awareness—hence this life is all a person has. Pliny filled every moment with activity and study. He slept little, preferring to write his many books at night rather than to repose. Besides *Natural History,* he wrote books on military affairs and the German people. It is *Natural History,* of course, for which he is best known, because of the book's influence for centuries after his death, because of its eclectic and universal approach to learning, and because it is accessible to a variety of readers of different skills and interests.

Pliny's ultimate concern was to make the sciences—human knowledge—accessible to all people. His attempt at universal knowledge is of mixed quality. *Natural History*'s presentation of astronomy is elementary, useful perhaps for the farmer but not the savant. Pliny, likewise, was not an expert in geodesy, the study of the shape of the earth. His approach to meteorology was also simple—but then a simple explication of natural events was his goal.

Pliny was at his best when discussing natural phenomena to which he was a witness. He had traveled throughout the empire as a soldier and administrator; during his travels he tirelessly recorded his observations and local

Portrait of Pliny the Elder (23–79 CE), the Roman polymath. (Bettmann/Corbis)

accounts of natural phenomena. Added to this was his broad reading and collection of useful facts from past experts in the sciences. His geographical descriptions of Western Europe were therefore very accurate. The overall extent of Europe, its size and limits, was unknown to Pliny, but he was not afraid to speculate. He assumed that Europe was wonderful enough to be half the size of the known world. He described credulously the Hyperboreans, who lived in northern Europe near the source of the winds, and who were reputedly extremely happy in their imagined utopia. Pliny's knowledge of Africa and Asia was, of course, limited, and Pliny made constant use of fabulous stories, exaggerating places, peoples, and landmarks, making them larger and grander than what was real. His imagination told him of strange peoples at the farthest extent of the world: men with no heads but faces on the chests, others with one large foot that gave them shade on particularly hot days. When Pliny used sources penned by actual observers, such as the scientific observations based on Alexander's expedition to Asia, Herodotus's stories of the eastern Mediterranean, and Polybius's account of north and west Africa, his descriptions were better, if dated.

Astronomy

Pliny's encyclopedic approach is clearly seen in his discussion of astronomy and meteorology. Pliny accepted contemporary Greek astronomical theories about a geocentric universe, the heavenly bodies of Sun, Moon, Mercury, Venus, Mars, Jupiter, Saturn, and stars revolving around the earth, which itself rotates at a remarkably high speed. He provided full descriptions of eclipses, the movement of the planets, constellations, comets, and other astronomical phenomena. Yet he was much too absorbed as were his contemporaries in the belief that the movements of the heavenly bodies affected human affairs, even natural phenomena. A case in point was the impact of planets and stars on meteorological events. Thunderstorms and other weather changes were caused by the influence of planets and stars in the heavenly sphere above Earth. Even if somewhat absurd, Pliny's discussion of some meteorological phenomena, such as rainbows, earthquakes, and the nature and force of winds, is remarkable.

Metallurgy

Pliny's discussion of metals and metallurgy had much common sense, being largely based on his own observations and analysis. He discussed the nature and uses of gold, silver, iron, lead, tin, copper, mercury, and bronze, providing some fascinating insights with little accompanying fantasy. He provided an extensive description of mining practices and the dangers miners endured in their quest for metals. He was fascinated with precious metals, yet he knew their limitations, and knew as well the greed and negative impact on the Roman character of gold and silver. One is surprised to find Pliny condemning the Roman obsession with gold and silver and its mining and wondering why it is necessary to disembowel the earth for the sake of metals used to satisfy greed and vanity. Pliny, always interested in the practical side of science, discussed a few of the apparent medicinal benefits of metals, such as the application of silver or lead on bodily parts needing cooling and passivity.

Biology, Botany, and Medicine

As one might expect from a compiler, Pliny's life and human sciences were rudimentary, based largely on hearsay. The anthropological discussion in *Natural History* reveals Pliny's utter credulity when it comes to world peoples. Likewise, his zoology was marred by a willingness to accept strange stories: he uncritically accepted remarkable tales about humanlike behavior, characteristics, emotions, and intelligence of animals such as elephants and lions. Pliny recorded accounts of mythical animals such as werewolves, although in this case he doubted their reality. His account of bees and their culture was a complete study based on close observation.

Pliny's discussion of flora was erudite and exhaustive, although generally derived from other botanical writers, such as the student of Aristotle, Theophrastus. His focus, as throughout *Natural History,* was on useful knowledge. Hence he provided a long discussion on papyrus, spice trees, viticulture, olive trees, the benefits of forest trees, and agriculture. Pliny saw enough of the effects of wine on Romans to condemn wine-drinking out of hand as a terrible vice.

Pliny provided as well an extensive materia medica, basing his study on the writings of physicians and other scientists as well as on his own experience. He cited Cato the Elder as a source for cabbage being used as a poultice on wounds and Asclepiades for using onion juice as a cure for ailments of the eyes and digestive tract. Pliny believed that vinegar used as a salve and rinse, as well as when gargled and ingested, was efficacious in curing and reducing pain in a variety of diseases and ailments. Vinegar is useful for asthma and other respiratory ailments and was a surprisingly good antidote for snake bite. Indeed, Pliny recorded a variety of antidotes for snake bite and poison.

Legacy

Although Pliny was not an original scientist, he was nevertheless significant as a compiler. His encyclopedic approach to learning had a profound effect on subsequent compilers, particularly of the Late Roman Empire and European Middle Ages. More significant is Pliny's willingness to cite other writers and to catalog systematically their writings. Modern students of the ancient world and science know of ancient writers and writings that would otherwise be unknown, save for Pliny's efforts.

> **See also** Astronomy; Life Sciences; Meteorology; Philo of Byzantium; Pliny the Younger; Roman Principate; Seven Wonders of the Ancient World; Social Sciences; Vesuvius
>
> **References**
> Pliny the Elder. *Natural History.* Translated by John F. Healy. London: Penguin Books, 1991.
> _____. *Natural History.* 2 vols. Translated by H. Rackham. Cambridge: Harvard University Press, 1938, 1947.
> Pliny the Younger. *The Letters of the Younger Pliny.* Translated by Betty Radice. Harmondsworth, Middlesex: Penguin Books, 1963.

Pliny the Younger (61–113 CE)

Gaius Plinius Luci was nephew and heir of Pliny the Elder. He was, like his uncle, interested in a variety of topics of inquiry, some of them scientific, which are revealed in his *Letters*. Pliny was a consul, senator, and lawyer. He was a warm supporter of the emperor Trajan (98–117 CE), who rewarded Pliny with the governorship of Bithynia and Pontus in the eastern Mediterranean. Pliny's intellectual interests were focused mostly on literature and rhetoric. He was not a scientist but rather an educated Roman. Yet his *Letters*

Portrait of Pliny the Younger (61–113 CE), whose letters provide insights into ancient Roman science. (Bettmann / Corbis)

contain important portraits of the culture and science of his time.

It is through the Younger Pliny that we obtain most of our information on the eruption of Mount Vesuvius in August 79 CE, which resulted in the death of his uncle and adopted father, Pliny the Elder. His description of the eruption of Mount Vesuvius was recorded at the bidding of Cornelius Tacitus, who was writing his history of the time and sought to record all remarkable phenomena. Pliny the Younger described the eruption as causing a massive cone of smoke and ash—white, yet spotted with a dark mixture—soaring above the mountain and then spreading out in all directions like an umbrella. As night fell, the mountain vomited unremitting fire. Daybreak on the morning of August 25 at Stabiae near Pompeii was indistinguishable because of the intense darkness. The nephew, meanwhile, and his mother remained in Misenum across the Bay of Naples from Pompeii. The eruption of Vesuvius caused everything to shake in a continual earthquake. The sea churned as well, and the tide receded to such an extent that marine animals were thrust upon the shore and stranded. Pliny and his mother joined an exodus from Misenum, the people wandering blindly in the utter darkness. Ash fell like heavy rain and covered everything. People cried out in fear of the end of the world and their abandonment by the gods.

Pliny claimed that he was terrified but less superstitious than others about the eruption of Vesuvius. Nevertheless, he painted an interesting portrait of the leading Roman intellectuals of his age, for example, his friends Cornelius Tacitus, the historian, and Suetonius Tranquillus, the biographer, as believers in the traditional Roman gods and goddesses and the prophetic nature of dreams and animal sacrifice.

Pliny's letters reveal the Roman fascination with water. Like many of his contemporaries, Pliny believed that bathing, particularly in cold water, was a guarantor of good health. He enjoyed watching natural hydraulics at work, the fall of springs and filling of ponds. As governor of Bithynia, he oversaw the building and maintenance of several public works, particularly aqueducts and canals.

See also Pliny the Elder; Roman Principate; Tacitus; Vesuvius

Reference
Pliny the Younger. *The Letters of the Younger Pliny.* Translated by Betty Radice. Harmondsworth, Middlesex: Penguin Books, 1963.

Plotinus (205–270 CE)

Plotinus was the leading Neoplatonic philosopher of the Later Roman Empire. A student of Plato (427–346 BCE), Plotinus sought to adapt the master's philosophy of the Intelligible world of ideal forms to a more universal conception of the absolute source of all things, the One, and the human ability to approach the One through intensive self-examination leading to a mystical union. Plotinus wrote the *Enneads* (literally, the nine

tracts in each of six books), which outlined his philosophy of the realms of existence in order from the Intelligible world of the One; the Intellectual world of the manifestation of the One through the logos, the word; the world of the Soul, both a universal world soul and the individual soul that makes each human unique; and the world of the body, of nature, and of demons, which is the counterpart of the Good, and the multiplicity that becomes somehow swept up in the encompassing One. Like Plato, Plotinus believed that a mystical union with the transcendent One could be achieved by intuition combined with reason built on a solid foundation of training in mathematics and logic.

Plotinus was a native Egyptian who taught at Alexandria and Rome. He lived during a time of civil unrest, economic dislocation, and cultural malaise. Plotinus compared his world to a Greek drama—the reality of the actors, the stage, and sets being highly questionable. Greek philosophy involved an unending repetition of the same theories, a continuing discussion of the same books by the great thinkers of the past. Plotinus sought to reinvigorate thought through his teachings and writings. Plato inspired him more than any other philosopher, and Plotinus adopted Plato's theories of ideal forms and methods to achieve knowledge and to approach the Good. Eunapius, writing about a century after Plotinus's death, claimed that Plotinus was still popular with intellectuals and altars to his genius continued to be well-attended to.

In the *Enneads,* Plotinus distinguished between his philosophy based on transcendent ideals that accommodate human freedom and the philosophies of his rivals. He thought the philosophy of the atomists, basing all truth on material forces, was absurd. Plotinus questioned how science could be erected from such uncertain foundations. Philosophers such as the Stoics argued that all events are fated by the creative principle, the divine fire—there is a necessity to all things. Plotinus, on the contrary, was a believer in the rational human acting according to free will. Other philosophers, astrologers in particular, believed in necessity and determination according to the motion of the stars and the arrangement of the planets. Plotinus believed in the Platonic notion that the heavenly bodies moved in perfect spheres and were themselves divine and ethereal. He did not deny the influence of the heavens upon man and nature, nor did he disapprove of astrologers involved in prophesying the future. He was adamant that the anonymous and passive One gave humans, collectively and individually, power over many of the details of corporeal, temporal existence.

Plotinus is notable for his penetrating study of the human psyche, its relationship to nature and the ultimate reality, and the deep well of the self. Anticipating modern psychologists such as Carl Jung, Plotinus believed that all reality is joined spiritually, that all humans commune with each other and with the Intellectual world and the Intelligible world. The One encompasses all, even each individual human. This is the Greek concept of *sympatheia*. Plotinus was one of the first philosophers to explore the self through his writings. In *Ennead* IV Plotinus wrote of transcendent moments during which he confronted the divine. Porphyry, his disciple, who wrote a biography of his teacher, described several moments of such spiritual union during Plotinus's life. Plotinus compared the longing of the individual soul for the unified world soul as the extended drink after an endless thirst. At times he felt conflict between his soul surrounded by the things of this world and the universal soul that has nothing to do with what is corporeal and transient. The individual longs for the ultimate reunification, coming home to the One, but until then must suffer through a divided life, being simultaneously pulled in two directions, to the transcendent and to the transient, good and evil. Plotinus believed that said union relies upon the human rather than the One. The individual soul cannot help but return to the world soul.

See also Iamblichus; Julian; Later Roman Empire; Neoplatonism; Plato; Porphyry; Psychology

References
Dodds, E. R. *Pagan and Christian in an Age of Anxiety.* New York: W. W. Norton, 1965.
Eunapius. *The Lives of the Sophists.* Translated by W. C. Wright. Cambridge: Harvard University Press, 1968.
Katz, Joseph, ed. *The Philosophy of Plotinus.* New York: Appleton Century Crofts, 1950.

Plutarch (46–120 CE)

The Greek philosopher and biographer Plutarch is best known for his moralistic biographies of great Greek and Roman statesmen and warriors. Plutarch was an eclectic, encyclopedic thinker who understood the philosophies and scientific theories of the past. He was willing to employ a given theory, especially from the masters Plato and Aristotle, whenever the biographical, historical, philosophical, or scientific needs of the moment demanded it. Plutarch was in some respects a compiler and commentator, particularly respecting the writings on the physical sciences contained in his massive *Moralia.* Plutarch was at his best as a biographer and student of human nature and behavior. As the sixteenth-century French philosopher Montaigne realized, Plutarch was particularly gifted in his ability to understand the human *psyche.*

Plutarch was a native of Chaeronea in Greece, where centuries before the Macedonian king Philip II had conquered the Greek city-states, forever depriving them of their freedom. Plutarch spent his life in Chaeronea, serving in various political capacities. He was for many years priest of Apollo at the nearby Oracle of Delphi. He traveled to Rome, where he came to know many of the leading intellectuals, and Egypt, where like his many philosophic predecessors he became inspired by the mysteries of the past. He was educated at Athens. His mentor was the Pythagorean philosopher Ammonius. Plutarch was a prolific writer, turning out not only his extensive *Parallel Lives* but a series of essays, *Moralia,* as well.

Psychology

Plutarch's psychology derived from his life-long study of human behavior and morality. This interest in the human motivation to act and its consequences led Plutarch to write the first great biographical portraits of individual humans. These are the *Parallel Lives,* fifty in all, somewhat incomplete portraits of men of mixed characters and accomplishments. Plutarch's aim, as he wrote in his *Life of Alexander,* was to draw individual portraits of life. He sought to penetrate the human soul, to go beyond the exterior behavior and appearance to find the essence of what is human.

Plutarch's biography of Alexander is a case in point. Modern scholars trained in historicism and the theories of personality development often point out the limitations of Plutarch's psychology, noting that it did not allow for changes in the stages of life. It is true that Plutarch was subject to the assumptions of his own time. Hence he could blame Alexander's drunken rage that killed his friend Cleitus on demons. Plutarch thought that Alexander's hot personality reflected his hot bodily constitution. Yet where in literature does one find a more penetrating portrait of insecurity propelling a person forward in constant acts of personal validation? Plutarch's Alexander is molded by his youth. Olympias, his mother, estranged from his father Philip, encouraged Alexander's suspicions and fears directed toward his gruff, one-eyed father, and suggested to the toddler that his true father was Zeus. Alexander's confusion was accentuated by constant comparisons to Heracles and Achilles. The hatred of his mother and father for each other instilled a deep void in Alexander's life that Alexander filled by continual activity. Childlike feelings of anger became warlike acts of violence against the enemies of Macedonia. As a man he used power and glory to erase the anxieties and fears of childhood. A contradictory self-image gave way to a godlike Great King of Persia. Uncertainty about self was buried in a series of conquests, victories, and unheard of, foolhardy accomplishments.

Plutarch claimed to write *bios,* stories of human life, discovering that, as he wrote in his *Life of Timoleon,* by studying past humans he came to identify, even empathize with, these people long dead.

As Michel de Montaigne discovered when he perused Plutarch's writings, Plutarch created a personal dialogue with an individual past human; this dialogue involved empathetic give and take on the part of Plutarch and, vicariously, his object of inquiry. Plutarch had the insight that the only sure way to uncover the deepest emotions in a person is to form a bridge to connect one's emotions and personal past with another. This empathetic tie remains today one of the fundamental approaches of psychoanalysis and counseling.

The individual struggle to sort reality from image and fantasy occurs on a broader human scale, as Plutarch revealed in his *Lives.* Plutarch lived in an age when philosophy struggled to make sense out of the fictions and myths of the past. The Platonic and Peripatetic schools refused to give credence to the Homeric gods and heroes. Epicureans and Stoics discounted any form of anthropomorphic gods. Stoics elevated the divine to the status of a universal *logos,* while Epicureans were practical atheists, joined in their sentiments by the Skeptics. Plutarch used the medium of the human past to sort through the rival claims to truth. When approaching the life of the legendary Theseus, for example, Plutarch was duly suspicious of the numerous myths and stories surrounding the life of the Athenian hero; yet at the same time Plutarch sensed that even in myth there is some truth.

One of the most perplexing anthropomorphic devices that Homer used to express the influence of the divine upon human actions was his anticipation of the modern idea of the human conscience in episodes wherein gods whispered direction to humans. In Book 1 of the *Iliad,* for example, Achilles prepares to strike Agamemnon in anger but is checked by the goddess Athena, who arrives just in time to forestall this hasty action by wise words of advice. Plutarch's explanation for tales of divine intervention was pragmatic and reasonable. He assumed that there must be a divine presence in some way or form in human events. Plutarch rejected the Epicurean argument that the gods exist but have absolutely no role in human affairs. Nor did he accept the Stoic ideal of a divine force that anonymously sets forth all things but then has an utterly passive role in human affairs. Plutarch assumed the existence of the divine and assumed that the divine had a role in human affairs and a concern for individual humans. Homer's portrayal of gods qua conscience fit perfectly well with Plutarch's assumptions that the divine has a subtle influence on human thought, encouraging and suggesting but never demanding and requiring, putting thoughts into one's head or calling out in a distant inner voice. Here, the god is invisible, anonymous, known only to the especially perceptive, sensitive human, who understands the divine as a message of hope.

Plutarch interpreted dreams in this fashion as well. Dreams reveal the inner workings of the mind, upon which the divine might act, again in an ever-so-subtle way. So when Alexander was trying to decide where he should found his city in Egypt, he had a dream in which a wise old man came to him and suggested the isle of Pharos. Alexander, who read Homer as a person would a Bible, awoke knowing that Homer was leading him to this place, which turned out to be the superb location upon which Alexandria was built. According to the Greeks the muses or some other deity inspired and spoke through the poets. On this occasion, Homer was Alexander's muse. Plutarch related a similar idea in his essay, *On Socrates' Personal Deity,* in which the idea that each human has a deity, one might say conscience, is defended, based in part on Socrates' own experience as Plato described in several of his dialogues, notably *Apology.*

Plutarch was often bold in his interpretations of human psychology. In *On the Use of Reason by 'Irrational' Animals,* he broke from the teachings of Plato and Aristotle to suggest the view that animals are naturally intelligent, even more intelligent than their human counterparts. Human reason is acquired by teaching, study, and practice—by artificial means ("art"), in other words. Animals, however, are instinctually wise, hence are less apt than humans to stray from their inherent proclivity toward wise and moral behavior. The context for this strange argument is an even stranger story involving Odysseus, held against his will on the isle of Circe, the witch, forced to debate with one of his men in the form of a pig (which was Circe's doing) over the question, Is it better to be a man or a hog? The hog, Gryllus, turns out to be much the better debater. He points out to the King of Ithaca that humans display courage, honor, or responsibility only to protect their reputations, or because they are afraid of customs or laws. They are so compelled by these outside forces that they lack free will, which cannot be said of an animal who willingly goes to battle to find food or to protect its young. Likewise, animals are not governed by greed for possessions like humans, and they exercise more restraint on their desires than humans do. Only humans are omnivorous, bisexual, and pleasure-seeking. In short, Gryllus shows that animals, being close to nature, are therefore more intelligent than humans, who do all that they can to separate themselves from nature by forming artificial environments.

Some scholars doubt that Plutarch really meant what he argued in *On the Use of Reason by 'Irrational' Animals.* But a student of Plutarch's thought, Michel de Montaigne, believed that Plutarch was serious. Montaigne's *Apology for Raimond Sebonde,* for example, relies heavily on Plutarch's apparent skepticism. Montaigne used Plutarch rather like a breviary for twenty years as he fought to control the obsessions and anxieties of his mind, perplexed with illness and images of death.

Montaigne finally arrived at the conclusion to which Plutarch had been guiding his readers all along, in his essay *On Contentment*. Plutarch believed that all humans, even the mentally ill, possess within themselves the basis of happiness, which derives from acceptance of self, position, responsibility, life, and death. The proclivity of humans is to find meanness, evil, suffering, and trouble in life rather than what is good and enjoyable. Obsessions about past actions destroy present moments and cast doom upon the future.

The future, as well as the past and the present, fascinated Plutarch, because he found in the passing of time, moment to moment, the source of discontent. Humans become obsessed with time, Plutarch wrote in *On Contentment*. Obsession with the future forces people to ignore the present, because they are always in anticipation of what will come next, and to ignore the past, as being irrelevant to upcoming moments. Like Augustine, Plutarch argued that time is a continuum of past, present, future—indistinguishable except by means of memory and anticipation in the present moment and held together by a sense of the unity and efficacy of time and life. Fighting depression caused by memory or dread is as simple as pushing the anxiety into the background of one's life portrait as it is being sketched moment by moment. Obsessions cannot be ignored, merely made unimportant. Anticipating modern psychology, Plutarch advocated that an individual suffering from depression should confront the fears, purposefully obsess and ritualize, to discover that obsessions brought into the light, out of the dark, become less terrifying.

Natural History

Plutarch directly tied human happiness with the human and natural past. The latter, he believed, was the product of the benevolence of the Good, which provides all that a human needs to survive, thrive, and be content. Plutarch's approach to the study of nature, then, had a therapeutic value to it. Science had the potential to provide the student of nature with insights necessary to understand the whole and one's place in it, which, in short, is the key to happiness. To this end Plutarch refused to limit his studies to any one discipline, but like his hero Plato tried to understand a variety of topics of inquiry by the use of reason, observation, and analysis. Plutarch was particularly interested in the principles of heat and cold and the action of heat and cold on the core elements of the earth. He wondered, in *On the Principle of Cold,* whether or not cold has an independent existence apart from heat—is there something that exists in nature that is simply *cold,* rather than dependent upon relationships with other phenomena? Plutarch like others before him recognized that the meeting of cold and warm air produces violent thunderstorms. He was fascinated by the interaction of cold and warm water and its effect on sea creatures, as seen in his *Causes of Natural Phenomena (Quaestiones Naturales). Natural Phenomena* is similar to a Peripatetic exercise in asking learned, open-ended questions about nature: plants, animals, meteorology. Indeed Plutarch relied heavily on Aristotle and Theophrastus in deriving the various possible answers to the questions that he asked. In other of his essays Plutarch wrote on a multitude of topics, such as the number of worlds in what appeared to be the fixed system of the heavens; the proclivity of fire to grow more bold in cold weather; the phenomenon of demi-gods in oracles; the close association of science and religion; whether or not the moon is inhabited and if so, by what sort of beings; the possibility of settled lands west of Britain in the Atlantic; and the possibility that animals have more sense than humans expect.

In his *Life of Camillus* Plutarch identified fire, or heat, as the basic principle of causation and motion, inaugurating movement in all things, which otherwise lie cold and still. In his *On the Principle of Cold,* he argued that cold derives not from air or water but from earth itself.

For the historian of science and philosophy, Plutarch's writings are a treasure of references and quotes from the great thinkers who preceded him. Many intellectuals of the Pax Romana have important parts in Plutarch's dialogues. Moreover, in his *Lives,* Plutarch included important vignettes of many noteworthy scientists. In the *Life of Marcellus,* for example, Plutarch provided a full description of the activities of Archimedes of Syracuse. We learn much about Plato from the *Life of Dion,* about Aristotle from the *Life of Alexander,* about Pythagorean thought from the *Life of Numa Pompilius,* and about the social sciences from the *Life of Solon.*

See also Alexander of Macedon; Dreams; History; Life Sciences; Philosophy; Physical Sciences; Psychology; Roman Principate; Solon

References
Barrow, R. H. *Plutarch and His Times.* New York: AMS Press, 1979.
Plutarch. *Essays.* Translated by Robin Waterfield. London: Penguin Books, 1992.
_____. *The Lives of the Noble Grecians and Romans.* Translated by John Dryden; revised by Arthur Hugh Clough. 1864; reprint ed., New York: Random House, 1992.
_____. *Moralia.* 15 vols. Cambridge: Harvard University Press, 1968–1976.

Polybius (208–126 BCE)

During the second century BCE, the Greek Polybius was sent to Rome as a prisoner, where he became the client of Scipio Aemelianus. Polybius, along with Panaetius, brought Stoic beliefs in reason and traditional morality to Rome, which had a profound impact on the Roman worldview. Polybius came to admire the Romans, who had already embraced a lifestyle very much like the Stoics; he brought his Stoic didacticism to the writing of a universal history of his time. Polybius's *Histories* narrates the rise of Roman power throughout the Mediterranean from the third to the second centuries BCE. His work was pragmatic and ecumenical, examining all affairs relating to Rome and the Mediterranean during this time. Polybius

traveled to many of the regions described in the books; thus the *Histories* are part geographical treatise. Polybius wrote in the tradition of Thucydides, seeking to describe the truth of human events but not to sacrifice truth to rhetorical flourish. He condemned the historian Timaeus in this regard, who used high rhetoric to mask the fact that he wrote about events in which he had no part and of places that he had not seen. Polybius wrote a chronological narrative using Olympiads as the basic framework of dates. He claimed to use all available documents as well as his firsthand knowledge of lands and peoples. Parts of Polybius's book contain a history of science, which is based on a scientific approach to history.

Polybius enlivened his history with firsthand accounts of the landscape and peoples of the Mediterranean. He described Italy as a triangle with the Apennine Mountains forming the center from which land and waters descend to the Adriatic in the east and the Tyrrhenian Sea in the west. The Po drains the northern region of Italy, its waters reaching flood stage about the time of the rising of the Dog Star, that is, mid-July. Likewise the Euphrates in Mesopotamia rises at the same time. The lotus of North Africa is useful in producing fruit from which wine can be fermented. Polybius traveled to Africa, and wrote of its geographical features, such as the behavior of wild animals, the habits of the Egyptians, and the environs of Mount Atlas. Unlike some ancient geographers, Polybius argued (in a lost treatise, *On the Parts of the Globe under the Celestial Equator*) that the equatorial zone of earth is a delightful place to live. Heat is concentrated in the tropic zones (Tropic of Cancer and Tropic of Capricorn) because the sun's rays settle dreadfully upon these spots, at the solstices, for about forty days. The geographer Strabo wrote that Polybius believed the equatorial zone to be higher in elevation, with more rainfall than the tropics. In lost parts of his *Histories,* Polybius discussed the supposed travels of Odysseus, making realistic assessments of actual locales to match the strange monsters and mythical forces described in Homer's poem *The Odyssey*. Polybius also described in detail but with much skepticism the supposed voyage of Pytheas of Massilia. After visiting the Alps of Europe, Polybius declared them uninhabitable because of snow and height. Astonished by the immensity of the Alps, Polybius imagined their extent to be at least a million feet. Indeed, all of the distances in Polybius's *Histories* are grossly overestimated.

One of the more famous parts of Polybius's massive history is Book 6, which describes in detail the Roman system of government. Polybius argued that a mixed government like that of the Roman Republic was the best form of government, because it combined democracy, aristocracy, and kingship, any one of which is on its own inadequate. Polybius formed his political science on a cyclical view of history. He believed that humans congregate together in herds like animals, but unlike beasts, humans use reason to form ideas of duty and justice. The initial form of government in human society is kingship, which is simply leadership by the best warrior and most courageous leader. As a hereditary principle worms its way into this natural form of leadership, oppression often results because inadequate leaders must use force and intimidation to secure their rule. Eventually the people rebel, led by wealthy aristocrats, who take charge of government upon the toppling of the king. But this leads to a new form of oppression, the oligarchy, which again is toppled by the will of the people, who form themselves into a body politic, a democracy. For a generation or so, Polybius argued, democracy works, but eventually the people grow lazily content with their freedom and let it slowly slip away into civil war and chaos, bringing the society around once again to primitive kingship.

See also Eratosthenes; Geography/Geodesy; Mountains; Pytheas of Massilia; Social Sciences; Stoicism; Strabo

Reference
Polybius. *The Histories.* Translated by W. R. Paton. 6 vols. Cambridge: Harvard University Press, 1922–27.

Porphyry (234–305 CE)

Porphyry was the student of Plotinus and one of the great Neoplatonic thinkers of the Later Roman Empire. He adopted Plotinus's Platonic beliefs in the division of existence into the Intelligible, Intellectual, and Natural worlds. He agreed with Plotinus that the essence of all things is the anonymous One. Porphyry also held the Platonic notions of the importance of human free will in dominating the corporeal passions and temporal limitations so as to gain reunification with the One and the transcendency of the human soul, encompassing a unified world soul. Porphyry was also a commentator on the works of Euclid.

Porphyry lived at a time of civil unrest and social despair followed by the autocratic reign of the emperor Diocletian. He was, perhaps, a Phoenician by birth, though he studied under Longinus the philosopher at Athens and at Rome under Plotinus. The biographer Eunapius claimed (probably in error) that Porphyry immigrated to Sicily and contemplated suicide because Plotinus taught him to hate his body. Porphyry claimed that Plotinus experienced a mystical union with the One on several occasions, while he only accomplished it once or twice. He was human enough to marry and have children. Porphyry was a polymath who mastered a variety of topics ranging from Pythagorean philosophy to mathematics and logic to rhetoric and astrology. He wrote biographies of Plotinus and Pythagoras, commentaries on Homer, and enjoyed quoting philosophical maxims to make a point. He agreed with Heraclitus that what is good and just to the gods is incomprehensible to humans and with Pythagoras that eating any kind of flesh was sinful (because of the transmigration of souls).

Porphyry conceived of the Greek pantheon of gods as representing manifestations of the One, the infinite and eternal. In *On Images,* Porphyry conceived of the One as being manifested in the Intellectual world as the Sun (Helios, or Apollo), although to the Greeks the One was worshipped as Zeus. Zeus's son Apollo represents the sun and Zeus's daughters the Muses are the seven heavenly spheres and the starry vault. Fertility goddesses—Hestia, Rhea, Demeter, Kore—represent the productive and regenerative natural world. Asclepius symbolizes the healing power of the sun. Hecate, Artemis, and Athena are like the moon, with its nocturnal light giving wisdom and blessing women with fertile wombs. Meanwhile, Aphrodite is the morning and evening stars, Kronos is time, and Hermes is the source of rational thought. Porphyry believed that the pantheons of gods in different cultures represented the same natural and transcendent powers of nature, the mind, and the universe.

See also Iamblichus; Julian; Later Roman Empire; Maximus of Ephesus; Neoplatonism; Plato; Plotinus

References

Eunapius. *The Lives of the Sophists.* Translated by W. C. Wright. Cambridge: Harvard University Press, 1968.

Dodds, E. R. *Pagan and Christian in an Age of Anxiety.* New York: W. W. Norton, 1965.

Katz, Joseph, ed. *The Philosophy of Plotinus.* New York: Appleton Century Crofts, 1950.

Porphyry. *On Images.* Translated by Edwin H. Gifford. In Eusebius, *Preparation for the Gospel.* Oxford: Clarendon Press, 1903.

Posidonius of Rhodes (135–50 BCE)

Posidonius, originally from Syria, was a Stoic philosopher and Greek thinker who was very influential in first-century Rome. A student of Panaetius, who first introduced Roman intellectuals to Stoic thought, Posidonius continued the Stoic influence upon the Romans particularly because of his friendship with Marcus Tullius Cicero. He was known to be the teacher of Gnaeus Pompey. Posidonius particularly made his mark in the science of geodesy, imitating Eratosthenes in his estimate of the circumference of the earth based on the use of the gnomon to measure the angle of the sun's shadow at Alexandria, then comparing it to a similar measurement made at Rhodes. He calculated the circumference of earth at 180,000 stades (a little over 20,000 miles, which is remarkably accurate). Much traveled, Posidonius reputedly journeyed all over the Mediterranean in search of scientific data. A polymath, he wrote on meteorology and history and penned a periplus based on his travels. Posidonius was also a student of geology (volcanoes) and meteorology (tides).

See also Cicero; Geography/Geodesy; Hellenism; Stoicism

Reference

Ogilvie, R. M. *Roman Literature and Society.* Harmondsworth, Middlesex: Penguin Books, 1980.

Potter's Wheel

See Engineering and Technology

Prometheus

The ancient Greeks penetrated ever deeper into the mystery of man. They realized that their own civilization was vastly different from the peoples to the north, east, and west of Greece. Greek writers and philosophers contrasted their culture, which included sophisticated literary discourse, the reflective art of mathematics, the physical and biological sciences, and technological and artistic achievements, with surrounding, "barbarian" cultures. How did the Greek achievement come about? Thoughtful Greeks, in search of answers, believed that in the distant past, in a golden age of gods and heroes, humans were somehow granted rational thought that enabled them to adapt to and seek to control their environment. The Greek poet Hesiod (about 700 BCE) believed that civilization

Prometheus. Lithograph by Rockwell Kent (1931). (Library of Congress)

Prometheus, whose name means *foresight,* could not give humans what they really needed, his own gift of looking into the future. Aeschylus echoed Hesiod in blaming Prometheus for dooming humans to live in blind confusion, driven by fate, uncertain of the future. Granted the power to control their material existence, to understand the workings of the universe, yet their uncertainty about the future guaranteed human impotence. Prometheus unwittingly cursed humans as he cursed himself. His punishment was to endure ceaseless torment, chained to the rocks of the distant Caucasus Mountains, visited daily by a vulture that ate his liver, which regenerated during the night, hence leading to an endless cycle of torture.

The myth of Prometheus was a fascinating attempt on the part of reflective Greeks to try to understand the varied contradictions in their society. Rational thought and science led to an apparent knowledge of man and the universe that, while it solved some problems of human existence and provided some of the comforts of civilized living, failed to release humans from war, disease, famine, and other forms of suffering. The curse of Prometheus, according to the Greeks, is the temptation to assume that science will provide the answers, will lead to a golden age. But the Greeks discovered, with the Hebrew poet of *Ecclesiastes,* that in much knowledge is much suffering.

was the result of the gift of fire. Prometheus, the titan, against the will of the king of the gods, Zeus, taught humans the uses of fire, which resulted in the civilizing arts and sciences. The myth of Prometheus had, perhaps, a Sanskrit origin, in which in some Indian epics Pramanthu invented the fire drill.

Several centuries after Hesiod, the Athenian playwright Aeschylus (525–456 BCE), in *Prometheus Bound,* was more explicit in assigning Prometheus the role of the paradoxical benefactor of mankind. According to Aeschylus, Prometheus was a primeval titan with human characteristics who defied the plan of the eternal mind and power, the god Zeus, to maintain humans in a primitive, animalistic state. Prometheus saved humans from their fate of ignorance and innocence. Humans were helpless, aimless, blind creatures to whom Prometheus introduced the deliberative arts of philosophy, astronomy, astrology, mathematics, poetry, prose, medicine, divination, and magic.

See also Greek Archaic Age; Hesiod; Myth
References
Aeschylus. *Prometheus Bound.* Translated by Rex Warner. In *Ten Greek Plays.* Boston: Houghton Mifflin, 1957.
Graves, Robert. *The Greek Myths.* Vol. 1. Harmondsworth, Middlesex: Penguin Books, 1960.
Hesiod. *Homeric Hymns, Epic Cycle, Homerica.* Translated by Hugh G. Evelyn-White. Cambridge: Harvard University Press, 1936.
Kerenyi, Karl. *Prometheus: Archetypal Image of Human Existence.* New York: Pantheon Books, 1963.
Vandvik, Eirik. *The Prometheus of Hesiod and Aeschylus.* Oslo: I Kommisjon hos J. Dybwad, 1943.

Psychology

One of the greatest accomplishments of ancient science was the discovery of the human psyche. Psychology, the study of the *psyche* (soul), was largely brought about by Greek philosophers, in particular the Platonists, Peripatetics, Stoics, Epicureans, Gnostics, and Christians. The Greeks were able to at once apply analysis, imagination, speculation, logic, and intuition to a thorny, mysterious, hidden object of inquiry—the mind. During the span of a millennium from the appearance of Homer's *Iliad* and *Odyssey* to Augustine's conversion experience, ancient thinkers were able to discover the existence of the individual, the singular mind tied to unique experiences; the emergence of the self from a sea of others, the collective mass of humanity; the identification of the self with the Other, the *numinous,* the sum and total of all existence; and how the individual's momentary awareness fits in the overall fluidity of time.

The Ancient Near East

Greek psychology did not develop in a vacuum. The Greeks built upon the insights of their predecessors, the Mesopotamians, Egyptians, and Hebrews. Mesopotamia, where the first civilization developed, hosted a people, the Sumerians, who engaged in speculation into the relation of humans to the divine, the ultimate purpose of existence, and the role of the individual in the whole. The human population increased dramatically during the third millennium BCE in Mesopotamia, and the Sumerians were able to isolate individual human achievements and personality traits. In the *Epic of Gilgamesh,* for example, we are able to read about an individual human who is complex, unique, and tragic. Gilgamesh's search for eternal life and happiness is a general human search made singular to the life of one man. Gilgamesh, moreover, is part god, and he can compete on the gods' level, which indicates a growing awareness of the significance and value of the individual person.

The Egyptians, meanwhile, expanded the human search for personal immortality and individual recognition both in the present and in the future. Although most Egyptians lived anonymous lives, the pharaohs and their families and close supporters became convinced of their own personal immortality and their greatness spanning the epochs, demanding monuments to direct future individuals not to forget *this one* commemorated in a monument or buried within a pyramid. The self-centered arrogance of the fourteenth-century BCE monotheist Akhenaten (Amenhotep IV) revealed a clear identification of himself with the divine, of his own inner light with the great light of the sun.

Amenhotep IV ruled during the eighteenth dynasty of Egyptian pharaohs, when Thebes was the religious capital of the New Kingdom dedicated to the worship of the sun, Amen. Upon assuming the throne in 1379 BCE, Amenhotep changed his name to Akhenaten, moved the religious center south to a new capital at Amarna, and devoted himself to the worship of the one god, Aten, the disk of the sun. Akhenaten's *Hymn to Aten* is a pious account of the god written by his own true worshiper, the pharaoh. Aten is the universal source of all light, warmth, and truth; only Akhenaten understands this, and therefore knows his true self as a reflection of the divine. Aten is with each human at the moment of conception; he nourishes the child in the womb; he determines his length of days and aims of life; he watches over each of his children, each human. Aten is the beginning and end of all things, the sum of time, the universal presence that chooses the sun's disk as his incarnation, visible to humans, especially to pharaoh. As the sun's rays reach deep into a person's being, so too does the Aten. Akhenaten feels the presence of the god within himself. It strengthens him to act on behalf of the Aten, spreading his worship, notwithstanding opposition and trials.

Akhenaten's *Hymn to Aten* sounds remarkably similar, of course, to the writings of the Hebrew Old Testament. Whereas ancient polytheistic religions typically portray the divine as humanlike and hence superficial, as powerful but not all-powerful, as being bound by fate like humans are, Akhenaten's Aten and the Hebrew Yahweh are blinding, omniscient, omnipotent, all-encompassing. When Moses asks God in the Book of Exodus who he is, God replies: "I am that I am." This is the most powerful proclamation of the divine in human history, yet it is a proclamation made to an individual man who is terrified out of his wits at a particular time and place. "I am" encompasses all things, all time, all life, all thought. And yet "I am" can become instantly knowable to anyone, not just to Moses. The Hebrew Yahweh had similar attributes to Aten, yet Yahweh was at the same time visibly grander and more powerful, yet more personal. The prophet Elijah discovered that he was less apt to be made known in thunder, lightning, and earthquakes than in the quiet moment, the gentle breeze. King David, the writer of the Psalms, knew a personal God who cares for each individual, king and commoner—who is a gentle shepherd to each of his children. David's interaction with Yahweh in the Psalms reveals anguish, fear, loneliness, hope, courage, love: the Psalms portray the breadth of human emotions and the search of the individual to find peace and redemption from pain, suffering, sin, and death. The Psalms provide a complete psychological portrait of humankind.

The Greeks

A very different approach to human psychology is found in the *Iliad* and *Odyssey* of the Greek poet Homer. Homer's tale is a timeless portrait of human struggle against fate. Unlike the Hebrews, fate in Homer's poems is anonymous and unknowable, and tremendous will and strength of character is required for the individual to forge his or her own life in time. Homer put a premium on the characteristics of the individual hero. In so doing he created a personality standard of the heroic individual who strives against fate by means of the peculiar human trait of *arete*—manly courage. The hidden presence of gods poetically describes the unconscious mind of individuals who typically heed the advice of this inner voice and act accordingly.

Subsequent Greek philosophers, particularly of the Ionian school—such as Anaxagoras, Socrates, Plato, and Aristotle—took this concept of *arete,* that is, individual free will in the face of overwhelming odds or fate, and fashioned it into a more universal presence of mind *(nous)* making itself known in each individual by means of the soul *(psyche),* an incorporeal presence, a being *(ousia)* that transcends time and place. Truth is a mental state scarcely achieved by humans living in time. But humans at least have the ability to recognize what they typically lack and have the freedom to pursue truth so as to achieve a sense of well-being that, more than strength of body, is a firm anchor in the storms of time. Plato and the Academy and Aristotle and the Peripatetics also hypothesized a transcendent truth expressed as knowledge, the logos, the word spoken in the creation throughout all time, recognized by the individual knower at a given point in time.

Aristotle was one of the greatest students of human psychology. He made extensive studies of sleep, discovering that human mental activity continues as during wakefulness. He examined dreams and declared them to be natural rather than supernatural and subject to scientific analysis rather than religious faith. In *On Memory and Reminiscence* he studied how the human mind responds to time and experience. He understood the role of sense-perception in observation and analysis, the chief means by which an Aristotelian scientist acquires knowledge. Aristotle referred to the *psyche,* or soul, as the force of being in the human upon which bodily actions are dependent.

Meanwhile, the Italian school countered the idealism of the Platonists and Aristotelians with a materialist psychology. Developed by Leucippus and Democritus, this materialism took the form of invisible atoms composing all existence. Even the mind,

Bas relief of the pharaoh Akhenaten (Amenhotep IV, eighteenth dynasty, fourteenth century BCE) and his wife, Nefertiti, basking in the rays of Aten, ca. 1345 BCE, Amarna, Egypt. (Kathleen Cohen / Egyptian Museum, Berlin)

thoughts, dreams, the soul, and being were composed of atoms constantly in movement. Life held them together into an individual being; death released them to scatter and form other arrangements. Mortality was nothingness for the individual, but not for the universe, which is constantly transforming and remaking itself. Epicureans such as Lucretius believed the aim of life was achieving contentment, a pleasant sense of self that is generally immune from fear of the future and unfazed by mental, emotional, or physical pain. Stoics such as Marcus Aurelius conceived of a material logos that created and governed (if distantly) the universe. Each human shares in the logos by means of the

mind and soul; but identity is restricted to the here and now, its future limited by death.

Plutarch, the Greek author of *Moralia* and *Parallel Lives* during the Pax Romana, is a good example of the Platonic philosopher who was influenced by, even if he rejected, materialist philosophy. Plutarch made human (and animal) psychology one of his favorite topics. Plutarch employed an empathetic approach to converse, as it were, with past humans such as Alexander the Great, to discover fresh insights into their personalities. Plutarch made a study of depression and its causes; he believed depression was the result of obsessive thoughts about the momentary present and the approaching future. One must enjoy the present by using the past, which is an extensive repository of pleasant memories, an encyclopedia of wisdom never to be equaled by oneself, and a peaceful balance to the irritations and fears of the present moment.

Plutarch believed that the mind was a powerful agent in arriving at contentment. Reason was not a foil but rather an aid to happiness. One must exercise control over depressing images and obsessive thoughts. Thoughts cannot always be avoided. In Plutarch's essay *On Contentment* he recommended that the anxious and depressed person purposely confront the fears and obsessions so as to make them less powerful. Modern psychologists often recommend the same technique to their patients.

Plutarch was not as original in his animal psychology as he was in human psychology. In *Whether Land or Sea Animals Are Cleverer* and *On the Use of Reason by 'Irrational' Animals* he argued that animals do possess reason. Nature itself provides animals with courage, acceptance, and patience, which are all too often lacking in humans. Plutarch's arguments are not too different from the Pythagorean belief in the transmigration of souls. *On the Use of Reason by 'Irrational' Animals,* for example, pits the wise Odysseus against a philosophic hog, who seems to get the better of the famous Ithacan. Plutarch as a young man went so far as to advocate vegetarianism in his essay *On the Eating of Flesh.*

Christianity and the Later Roman Empire

Christianity as it developed during the first few centuries CE brought together into one system of thought the psychology of antiquity as it was developed over the course of several millennia by the Mesopotamians, Egyptians, Hebrews, and Greeks. The Gospels and Epistles of the Greek New Testament present an approach to the human psyche that is at the same time spiritual and materialist, based on surrender as well as freedom, in direct contrast to the omniscience of God, yet sharing

in the mind of God. The crucial development in ancient Christian psychology revolves around the life and teachings of Jesus of Nazareth combined with the belief by the early Christian church that he was the Christ, the Logos.

The fourth gospel, the Gospel of John, is the crucial text in the emergence of Christianity from the psychology of the ancient Near East and ancient Greeks. John interpreted Jesus as the Greek logos, the creative force of the universe, the source of reason, knowledge, and being. The Jesus of the Gospel of John is, as well, the begotten, co-eternal *word* of the Hebrew conception of God, Yahweh. What was completely new and unique amid the religious and philosophical history of the ancient Mediterranean was that Jesus, besides being the *logos,* the *nous,* and the *ousia,* was also a simple peasant born to a carpenter and his wife in the poor rural society of first-century BCE Palestine.

That Jesus was a man, or as he called himself, the Son of Man, had a profound effect on the development of Christian psychology. It is altogether a different experience to find within oneself a sense of knowing, being, feeling, and thinking that is human rather than eternal, infinite, transcendent, and anonymous. One knows, knowing that Jesus knew. One feels, knowing that Jesus felt. One thinks, knowing that Jesus thought. Christian psychology is so overwhelmed with human feelings and experiences of love, joy, faith, hope, sorrow, suffering, and pain that the believer, by believing in Jesus as the Son of Man and Christ, feels less alone, a part of something encompassing the whole of human experience, akin to a man who was god incarnate who suffered and died, the fear of which is precisely the source of anxiety, obsession, and depression among humans. Christ is the means of contentment for the Christian. Christ is the means of achieving a satisfactory sense of identity, of having a meaningful understanding of life, of accepting oneself, life and death, the universe itself.

Harkening back to Yahweh's proclamation

to Moses that "I am that I am," the Gospel of John quotes Jesus proclaiming to his disciples and the Jews, "I am" *(ego eimi)*. Jesus, a man, proclaimed himself the transcendent logos. But he also set forth an invitation to the human who seeks to know the transcendent, that to simply proclaim "I am" is to know the truth, the source of freedom.

Christianity combined with other religious and philosophical sects flooding the Roman Empire of the second and third centuries CE to produce one of the most intellectually dynamic times in human history. Gnostics such as Valentinus, Stoics such as Marcus Aurelius, Neoplatonists such as Plotinus, and Christians such as Origen tried to find meaning at a time when the ancient world was coming to an end, the Roman Empire was showing signs of collapse, the world seemed old and decayed, and humans were weighed down with sin and suffering. For many, the mind was the best escape to a new and better reality. This was certainly true of Plotinus, who believed that the self was the means of achieving the divine, to unite with the ultimate reality, the One, in an ecstatic transformation. Gnostic philosophers and Christians believed that reality was nonmaterial, noncorporeal, and hence the body had to be ignored, neglected, or punished. This period from the third to the fifth century CE was the time of the great desert hermits and self-mutilators such as Simon Stylites. The body had nothing to do with personal identity, indeed it hampered man's experience with the divine world. Total sexual abstinence was extremely popular; some fanatics castrated themselves; others refused to bathe; some loaded chains on their bodies to purge it of sin; others practically starved themselves in the name of purity. Such actions imply tremendous guilt, which appears to have been a common experience as a response by individuals and groups to the growing problems of the Roman Empire, such as civil war, famine, epidemics, violence, apathy, and so on.

That the individual search for identity continued as the Roman Empire of the West reached its last stages is seen in the life of Aurelius Augustine, who was at various times a Neoplatonist, Stoic, and Manichee before he turned to Christianity. Augustine was the typical obsessive individual who was overwhelmed with feelings of guilt that resulted in depression even as he was becoming rich and famous in fourth-century Italy. Having tried to find happiness by exorcising his guilt by means of self-examination, self-control, and the use of reason, and finding himself even more miserable, Augustine turned to Christianity in response to a religious experience in which he heard the call of a child telling him to "take and read" the Bible. Augustine did, and became a completely new man, born again, free from the oppressive feelings of guilt, confident that his life was valid. Augustine discovered that he could not think or will himself happy, he had to surrender, accept, and embrace something larger than himself to find himself. He wrote the *Confessions* to describe his journey to contentment and the connection of his psyche to the logos, Jesus Christ. The *Confessions* is in many ways the beginning of modern psychology. Few people have documented so completely depression and recovery, the obsessive-compulsive personality, and the sources and resolution of anxiety and the identity crisis. Martin Luther, who suffered from many of the same problems as Augustine, was an Augustinian monk deeply influenced by the *Confessions* and *City of God,* Augustine's other grand treatise dealing with the duality of mind and body. Jonathan Edwards, eighteenth-century America's great theologian, was a student of Augustine's psychology. Sigmund Freud and Carl Jung were also similarly influenced.

Modern psychological study continues to learn from the ancients, thanks to the experiences of Renaissance intellectuals such as Francesco Petrarca and Michel de Montaigne. The philosophy and psychology of the ancient world inspired Petrarch to write his incredible works of self-examination, such as the *Secret,* and Montaigne's great essay on self, the *Essays.* Petrarch learned from his study of Augustine that the path to contentment lies in self-examination in the context of a full understanding of time and the impact of the fleeting nature of time on the human psyche. Montaigne learned from Stoic thinkers such as Seneca and Platonists such as Plutarch a similar lesson of finding in the present sufficient contentment from the active recollection of the past and passive anticipation of the future. Montaigne gained assistance in combating his depression and anxiety by engaging in a dialogue with the past, conversing with past humans, by means of which Montaigne was able to see his life as hardly unique, as a common human experience of guilt, regret, suffering, and unhappiness. Accepting his *humanness* helped Montaigne "to live appropriately," which he discovered was the means of contentment.

See also Aristotle; Aurelius, Marcus; Aurelius Augustine; Egypt; Greek Classical Age; Later Roman Empire; Mesopotamia; New Testament; Old Testament; Plato; Plotinus; Plutarch

References

Aristotle. *On Sleep and Sleeplessness; On Prophesying by Dreams; On Memory and Reminiscence.* Translated by J. I. Beare. In *The Parva Naturalia.* Oxford: Clarendon Press, 1908.

De Montaigne, Michel. *Essays.* Translated by Donald Frame. Stanford: Stanford University Press, 1957.

Dodds, E. R. *Pagan and Christian in an Age of Anxiety.* New York: W. W. Norton, 1965.

Hallo, William, and William Simpson. *The Ancient Near East.* New York: Harcourt Brace Jovanovich, 1971.

Jacobsen, Thorkild. *The Treasures of Darkness: A History of Mesopotamian Religion.* New Haven: Yale University Press, 1976.

Plutarch. *Essays.* Translated by Robin Waterfield. London: Penguin Books, 1992.

———. *The Lives of the Noble Grecians and Romans.* Translated by John Dryden; revised by Arthur Hugh Clough. 1864; reprint ed., New York: Random House, 1992.

St. Augustine. *Confessions.* Translated by R. S. Pine-Coffin. Harmondsworth, Middlesex: Penguin Books, 1961.

Wilcox, Donald. *The Measure of Time's Past: Pre-Newtonian Chronologies and the Rhetoric of Relative Time.* Chicago: University of Chicago Press, 1987.

Ptolemaeus, Claudius (100–170 CE)

Claudius Ptolemaeus, or Ptolemy, of Alexandria was one of the most influential scientists of the ancient world. Ptolemy was the head of the Library of Alexandria. He was a mathematician, geographer, and astronomer of note whose conception of the world and the universe influenced thinkers of Medieval and Renaissance Europe and the Islamic East. His works were translated into Arabic as *Almagest,* and have been known as such ever since.

Ptolemy worked in the shadow of Eratosthenes and other Alexandrian geographers to develop the most sophisticated system of geography in the ancient world. His ideas were, however, erroneous in several respects. Ptolemy's measurement of the earth's circumference underestimated the earth by 80 degrees or 2/9 of the earth's surface, and conceived of the earth as being largely composed of land rather than water. Not knowing of the Pacific Ocean or the Americas, Ptolemy's conception of the earth was of three continents (Europe, Asia, Africa), a world-encircling ocean (the Atlantic), and a landlocked Indian Ocean. He assumed that Asia and Africa were connected, Asia dipping farther south and west than in reality, and he conceived of a vast terra incognita in the southern hemisphere.

Ptolemy's astronomy was informed by his predecessors, especially Hipparchus, as well as Babylonian astronomy. Because of his position as Librarian at Alexandria, Ptolemy had before him the vast corpus of Babylonian observations: ephemerides covering many centuries and lunar and solar eclipse records. Indeed, in the *Almagest,* Ptolemy provided numerous tables to describe astronomical phenomena. Ptolemy's geocentric universe was very similar to the Babylonian universe and theories of Greek astronomers before him. In it, Ptolemy assumed that the earth is the center around which the sun orbits. The planets are generally on the same plane as the sun. And from earth the observer can see their movement. Ptolemy explained a planet's retrograde motion by assuming that planets rotated on an epicycle around the spherical path that took them around the earth. When a planet is rotating about the earth in the distant semicircle of the epicycle it appears to move rapidly in the direction of the sun. But when it is rotating about the earth in the semicircle of the epicycle closest to earth it appears to reverse its orbit and then go back again—retrograde motion. Ptolemy's explanation of the morning and evening stars, that Mercury and Venus are visible for short times in the eastern horizon and western horizon, depended on the daily location of these planets in the direction of the sun. The morning star is visible until it reaches an area where it is blocked by sunlight, but then it reappears again on the opposite horizon when the sun sets in the west.

Ptolemy's concern was to create a theoretical model that could explain for the geometer and astronomer the positions of the planets relative to the fixed stars at a given time. Whereas in another work, *Planetary Hypotheses,* Ptolemy treated the planets as physical phenomena and tried to estimate distances from earth, the *Almagest* is entirely theoretical, and one wonders whether he intended his complex system of epicycles to be real or just a good theoretical plan. In the preface to the *Almagest,* Ptolemy claimed that theoretical rather than practical philosophy is best, and that that would be the approach he would take in his book. He followed Aristotle in defining the three areas of investigation as theology, the study of the First Cause; mathematics, the study of forms and motions of heavenly bodies both physical and immaterial; and physics, the study of the actual physical motions and attributes of material phenomena. Ptolemy concluded that of these three areas, the second, mathematics, was most appropriate for the scientist, as the former is unknowable by humans, and the latter is subject to the distressing uncertainty and corruptibility of material objects.

See also Alexandria; Astronomy; Geography/Geodesy; Hellenism
References
Crowe, Michael J. *Theories of the World from Antiquity to the Copernican Revolution.* New York: Dover Books, 1990.
Kuhn, Thomas S. *The Copernican Revolution: Planetary Astronomy in the Development of Western Thought.* Cambridge: Harvard University Press, 1957.
Neugebauer, O. *The Exact Sciences in Antiquity.* New York: Dover Books, 1969.

Pythagoras (570–490 BCE)

Pythagoras, along with Thales and Anaximander, ranks as one of the founders of Greek philosophy. Legends told of Pythagoras emphasized his great wisdom, his ability to foretell future events, his relationship with the gods (particularly the god of wisdom, Apollo), and his understanding and control of nature. Like other holy men, many miracles and aphorisms were associated with Pythagoras that cannot be confirmed by his own words as he apparently never recorded them, or they were irrevocably lost. Later writers such as Plutarch, Aristotle, Porphyry, and Diogenes Laertius recorded the bases of his philosophy. He believed in the transmigration of souls, which necessitated a vegetarian diet. The belief in reincarnation necessitated a refusal to abide by the norm of animal sacrifice to the gods. Likewise Pythagoras chose to wear clothes of linen rather than animal skin. He preached the virtue of silence, which is contradicted by other anecdotes of his life. A fragment from the writings of Xenophanes, for example, portrays humorously Pythagoras's belief in reincarnation, that he was moved to prevent the beating of a dog because in the animal's yelps he heard the voice of an old (dead) friend. Pythagoras was a metaphysician who emphasized the transcendent nature of being. The best way to approach an understanding of this invisible, universal truth is through mathematics. Number is the essence of being.

Pythagoras (570–490 BCE), the great Greek mathematician and philosopher. (Courtesy of the National Library of Medicine)

Pythagoras was reputedly of Ionian origin, possibly born in Samos to the engraver Mnesarchus. As an adult Pythagoras migrated to Croton in southern Italy. Herodotus, a famous traveler to such places as Egypt, believed that Pythagoras traveled to Egypt to learn the mysteries of the transmigration of souls. Porphyry in his *Life of Pythagoras* claimed that Pythagoras was taught by Chaldean astrologers—the magi of Asia. Diogenes Laertius named his teacher as Pherecydes of Syros. Pherecydes wrote on astronomy and the spheres of the heavenly bodies, reputedly learned to predict eclipses, constructed the gnomon to gauge time according to the movement of the sun, and learned much on his travels in Egypt.

Pythagoras astonished his contemporaries with his extravagant claims, one of which was that he had been blessed with being able to remember his past lives. Hence he recalled being Aethalides, the son of Hermes; then he was Euphorbus at the time of the Trojan War;

followed by Hermotimus and then Pyrrhus, a fisherman. After Pyrrhus, he became Pythagoras. In this last life (that we know of) Pythagoras opened a school and got involved in politics at Croton and died at Metapontum.

Changing seasons, unending cycles, allow humans to conceive of number, a quantitative aspect to life. Pythagoras found numerical harmony in music, shapes, and quantities of things. He is known for the theorem that states that the square of the length of the hypotenuse of a right triangle equals the sum of the squares of the lengths of the other two sides. The Babylonians had, however, made use of this technique a millennium earlier. Such theorems as the Pythagorean, abstract conceptions based on measurement of lines and spaces, gave rise among his followers to a general approach to life—that reality is not concrete and is rarely seen but yet can be approximated by mathematics. Time, for example, is not seen, not "real," but movement can be traced according to set measurements, numbers, which gives us an idea of some metaphysical reality that we call time.

It is entirely possible that Pythagoras was the first to hypothesize the spherical shape of the earth based on geometry. Diogenes Laertius asserted that Pythagoras thought that the earth was perfect, that the sphere was the most perfect shape, and thus the earth must be a sphere. But a perfect sphere would naturally be the center of all things; hence Pythagoras had a geocentric conception of the universe. Plutarch, however, in his life of Numa Pompilius, who was reputedly a Pythagorean, claimed that the Pythagoreans believed that the earth orbited the central fire, and that Plato, under their influence, adopted a similar heliocentric view.

Much of what is attributed to Pythagoras derived from his followers, which included philosophers and scientists such as Telarges, his son, Philolaus, Hippo, and Hippasus. Philolaus was the leading Pythagorean and perhaps the source for the ideas of the central fire, the counter-earth, the *tetractys* (10 is a perfect number derived from adding 1, 2, 3, and 4), and the music of the spheres. Hippasus reportedly discovered the mathematical harmonies of the musical scales, the dodecahedron (a twelve-sided figure), and irrational geometric constructs.

See also Astronomy; Greek Archaic Age; Hippo of Croton; Iamblichus; Mathematics; Neoplatonism; Philolaus; Plato; Plotinus; Porphyry

References

Barnes, Jonathan, trans. *Early Greek Philosophy.* London: Penguin Books, 1987.

Burnet, John, ed. and trans. *Early Greek Philosophy.* London: Adam and C. Black, 1930.

Heath, Sir Thomas. *Aristarchus of Samos.* New York: Dover Books, 1913.

Laertius, Diogenes. *Lives of the Philosophers.* Translated by R. D. Hicks. 2 vols. Cambridge: Harvard University Press, 1931, 1938.

Plutarch. *The Lives of the Noble Grecians and Romans.* Translated by John Dryden; revised by Arthur Hugh Clough. 1864; reprint ed., New York: Random House, 1992.

Russell, Bertrand. *A History of Western Philosophy.* New York: Simon and Schuster, 1945.

Pytheas of Massilia (floruit late fourth century BCE)

Pytheas of Massilia lived about 300 BCE. Little is known about his journeys and even less about his life. The account of his journey to the North Atlantic is lost. But ancient authors and geographers, such as Strabo and Polybius, wrote about Pytheas and provided some details of his journey. Pytheas was an ad hoc scientist, an explorer who in the process of penetrating the unknown had to adopt a scientific methodology of observation, forming and testing hypotheses, and recording data. Some ancient critics, particularly Strabo, doubted the authenticity of Pytheas's account; others, such as Eratosthenes, believed

his voyage took place. The few details that do survive provide compelling evidence that Pytheas of Massilia did indeed journey to the North Atlantic.

Massilia in Pytheas's time was a city situated at the mouth of the Rhone River in what is today southern France. Massilia was a seafaring city engaged in shipbuilding and trade. Carthage, across the Mediterranean in North Africa, dominated the trade of the western Mediterranean. Mariners such as Pytheas frequently looked for the rare opportunity to sail undetected through the Strait of Gibraltar. Somehow Pytheas was able to do so around 300 BCE. Knowing of the Carthaginian tin trade with the British Isles, Pytheas and crew made their way up the coast of Spain and hugged the shores of France until they reached England. He claimed to have circumnavigated the Isles, making measurements and taking notes, and to have explored the islands on foot.

The most tantalizing and incredible part of Pytheas's journey was his exploration of Thule. Strabo reported that Pytheas claimed Thule was several days of sailing north of the Tin Islands, Britain. Thule was never clearly defined by the ancients, or by later authors; even as late as the sixteenth century CE, the son and biographer of Christopher Columbus, Ferdinand, recorded a visit by his father to the North Atlantic, where he had heard of Thule. Candidates to be Thule are northern Scotland, the Orkney Islands, the Shetland Islands, Iceland, or Scandinavia—some have claimed that Thule was Greenland or even Baffin Island in Canada. Pytheas's description of the environs of Thule leads one to speculate that it was Norway or Iceland. Pytheas described the icy fog that enveloped the sea in that arctic region; his description could only have been gained by experience.

As a scientist, Pytheas's knowledge of celestial navigation helped him on the outward and return voyages. The report of his exploits included precise measurements of the British coastline, which he estimated to be about 40,000 stadia, or 4,600 miles, in extent. Pytheas believed that there was a relationship between the moon and the ocean tides. He made calculations of the position of the North Star and also used the sundial to determine the solstices and equinoxes. Like most inquisitive Greeks of his time, Pytheas's questions resulted in reasonable answers based on experience and observations made on the spot.

See also Geography/Geodesy; Greek Archaic Age; Polybius; Strabo

References

Freeman, Kathleen. *Greek City-States.* New York: W. W. Norton, 1950.

Heath, Sir Thomas. *Aristarchus of Samos.* New York: Dover Books, 1913.

Polybius. *The Histories.* Translated by W. R. Paton. 6 vols. Cambridge: Harvard University Press, 1922–27.

Strabo. *Geography.* Translated by H. L. Jones. Cambridge: Harvard University Press, 1917, 1923.

R

Roman Principate (31 BCE–180 CE)

Augustus

The Roman Principate is named for the preferred title of Augustus (Octavian) Caesar, who was only eighteen years old when his great-uncle and adopted father Julius Caesar was assassinated by Republican senators at Rome. Yet Octavian quickly gained the loyalty of Caesar's troops and supporters, made war against the leaders of the conspiracy, Brutus and Cassius, and then gradually became the most powerful man in the empire. In 31 BCE, he defeated his rival Antony at the Battle of Actium and assumed control of the Roman Empire. Octavian ostensibly returned power to the "Senate and People of Rome" but was given the special powers of Proconsul, commander of Roman military forces, and Tribune, defender of the people, with veto power. Octavian also had personal control over the province of Egypt, which gave him unlimited wealth and put him in charge of a primary source of food in Rome. In 27 BCE, the Senate conferred upon Octavian the titles of Augustus (honored, revered) and Imperator (conqueror, one holding imperium, power). Augustus preferred, however, the title Princeps, which Roman leaders in good standing in the Republic had long used; it meant simply First Citizen. Henceforth Augustus and his successors during the two-hundred-year Principate would rule Rome with almost total power, yet style themselves as the Princeps of Rome.

Julio-Claudians

Augustus, after years of civil conflict, tried to restore the empire to health and prosperity. He initiated a campaign to bring back the old morality of the Romans, and he sponsored the work of many poets and historians, such as Virgil and Horace. This atmosphere of prosperity and achievement inspired others to engage in science and medicine. Three dynasties of Roman emperors oversaw a relatively peaceful time in the history of Rome that encouraged thought and speculation about nature. The three dynasties were the Julio-Claudian dynasty (31 BCE–68 CE) under the emperors Augustus (31 BCE–14 CE), Tiberius (14–37), Caligula (37–41), Claudius (41–54), and Nero (54–68); the Flavian dynasty (69–96) under the emperors Vespasian (69–79), Titus (79–81), and Domitian (81–96); and the Antonine dynasty under the emperors Nerva (96–98), Trajan (98–117), Hadrian (117–138), Antoninus Pius (138–161), and Marcus Aurelius (161–180).

Stoics

Roman science during the final centuries BCE had become heavily dependent upon the Greeks. The Epicurean view of a material universe was eloquently expressed by Lucretius in *On the Nature of Things*. Stoicism, founded by Zeno, a Greek, was the most popular philosophy among Roman intellectuals. Its leading advocate during the late Republic was Cicero, who, although he was primarily an orator and statesman, produced works such as *On the Nature of the Gods* and *On Divination*. A century later during the reign of Nero another great Stoic thinker of the Principate, Seneca, in his daily practice of philosophy, engaged in spirited inquiries into the nature of things. His surviving *Epistles* reveal his preoccupation with morality, nature, and science. Seneca wrote other works, too, such as *Problems in Natural Science*. A half century later during the reign of Trajan the Younger, Pliny revealed his scientific inclinations in his correspondence. The emperor Marcus Aurelius was a fine example of a Stoic philosopher. His *Meditations* reveal his inquisitiveness about history, nature, the origin of things, and their final end. Other emperors likewise considered themselves to be philosophers: Nero engaged in verse and architecture; Hadrian loved Greek philosophy and also delved into architecture; Claudius was a biographer, philologist, and historian.

History and Geography

Historical writing was the art and science par excellence during the Principate. Roman historians, as students of the entire experience of humankind, of necessity engaged in speculation on human nature and natural history. During Augustus's reign, Titus Livius produced a massive history of Republican Rome that included wonderful descriptions of the imposing forces of nature, such as the Alps. C. Julius Hyginus, a native of Spain and a freedman, was the librarian of the Palatine library who wrote biographies and histories as well as treatises on geography, agriculture,

aviculture, and religion. The polymath Cornelius Tacitus, who wrote during the reign of Trajan, explored the human psyche (in his study of Tiberius, for example) and described the culture of the Germanic tribes of northern Europe in the *Germania*. Plutarch, a Greek writing during the Principate, composed not only *Lives* but *Moral Essays* as well, in which he explored a variety of scientific issues ranging from human behavior to world geography to astronomy. Plutarch was a polymath, as was his predecessor in the art of knowing a little about a lot, the Elder Pliny. Pliny was a historian and geographer, a tirelessly inquisitive man who lost his life when Mount Vesuvius erupted in 79 CE. Pliny's *Natural History*, a wonderful catalog of hearsay and observation, was published posthumously.

The works of Livy, Tacitus, and Plutarch reveal that historical writing requires the complement of geographical investigation. The Greek Strabo produced a massive compendium of geographical facts and observations about nature ranging from Europe to Africa to Asia. Pomponius Mela of Spain produced a multivolume *Chorographia* during the reign of the emperor Claudius wherein he described the many lands subjugated by the Romans. Augustus sponsored the work of Hyginus on the geography of Italy.

Roman Pragmatism

The Roman mind-set was less speculative and metaphysical than that of the Greeks, who excelled at philosophy and the search for *being*. The Roman scientist was interested in knowledge that could be usefully applied to problems of everyday life as well as issues of order, mobility, structure, power, and majesty. Roman road-building is a good example. Roads are useful for travel and trade, of course, but initially the Romans constructed roads as a consequence, or to facilitate, military activity. Logistics, unimpeded communications and supply lines, were keys to Roman military success. Roman surveyors solved the problem of drainage and picked the best routes with the least fluctuation in elevation. Surveyors solved the problem of elevation and gravity in the construction of aqueducts, some of which still exist, which brought fresh water to towns using the force of gravity: water flows as long as there exists an uninterrupted declivity. The aqueducts were astonishing structures of elegance and utility, which relied on sophisticated engineering techniques. Roman engineers learned how to distribute the material forces of weight and gravity by means of the vaulted arch. The emperor Hadrian showed his ability as an engineer in the design of the domed Pantheon, which became the form of choice for builders of public buildings for centuries to come. The Roman Coliseum, completed during the reign of Titus (79–81 CE) was not only a magnificent engineering achievement but featured an intricate design for a partial cloth covering or shade to be used on sunny days. Many of the ideas and techniques of Roman construction, engineering, and architecture are preserved in Vitruvius's *On Architecture*.

Agriculture was the mainstay of the Roman economy. Thus many Romans studied and wrote on agricultural practices. Varro, best known for his study of language, wrote *On Agriculture* during the period of civil conflict after the assassination of Caesar. Varro believed in practical experience gained by years of working with the land as well as experimentation with crops and soils. Columella, surpassing Varro, wrote *On Agriculture* and *On Trees*. He was interested in aviculture (birdkeeping), relying on the work of Hyginus in this regard. Viticulture was also important for the wine-imbibing Romans, and several notable authors, such as Julius Graecinus, penned works on the cultivation of grapes.

See also Aurelius, Marcus; Cicero; Columella; Engineering and Technology; Epicureanism; Lucretius; Pliny the Elder; Pliny the Younger; Plutarch; Roman Roads and Bridges; Seneca, Lucius Annaeus; Stoicism; Tacitus; Varro; Vitruvius

References
Barrow, R. H. *The Romans.* Harmondsworth, Middlesex: Penguin Books, 1949.
Durant, Will. *Caesar and Christ.* New York: Simon and Schuster, 1944.
Lucretius. *The Nature of the Universe.* Translated by R. E. Latham. Harmondsworth, Middlesex: Penguin Books, 1951.
Ogilvie, R. M. *Roman Literature and Society.* Harmondsworth, Middlesex: Penguin Books, 1980.
Sinnigen, William, and Arthur Boak. *A History of Rome.* 6th ed. New York: Macmillan Publishing, 1977.
Suetonius. *The Twelve Caesars.* Translated by Robert Graves. London: Penguin Books, 1957.
Tacitus. *The Annals.* Translated by Michael Grant. London: Penguin Books, 1971.

Roman Roads and Bridges

The great builders of antiquity were the Romans. The Roman practical genius combined with military necessity, the riches of empire, and soldiers who knew how to work and to build to create lasting roads and bridges that have withstood the passing millennia. The Roman legions built as they marched, confident that they would be returning the same way again and again once enemy territory was pacified and brought into the Roman Empire. The empire, as it expanded throughout the Mediterranean world, required good roads for communications. Often the roads traversed hilly, wet land that necessitated numerous bridges. The demands of civilization meant that the Roman road- and bridge-builders were constantly at work.

The first Roman road is in many ways still the most grand. The Via Appia, or Appian Way, connects the city of Rome with Capua to the south. It was built at the insistence of the Roman senator Appius Claudius Crassus in 312 BCE. The Via Appia, like subsequent roads, was built by Roman engineers using soldiers to do the labor. They dug a running pit three feet deep and fifteen feet wide and

Roman engineering genius applied to roads is evident in the modern ruins of this Roman road in Algeria. (Corel Corporation)

layered it with gravel and stone. No cement was used. The stones, basalt and silex, were quarried from ancient volcanic sites, brought to the construction site and carefully cut. Workers placed the octagonal stones in a bed of gravel and heated sand. Workers wedged the stones together so tight as not to allow even a knife's edge to penetrate. The use of a surveying instrument, the *groma,* which relied on plumb lines, ensured that the road would be level. Low-lying, marshy regions required additional care and the building of causeways. The Via Appia traversed the Pontine Marshes and was forced to end at Lake Pontia in Campania at the Forum Appii. After the lake the Via Appia continued to Capua. Along the road, numerous tombs were built, beginning with that of its creator, Appius, who died shortly after the completion of the road that bears his name.

As the centuries passed Roman roads changed to meet the conditions of different lands. Some roads were built with curbs. Lands such as Africa did not have volcanic stone, so other rock, such as limestone, was cut by masons into rectangles and laid closely together. Engineers learned how to build a road with a delicate slant from center to sides to allow for drainage. By the mid-first century CE there were over three hundred roads covering over fifty thousand miles. Roads connected the empire. Dozens of roads spread from Italy to the Alps, connecting Rome with Ravenna, Marseilles, Lyons, Milan, Naples, and Syracuse. Roads followed conquests. Thus they extended into Spain, Gaul, and England, connecting the cities of Toledo, Cadiz, Tarrogona, Barcelona, Bordeaux, Paris, Cologne, London, and York. Under Hadrian, roads in England ended at a seventy-six-mile wall built to hold back the

Picts and Scots to the north. Hadrian's Wall was built of stone and cement and was fortified every mile with a small fort or castle. Roads later extended beyond Hadrian's Wall to the Antonine Wall, built under his successor Antoninus Pius. To the south, eight roads entered London. Eighteen entered Rome. Throughout the empire there was a sophisticated post system with hostels every eighteen miles where travelers could find refreshment and a place to stay. Perhaps the Romans borrowed the idea from the Persians, who once had the great Royal Road spanning their Asian empire, which had hostels every fifteen miles. The Roman system was called during the later Roman Empire the *cursus publicus.* Beginning during the second century BCE, Romans set up milestones every mile (4,800 feet) to indicate distance. Cartographers drew early road maps to gauge distance and direction, especially for imperial and military purposes. Of these maps, called *itineraria,* which were drawn on goat's skin or papyrus, only one survives, the Peutinger Table, a copy of an *itinerarium* of the Late Roman Empire.

The Romans were also the greatest bridge-builders in antiquity. Few people before the Romans understood the art and science of bridging rivers and streams. One reads about pontoon bridges and bridges formed by lashing boats together, but no country except Rome made bridges of stone that spanned rivers and time. Some of the most famous Roman bridges included the Milvian Bridge that crossed the Tiber, at the place where Constantine defeated Maxentius in 311 CE; the mile-long bridge spanning the Danube, built by the emperor Trajan under the direction of the engineer Apollodorus of Damascus; the Pont du Gard, a bridge and aqueduct, still standing, built by Marcus Agrippa during the reign of Augustus; the Alcántara in Spain, also designed by Apollodorus; the aqueduct at Segovia, Spain, built during the reign of Augustus; Valen's aqueduct, built during the late fourth century,

which lasted 800 years and spanned the 150-mile breadth of the Balkans to Constantinople. Some of these imposing works were built with stone blocks arranged together with such precision as to withstand gravity, time, and geologic events. Others used cement, which the Romans developed, combining volcanic rock with lime, sand, and water. Bridges required a firm base in the marsh or river; engineers dug through silt to rock, to which they cemented ashlars of stone or pylons kept upright with huge boulders.

See also Engineering and Technology; Hydraulics; Roman Principate

References

Dal Maso, Leonard B. *Rome of the Caesars.* Translated by Michael Hollingsworth. Florence: Bonechi-Edizioni, 1974.
Von Hagen, Victor W. *Roman Roads.* London: Werdenfeld and Nicholson, 1966.

Rome

Rome, built on the Tiber River of central Italy in (according to tradition) 753 BCE, was a scientific center during the ancient world due more to its place as a governmental center of great power, wealth, and population than to its promotion of the sciences. The Romans purposely cultivated a practical, active mind-set rather than metaphysics and speculation, which they thought to be less manly and suitable more for conquered peoples such as the Greeks. Roman science was devoted to the arts linked to empire, power, and war, such as engineering, hydraulics, military science, and architecture. Their great accomplishments were construction of roads, buildings, aqueducts, and engines of war. As a society that enslaved the conquered and relied on slavery for labor and production, the Romans had little incentive to devise new forms of technology to expand production. And speculative sciences that seemed to have no pragmatic result they eschewed. Yet the Romans embraced science

The Roman Coliseum, built from 72 to 80 CE, illustrates Roman sophistication in monumental architecture. (Corel Corporation)

against their better judgment, particularly during the Augustan Age and after, when the empire included tens of millions of peoples living in three continents with diverse and cosmopolitan ideas. The Greeks in particular exercised a tremendous influence on Roman thought and belief during the first few centuries CE.

The beginnings of Greek philosophy in Rome occurred with the Roman conquest of Greece during the second century BCE. Greek thinkers such as Panaetius and Polybius arrived in Rome, some such as Polybius under compulsion, where they introduced such ideas as Stoicism to the Romans. The focus on reason, on duty, on self-control, on living according to the rules of nature, appealed to the pragmatic Romans. Posidonius of Rhodes during the first century influenced Cicero, who took Stoicism to heart in his political activities and in his many writings on politics, rhetoric, and science. Epicureanism came to Rome about the same time as did Stoicism. The Epicurean Philodemus of Gadara wrote varied scientific treatises in the first century that appealed to many Romans, who might have otherwise found the tenets of Epicureanism difficult to accept. Lucretius's *On the Nature of Things,* which presented Epicurean tenets of acceptance of life, of the physical nature of the universe, and of

complete free will, found an audience in Rome during the mid first century. Epicureanism had less of an enduring hold on the Romans than Stoicism. Some of Rome's greatest thinkers and scientists during the first several centuries CE, such as Seneca, Pliny the Elder, Epictetus, and Marcus Aurelius, were Stoics.

Stoicism appealed to Romans in part because of its focus on the practical, on action rather than words. Romans eschewed metaphysics for ideas and things that worked. It took Polybius, a Greek, to write a complete political analysis of the Roman Republic. The Roman love for practical knowledge was emphasized in particular during the reign of Augustus Caesar (31 BCE–14 CE), who patronized great writers and thinkers such as Titus Livius, Virgil, and Vitruvius. Building and architecture were activities that exhibited the Roman love for monuments to Roman glory and reminders of personal military achievements, as well as the means to achieve more. The city, by the end of the Pax Romana, featured numerous forums that commemorated the victories of emperors such as Trajan and the love for building of emperors such as Hadrian. Hadrian, for example, had a hand in designing the pantheon, the temple to all deities, which had a large dome with a hole at the top to let the sunlight in; light moved across the towering walls during the course of the day. The pantheon used concrete and a series of panels that grow larger and heavier as they descend from the cupola. Other emperors built baths, theatres, circuses, and stadiums. The emperor Vespasian began the Coliseum, which was finished under his son and successor Titus. Trajan and Marcus Aurelius set up great columns to commemorate military victories. Titus, Septimius Severus, and Constantine constructed grand arches for the same purpose. The city featured several obelisks and numerous temples as well. The vast wealth that sponsored such public works was based on agriculture, trade, and military conquest. The importance of the former led to a variety of handbooks and treatises on farming, viticulture, and olive growing. Authors included Cato, Celsus, Columella, and Pliny. Perhaps the most important key to the success of the empire was the network of roads, beginning with the Via Appia, constructed in 312 BCE. A maze of thousands of miles of roads crisscrossed Spain, Gaul, Britain, Italy, Africa, Greece, Turkey, and Palestine. Roads were built by the Roman legions using sand, gravel, basalt, and limestone. They were built so efficiently that many are in use even today.

See also Engineering and Technology; Epicureanism; Roman Roads and Bridges; Stoicism

References

Barrow, R. H. *The Romans.* Harmondsworth, Middlesex: Penguin Books, 1949.

Dal Maso, Leonard B. *Rome of the Caesars.* Translated by Michael Hollingsworth. Florence: Bonechi-Edizioni, 1974.

Ogilvie, R. M. *Roman Literature and Society.* Harmondsworth, Middlesex: Penguin Books, 1980.

Rowell, Henry Thompson. *Rome in the Augustan Age.* Norman: University of Oklahoma Press, 1962.

S

Seneca, Lucius Annaeus (5–65 CE)

Seneca was an extremely influential statesman and Stoic philosopher of the mid-first century CE. He was primarily a moralist, but he also speculated on nature in his *Natural Questions,* and he explored the human psyche in the *Moral Letters.* A native of Spain, Seneca gained a reputation in Rome for his essays and plays. He served under the emperor Claudius and was made tutor to Claudius's adopted son Nero. Upon Nero's accession in 54 CE, Seneca served as the young emperor's chief adviser. After about ten years, Nero grew suspicious of Seneca, who retired to his villas and his books. He was compelled to commit suicide in 65 CE, after a plot to topple Nero was discovered. Nero thought that Seneca was behind it.

Seneca was one of the leading Stoics of his day. Stoicism had as one of its chief tenets that nature is rational and orderly, and the man who imitates such reason and order will enjoy the best sort of existence. Natural history was therefore important to a Stoic such as Seneca. His *Natural Questions,* addressed to Lucilius, like the *Moral Letters,* reveals this concern. The book examines meteorology, astronomy, and geosciences. Seneca explained meteors according to changes in the atmosphere. He described the origin of winds, the varied precipitation falling from clouds, the weather of Egypt compared to Italy, the causes of earthquakes, and the nature of comets.

The *Moral Letters* reveal Seneca to have deeply pondered the nature of happiness and how to achieve it. His psychology focused on the constant fear of death, the ongoing awareness of the passage of time and mortality, and the resulting anxiety that overwhelms, depresses, imprisons, and freezes human action. Seneca advocated a form of *apatheia,* the ability to withstand change and contingency, which are the forerunners of death. One must treat death, he preached in letters to his friend Lucilius, as another act of life, as something one simply does, like eating, sleeping, and bathing. The key is to avoid a constant focus on the future. One must rid oneself of thoughts or sensations of fear as well as of hope—anything that represents the utter unknown of the future. Seneca's argument regarding the quandary of hope and fear was very similar to St. Augustine's of centuries later. Time involves anticipation of the future, awareness of the present, and recollection of the past. But if memory brings on obsessions about past wrongs and sins, while anticipation of the future suggests all sorts of awful possibilities, and the present moment goes by too quickly to make sense of it, then humans are destined, it seems, to suffer unhappiness.

Seneca (5–65 CE), the Roman Stoic philosopher. Photographische Gesellschaft, Berlin, 1880 to 1930. (Library of Congress)

Seven Sages

The Seven Sages were legendary thinkers identified by ancients of the Greco-Roman world to explain the origins of thought, literature, and science. Diogenes Laertius's *Lives of the Philosophers* lists the seven as Thales, Solon, Periander, Cleobulus, Chilon, Bias, and Pittaeus, although Diogenes noted that sometimes these were replaced by others: Anacharsis the Scythian, Myson of Chen, Pherecydes of Syros, Epimenides the Cretan, and Pisistratus, tyrant of Athens. Thales of Miletus was, perhaps, the only physical scientist among the lot. He was an astronomer, engineer, and metaphysician who was clearly influenced by Egyptian and Mesopotamian scientists. The Athenian Solon was known for his wisdom and statesmanship in creating the Athenian state. Besides Thales and Solon, most of the other Seven Sages are known only by anecdotal information. Diogenes Laertius called Chilon, Pittaeus, Bias, and Cleobulus moral philosophers, although the latter was familiar with Egyptian philosophy. Anacharsis was reputed by some to be the inventor of the anchor and potter's wheel. Diogenes claimed that Myson argued for a concrete approach to acquiring knowledge based on accumulating facts with which to support arguments. Epimenides, according to Diogenes, saved Athens from the ravages of plague. According to Pliny the Elder he lived for 157 years, having spent 57 of those asleep in a cave. Plutarch claimed he was a soothsayer. Pherecydes, whom some call the teacher of Pythagoras, was, perhaps, a philosopher and scientist of time, inventing the sundial. Pliny the Elder claimed (without giving details) that Pherecydes was able to predict earthquakes.

See also Diogenes Laertius; Solon; Thales
References
Laertius, Diogenes. *Lives of the Philosophers.* Translated by R. D. Hicks. 2 vols. Cambridge: Harvard University Press, 1931, 1938.
Pliny the Elder. *Natural History.* Translated by John F. Healy. London: Penguin Books, 1991.
Plutarch. *The Lives of the Noble Grecians and Romans.* Translated by John Dryden; revised by Arthur Hugh Clough. 1864; reprint ed., New York: Random House, 1992.

Seneca's solution to the dilemma of human suffering was to assume that he was in constant recovery from the illness of anxiety: the only medicine that works is acceptance of life and self. The latter involves knowing oneself, one's faults and virtues, and accepting one's existence and, especially, one's mortality.

Seneca's psychology of self had a profound influence on many subsequent psychologists and philosophers such as Epictetus, Augustine, Montaigne, and Erasmus, and through them the modern study of the mind, emotions, and behavior.

See also Roman Principate; Psychology; Stoicism
References
Clarke, John, trans. *Physical Science in the Time of Nero: Being a Translation of the Quaestiones Naturales of Seneca.* New York: Macmillan, 1910.
Seneca. *Letters from a Stoic.* Translated by Robin Campbell. London: Penguin Books, 1969.

Seven Wonders of the Ancient World

The Seven Wonders of the Ancient World were selected by the ancients themselves as being astonishing examples of human creativity and construction.

The Great Pyramid of Cheops, built about 2650 BCE, was observed by Herodotus on his visit to Egypt during the fifth century CE. Herodotus learned from Egyptian priests that the pyramid was built with the labor of 100,000 men who dragged massive limestone blocks from barges that had sailed up canals filled with water from the flooding Nile. Levers were used to raise the blocks from each level or step to the next. The height of the pyramid was the same as each side of its base. Pliny the Elder considered the pyramids unforgivable examples of hubris, built by peasants in massive building projects. The largest, he said, covered five acres and was 725 feet high. The ancients were uncertain how they were built—Pliny thought perhaps by means of mud brick ramps or heaps of salt. The theory that the huge limestone blocks were brought to the building site during the Nile's flooding was doubted by Pliny.

The Colossus of Rhodes, designed and constructed by Chares of Lindos on the island of Rhodes, was a massive bronze statue over one hundred feet high of the sun god Apollo. The statue took twelve years to build, from 292 to 280 BCE. Bronze covered an iron structure that was built by piling up hills of sand around the statue as it rose in height. Pliny the Elder recorded that the colossus stood for sixty-six years, falling to pieces during an earthquake.

The lighthouse of Alexandria at Pharos was designed and built by Sostratos of Cnidus. The tower was built in three levels and was four hundred feet high. Pliny the Elder claimed that the lighthouse cost eight hundred talents—a talent was a unit of measure of silver or gold that equaled roughly 6,000 drachmas in classical Athens.

The Mausoleum of Halicarnassus was designed by Pythius of Halicarnassus from 355 to 350 BCE as a marble monument to the king of Caria Mausolus. It was fifty-five meters high, was supported by thirty-two columns, and had a step-pyramid at the top.

According to legend, King Nebuchadnezzar II (604–562) built gardens for his wife, who missed the forested mountains of her native land. Authorities such as Diodorus Siculus, Strabo, and Philo of Byzantium described the gardens from hearsay. Reputedly an elaborate system of irrigation kept the trees and shrubs blooming in constant dazzling colors. The ruins of the Hanging Gardens of Babylon at the southern palace of King Nebuchadnezzar II suggest layered walls that hosted a diverse flora.

The Temple of Artemis (Roman Diana) at Ephesus was, according to Pliny the Elder, 425 long and 225 feet wide, with 127 columns of up to 60 feet in height. The architect, Chersiphron of Knossos, received guidance in building the temple from Artemis herself in dreams. The temple was built on low-lying, marshy ground to escape the impact of earthquakes. Sand bags, stacked one upon another, supported the weighty stone; once the capital and lintel were in place, Chersiphron had the sand released from the bags, one after another, so gently easing the massive stones into place. Fire destroyed the Temple of Artemis in 356 BCE, the same day, it was claimed, as the birth of Alexander of Macedon. Soothsayers interpreted the omen as indicating that Alexander would scorch all of Asia. The temple was rebuilt in 334 BCE by Deinocrates of Rhodes, the urban planner of the city of Alexandria.

The Temple of Zeus at Olympia was designed by Libon of Ellis and was completed in 456 BCE. The wonder, a statue of Zeus designed and sculpted by the art director of the Parthenon, Phidias, was forty-four feet tall and twenty-two feet wide.

The Great Pyramid of Khufu (Cheops) at Giza, built during the twenty-sixth century BCE, is the most amazing of the Seven Wonders of the Ancient World. (Corel Corporation)

See also Alexandria; Engineering and
Technology; Egypt; Philo of Byzantium
References
Herodotus. *The Histories.* Translated by Aubrey
de Selincourt. Harmondsworth, Middlesex:
Penguin Books, 1972.
Oates, Joan. *Babylon.* London: Thames and
Hudson, 1986.
Pliny the Elder. *Natural History.* Translated by
John F. Healy. London: Penguin Books,
1991.
"The Seven Wonders of the Ancient World":
http://ce.eng.usf.edu/pharos/wonders/in
dex.html.

Sextus Empiricus
See Philosophy

Shipbuilding and Design
See Marine Science

Skepticism
See Philosophy

Social Sciences
Social science is literally the scientific study of society in all its forms: family, community, kinship, nation, institutions, laws and norms, ethnic groups, human culture. Although the social sciences are modern scientific disciplines of study, one finds the roots of the formal study of sociology, anthropology, ethnology, geography, economics, and political science in the ancient world, particularly among the Greeks. Social science is, of course, vastly different in scope and method from the physical and life sciences. The latter scientists manipulate the objects of study in ways that social scientists refuse to do. There are few laboratory experiments in the study of society. Ancient scientists, however, per-

formed few experiments, and therefore science was less empirical and more reliant upon reason, logic, observation, and analysis. In short, social science was scarcely different from the physical and life sciences in the ancient world.

In ancient Mesopotamia at the end of the third millennium and beginning of the second millennium BCE, the first law codes were recorded, that of Ur Nammu at Ur in the twenty-first century BCE and the Code of Hammurapi at Babylon in the eighteenth century BCE. These law codes, although barbaric in some ways with an unrelenting focus on violence and capital punishment, nevertheless began the process of the state determining right and wrong, releasing humans from the hitherto endless cycle of blood vengeance. The Code of Hammurapi was a code of justice, which was in the hands of the state and determined by the state. The idea of a public to which the individual must conform had begun.

The Greeks

The Greek historian Herodotus has been called the father of history, the father of geography, and even the father of lies. Arguably he was the father of anthropology as well. His accounts of Asian and African cultures, gained by personal observation over the course of several years journeying through Asia Minor, Palestine, and Egypt, sometimes contained the ludicrous and stories that challenge one's credulity. Yet his writings also give fascinating and highly accurate and sensitive portraits of contemporary customs and beliefs. In Egypt, for example, Herodotus found a society where the women and men had distinct roles and habits, the women being involved in trade and going to market, the men staying home to perform domestic duties such as making clothing. Egyptians mourned by growing their hair rather than cutting it, as in other cultures. Although they lived with their animals and handled dung, in other ways they had singular ideas of cleanliness: for example,

unlike most people, the Egyptians practiced circumcision, which they thought was more sanitary. And Egyptian priests shaved their entire bodies to ensure that lice and other vermin would not plague them. Herodotus was fascinated by the Egyptian obsession with cats—Egyptians even had their house pets mummified.

Athens

Sixth- and fifth-century BCE Athens was the place and time during which the basic ideas of social science were developed, primarily by such thinkers as Solon, Pericles, Thucydides, Socrates, and Plato. The lawgiver Solon made the Athenian law code more equitable and fitting to the people and place of ancient Attica. Pericles oversaw the implementation of the basic core values and institutions of democracy—such as trial by jury, equality among citizens, public responsibility and service, and the secret ballot. Thucydides the historian used the Peloponnesian War to make lasting observations about human behavior. Socrates and Plato, as revealed in Plato's dialogues such as the *Republic,* developed such core ideas of political and social science as the social compact, where government is a voluntary association among free humans who join together to promote their own survival; the reliance of society upon a division of labor, wherein each human performs the task that most benefits the public good; ideals of political and social responsibility, of leaders who dedicate their lives to bringing truth into the workings of the state. The Greeks invented the science of political oratory, the greatest orators being Lysias, Isocrates, and Demosthenes.

Aristotle was one of the first scientists of human behavior. His study *Ethics* is based on correct behavior in the human community. Selfless motives lead to virtuous actions as opposed to selfish motives that result in vice. Society clearly benefits from actions done for their own sake and not from ulterior motives. The best society promotes virtuous actions by means of the body politic—this was Aristotle's argument in his treatise *Politics*. Aristotle studied human and animal behavior to see how they were similar and different. He believed that by observation, analysis, deduction, and induction an understanding of patterns in human behavior can be acquired.

Rome

The Romans, ever practical and concerned with building successful communities, government, and empire, developed social and political systems based on observations of human nature and experience. Polybius, the Greek who wrote a history of Rome in the second century BCE, argued that only by means of history, an examination of human experience, may correct behavior be molded and successful institutions be adopted. Livy echoed Polybius in his history of Rome, declaring that morality is gained by the reading of history and an imitation of good behavior and an avoidance of the bad.

The Roman Constitution as presented by Polybius was a masterly experiment in political science. Polybius argued that Rome balanced power by combining the rule of one person (kingship) with the rule of many people (aristocracy and oligarchy) with the rule of the people en masse (democracy). Rome's mixed constitution gave executive power to the Consuls, deliberative power to the Senate, and legislative power to the people in the Assembly. The two Consuls served annually and could not be reelected. They were elected by the people: one came from the lower and middle classes, the Plebeians; the other from the aristocracy, the Patricians. Each had a veto over the other's actions; the Senate exercised a powerful influence over both Consuls. The numbers of the Senate constantly changed as its membership was not dependent upon election—rather Consuls immediately joined the Senate after their one-year term expired. Senators served for life. It was their job to advise the Consuls and recommend legislation for the Assembly to consider. The Assembly was composed of the male citizens. It passed the laws and elected the Consuls. The rights of the Assembly were also represented by the Tribune, which had veto power and was bound to exercise it in the protection of the people from wanton abuse of power.

The Republican Marcus Tullius Cicero, lamenting the loss of the Republic to the aggressive ambition of dictators such as Julius Caesar, argued in *On the Character of the Orator* that the laws of the Roman Republic are based on a systematic approach to society and government; thus, following Aristotle, the laws are based on a science of politics. In *On Laws* and *On the Republic* Cicero advocated a return to the Rome of the past, when the Senate held ultimate authority, providing through its conservative guidance for a relatively free state.

A century later, after the imperial structure of rule by the emperors had established itself in Rome, Pliny the Elder wrote *Natural History*, in which he provided a long pseudoscientific discussion of human culture compared to the habits of animals. Notwithstanding his credulity in accepting stories of the remarkable and strange among humans in Asia, Africa, and northern Europe, Pliny made an attempt at an anthropology: a description of world culture, institutions, habits, geographic and racial similarities and differences, and differing physical characteristics.

The last and perhaps greatest contribution of the ancient world to the origins of social science were the two great law codes of the Later Roman Empire, the Codex Theodosius and Codex Justinius. The Theodosian Code was published under the auspices of the emperor Theodosius in 438 CE. It summarized the edicts of Roman emperors for previous centuries, showing how earlier lawgivers dealt with certain crimes and setting precedent for later jurists. The Justinian Code, and its offshoots the *Digest* and *Institutes*, were the result of intense research by a group of lawyers and jurists, led by Tribonian, working at the command of the emperor Justinian, who ruled from Constantinople during the years 527 to 565 CE.

See also Aristotle; Athens; Cicero; Geography/Geodesy; Herodotus of Halicarnassus; History; Mesopotamia; Pliny the Elder; Polybius; Rome; Solon

References

Herodotus. *The Histories.* Translated by Aubrey de Selincourt. Harmondsworth, Middlesex: Penguin Books, 1972.

Justinian. *The Digest of Roman Law.* Translated by C. F. Kolbert. Harmondsworth, Middlesex: Penguin Books, 1979.

Pliny the Elder. *Natural History.* Translated by John F. Healy. London: Penguin Books, 1991.

Taylor, Lily Ross. *Party Politics in the Age of Caesar.* Berkeley: University of California Press, 1949.

Socrates (470–399 BCE)

Socrates of Athens was one of the greatest philosophers of all time. He inspired the work of countless other philosophers and scientists such as Plato, Aristotle, and Xenophon. Socrates was a philosopher of *being,* perfectly in line with Ionian thinkers such as Anaxagoras and Archelaus. Socrates believed that reality is incorporeal and transcendent, perceived by the very few thinkers who have the intellect and discipline to penetrate the generally unknowable ideal forms of the universe. Socrates did not write anything, but we know of his thought from his disciples Plato and Xenophon.

Plato's dialogues indicate that Socrates believed that constant questioning would lead to the truth. His technique in conversation, teaching, and debate was to pose a question, responding to the answer with another question, and so on. Each question became more penetrating and was posed in such a way to yield a desired response from the respondent. Plato's dialogues show that Socrates had already deduced the truth that he was carefully and patiently trying to elicit from

This eighteenth-century engraving by L. P. Boitard (in Cooper, The Life of Socrates, *London, 1750, p. 115) shows the philosopher Socrates lecturing to his students in Athens. (Library of Congress)*

his conversants. This technique of assuming an a priori truth that one will certainly arrive at through a mental process is the hallmark of deductive reasoning, of which Socrates was the greatest practitioner.

Socrates was unafraid to challenge the beliefs and knowledge of others in his pursuit of truth and his goal of revealing this truth and the correct methods by which to achieve a knowledge of the truth to others. His challenging intellectual demeanor eventually got him into trouble after the Athenians had lost the Peloponnesian War to the Spartans and Athenian democracy was crumbling at the end of the fifth century. Socrates was put on trial for corrupting the youth of Athens, charges that he vigorously denied and showed to be absurd in his trial, recorded by Plato in the *Apology*. Nevertheless Socrates was convicted and sentenced to die, which he could avoid by exile. Athenian to the end, Socrates chose to end his life by drinking the hemlock provided by the executioner, discoursing with his disciples on life and death to the very end.

See also Anaxagoras of Clazomenae; Archelaus of Athens; Athens; Greek Classical Age; Plato; Xenophon

References

Jowett, Benjamin, trans. *The Portable Plato.* Harmondsworth, Middlesex: Penguin Books, 1976.

Tredennick, Hugh, trans. *The Last Days of Socrates.* Harmondsworth, Middlesex: Penguin Books, 1959.

Solar System
See Astronomy

Solon (640–560 BCE)

The Greeks considered Solon, the Athenian statesman, to be one of the Seven Sages because of his wisdom in framing laws for Athens. In his *Lives of the Philosophers*, Diogenes Laertius claimed that, of the Seven Sages, all were statesmen except Thales, who was the only naturalist. Plutarch's *Life of Solon*

points out, however, that if Solon was not a naturalist, he was a political thinker who devised laws to promote equality and democracy in sixth-century Athens. Solon was a political scientist, the first and perhaps greatest in antiquity, one who applied reason to law and government.

Little is known of Solon's life except through anecdote. The sources indicate that he was born in Salamis, the little island south of Athens. He came to Athens at an early age and gained a reputation for wisdom. He was a merchant who earned great wealth and came to see that Athens's hope for political and economic greatness lay in production, trade, and the sea. As archon, an executive office in early Athens, Solon suggested that Athenians open their city and citizenship to foreign craftsmen and traders in order to rid the city of its reliance upon the land and decrease the power of the landed aristocracy in the process. A city of merchants, craftsmen, and laborers necessarily moved toward a more open society politically—an important precondition for democracy in Athens. Such was Solon's reputation that he gained the respect of the Athenians to reform their law code to conform to their more middle-class society. The focus of his laws was on fairness, equity, and reason. His legislation led to reforms based on advancement and participation in government on merit and wealth. The reforms linked an expectation of public responsibility to the accumulation of wealth, relieved the burdens of the poor by canceling debts, and established the institutions upon which democracy in Athens would be based.

According to Plutarch, Solon reformed the Athenian lunar calendar by not relying on the phases of the moon but instead on the point in the lunar cycle when the moon appears before the sun appears and sets before the sun sets. This day Solon called "the old and the new," declaring that it should be the watershed between the end of the old month and beginning of the new.

Aristotle, in his *Athenian Constitution*, praised Solon for his government reforms, in particular three of them: first, to prevent corruption in using humans as collateral in loans; second, to assist any Athenian, rich or poor, in suing for damages; third, to empower the citizenry by instituting trial by jury.

According to ancient writers, upon completing his legal reforms Solon decided to leave the city for ten years to allow the reforms to take shape without the constant presence of their creator. He traveled to Egypt, as all wise men of antiquity apparently did, and spoke with the Egyptian priests and learned from them as well. He traveled to Lydia where he met King Croesus, wealthy, powerful, and vain. Croesus sought compliments from all who visited him, but wise Solon refused to accommodate the king. Instead he tried to convince Croesus that happiness had nothing to do with wealth, but rather resulted from a useful life and honorable death. Croesus, according to Herodotus, learned this lesson later when he was captured by Cyrus, the king of Persia. According to anecdotal accounts, Solon visited just about everywhere on his ten-year sojourn, making a point to visit the other sages like himself and giving advice wherever he went. He became the legendary legal sage of antiquity, whose life demonstrated that wisdom, reason, sound judgment, and a clear understanding of human experience have much to do with the science of government. Aristotle was impressed, and so too were the framers of the U.S. Constitution centuries later.

See also Athens; Greek Archaic Age; Seven Sages; Social Sciences

References

Aristotle. *On the Athenian Constitution.* Translated by Frederic G. Kenyon. London: G. Bell and Sons, 1891.

Durant, Will. *The Life of Greece.* New York: Simon and Schuster, 1939.

French, A. "The Economic Background to Solon's Reforms." *Classical Quarterly* 6 (1956).

Plutarch. *The Rise and Fall of Athens.* Translated by Ian Scott-Kilvert. London: Penguin Books, 1960.

Robinson, Charles A., Jr. *Athens in the Age of Pericles.* Norman: University of Oklahoma Press, 1959.

Illustration of Solon—lawgiver, sage, and Athenian (640–560 BCE). (Bettmann/Corbis)

Steam Power
See Hero

Stoicism

Stoicism, a Greek philosophy named for the *stoa* or colonnade of ancient Athens, was a system of thought based on a conception of a material universe composed exclusively of atoms in constant motion creating varying combinations that compose the stuff of matter and spirit. Atoms move in a void of no substance. A material universe of constant movement does not easily accommodate the supernatural. Indeed, the Stoics generally removed divine forces from their system of thought, though not going so far as the Epicureans. Rather, Stoics could not conceive of a completely random origin of the universe and assumed the presence of some mind or thought (composed of atoms, of course) that conceived of and directed, if passively, the universe. This eternal force at once material and spiritual was the logos, variously translated as word, defining principle (Aristotle), or Holy Spirit. The Stoics conceived of a reality in which the logos creates and destroys in an unending cycle of change. What remains the same are the atoms and the void, which constitute over the everlasting cycles an infinite number of combinations. This accounts for all beings—plant, animal, and humans. Each human is one of a kind with a unique soul. Upon the completion of life the atoms of the unique human disintegrate into the collective, anonymous whole to be resurrected, as it were, in completely different forms of matter, life, and spirit. The logos conceives of and directs the process but is necessarily distant and unapproachable. Stoicism is thus a philosophy based on determinism that is impersonal and ultimately unknowable. The best the human can do is try to understand the mind of the logos reflected in the laws of the universe; in so doing the rational and scientific-minded may comprehend some of the natural laws upon which the universe is based. Such understanding of natural law became an important ingredient in the pursuit of scientific knowledge in subsequent centuries.

The great Stoic philosophers were Greeks such as Zeno, Cleanthes, Chrysipus, and Epictetus and Romans such as Cicero, Seneca, and Marcus Aurelius. The Greeks Polybius and Panaetius brought Stoicism to Rome in the second century BCE. Cicero learned of Stoicism by means of Posidonius of Rhodes. The Romans, from Cicero on, found Stoic philosophy so much to their liking that they adopted it as the only way to understand the overwhelming mystery of the universe, the apparent arbitrariness of fate, and the qualities that humans can adopt to find the means of happiness in a universe that otherwise does not promise very much.

Pliny the Elder's *Natural History* provides an interesting example of Stoicism applied to Roman science. Pliny advocated the Stoic belief in the wisdom and benevolence of God or Nature that created a universe based on reason. Rational humans can uncover the workings of nature and the laws of the universe and base their communities upon such knowledge. Pliny repeatedly revealed his awe at the remarkable and rational workings of nature: for example, the orderliness and humanlike behavior of bees, who are selfless, productive, and fearless—a perfect example of the Stoic belief that humans (like all creatures) must accommodate nature in order to thrive.

The most profound Stoic psychologists were Epictetus and Marcus Aurelius. Epictetus, the former slave and Greek writer of *Discourses,* had a profound influence on the emperor Marcus Aurelius, who tried to use Epictetus's techniques of acceptance of self and circumstances to rise above life's contingencies to achieve happiness. Aurelius's *Meditations,* however, reveals the limitations of Stoic thought when confronted with the various anxieties of life.

See also Aurelius, Marcus; Cicero; Epictetus; Pliny the Elder; Polybius; Posidonius of Rhodes; Seneca, Lucius Annaeus

References

Epictetus. *The Discourses.* Edited by Christopher Gill. Everyman's Library. Rutland, Vt.: Tuttle Publishing, 2001.

Ogilvie, R. M. *Roman Literature and Society.* Harmondsworth, Middlesex: Penguin Books, 1980.

Pliny the Elder. *Natural History.* Translated by John F. Healy. London: Penguin Books, 1991.

Sandbach, F. H. *The Stoics.* New York: W. W. Norton, 1975.

Strabo (63 BCE–21 CE)

Strabo was the Greek writer of *Geography,* an influential treatise on history and geography. Strabo was a Stoic philosopher influenced by Athenodorus, a contemporary Stoic philosopher, Xenarchus, a notable Peripatetic philosopher, and the geographer Tyrannion. Strabo spent time in Alexandria, journeyed throughout the Near East, and ascended the Nile River to Ethiopia. His *Geography* was based in part on his personal experiences and reveals him to have been a polymath interested in a variety of topics of inquiry.

Strabo's concept of the earth was typical for his time. He unquestioningly relied on Homer for the geographic essentials. He envisioned three continents—Europe, Asia, and Africa—which combined together to form a great island surrounded by the vast encircling river Ocean. The sun orbited the Earth, appearing out of Ocean in the East and setting in Ocean in the West. The Caspian Sea flowed into the outer ocean. The Isles of the Blessed lay to the West in the Atlantic. Ocean was a river, flowing in and about, which explained the tides.

Strabo went beyond Homer, however, in his hypothesis that the world could be circumnavigated by sailing west from Europe to Asia on the same latitude. The distance, only, would prevent the fulfillment of the journey. Strabo had the support of Posidonius and Athenodorus, the Stoics, partly because the greater the water on the surface of the earth, the Stoics thought, the stronger was the bond that held the planets and stars in place. Strabo indicated Hipparchus's disagreement with both ideas, the former because of the possibility of an interrupted ocean, the latter because of its absurdity. Strabo condemned Eratosthenes for his criticism of Homer, arguing that Homer's myths were meant to bring his hearers and readers to an awareness of the core of truth found in the *Iliad* and *Odyssey*.

The reader of Strabo, in short, finds an author who was skeptical of many of the stories told of other lands and peoples. He used reason to sort through anecdote to arrive at plausible cause and effect. For example, Strabo spent much time in Book 1 of his *Geography* examining Posidonius of Rhodes and his stories, particularly one about Eudoxus of Cyzicus. Posidonius gave as fact the account of Eudoxus's voyages in and about Africa, which Strabo, checking for internal consistency in the stories, branded as spurious. Strabo also doubted the accounts of Pytheas that Polybius and other writers had passed along as true.

The structure of Strabo's *Geography* is as follows: Books 1 and 2 provide useful summaries of the lost works of writers such as Eratosthenes while allowing Strabo to engage in long dissertations defending writers such as Homer and attacking others such as Posidonius of Rhodes. Books 3 and 4 analyze the peoples, places, and sources of information regarding Spain and Gaul. Book 5 provides a description of Italy, including an extensive discussion of the city of Rome. Books 6 through 10 discuss Magna Graecia, Sicily, Germany, and Greece, while Books 11 through 14 discuss Asia Minor and the Near East. Books 15, 16, and 17 describe India and Africa.

See also Eratosthenes; Geography/Geodesy; Posidonius of Rhodes; Pytheas of Massilia; Roman Principate

Reference

Strabo. *Geography.* Translated by H. L. Jones. Cambridge: Harvard University Press, 1917, 1923.

Surgery
See Medicine

T

Tacitus (56–117 CE)

Cornelius Tacitus was a historian, biographer, and ethnographer. He was a senator during the Flavian and Antonine dynasties of the Roman Principate. His works included the *Annals, Histories, Agricola,* and *Germania.* He was a friend and correspondent of Pliny the Younger. Tacitus was one of the most sophisticated Roman authors, a polymath of note, who, as an ethnologist, penned an enduring portrait of the peoples of Germany.

Tacitus's *Annals* has often been praised for its penetrating psychological analyses of emperors such as Tiberius and for its ability to portray collective behavior. Tacitus was keenly aware of the abuse of power by the Princeps and the army during the age of the Julio-Claudian emperors (31 BCE–68 CE). Tacitus yearned for the Republican past when Romans worked together as a supportive community and selfishness and lust for power—the products of inequality and increasing wealth—had not yet set in.

Generally Tacitus, as an objective thinker, falls short. He believed completely in Roman polytheism and the pantheon of gods, Stoic and Epicurean skepticism having not, apparently, caused sufficient doubts. Like many historians, Tacitus recorded miracles, wonders, omens, and prophecy. Tacitus's *Histories* relates an incident involving the future emperor Vespasian, who received clear messages from the gods and even restored sight to a blind man (81–82). The healing was not science, but rather miracle.

The best example of Tacitus as a social and behavioral scientist is his *Germania.* Tacitus relied on a variety of Greek and Roman sources, such as Pliny the Elder, who had written histories of the wars with the Germans, and Posidonius of Rhodes, who had lived during the previous century. Tacitus was also the son-in-law of the Roman commander Agricola, who had served as governor of Britain. In his biography of *Agricola,* Tacitus described the customs and lifestyle of the Britons and provided an interesting account of Roman explorations around the British Isles, approaching almost to Thule. The *Germania,* however, provided a fuller and more sensitive account of the Germanic peoples. The Romans considered the Germans as barbarians, and Tacitus clearly echoed this point of view. Yet the *Germania* is less a condemnation of the German peoples and more a full description of their physical characteristics, the land in which they lived, and their customs, institutions, way of life, and communities. The loyalty, constancy, and self-sacrifice of the Germans toward one another

Bust of the Roman historian Tacitus (55–117 CE).
(Bettmann / Corbis)

impressed Tacitus. He believed that if they were uncivilized compared to the Romans, the Germans were morally superior to the Romans.

See also Geography / Geodesy; History; Pliny the Younger; Roman Principate; Social Sciences
References
Tacitus. *The Agricola and the Germania.* Translated by H. Mattingly. Harmondsworth, Middlesex: Penguin Books, 1970.
———. *The Histories.* Translated by Kenneth Wellesley. Harmondsworth, Middlesex: Penguin Books, 1972.

Thales (625–545 BCE)

Ancient Greek writers identified Thales of Miletus as the first great scientist of the Mediterranean world. Thales was one of the famed Seven Sages of the Hellenic world; of the seven, Thales was the natural philosopher. He hailed from Miletus, a town in Western Turkey on the eastern shores of the Aegean Sea, to which centuries before Greeks had migrated; they called themselves Ionians, and their new Asian home, Ionia. Diogenes Laertius, in *Lives of the Philosophers,* related one tradition that Thales was a native Phoenician who immigrated to Miletus. Herodotus, the Greek historian, wrote that Thales was a contemporary of Croesus, King of Lydia, and that he moved to Miletus from Phoenicia, which explains his interest and skill at celestial navigation. Legend has it that he diverted the Halys River to allow Croesus's army to advance across it and that he predicted a solar eclipse in 585 BCE. Plutarch recorded in his *Life of Solon* that the two men knew each other and that Thales tried to convince Solon that a philosopher must not have distractions such as a wife and children, a view that Plutarch was highly critical of.

To know his thought one must rely on the reports of other ancient writers. Diogenes Laertius, who presented a twofold division of Hellenic philosophy, the Ionian and the Italian, lauded Thales as the founder of the former by means of his influence on Anaximander. Diogenes also gave Thales the title of first ancient astronomer because of two books he reputedly wrote, *On the Solstices* and *On the Equinoxes.* Thales was the first to identify Ursa Minor, Little Bear, the basis of sailing the Mediterranean by the North Star. Some Greeks believed Thales explained this in his book *Nautical Astronomy.* If Diogenes Laertius was correct, Thales measured the movement of the sun on the zodiac from the sun's southern progression toward the Tropic of Capricorn from June to December and its northern progression toward the Tropic of Cancer from December to June. From Thales' solar observations, he arrived at an estimate of the size of the sun by hypothesizing that the size of the sun's disk as it was observed traversing the zodiac is 1/720 of its actual size. Thales made similar studies of the moon's path of movement and relative size.

Diogenes Laertius ascribed to Thales the ability to estimate the size of the sun, to measure the height of the pyramids of Egypt, to argue for the immortality of the soul, to identify souls in other natural phenomena, and to be the first to proclaim "know thyself." Proclus, a Neoplatonist living in the Later Roman Empire, believed that Thales was a geometrician who discovered theorems about the diameter of a circle and right angles at perpendicular lines. Aristotle claimed that Thales believed that water holds the earth in place, although he ignored the equally significant question of what holds water in place. Thales thought that water served as the primal element because it was a fluid that could congeal into a solid or be dispersed into a gas.

Thales was clearly a Greek thinker of amazing breadth and originality. The ancient sources indicate that his predecessors in scientific inquiry, the Egyptians and Mesopotamians, influenced the scope and technique of his investigations. He was not the first to consider the origins of the universe, but perhaps he was the first to divorce such investigation from superstition. Indeed he apparently refused to adopt the Mesopotamian (Chaldean) propensity to assign magical explanations to natural phenomena. Modern scholars doubt that Thales had the knowledge and observational skills to predict an eclipse. The story in Herodotus that he learned the techniques from Babylonian astronomers is doubtless untrue, because they did not have sufficient knowledge to predict lunar or solar eclipses. Besides, Herodotus noted that Thales predicted the *year* rather than the day or week of the solar eclipse, which makes the prediction a little less astonishing. Thales believed that the earth was a round arched disk, perhaps hollow underneath.

The ancients believed that Thales either discovered or learned from others (such as the Egyptians) the technique of using the gnomon, or sundial, to determine the equinoxes and solstices. Herodotus claimed that Thales followed the Egyptian solar calendar rather than the Greek lunar calendar. Some scholars such as Neugebauer doubt Thales' understanding of Egyptian (or Babylonian) science.

In short, Thales was a thinker and scientist learned in the theories and techniques of Egyptian, Mesopotamian, and Phoenician philosophers, astronomers, and mathematicians. He is significant in the history of science for his ability to bring the work of his Asian and African predecessors to the Greeks. Thales tempered the superstition of the Chaldean and Egyptian priests with the rational mind-set of the Ionian Greeks. Most important, Thales was not content to merely describe natural phenomena; rather, he sought the cause of things in the workings of nature.

See also Anaximander of Miletus; Anaximenes of Miletus; Astronomy; Calendars and Dating Systems; Diogenes Laertius; Egypt; Ionians; Miletus; Physical Sciences

References
Barnes, Jonathan, trans. *Early Greek Philosophy.* London: Penguin Books, 1987.
Heath, Sir Thomas. *Aristarchus of Samos.* New York: Dover Books, 1913.
Laertius, Diogenes. *Lives of the Philosophers.* Translated by R. D. Hicks. 2 vols. Cambridge: Harvard University Press, 1931, 1938.
Leicester, Henry M. *The Historical Background of Chemistry.* New York: Dover Books, 1971.
Neugebauer, O. *The Exact Sciences in Antiquity.* New York: Dover Books, 1969.

Themistius (317–388 CE)

Themistius was one of the greatest commentators on the science of Aristotle during the Later Roman Empire. He was a pagan philosopher whose tact, learning, and approach to philosophy earned him the admiration of pagan as well as Christian emperors.

Themistius was born in 317 CE, just a few years after the emperor Constantine had converted to Christianity. Themistius's father Eugenius was a Greek Sophist at Constantinople, Constantine's new capital of his Christian Roman Empire. Themistius followed the path of his father, operating a school at Constantinople from 345 to 355. During this time he attracted the attention of the student and future emperor Julian, who was delighted to find a pagan philosopher who was the equal to any Christian counterpart. Themistius served as an orator, panegyrist, tutor, and adviser to six emperors until his death in 388 CE.

Themistius was one of the many philosophers of the Later Roman Empire who tried to reconcile the apparent disparity between the teachings of Plato and Aristotle. Platonic (Neoplatonic) thinkers believed in the contemplative life removed from the demands of public service, which fit their view that the activities, sights, and sounds of daily life are in the end insignificant, mere shadows of what is true and real. Aristotelian (Peripatetic) thinkers on the other hand embraced the apparent reality of everyday life, believing that in the everyday lie the hints of truth to the observant philosopher and scientist. Themistius believed in personal enlightenment used in public service. For example, in his orations to the emperor Constantius II Themistius argued that *philanthropia* is the most important quality for a ruler to have— to the ancient world, that meant love, clemency, mildness, justice, humanity. Themistius hoped that the emperor, the ruler of the Roman world, would imitate God, the ruler of the universe. Here is the Platonic concern for the awareness of truth combined with the statesman's concern for its proper application in government and society.

Themistius's contribution to the study of Aristotle was his *Paraphrase,* which featured an important discussion of Aristotle's *On the Soul, Metaphysics, Posterior Analytics,* and *On Heaven.* Themistius's work was translated into Arabic, Hebrew, Latin, and, in some cases, English. It was through the work of such Aristotelian commentators that Aristotle's science came to be known to the Muslim world as well as to late medieval thinkers such as Thomas Aquinas. Constantinople, where Themistius taught, became in the fourth century an important center of learning. Along with other Greek cities of the Eastern Roman Empire, Constantinople survived the destruction of the Western Roman Empire during the fifth century. During subsequent centuries, Constantinople served as the capital (the second Rome) of the Byzantine Empire, thereby ensuring that the works of ancient science would continue to be studied for years to come.

See also Aristotle; Julian; Later Roman Empire; Neoplatonism; Peripatetic School

References
Downey, Glanville. "Philanthropia in Religion and Statecraft in the Fourth Century after Christ." *Historia* 4 (1955): 199–208.
Todd, Robert, trans. *Themistius: On Aristotle's On the Soul.* Ithaca: Cornell University Press, 1996.
Wright, W. C., trans. *The Works of the Emperor Julian.* Cambridge: Harvard University Press, 1962, 1969.

Theon of Alexandria
See Hypatia of Alexandria

Theophrastus (370–286 BCE)

Theophrastus, a student of both Plato and Aristotle, was a native of the isle of Lesbos and an early Peripatetic philosopher, famous for his work in flora. Theophrastus, like his teacher Aristotle, was at the same time a deep yet practical thinker. A polymath, his creative output was immense. Diogenes Laertius listed dozens of titles that came from Theophrastus's pen. These included works on astronomy, logic, physics, meteorology, morality, zoology, psychology, political science, mathematics, history, poetry, music, and commentaries on earlier philosophers.

Theophrastus's *Book of Signs* examined clouds and other environmental conditions with which to predict the weather. Upon the death of Aristotle, Theophrastus took over leadership of the Lyceum, Aristotle's school in Athens. The Lyceum had a wonderful garden that Aristotle enjoyed strolling through as he taught; Theophrastus maintained it and used it as an herbarium. Proclus, the fifth-century CE writer, recorded Theophrastus's beliefs that Chaldean astrologers could predict the future, including the time of one's death. Whether or not they predicted Theophrastus's own death is not known, although Diogenes Laertius does transcribe his extensive will.

Theophrastus's *Enquiry into Plants* provides a full description of the flora of the ancient Mediterranean; it is an indispensable tool for those researching the history of botany. Theophrastus classified and described trees, shrubs, and flowers, building a materia medica of those plants with medicinal properties. Like Aristotle, Theophrastus was interested in classifying plants; his *Enquiry* provided detailed discussions of plant types and morphology. All aspects of plants—roots, leaves, buds, fruit, propagation, uses, and types according to place and climate—were described in detail. Theophrastus provided encyclopedic accounts of trees, shrubs, flowers, wild and cultivated plants, herbs, edible and inedible plants, cereals, spice-bearing plants, and the odors of plants. The writing was dry, although detailed and without parallel in scope for centuries.

> *See also* Aristotle; Athens; Life Sciences;
>   Peripatetic School; Plato
> *References*
> Laertius, Diogenes. *Lives of the Philosophers.*
>   Translated by R. D. Hicks. 2 vols. Cambridge:
>   Harvard University Press, 1931, 1938.
> Neugebauer, O. *The Exact Sciences in Antiquity.* New
>   York: Dover Books, 1969.
> Theophrastus. *Enquiry into Plants and Minor Works on
>   Odours and Weather Signs.* Translated by Arthur
>   Hort. Vol. 2. Cambridge: Harvard University
>   Press, 1916.

Thucydides (460–400 BCE)

Thucydides was the greatest historian in antiquity. He penned *The Peloponnesian War* to describe what he thought would be one of the most fundamental conflicts in human history, the war between the Ionians (led by Athens) and the Dorians (led by Sparta) from 431 to 404 BCE. Thucydides was an Athenian general who lost his commission early in the war; he decided to stay involved by observing events, talking to participants, and recording his own assessments of the war. He lived in Thrace for most of the war and returned to Athens at its conclusion in 404. Thucydides purposely treated historical inquiry like a science by asking questions, collecting available facts, and setting forth answers based on reason, analysis, and an objective mind-set.

In the first book of his history, Thucydides, seeking an accurate picture of the Trojan War and the Mycenaean kings, engaged in deductive analysis based on reason and experience to try to reconstruct in general terms the Greek past. He set himself apart from his predecessors Homer, Hecataeus, Hellanicus, and Herodotus. He condemned their uncritical use of sources and reliance upon myth and poetry. History has little to do with poetry, Thucydides argued. Aristotle, in the *Poetics* (Book 9) would echo this same sentiment half a century later. Aristotle compared history unfavorably to poetry, in that the former refers to particulars, the latter to universals and thus to the truth. Thucydides, however, believed the exact opposite, seeing in the particulars of human experience the true kernels of universal human truth.

Thucydides argued that by examining an event such as a war we might see how human behavior will repeat itself, not in the particulars of time and place but in the general behavioral response of humans to certain conditions. In this way history can become a science of human behavior, wherein patterns will be found to occur again and again. His portrait of the whims of public opinion and the power of demagoguery at Athens will be seen again and again over the course of centuries in similar democracies and republics. The unexpected and irrational in human affairs, so clearly seen in the case of Alcibiades, accused of impiety and driven to the Spartan side, is a constant feature of Thucydides' work. His account of the plague that raged through Athens early in the war is a realistic portrait of the impact of fear and disaster upon human institutions, morality, and decency. Thucydides was impatient with the beliefs among the Greeks that healing could come from the gods, particularly in the sanctuary of a temple of Asclepius or Apollo. The gods, he believed, have no apparent impact on prevention of illness or recovery. This rational approach to medicine was being practiced by a contemporary of Thucydides, Hippocrates of Cos. Indeed Thucydides' description of the plague in The Peloponnesian War shows clear indications that he was influenced by Hippocrates.

There were many imitators of Thucydides in subsequent centuries; yet few could match his tight narrative and seemingly scientific precision. True, Thucydides began the practice imitated by other Greek and Roman historians and biographers of recreating speeches based on his understanding of human character and the particulars of time and place. This merely showed his genius for interpretation, for portraying the generalities of human existence from sporadic, uncertain, or nonexistent sources. Thucydides' greatness lay in his ability to organize a clear narrative of sequential events over time, to see time as one episode after another, moving from future possibilities to present existence and awareness to past recollection. Humans are typically blinded by the present moment, which is fleeting (while the future is unknown and the past unclear). Through the chronological historical narrative, the reader can escape from the dependence on the present moment, to see human existence and behavior over a broad expanse of time, and thereby gain an appreciation of what it means to be human.

See also Athens; Greek Classical Age; Hecataeus of Miletus; Herodotus of Halicarnassus; Hippocrates; History; Homer; Medicine; Psychology; Social Sciences; Time

References
Breisach, Ernst. *Historiography: Ancient, Medieval and Modern.* Chicago: University of Chicago Press, 1983.
Finley, M. I. *Aspects of Antiquity: Discoveries and Controversies.* Harmondsworth, Middlesex: Penguin Books, 1977.
Thucydides. *The Peloponnesian War.* Translated by Rex Warner. Harmondsworth, Middlesex: Penguin Books, 1972.

Time

Time, its nature, meaning, and origins, was one of the most difficult subjects of philosophical and scientific inquiry for ancient thinkers. Scientists, theologians, philosophers, and historians have for centuries tried to comprehend time. But because humans are so much a part of, so dependent upon, time, a true understanding has been and continues to be elusive. The questions of today were the questions the ancients asked about time. Is time an artificial measure, a tool by which humans trace their own existence? Or does time have an independent existence—a phenomenon separate from human experience? Is it true that there is geologic time, that the universe carves a temporal path from its beginning to its end? Or is time separate from human awareness?—without humans to know and trace it, time is meaningless, nonexistent. Is time therefore an absolute, a constant that can be measured with mechanical devices, a certainty that, as Newton believed, has very little fluctuation, and thus allows humans the confidence to base their lives upon it? Clocks, chronometers, and calendars help us to safely trace the passing of years, days, months, which gives us meaning, helps us to know ourselves and our world. Perhaps time is relative, as Einstein believed: Since it depends upon the individual observer, time is inconstant and fluctuating, governed by outside forces, significant only insofar as it yields for us a sense of uncertainty, inconstancy, meaninglessness, and anomie. Is one human's time the same as another human's time? Is the time of twenty-first-century America the same as the time of first-century Rome? What does it mean to say that we live in the year 2005? How does it help to know one's age? What does it mean to guide one's life by the clock? What does it mean to regulate institutions, government, the most minute human events, according to the passage of seconds, minutes, and hours?

Two of the most fundamental explanations of the nature of time were developed in the ancient Mediterranean. Time as an objective phenomenon is an external, natural force separate from human thought and experience. Time as a component of nature exists even if humans do not—time has an independent existence that humans struggle to perceive and understand. Time as a subjective phenomenon, on the contrary, is an internal human experience understood best by those who understand self. A personal sense of time is a unique experience enjoyed by each person individually over the course of life.

Cronos

The earliest Greek writers and philosophers considered time as a divine phenomenon, often subjective and personal yet at times distant and untouchable. Cronos, the son of heaven (Uranos) and earth (Gaia) was, according to Greek mythology, the god of time. Cronos was an odd one, jealous of his own power, suspicious of his own children—he ate his daughters Hestia (hearth), Demeter (grain), and Hera (fertility) and sons Hades (hell) and Poseidon (sea) until Zeus (sky) conquered his father and sent him to the depths of Tartarus. Perhaps Cronos's confusion about power and responsibility explains why the poets such as Homer ignored the precise movement and logic of time and cast human events in isolated, sporadic moments seemingly unconnected with the continuum of past/present/future. So contradictory was Homer's sense of time that his poems are models of *anachronism,* which means literally *against time,* a confusion of chronology. Homer's *Iliad* and *Odyssey* record the people and events of the distant Mycenaean Age (which ended during the twelfth century BCE) joined to a portrait of society, institutions, and culture at the height of the Greek Dark Ages (1000 BCE), while adding random perspectives of the time (eighth century BCE) in which the poems were written down after centuries of oral telling and retelling.

Time in Classical Greek Thought

At the end of the Greek Dark Ages in the eighth century BCE, Greek society was increasingly sophisticated. The city-state *(polis)* was the center of trade, organized government, and intellectual speculation. The order and structure of civilization usually requires a concrete perspective on the passing of events and a record of what has happened. Greek thinkers developed a sense of objective time as external to human affairs. One Pherecydes of Syros (according to the Neoplatonist writer Damascius) conceived of time as the creative force of earth's primal elements. But time itself was not begotten, therefore was uncreated, eternal, and infinite. Anaximander of Miletus (610–540 BCE), according to Aristotle, conceived of the *infinite,* which is the unending of space and time. Hippolytus in *Refutation of All Heresies* explained that Anaximander believed that time is the eternal action of "being, existence, and passing away" (Heath 1913). Aristotle claimed that Pythagoras believed "that *time* is the *motion of the whole* (universe)" (Heath 1913). According to the Greek mathematician Eudemus, Pythagoras argued that all phenomena experience eternal recurrence. The heavenly spheres of the universe move according to mathematical precision, in constant repetition of the same harmonic circles. If the heavenly spheres constantly return to the beginning, then why not humans as well? Socrates, in Plato's *Phaedo,* professed his belief in the recollection of ideas and phenomena previous to this life, which implies a fundamental cyclical state of time. Plato in the *Timaeus* explained the nature of time as due to the eternal nature of the Good and the fixity of number.

At the same time the Greek awareness of their spectacular accomplishments in the Mediterranean world of the first century spawned a complex sense of history to record the passage of time in light of political events. Herodotus, the first Greek historian of note, relied on the works of his predecessors Hecataeus of Miletus and Hellanicus of Lesbos to develop a subjective sense of time as inquiries, *historia*. The Greek sense of time in historical writing was chronologically imprecise and episodic because dating systems were imprecise and far from standardized. Olympiads were a favorite chronological marker, as were the term of office of archons, the election of priests and priestesses, the reigns of kings or, under the Roman Empire, the annual terms of consuls. Such points on the human scale of time were overall unsatisfactory. Historians and biographers were less apt to place the lives of humans in a broader context of linear events and more apt to isolate the object of inquiry in a subjective profile of life, character, and personality.

The Atomists

Hellenistic philosophy and historiography continued the balancing of objective and subjective notions of time. Epicurean and Stoic philosophers argued for recurrence and infinite cycles of life and death, creation and destruction. What was indestructible and infinite—atoms—were also uncreated, forming and re-forming in countless combinations of matter, alive and dead. Lucretius, the Roman Epicurean, wrote in *On the Nature of the Universe* that time is objective, and thus exists only insofar as an observer might recognize and trace the ongoing transformation of matter. Time is completely merged with natural movement, and otherwise has no existence.

One finds in the Stoic philosopher Marcus Aurelius's *Meditations,* however, a strong sense of the subjective human experience of time.

Aurelius could make little sense out of life and death because of his materialistic assumptions about the indestructibility of matter, the material basis of the soul, and the insignificance of human existence. He believed that time is an unending series of moments over which the individual has absolutely no control. Life is random; the self is a product of random atoms in constant movement. Each individual's life is a solitary moment in a vast whole. There is no meaning in the duration of time; the only meaning is in the fleeting moment. Ironically, as Aurelius professed the meaninglessness of life he desperately sought meaning. As he proclaimed the anonymity of time he sought to personalize it, make it his own. In this he ultimately failed because of his materialistic fatalism. The self, according to Marcus Aurelius, yearns for significance but cannot find it in a purposeless, godless world.

Aurelius Augustine

A one-time Stoic turned Neoplatonist and then Christian, Aurelius Augustine (354–430 CE) reassessed ancient theories of time in light of Hebrew and Christian theology to arrive at a completely original and personal view of time. The societies of the ancient Near East such as the Sumerians, Egyptians, and Hebrews lacked a clear chronological dating system and like the Greeks and Romans dated events according to pharaohs, kings, prophets, and the passage of generations of father and son. Hebrew historical narratives, such as Chronicles and Kings in the Old Testament, are clear narratives of events with but a simple sense of the linear movement of time. The Hebrews lived their lives in between the past and future, the previous greatness of their ancestors and the future coming of the Messiah. This obsessive sense of concern for the past and future found its way into Christian theology during and after the first century CE because of the teachings of Jesus of Nazareth described in the Gospels and the Acts of the Apostles. Luke the physician, who wrote the third Gospel as well as Acts, used the same episodic, subjective time frame to couch his narrative of events that are otherwise chronologically imprecise. Christians made their mark in the history of human comprehension of time by seeing the birth of Jesus as the most significant event in human history. This event required a sense of division—before the Incarnation of God to Man, before Jesus, and after his crucifixion and resurrection. It was not until the sixth century, and the chronology of Dionysus Exiguus, that the dating system of BC *(ante Christos)* and AD *(anno domini)* came into being. More significant than this new dating system was Aurelius Augustine's sophisticated study of the nature of time.

Augustine personalized time in a way no one had before him. His *Confessions* recounts his own life from birth to conversion and baptism at middle age. There are no dates, and the passage of time is not marked by clear references to the reign of kings and the like, the typical Greek and Roman approach of providing an external, objective human or natural reference. Yet the narrative is temporal and linear, and the reader does achieve a clear sense of Augustine's path through his own life, in terms of his own time. Augustine's time is his own; no one else experiences his time—each has his own. Each person experiences time according to the pattern of his own life. Augustine's philosophy appears to be an extreme form of relativism, yet he tempers it and provides a universal standard—in other words he provides an objective time frame from which to gauge one's own time. This objective standard is unexpected and untraditional in terms of Greco-Roman writing. It is the Incarnation—the birth of Jesus of Nazareth. Augustine's life is understood only by means of reference to this event that occurred centuries before, but which according to Christian theology is made personal and real to each individual Christian. Here in the thought of Augustine is the culmination of the ancient approach toward time: the objective and subjective, the external and personal experiences of time, are combined in the life of the Christian who lives in reference to, and fully in, the life of the Son of Man, Jesus of Nazareth.

See also Aurelius, Marcus; Aurelius Augustine; Epicureanism; Herodotus of Halicarnassus; History; Myth; New Testament; Plato; Pythagoras; Stoicism

References

Barnes, Jonathan, trans. *Early Greek Philosophy.* London: Penguin Books, 1987.

Heath, Sir Thomas. *Aristarchus of Samos.* 1913; reprint edition. New York: Dover Books, 1981.

Russell, Bertrand. *A History of Western Philosophy.* New York: Simon and Schuster, 1945.

St. Augustine. *Confessions.* Translated by R. S. Pine-Coffin. Harmondsworth, Middlesex: Penguin Books, 1961.

Wilcox, Donald. *The Measure of Time's Past: Pre-Newtonian Chronologies and the Rhetoric of Relative Time.* Chicago: University of Chicago Press, 1987.

V

Varro (116–27 BCE)

Marcus Terrentius Varro was one of the great scholars of the Roman republic. His many works included *On Country Life, Antiquities,* and *On the Latin Language,* which provided a scientific account of Roman agriculture, an analysis of the human and natural past, and a scholarly study of Latin. Augustine, who used *On the Latin Language* as well as Varro's histories, thought Varro was one of the most important thinkers of the past. Varro's agricultural writings influenced others such as Columella and Palladius. Varro wrote on farming and ranching, advocating an empirical approach to the study of plants and animals. Varro's *On the Latin Language* argued the belief, especially prevalent in first century BCE Rome, that truth is dependent upon how it is presented in speaking and writing. The *Antiquities* consisted of forty-one books devoted to anthropology and theology. Augustine despised Varro's paganism but approved his rational approach toward the Roman pantheon of gods. Varro described the varied approaches of Greek philosophers to the divine but reserved judgment as to which theory was most accurate. In the end, Augustine relied on Varro's natural theology to condemn the paganism of the Romans and support his own views on the supremacy of Christianity.

See also Agriculture; Aurelius Augustine; Cato, Marcus Porcius; Celsus; Columella; Palladius

References

Ogilvie, R. M. *Roman Literature and Society.* Harmondsworth, Middlesex: Penguin Books, 1980.

St. Augustine. *City of God.* Translated by Henry Bettenson. London: Penguin Books, 1984.

Vesuvius

One of Rome's leading scientists, Pliny the Elder, was killed in August of the year 79 CE when Vesuvius erupted. Pompeii and Herculaneum were two small cities to the south and west of Mt. Vesuvius in the province of Campania. Both cities looked out upon the Bay of Naples. It was a beautiful place to live, a place of wealth and culture. But when Mt. Vesuvius erupted, lava, stone, and ash destroyed and buried the two cities. Thousands of people died, including the fifty-six-year-old Gaius Plinius Secundus—known to history as Pliny the Elder.

Mt. Vesuvius has been an active volcano for thousands of years. The region of western Italy dominated by the four-thousand-foot volcano experienced many warnings of the mountain's volatility before the massive explosion of 79 CE. Cassius Dio, who was not a scientist, described how for years Vesuvius

Mount Vesuvius as it appeared in an early-seventeenth-century illustration. (Library of Congress)

had erupted, sending up flames, smoke, and ash. The curious had climbed to the crater at its summit, which appeared like an amphitheater. Quite often inhabitants had heard the rumbling of the mountain, had seen the frequent orange glow at night—the warnings of what might occur. But Dio implied that the inhabitants of Pompeii and Herculaneum were so familiar with the mountain's habits that the roars, quakes, and fires preceding the August 24 eruption were ignored.

Seneca, the Roman stoic and naturalist, described the earthquake of 62 CE that presaged the total destruction of the year 79. The earthquake hit in February, causing great damage. Herculaneum was partially destroyed, and Pompeii almost totally. But the people immediately set to rebuilding, and were still doing so in August 79.

Pliny the Elder, in his *Natural History,* also described the region, its fertility and beauty. He knew Campania well, had observed Vesuvius and the surrounding mountains repeatedly. As a commander of the Roman navy, he was stationed at a nearby port, Misenum, on August 24. Pliny's nephew, the letter writer and naturalist Pliny the Younger, then seventeen years old, was present the morning of August 24. He recalled later, in a letter to the historian Cornelius Tacitus, that his uncle had determined to investigate the reason for the large dark cloud rising from Vesuvius and called for a boat to be made ready. Science then had to make way for official duties. Having received word that the people of the coast at Pompeii and Herculaneum were in danger, he ordered galleys to be launched to rescue the inhabitants. As he sailed across the Bay of Naples directly toward the massive cloud looming above the mountain, spreading outward, Pliny took notes of his observations. The boats were blocked by the number of volcanic rocks falling from the sky, making hazardous the shallow water along the eastern shore of the bay. Pliny ordered the ships south to the town of Stabiae, where the wind, current, and quakes made escape impossible. Pliny ordered a bath and dinner and then slept. Meanwhile pumice stones and ash fell, darkening the sky. Buildings were rocking and threatening to collapse. Pliny and his followers rushed to the seashore but found there was no escape. The stench of sulphur was overwhelming. Poisonous gas, heat, and ash finally brought death.

Scientists such as Pliny the Elder and his nephew took a rational, scientific approach to the eruption and earthquakes of Vesuvius. The credulous, however, interpreted the calamity of the eruption of Vesuvius as the work of the gods and demons. Cassius Dio, writing years later in his *History of Rome,* recorded the perceptions of many survivors, that the eruption was the work of demons. The more thoughtful wondered if it presaged the coming destruction of the universe by fire. Such was the belief of Stoic philosophers and scientists. Mt. Vesuvius buried Herculaneum and Pompeii in feet of ash, mud, and pumice. In time, nature took over, covered the region with new growth, and the towns were forgotten. The dead of Pompeii and Herculaneum lay buried for fifteen hundred years. Finally in the 1700s and 1800s Italian archeologists uncovered the city, rediscovering what had been wealthy, productive towns and busy scenes of humanity that came to an end in 79 CE when Vesuvius erupted.

See also Pliny the Elder; Pliny the Younger; Roman Principate; Stoicism; Strabo

References

Cassius Dio. *Roman History.* Translated by Earnest Cary. Cambridge: Harvard University Press, 1914–1927.

Pliny the Elder. *Natural History.* 2 vols. Translated by H. Rackham. Cambridge: Harvard University Press, 1938, 1947.

Pliny the Younger. *The Letters of the Younger Pliny.* Translated by Betty Radice. Harmondsworth, Middlesex: Penguin Books, 1963.

Strabo. *Geography.* Translated by H. L. Jones. Cambridge: Harvard University Press, 1917, 1923.

Vanags, Patricia. *The Glory That Was Pompeii.* New York: Mayflower Books, 1979.

Vitruvius (floruit 25 BCE)

Marcus Vitruvius Pollio was a Roman architect during the age of Augustus and the learned author of *On Architecture.* Little is known of his life except for his book, in which he addressed the Emperor Augustus and his interest in the Roman infrastructure of public buildings and forums, hydraulics, and engineering. Vitruvius discussed in detail building materials; the impact of climate on building; the functionality of rooms in a dwelling; interior design and wall paintings; and the dangers of lead pipes. Vitruvius argued for the active sharing of scientific knowledge. An engineer, he examined aqueducts, Archimedes' discoveries on the displacement of water, the water screw, the lever, rotary power, and the use of machinery in making weapons of war.

On Architecture describes in detail the science of acoustics. Vitruvius compared the human voice in speech or song to the waves spreading out from a stone tossed into still water; the voice moves both vertically and horizontally. The human voice, he argued, has three types of modulation in tone. An advocate for using the pure shapes of the universe, the knowledge of geometry, in building, Vitruvius was a student of the Pythagorean theorem and the works of Archimedes. He argued that the Roman theater should be built with four equilateral triangles coming to a point in the center. He hoped that the theater's acoustics would rival the music of the heavenly spheres. Vitruvius also discussed the building of a hydraulic organ.

Vitruvius was interested as well in astronomy and its practical uses in time-keeping. He discussed sundials, water clocks, and how the gnomon can measure the sun's shadow at the winter solstice to get an idea of the extent of the world. A long section of *On Architecture* focused on the geocentric view of the planets, moon, and sun and the revolution of the heavens about the two poles on the earth. Fascinated by astrology, Virtruvius discussed in detail the zodiac and constellations. He claimed that the greatest astrologists were the Chaldeans, in particular Berossus (a Babylonian), who had a school at Cos in the Aegean. Vitruvius is often remembered for his conception of the perfect dimensions of man, his hands and legs outstretched within a square and circle.

See also Engineering and Technology; Hydraulics; Roman Principate

References

Ogilvie, R. M. *Roman Literature and Society.* Harmondsworth, Middlesex: Penguin Books, 1980.

Radice, Betty. *Who's Who in the Ancient World.* Harmondsworth, Middlesex: Penguin Books, 1973.

Vitruvius. *On Architecture.* Translated by Joseph Gwilt. London: Priestley and Weale, 1826.

W

Wheeled Vehicles

See Engineering and Technology

Women and Science

The ancient sources provide only scarce information about the role of women in science. The sources were written by men—women in most classical societies were not encouraged to participate in intellectual activities, and those who did risked a tarnished reputation or worse. It took an exceptional person to rise above such constraints and participate in the man's world of science. One such person was Theono of Thurii, who lived in the sixth century BCE and was reputedly the wife (and disciple) of Pythagoras. She was much younger than Pythagoras; upon his death she continued his work, writing treatises on astronomy and number. She wrote *Theory of Numbers* and *Construction of the Universe*. In the latter she hypothesized (along with another of Pythagoras's students Philolaus) that there were ten heavenly bodies moving about a central fire. She also hypothesized that the distances between the heavenly bodies is proportional to the distances between notes on a musical scale.

Similar, perhaps, was Aspasia, the consort of Pericles. Aspasia was from Miletus, a leading center of science during the fifth century BCE. She was possibly associated with Anaximander and Archelaus, Pericles' and Socrates' teachers, respectively. A hetaira, one of the elegant, promiscuous consorts of the rich and famous of Athens, she was Pericles' companion for many years, holding forth in salon fashion among the intellectual elite of mid-fifth-century Athens. She reputedly opened a school of philosophy, having not only well-born women but some of Athen's most important men as her students.

Another wife of a great man who drew around her the leading intellectuals of her time was Julia Domna, wife of the third-century CE Roman emperor Septimius Severus and mother to the emperor Caracalla. She was foretold by a horoscope to be an empress, which compelled the astrologist Septimius Severus to marry her. She cultivated the pagan arts and literature, patronizing Philostratus, who wrote *Lives of the Sophists* and *Life of Apollonius of Tyana,* at her bidding. Aelian, the author of *On the Characteristics of Animals,* was also patronized by Julia.

The greatest woman scientist lived toward the end of the ancient period at the intellectual center of Alexandria—appropriately. Hypatia was the daughter of the mathematician and astronomer Theon, with whom she

The Athenian patroness of science and consort of Pericles, Aspasia (fifth century BCE). From G. Staal and F. Holl, New York: D. Appleton & Co., between 1860 and 1888. (Library of Congress)

dent was the Christian philosopher Synesius. A pagan, Neoplatonist, and astrologist in Christian Alexandria, Hypatia was killed by mob violence.

See also Aelian, Claudius; Alexandria; Athens; Hypatia of Alexandria; Philolaus; Philostratus; Pythagoras

References

Aelian. *On the Characteristics of Animals*. 3 vols. Translated by A. F. Scholfield. Cambridge: Harvard University Press, 1971.

Durant, Will. *Caesar and Christ*. New York: Simon and Schuster, 1944.

_____. *The Life of Greece*. New York: Simon and Schuster, 1939.

Jones, Tom B. *In the Twilight of Antiquity*. Minneapolis: University of Minnesota Press, 1978.

Philostratus. *Lives of the Sophists*. Translated by W. C. Wright. Cambridge: Harvard University Press, 1921.

Technology Museum of Thessaloniki website: www.tmth.edu.

collaborated on commentaries of Claudius Ptolemaeus. Besides her father, Hypatia was influenced by the geometer Pappas, the arithmetician Diophantus, the Neoplatonist Proclus, and the work of mathematicians such as Archimedes, Apollonius of Perga, and of course Ptolemy. Hypatia's most famous stu-

Xenophanes of Colophon (570–478 BCE)

Xenophanes was a poet whose elegies and satires portrayed philosophers and their theories, as well as provided insights into the nature of the universe. Xenophanes was from the Ionian town of Colophon; like his fellow Ionians Thales, Anaximander, Anaximenes, and Anaxagoras, Xenophanes believed in a transcendent cause for all things and was uncomfortable explaining phenomena as the results of proclivities of anthropomorphic gods. At some point during his life, Xenophanes emigrated to Magna Graecia, where he lived at Elea. A tradition grew over time that he was the teacher of Parmenides—their philosophies are indeed similar. In short, Xenophanes was an original philosopher, perhaps the first skeptic, who challenged contemporary beliefs about nature and the divine.

Xenophanes' beliefs about the divine are preserved in several fragments. He condemned the ancient poets for their anthropomorphism respecting the divine. Xenophanes proposed a singular, all-powerful god of thought who exercised control over the universe.

Xenophanes' verse obscures many of his beliefs about the universe, or rather his beliefs were obscure and verse was the best way to portray them. According to Hippolytus, Xenophanes believed that the universe is neither finite nor infinite, a contradiction that may be resolved by considering that Xenophanes, like the materialists, hypothesized an ongoing creation and destruction of the universe. Xenophanes also was indebted to Thales, perhaps, in assigning to water (that is, mud) a creative force. Xenophanes also held the contrary view that above the earth is a limited region of air, sun, moon, planets, and stars, while below the earth is an infinite void. This appears to reflect a view of the earth as flat. More perplexing was his belief that clouds of fire form the heavenly bodies, and that the sun only appears to be one phenomenon, but is in reality a multitude, indeed an infinite number. How? Xenophanes, according to the first century CE commentator Aëtius, believed "that there are many suns and moons according to the regions, divisions, and zones of the earth; and at certain times the disc lights upon some division of the earth not inhabited by us and so, as if it were stepping on emptiness, suffers eclipse." Also, Xenophanes "maintains that the sun goes forward *ad infinitum,* and that it only appears to revolve in a circle owing to its distance" (Heath 1913). In short, the flat earth is infinitely long, over which are infinite numbers of suns moving east to west; as one appears, moves by, and disappears from the eyes of the observer the sun seems to be one body appearing and reappearing, but the senses fool us.

Xenophanes' ideas appear ludicrous today, but he did rely on observation more than on blind faith in the same old Homeric gods. Xenophanes took a fresh approach, and, although he was in error, his was the same scientific approach of his contemporaries and his forebears, the Ionians.

See also Astronomy; Eleatic School; Greek
    Archaic Age; Ionians; Magna Graecia
References
Barnes, Jonathan, trans. *Early Greek Philosophy.*
    London: Penguin Books, 1987.
Burnet, John, ed. and trans. *Early Greek Philosophy.*
    London: Adam and C. Black, 1930.
Heath, Sir Thomas. *Aristarchus of Samos.* New York:
    Dover Books, 1913.

Xenophon (430–355 BCE)

Xenophon was a native Athenian writer, philosopher, historian, adventurer, and soldier. He is famous for his *Anabasis,* an account of a dangerous journey into the heart of Persia and a successful retreat back to Greece led by Xenophon himself. He also wrote *Hellenica,* a continuation of Thucydides' brilliant historical narrative; *Oeconomicus,* about running one's personal household *(oikos);* and *Symposium* and *Memorabilia,* both of which are reminiscences of former times when he was a student of the great Athenian philosopher Socrates. Xenophon's philosophy was not as good as Plato's. His history was not as good as Thucydides'. And his *Oeconomicus* had limited value. And Xenophon was not much of a scientist. Nevertheless it was through the *Anabasis* that Xenophon made his mark on the history of literature, of thought, and even of science.

Xenophon was a young Athenian nobleman, a veteran of the Peloponnesian War, and a student of Socrates when a friend asked him to join a contingent of Greek hoplites (heavily armed infantrymen) who were to march into Asia Minor on an expedition against the Persians. They were to be led by Cyrus, a brother of the king of Persia Artaxerxes. Xenophon agreed but claimed later that he did not realize Cyrus's real intent, to topple his brother. They marched, however, in 401, into the heart of Persia, where Cyrus was killed in an engagement with the Persian army under Artaxerxes. The Greeks, leaderless and surrounded in hostile territory, began a dramatic journey amid sporadic fighting to return to Asia Minor, the Black Sea, and eventually Greece. During this journey Xenophon rose to be one of the commanders. He and most of the soldiers survived, after which Xenophon used his sword to fight for the Spartans. He lived in the Peloponnesus for many years, returning near the end of his life to Athens.

The *Anabasis* is a wonderful adventure story that provides a fairly good historical narrative filled with action, speeches, and descriptions of Asia. Xenophon imitated Thucydides' style of writing, presenting a no-nonsense narrative that provides a chronological viewpoint following a clear temporal order. Xenophon rarely digressed, but stayed with his story. Although he clearly believed in the Olympian gods, there is little that is ridiculous in the *Anabasis.* From a historical point of view, it is unique as a first-hand account of historical events—history as personal experience. Xenophon was observant and intelligent, and he provided some good descriptions of the Asian peoples, cultures, and institutions and the landscapes of Mesopotamia, Armenia, and Asia Minor. Xenophon was not trained in the study of human culture, but he became a reasonably good anthropologist out of the necessity of escaping Persian troops through a foreign and dangerous country.

Xenophon's significance from a scientific standpoint was limited. He influenced others who sought to discover more about Asia's geography and people. Notably he inspired

Aristotle's interest in the Persian Empire, which was passed on to his student Alexander, who used the *Anabasis* as a guide to Persia, its peoples and way of life. That Alexander became an ad-hoc geographer and anthropologist like Xenophon was not a coincidence. Out of Alexander's anabasis came some other good narrative adventures filled with geographical, anthropological, and natural insights—for example, Nearchus's *Indica*.

See also Alexander of Macedon; Greek Classical Age; Nearchus of Crete; Plato; Socrates; Thucydides

References

Brunschwig, Jacques, and Geoffrey Lloyd. *Greek Thought: A Guide to Classical Knowledge.* Cambridge: Harvard University Press, 2000.

Grant, Michael. *Readings in the Classical Historians.* New York: Scribner's, 1992.

Xenophon. *A History of My Times.* Translated by Rex Warner. Harmondsworth, Middlesex: Penguin Books, 1979.

_____. *The Persian Expedition.* Translated by Rex Warner. Harmondsworth, Middlesex: Penguin Books, 1972.

Zeno
See Stoicism

Zeno of Elea
See Eleatic School

Zodiac
See Astronomy

Zoology
See Life Sciences

Chronology

Before the Common Era

10,000   Neolithic Era begins at
            Mesopotamia.

6000   Pottery developed at
            Mesopotamia.

3500   Bronze Age in Mesopotamia:
            Cities, irrigation, social structure,
            labor specialization.

3100   First Dynasty in Egypt.
            Cuneiform developed in
            Mesopotamia.

3000   Hieroglyphics in Egypt. Trade
            begins between Mesopotamia and
            Egypt.

2800–   Construction of different phases
1500   of Stonehenge in England.

2700   First step pyramid built at Egypt
            under supervision of architect
            Imhotep.

2650   Great Pyramid of Cheops built at
            Egypt.

2500   Indus River civilization emerges.

2350   Sargon of Akkad creates first
            world empire at Mesopotamia.

2000   *Epic of Gilgamesh* written after
            having first been orally composed.
            Bronze developed at Crete.
            Achaean migration into Greece.

1900   Mycenaean Age begins at Greek
            Peloponnesus.

1800   Civilization at Chinese Yellow
            River developed.

1792–   Reign of Hammurapi of Babylon.
1750

1650   Linear A script developed at
            Crete.

1570   New Kingdom begins at Egypt.

1450   Rise of Hittite Empire at Turkey
            and Syria. Decline of Cretan
            power in Mediterranean.
            Mycenaean control of Greece and
            Aegean Sea region.

1400   Appearance of Linear B script in
            Greece.

1379–1362	Reign of Amenhotep IV (Akhenaten), pharaoh of Egypt.
1300	Development of Chinese solar calendar.
1200	Invasions of Sea Peoples throughout eastern Mediterranean. Dorian invasion of Greece.
1150	Beginning of Greek Dark Ages.
1000	Homer's *Iliad* and *Odyssey* composed orally.
1000–962	Reign of Hebrew King David.
800–500	Greek Archaic Age.
800	Carthage founded by Phoenicians. Greek *poleis* (city-states) dominate Mediterranean.
776	Olympic games begin.
753	Legendary founding of Rome.
750–700	Appearance of written *Iliad* and *Odyssey*.
733	Syracuse in Sicily founded by Corinth.
700	Hesiod's poems *Theogony* and *Works and Days* appear.
672	Height of Assyrian Empire in Mesopotamia.
650	Byzantion founded at Bosphorus.
640–560	Athenian lawgiver Solon.
625–545	Ionian philosopher and scientist Thales.
610–540	Ionian scientist and philosopher Anaximander.
604–562	Reign of Nebuchadnezzar, King of Babylon.
600	Massilia founded in southern France.
590	Solon reforms laws of Athens.
586	Babylonians destroy Jerusalem.
585–525	Milesian scientist and philosopher Anaximenes.
585	Eclipse reputedly predicted by Thales.
570–490	Philosopher and mathematician Pythagoras.
570–478	Philosopher and scientist Xenophanes.
540–480	Philosopher and scientist Heraclitus of Ephesus.
510	Scylax of Caryanda explores the Indus River, Arabian Sea, and Red Sea.
509	Roman Republic founded.
500–331	Greek Classical Age.
500	Explorer Euthymenes explores the west coast of Africa.
500–428	Philosopher and scientist Anaxagoras.
500	Geographer Hecataeus of Miletus flourishes.
500	Carthaginian Hanno explores west coast of Europe and Africa.

495–435   Philosopher Empedocles.

490–430   Greek historian Herodotus.

490   Greek defeat of Persians at Marathon.

480   Greek defeat of Persians at Salamis.

470–399   Athenian philosopher Socrates.

460–370   Epicurean Democritus.

460–473   Greek physician Hippocrates.

460–400   Greek historian Thucydides.

456   Temple of Zeus at Olympus completed.

447–438   Parthenon built under supervision of Callicrates.

431–404   Peloponnesian War.

430–427   Plague in Athens.

430–355   Philosopher and historian Xenophon.

427–347   Athenian philosopher Plato.

408–352   Student of Plato, Eudoxus of Cnidus.

401–399   March of the Ten Thousand led by Xenophon.

384–322   Athenian philosopher and scientist Aristotle.

384–322   Athenian orator Demosthenes.

370–286   Student of Aristotle, Theophrastus.

365–279   Skeptic Pyrrho of Elis.

360–312   Explorer Nearchus of Crete.

356   Temple of Artemis at Ephesus destroyed. Birth of Alexander of Macedon.

350   Completion of Mausoleum at Halicarnassus.

341–271   Founder of Epicureanism Epicurus.

333–262   Founder of Stoicism Zeno.

331–31   Greek Hellenistic Age.

331   Founding of Alexandria.

325   Voyage of Nearchus along the southern coast of Asia.

323   Death of Alexander of Macedon.

315–240   Astronomer Aratus of Soli.

312   Construction of Appian Way.

310–230   Astronomer and mathematician Aristarchus of Samos.

300   Massilian explorer Pytheas explores North Atlantic.

300   Greek geometer Euclid flourishes.

287–212   Syracusan mathematician and engineer Archimedes.

280   Completion of the Colossus of Rhodes.

279   Completion of the Lighthouse of Alexandria.

276–195   Astronomer Eratosthenes.

275–194   Physician Erasistratus.

260–180   Greek scientist Philo of Byzantium.

235   Mathematician Apollonius of Perga flourishes.

234–149   Roman agriculturalist Marcus Porcius Cato.

208–126   Greek historian Polybius.

190–120   Astronomer Hipparchus.

146   Roman destruction of Carthage.

145–90   Chinese historian Ssu-Ma Ch'ien.

135–50   Stoic scientist Posidonius of Rhodes.

116–27   Roman polymath Varro.

106–43   Roman philosopher Cicero.

98–55   Epicurean Lucretius.

86–35   Roman historian Sallust.

70–19   Roman poet Virgil.

63–21 CE   Geographer Strabo.

59–17 CE   Roman historian Livy.

58–50   Caesar's conquest of Gaul.

49–45   Civil War between Caesar and Pompey.

44   Assassination of Caesar.

31   Battle of Actium. Augustus begins 45-year reign (31 BCE–14 CE).

31–180 CE   Pax Romana.

25   Roman physician Celsus flourishes.

25   Aelius Gallus explores the Arabian peninsula.

25   Roman architect Vitruvius flourishes.

5–60 CE   Roman agriculturalist Columella.

4 (?)   Birth of Jesus of Nazareth.

Common Era

5–65   Roman Stoic Seneca.

14–37   Reign of Roman Emperor Tiberius.

23–79   Roman polymath Pliny the Elder.

30   Crucifixion and death of Jesus.

37–100   Jewish historian Josephus.

37–41   Reign of Roman Emperor Caligula.

41–54   Reign of Roman Emperor Claudius.

43   Roman conquest of Britain.

46–120   Biographer and essayist Plutarch.

54–68   Reign of Roman Emperor Nero.

55–135   Stoic philosopher Epictetus.

56–117   Roman historian Tacitus.

61–113   Pliny the Younger.

62–152   Engineer Hero of Alexandria.

64   Great Fire at Rome.

67 (?)   Death of St. Paul in Rome.

69–96   Flavian Dynasty of Roman Emperors (Vespasian, Titus, Domitian).

71   Roman destruction of Jerusalem.

79   Eruption of Mt. Vesuvius. Death of Pliny the Elder.

88–175   Biographer of Alexander, Arrian.

96–193   Antonine Dynasty of Roman Emperors (Nerva, Trajan, Hadrian, Antoninus Pius, Marcus Aurelius, Commodus).

100–167   Friend and tutor of Marcus Aurelius, Fronto.

100–170   Astronomer, mathematician, geographer Claudius Ptolemaeus.

130–200   Roman physician Galen.

150–215   Theologian and commentator Clement of Alexandria.

163–225   Roman historian Dio Cassius.

170–250   Sophist Philostratus.

180–235   Commentator Hippolytus.

180–565   Later Roman Empire.

185–254   Theologian Origen.

193–235   Severan Dynasty of Roman Emperors (Septimius Severus, Caracalla, Gela, Elagabalus, Severus Alexander).

205–270   Founder of Neoplatonism, Plotinus.

216–276   Life of Mani, founder of Manicheism.

234–305   Neoplatonist and disciple of Plotinus, Porphyry.

235–284   Civil War in the Roman Empire: twenty-six emperors.

250–325   Neoplatonist Iamblichus.

251–356   Desert hermit St. Anthony.

264–340   Church historian Eusebius of Caesarea.

284–305   Reign of Diocletian and administrative reform of the Roman Empire.

306–337   Reign of Roman Emperor Constantine I.

312   Edict of Religious Toleration.

312   Conversion of Constantine.

314–393   Orator Libanius.

317–388   Aristotelian commentator and orator Themistius.

325   Council of Nicaea.

330   Dedication of Constantinople as capital of Christian Roman Empire.

337–361   Reign of Constantine's son Constantius II.

340–402   Orator Symmachus.

340–420   Theologian and Bible translator
St. Jerome.

354–430   St. Augustine of Hippo.

361–363   Reign of Roman Emperor Julian.

363–392   Reigns of Roman Emperors
Jovian, Valentinian I and II,
Gratian, Valens.

370–415   Alexandrian mathematician
Hypatia.

378   Battle of Adrianople.

379–395   Reign of Roman emperor
Theodosius the Great.

395–408   Reign of Roman emperor
Arcadius.

395–423   Reign of Roman emperor
Honorius.

395   Permanent political division of
Roman Empire (Western Roman
Empire and Eastern Roman
Empire).

395   Christianity made official religion
of Roman Empire.

397   Augustine becomes Bishop of
Hippo in North Africa.

398   Augustine completes the writing
of *Confessions*.

410   Sack of Rome by the Goths.

412–485   Commentator Proclus.

426   Augustine completes the writing
of *City of God*.

430   Augustine dies at Hippo while the
city is under siege.

438   Publication of Theodosian Code.

476   Abdication of last Western Roman
Emperor Romulus Augustulus.

480–524   Philosopher Boethius.

500–540   Commentator Simplicius.

527–565   Roman/Byzantine emperor
Justinian.

585   Dionysius Exiguus develops Easter
table with December 25 date of
Christ's birth.

Bibliography

Primary Sources—General

Grant, Michael. *Readings in the Classical Historians.* New York: Scribner's, 1992.

Holy Bible, Containing the Old and New Testaments. New York: American Bible Society, 1865.

New Oxford Annotated Bible with the Apocrypha. Oxford: Oxford University Press, 1977.

Primary Sources—Near East

Budge, E. A. Wallis, trans. *Papyrus of Ani: Egyptian Book of the Dead.* New York: Dover Books, 1967.

Josephus. *The Jewish War.* Translated by G. A. Williamson. Harmondsworth, Middlesex: Penguin Books, 1969.

Neugebauer, O. *Astronomical Cuneiform Texts.* 3 vols. London: Institute for Advanced Study, 1955.

Pritchard, James B., ed. *Ancient Near Eastern Texts Relating to the Old Testament.* Princeton: Princeton University Press, 1969.

Sandars, N. K., trans. *Epic of Gilgamesh.* London: Penguin Books, 1972.

Thompson, R. Campbell. *Assyrian and Babylonian Literature: Selected Transactions.* With a critical introduction by Robert Francis Harper. New York: D. Appleton and Company, 1901.

Primary Sources—Greece

Aelian. *On the Characteristics of Animals.* Translated by A. F. Scholfield. 3 vols. Cambridge: Harvard University Press, 1971.

Aeschylus. *Prometheus Bound.* Translated by Rex Warner. In *Ten Greek Plays.* Boston: Houghton Mifflin, 1957.

Apollonius of Rhodes. *The Voyage of Argo.* Translated by E. V. Rieu. Harmondsworth, Middlesex: Penguin Books, 1971.

Aristarchus. "On the Sizes and Distances of the Sun and Moon." In Sir Thomas Heath, *Aristarchus of Samos.* 1913. Reprint edition, New York: Dover Books, 1981.

Aristotle. *On Sleep and Sleeplessness; On Prophesying by Dreams; On Memory and Reminiscence.* Translated by J. I. Beare. In *The Parva Naturalia.* Oxford: Clarendon Press, 1908.

_____. *On the Athenian Constitution.* Translated by Frederic G. Kenyon. London: G. Bell and Sons, 1891.

Arrian. *Anabasis* and *Indica.* Translated by P. A. Brunt and E. Iliff Robson. 2 vols. Cambridge: Harvard University Press, 1933, 1976.

_____. *The Campaigns of Alexander.* Translated by Aubrey de Selincourt. Harmondsworth, Middlesex: Penguin Books, 1971.

Athenaeus. *The Deipnosophists.* Translated by C. B. Gulick. 7 vols. Cambridge: Harvard University Press, 1963.

Aurelius, Marcus. *Meditations.* Translated by Maxwell Staniforth. Harmondsworth, Middlesex: Penguin Books, 1964.

Bambrough, Renford, ed. and trans. *The Philosophy of Aristotle.* New York: New American Library, 1963.

Barnes, Jonathan, trans. *Early Greek Philosophy.* London: Penguin Books, 1987.

Burnet, John, ed. and trans. *Early Greek Philosophy.* London: Adam and C. Black, 1930.

Epictetus. *The Discourses.* Edited by Christopher Gill. Everyman's Library. Rutland, Vt.: Tuttle Publishing, 2001.

Euclid. *The Thirteen Books of the Elements.* Translated by Sir Thomas Heath. New York: Dover Books, 1925.

Eunapius. *The Lives of the Sophists.* Translated by W. C. Wright. Cambridge: Harvard University Press, 1968.

Galen. *On the Natural Faculties.* Translated by A. J. Brock. Cambridge: Harvard University Press, 1916.

Hero of Alexandria. *The Pneumatics.* Translated by Bennet Woodcroft. London: C. Whittingham, 1851.

Herodotus. *The Histories.* Translated by Aubrey de Selincourt. Harmondsworth, Middlesex: Penguin Books, 1972.

Hesiod. *Homeric Hymns, Epic Cycle, Homerica.* Translated by Hugh G. Evelyn-White. Cambridge: Harvard University Press, 1936.

_____. *Theogony and Works and Days.* Translated by Richard Lattimore. Ann Arbor: University of Michigan Press, 1959.

Homer. *Iliad.* Translated by Robert Fitzgerald. New York: Doubleday, 1989.

_____. *Odyssey.* Translated by Robert Fitzgerald. New York: Random House, 1990.

Jones, W. H. S., trans. *Hippocrates.* Vol. 1. Cambridge: Harvard University Press, 1923.

Jowett, Benjamin, trans. *The Portable Plato.* Harmondsworth, Middlesex: Penguin Books, 1976.

Katz, Joseph, ed. *The Philosophy of Plotinus.* New York: Appleton Century Crofts, 1950.

Laertius, Diogenes. *Lives of the Philosophers.* Translated by R. D. Hicks. 2 vols. Loeb Classical Library. Cambridge: Harvard University Press, 1931, 1938.

Philostratus. *Life of Apollonius of Tyana.* Translated by F. C. Conybeare. Cambridge: Harvard University Press, 1912.

_____. *Lives of the Sophists.* Translated by W. C. Wright. Cambridge: Harvard University Press, 1921.

Plutarch. *Essays.* Translated by Robin Waterfield. London: Penguin Books, 1992.

_____. *Life of Alexander.* Translated by Bernadotte Perrin. Cambridge: Harvard University Press, 1986.

_____. *The Lives of the Noble Grecians and Romans.* Translated by John Dryden. Revised by Arthur Hugh Clough, 1864. Reprint ed., New York: Random House, 1992.

_____. *Moralia.* 15 vols. Loeb Classical Library. Cambridge: Harvard University Press, 1968–1976.

Polybius. *The Histories.* Translated by W. R. Paton. 6 vols. Cambridge: Harvard University Press, 1922–27.

Porphyry. *On Images.* Translated by Edwin H. Gifford. In Eusebius, *Preparation for the Gospel.* Oxford: Clarendon Press, 1903.

Strabo. *Geography.* Translated by H. L. Jones. Cambridge: Harvard University Press, 1917, 1923.

Theophrastus. *Enquiry into Plants and Minor Works on Odours and Weather Signs.* Translated by Arthur Hort. Vol. 2. Cambridge: Harvard University Press, 1916.

Thucydides. *The Peloponnesian War.* Translated by Rex Warner. Harmondsworth, Middlesex: Penguin Books, 1972.

Todd, Robert, trans. *Themistius: On Aristotle's On the Soul.* Ithaca: Cornell University Press, 1996.

Tredennick, Hugh, trans. *The Last Days of Socrates.* Harmondsworth, Middlesex: Penguin Books, 1959.

Wheelwright, Philip, ed. and trans. *Aristotle.* New York: Odyssey Press: 1951.

Wright, W. C., trans. *The Works of the Emperor Julian.* Cambridge: Harvard University Press, 1962, 1969.

Xenophon. *A History of My Times.* Translated by Rex Warner. Harmondsworth, Middlesex: Penguin Books, 1979.

_____. *The Persian Expedition.* Translated by Rex Warner. Harmondsworth, Middlesex: Penguin Books, 1972.

Primary Sources—Rome

Caesar. *The Civil War.* Translated by Jane F. Gardner. Harmondsworth, Middlesex: Penguin Books, 1976.

_____. *The Conquest of Gaul.* Translated by S. A. Handford. Harmondsworth, Middlesex: Penguin Books, 1951.

Cassius Dio. *Roman History.* Translated by Earnest Cary. Cambridge: Harvard University Press, 1914–1927.

Cicero. *Basic Works.* Edited by Moses Hadas. New York: Modern Library, 1951.

Clarke, John, trans. *Physical Science in the Time of Nero: Being a Translation of the Quaestiones Naturales of Seneca.* New York: Macmillan, 1910.

Columella. *On Agriculture.* Translated by Edward H. Heffner. Cambridge: Harvard University Press, 1989.

Eusebius. *History of the Church.* Translated by G. A. Williamson. Harmondsworth, Middlesex: Penguin Books, 1965.

Frontinus. *The Aqueducts of Rome.* Translated by Charles E. Bennett. Cambridge: Harvard University Press, 1925.

Galen. *On the Natural Faculties.* Translated by A. J. Brock. Cambridge: Harvard University Press, 1916.

Grant, Mark, ed. and trans. *Galen on Food and Diet.* New York: Routledge, 2000.

Justinian. *The Digest of Roman Law.* Translated by C. F. Kolbert. Harmondsworth, Middlesex: Penguin Books, 1979.

Livy. *The Early History of Rome.* Translated by Aubrey de Selincourt. Harmondsworth, Middlesex: Penguin Books, 1971.

_____. *Rome and the Mediterranean.* Translated by Henry Bettenson. Harmondsworth, Middlesex: Penguin Books, 1976.

Lucretius. *The Nature of the Universe.* Translated by R. E. Latham. Harmondsworth, Middlesex: Penguin Books, 1951.

Palladius. *On Husbandrie.* Translated by Barton Lodge. London: Early English Text Society, 1879.

Pharr, Clyde, trans. *The Theodosian Code and Novels.* Princeton: Princeton University Press, 1952.

Pliny the Elder. *Natural History.* Translated by John F. Healy. London: Penguin Books, 1991.

_____. *Natural History.* Translated by H. Rackham. 2 vols. Loeb Classical Library. Cambridge: Harvard University Press, 1938, 1947.

Pliny the Younger. *The Letters of the Younger Pliny.* Translated by Betty Radice. Harmondsworth, Middlesex: Penguin Books, 1963.

Rolfe, John C., trans. *Ammianus Marcellinus.* 2 vols. Cambridge: Harvard University Press, 1950.

Seneca. *Letters from a Stoic.* Translated by Robin Campbell. London: Penguin Books, 1969.

St. Augustine. *City of God.* Translated by Henry Bettenson. London: Penguin Books, 1984.

_____. *Confessions.* Translated by R. S. Pine-Coffin. Harmondsworth, Middlesex: Penguin Books, 1961.

Suetonius. *The Twelve Caesars.* Translated by Robert Graves. Harmondsworth, Middlesex: Penguin Books, 1957.

Tacitus. *The Agricola and the Germania.* Translated by H. Mattingly. Harmondsworth, Middlesex: Penguin Books, 1970.

_____. *The Histories.* Translated by Kenneth Wellesley. Harmondsworth, Middlesex: Penguin Books, 1972.

Thatcher, Oliver J., ed. *The Roman World*. Vol. 3, in *The Library of Original Sources,* pp. 286–292. Milwaukee: University Research Extension, 1907.

Valesius, Henri de, trans. *The History of the Church . . . Written in Greek by Eusebius Pamphilus, Socrates Scholasticus, Evagrius.* 1692. Reprint ed., London: Henry Bohn, 1853.

Vegetius. *Epitome of Military Science.* Translated by N. P. Milner. Liverpool: Liverpool University Press, 1993.

Vitruvius. *On Architecture.* Translated by Joseph Gwilt. London: Priestley and Weale, 1826.

Wippel, John, and Allan Wolter, eds. *Medieval Philosophy.* New York: Free Press, 1969.

Secondary Sources—General

Abell, George O. *Exploration of the Universe.* 3d ed. New York: Holt, Rinehart Winston, 1975.

Ahrens, C. Donald. *Meteorology Today: An Introduction to Weather, Climate, and the Environment.* St. Paul: West Publishing, 1988.

Bass, George F. "Sea and River Craft in the Ancient Near East." Vol. 3, in *Civilizations of the Ancient Near East,* edited by Jack Sasson et al. 4 vols. New York: Charles Scribner's Sons, 1995.

Boardman, John, Jasper Griffin, and Oswyn Murray. *Oxford History of the Classical World.* Oxford: Oxford University Press, 1986.

Boorstin, Daniel. *The Discoverers.* New York: Random House, 1983.

Bowersock, G. W. *Fiction as History: Nero to Julian.* Berkeley: University of California Press, 1994.

Breisach, Ernst. *Historiography: Ancient, Medieval and Modern.* Chicago: University of Chicago Press, 1983.

Cary, M. *The Geographical Background of Greek and Roman History.* Oxford: Clarendon Press, 1949.

Cary, M., and E. H. Warmington. *The Ancient Explorers.* Harmondsworth, Middlesex: Penguin Books, 1963.

Cassirer, Ernst. *An Essay on Man.* New Haven: Yale University Press, 1944.

Casson, Lionel. *Ships and Seamanship in the Ancient World.* Princeton: Princeton University Press, 1971.

Childe, Gordon. *What Happened in History.* Harmondsworth, Middlesex: Penguin Books, 1946.

Crowe, Michael J. *Theories of the World from Antiquity to the Copernican Revolution.* New York: Dover Books, 1990.

Davies, Paul. *God and the New Physics.* New York: Simon and Schuster, 1983.

De Camp, L. Sprague. *Ancient Engineers.* New York: Doubleday, 1963.

Encyclopedia Britannica. 24 vols. Chicago: Encyclopedia Britannica, 1962.

Finley, M. I. *Aspects of Antiquity: Discoveries and Controversies.* Harmondsworth, Middlesex: Penguin Books, 1977.

Gross, M. Grant. *Oceanography: A View of the Earth.* Englewood Cliffs, N.J.: Prentice-Hall, 1987.

Hawkes, Jacquetta. *Prehistory: History of Mankind: Cultural and Scientific Developments,* vol. 1, pt. 1. New York: Mentor Books, 1965.

Heyerdahl, Thor. *Early Man and the Ocean: A Search for the Beginning of Navigation and Seaborne Civilizations.* New York: Vintage Books, 1980.

_____. *Kon-Tiki: Across the Pacific by Raft.* Translated by F. H. Lyon. New York: Washington Square Press, 1984.

Jung, Carl. *Man and His Symbols.* New York: Doubleday, 1964.

Kelsey, Morton. *Healing and Christianity.* New York: Harper and Row, 1973.

Kuhn, Thomas S. *The Copernican Revolution: Planetary Astronomy in the Development of Western Thought.* Cambridge: Harvard University Press, 1957.

_____. *The Structure of Scientific Revolutions.* Chicago: University of Chicago Press, 1970.

Kuriyama, Shigehisa. *The Expressiveness of the Body and the Divergence of Greek and Chinese Medicine.* New York: Zone Books, 1999.

Leicester, Henry M. *The Historical Background of Chemistry.* New York: Dover Books, 1971.

Ogden, Daniel. *Greek and Roman Necromancy.* Princeton: Princeton University Press, 2001.

Otto, Rudolf. *The Idea of the Holy.* New York: Oxford University Press, 1968.

Oxford Companion to the Bible. Oxford: Oxford University Press, 1993.

Oxford English Dictionary. 20 vols. Oxford: Oxford University Press, 1989.

Radice, Betty. *Who's Who in the Ancient World.* Harmondsworth, Middlesex: Penguin Books, 1973.

Raven, Charles E. *Natural Religion and Christian Theology.* Cambridge: Cambridge University Press, 1953.

Russell, Bertrand. *A History of Western Philosophy.* New York: Simon and Schuster, 1945.

Sasson, Jack, et al., eds. *Civilizations of the Ancient Near East.* 4 vols. New York: Charles Scribner's Sons, 1995.

Sullivan, Richard E. *Aix-la-Chapelle in the Age of Charlemagne.* Norman: University of Oklahoma Press, 1963.

Tillinghast, William H. "The Geographical Knowledge of the Ancients Considered in Relation to the Discovery of America." In *Narrative and Critical History of America,* vol. 1, ed. Justin Winsor. Boston: Houghton, Mifflin, 1889.

Wilcox, Donald. *The Measure of Time's Past: Pre-Newtonian Chronologies and the Rhetoric of Relative Time.* Chicago: University of Chicago Press, 1987.

Woolley, Leonard. *The Beginnings of Civilization: History of Mankind: Cultural and Scientific Developments,* vol. 1, pt. 2. New York: Mentor Books, 1965.

Zimmerman, J. E. *Dictionary of Classical Mythology.* New York: Harper and Row, 1971.

Secondary Sources—Near East and Asia

Beasley, W. G., and E. G. Pulleyblank, eds. *Historians of China and Japan.* London: Oxford University Press, 1961.

Cimok, Fatih. *Istanbul.* Istanbul: A Turizm Yayinlari Ltd., 1989.

Daniel, Glyn. *The First Civilizations: The Archaeology of Their Origins.* New York: Thomas Y. Crowell, 1968.

Downey, Glanville. *Constantinople in the Age of Justinian.* Norman: University of Oklahoma Press, 1960.

————. *Gaza in the Early Sixth Century.* Norman: University of Oklahoma Press, 1963.

Erman, Adolf. *Life in Ancient Egypt.* Translated by H. M. Tirard. New York: Dover Books, 1894.

Fairbank, John K., Edwin O. Reischauer, and Albert M. Craig. *East Asia: Tradition and Transformation.* Boston: Houghton Mifflin, 1978.

Ghirshman, R. *Iran: From the Earliest Times to the Islamic Conquest.* Harmondsworth, Middlesex: Penguin Books, 1954.

Glassner, Jean-Jacques. *The Invention of Cuneiform: Writing in Sumer.* Translated by Zainab Bahrani and Marc Van De Mieroop. Baltimore: Johns Hopkins University Press, 2003.

Grant, Michael. *Jesus: An Historian's Review of the Gospels.* New York: Charles Scribner's Sons, 1977.

Hallo, William, and William Simpson. *The Ancient Near East.* New York: Harcourt Brace Jovanovich, 1971.

Hunger, Hermann, and David Pingree. *Astral Sciences in Mesopotamia Handbook of Oriental Studies: The Near and Middle East.* Leiden, Boston: Brill, 1999.

Jacobsen, Thorkild. *The Treasures of Darkness: A History of Mesopotamian Religion.* New Haven: Yale University Press, 1976.

Kramer, Samuel Noah. *History Begins at Sumer.* Philadelphia: University of Pennsylvania Press, 1980.

Mote, Frederick W. *Intellectual Foundations of China*. New York: Knopf, 1971.

Neugebauer, O. *The Exact Sciences in Antiquity*. New York: Dover Books, 1969.

Oates, Joan. *Babylon*. London: Thames and Hudson, 1986.

Orlinsky, Harry M. *Ancient Israel*. Ithaca: Cornell University Press, 1960.

Pedley, John G. *Sardis in the Age of Croesus*. Norman: University of Oklahoma Press, 1968.

Riefstahl, Elizabeth. *Thebes in the Time of Amunhotep III*. Norman: University of Oklahoma Press, 1964.

Sandars, N. K. *The Sea Peoples*. London: Thames and Hudson, 1985.

Scholz, Piotr O. *Ancient Egypt: An Illustrated Historical Overview*. Hauppauge, N.Y.: Barron's Education Press, 1997.

Steiner, Rudolph. *Christianity as a Mystical Fact*. New York: Anthroposophic Press, 1947.

Vasiliev, A. A. *History of the Byzantine Empire*. 2 vols. Madison: University of Wisconsin Press, 1958.

Watson, Burton. *Early Chinese Literature*. New York: Columbia University Press, 1962.

_____. *Ssu-Ma Ch'ien: Grand Historian of China*. New York: Columbia University Press, 1958.

White, Jon Manchip. *Everyday Life in Ancient Egypt*. New York: Capricorn Press, 1967.

Secondary Sources—Greece

Barnes, Jonathan. *Aristotle*. Oxford: Oxford University Press, 1982.

Botsford, George, and Charles A. Robinson. *Hellenic History*. Revised by Donald Kagan. New York: Macmillan Publishing, 1969.

Brunschwig, Jacques, and Geoffrey Lloyd. *Greek Thought: A Guide to Classical Knowledge*. Cambridge: Harvard University Press, 2000.

Burkert, Walter. *Structure and History in Greek Mythology and Ritual*. Berkeley: University of California Press, 1979.

Burn, A. R. *The Pelican History of Greece*. Harmondsworth, Middlesex: Penguin Books, 1974.

_____. *The World of Hesiod*. Harmondsworth, Middlesex: Penguin Books, 1936.

De Montaigne, Michel. *Essays*. Translated by Donald Frame. Stanford: Stanford University Press, 1957.

Doumas, Christos G. *Thera: Pompeii of the Ancient Aegean*. London: Thames and Hudson, 1983.

Durant, Will. *The Life of Greece*. New York: Simon and Schuster, 1939.

Ehrenberg, Victor. *Alexander and the Greeks*. Oxford: Oxford University Press, 1938.

Empereur, Jean-Yves. *Alexandria Rediscovered*. New York: George Brazziler, 1998.

Faraone, Christopher A. *Magika Hiera: Ancient Greek Magic and Religion*. New York: Oxford University Press, 1991.

Finley, M. I. *The World of Odysseus*. Harmondsworth, Middlesex: Penguin Books, 1972.

Fowler, David. *The Mathematics of Plato's Academy: A New Reconstruction*. New York: Oxford University Press, 1999.

Fox, Robin Lane. *The Search for Alexander*. Boston: Little, Brown, 1979.

Freeman, Kathleen. *Greek City-States*. New York: W. W. Norton, 1950.

French, A. "The Economic Background to Solon's Reforms." *Classical Quarterly* 6 (1956).

Grant, Michael. *From Alexander to Cleopatra: The Hellenistic World*. New York: History Book Club, 2000.

Graves, Robert. *The Greek Myths*. Vol. 1. Harmondsworth, Middlesex: Penguin Books, 1960.

Griffin, Jaspar. "Greek Myth and Hesiod." In *Oxford History of the Classical World*. Oxford: Oxford University Press, 1986.

Hadas, Moses. *Humanism: The Greek Ideal and Its Survival*. New York: Mentor Books, 1972.

Hamilton, J. R. *Alexander the Great*. Pittsburgh: University of Pittsburgh Press, 1974.

Hare, R. M. *Plato.* Oxford: Oxford University Press, 1982.

Heath, Sir Thomas. *Aristarchus of Samos.* 1913. Reprint edition, New York: Dover Books, 1981.

Hussey, E. *The Presocratics.* London: Duckworth, 1972.

Kerenyi, Karl. *Prometheus: Archetypal Image of Human Existence.* New York: Pantheon Books, 1963.

Mayor, Adrienne. *Greek Fire, Poison Arrows, and Scorpion Bombs: Biological and Chemical Warfare in the Ancient World.* Woodstock: Overlook Duckworth, 2003.

Netz, Reviel. *The Shaping of Deduction in Greek Mathematics: A Study in Cognitive History.* Cambridge: Cambridge University Press, 1999.

Phillips, E. D. *Greek Medicine.* London: Thames and Hudson, 1973.

Robinson, Charles A., Jr. *Athens in the Age of Pericles.* Norman: University of Oklahoma Press, 1959.

Schmitt, Charles B. *Aristotle and the Renaissance.* Cambridge: Harvard University Press, 1983.

Starr, Chester. *The Awakening of the Greek Historical Spirit.* New York: Knopf, 1968.

Taplin, Oliver. "Homer." In *Oxford History of the Classical World.* Oxford: Oxford University Press, 1986.

Turner, William. "Aristotle." *Catholic Encyclopedia.* New York: The Encyclopedia Press, 1913.

Vandvik, Eirik. *The Prometheus of Hesiod and Aeschylus.* Oslo: I Kommisjon hos J. Dybwad, 1943.

Warmington, E. H. *Greek Geography.* London: J. M. Dent, 1934.

Secondary Sources—Rome

Barrow, R. H. *Plutarch and His Times.* New York: AMS Press, 1979.

_____. *The Romans.* Harmondsworth, Middlesex: Penguin Books, 1949.

Birley, Anthony. *Marcus Aurelius.* Boston: Little, Brown, and Co., 1966.

Bowersock, G. W. *Julian the Apostate.* Cambridge: Harvard University Press, 1978.

Brown, Peter. *Augustine of Hippo.* Berkeley: University of California Press, 1967.

_____. *The Making of Late Antiquity.* Cambridge: Harvard University Press, 1978.

Browning, Robert. *The Emperor Julian.* Berkeley: University of California Press, 1976.

Chadwick, Henry. *Augustine.* Oxford: Oxford University Press, 1986.

Chadwick, Nora. *The Celts.* Harmondsworth, Middlesex: Penguin Books, 1970.

Dal Maso, Leonard B. *Rome of the Caesars.* Translated by Michael Hollingsworth. Florence: Bonechi-Edizioni, 1974.

De Kleijn, Gerda. *The Water Supply of Ancient Rome: City Area, Water, and Population.* Amsterdam: Gleben, 2001.

Dodds, E. R. *Pagan and Christian in an Age of Anxiety.* New York: W. W. Norton, 1965.

Durant, Will. *Caesar and Christ.* New York: Simon and Schuster, 1944.

Gibbon, Edward. *The Decline and Fall of the Roman Empire.* New York: Modern Library, 1932.

Grant, Michael. *The Climax of Rome.* Boston: Little, Brown, 1968.

Jones, A. H. M. *The Decline of the Ancient World.* London: Longman, 1966.

_____. *The Later Roman Empire.* 2 vols. Norman: University of Oklahoma Press, 1964.

Jones, Tom B. *In the Twilight of Antiquity.* Minneapolis: University of Minnesota Press, 1978.

McCluskey, Stephen C. *Astronomies and Cultures in Early Medieval Europe.* Cambridge: Cambridge University Press, 1998.

Meagher, Robert. *Augustine: An Introduction.* New York: Harper and Row, 1978.

Ogilvie, R. M. *Roman Literature and Society.* Harmondsworth, Middlesex: Penguin Books, 1980.

Rowell, Henry Thompson. *Rome in the Augustan Age.* Norman: University of Oklahoma Press, 1962.

Sandbach, F. H. *The Stoics.* New York: W. W. Norton, 1975.

Sinnigen, William, and Arthur Boak. *A History of Rome.* 6th ed. New York: Macmillan Publishing, 1977.

Taylor, Lily Ross. *Party Politics in the Age of Caesar.* Berkeley: University of California Press, 1949.

Vanags, Patricia. *The Glory That Was Pompeii.* New York: Mayflower Books, 1979.

Von Hagen, Victor W. *Roman Roads.* London: Werdenfeld and Nicholson, 1966.

Websites

O'Connor, J. J., and E. F. Robertson. *History of Mathematics:* http://www-history.mcs.st-andrews.ac.uk/history/References/Heron.html (website of School of Mathematics and Statistics, University of St. Andrew's Scotland).

"The Seven Wonders of the Ancient World": http://ce.eng.usf.edu/pharos/wonders/index.html.

Technology Museum of Thessaloniki website: www.tmth.edu.

Index

About the Author

Russell M. Lawson, Ph.D., is an associate professor of history and chair of the Division of General Studies at Bacone College, Muskogee, Oklahoma. His published works include *The Land between the Rivers: Thomas Nuttall's Ascent of the Arkansas, 1819,* and *Passaconaway's Realm: Captain John Evans and the Exploration of Mount Washington.*

CPSIA information can be obtained at www.ICGtesting.com
Printed in the USA
BVOW08*2013131014

370398BV00008B/11/P